The Defended Border

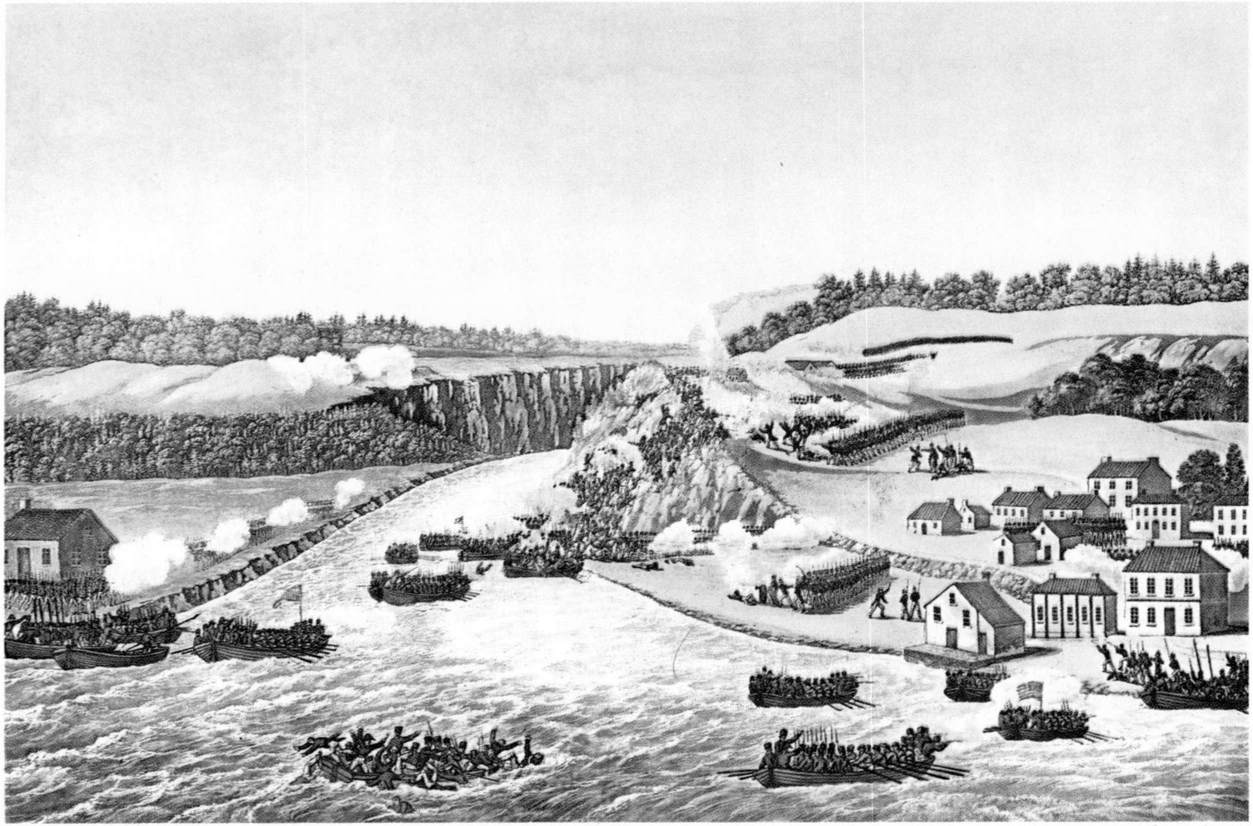

Drawn by Major Dennis. London: Pub.d April 12th 1836 for I.W. LAIRD's Martial Achievements, at 1, Leadenhall St. Engraved by T. Sutherland.

THE BATTLE OF QUEENSTON, OCT.R 13TH 1812,

Which ended in a complete Victory on the part of the British, having captured 927 Men, killed or wounded about 500, Taken 1400 Stand of Arms, a six Pounder, and a Stand of Colours.

The Defended Border

UPPER CANADA AND THE WAR OF 1812

A collection of writings giving a comprehensive picture of the War of 1812 in Upper Canada: the military struggle, the effects of the war on the people, and the legacies of the war.

Edited for the Ontario Historical Society by

MORRIS ZASLOW

Department of History, University of Toronto

Assisted by Wesley B. Turner

1964

TORONTO

THE MACMILLAN COMPANY OF CANADA LIMITED

Printed in Canada by the Hunter Rose Co. Limited

Contents

Maps

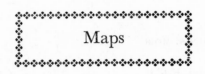

BY GEOFFREY MATTHEWS

Illustrations

FRONTISPIECE: The Battle of Queenston Heights, October 13, 1812.

From a drawing by Major Dennis, engraved by T. Sutherland, London, 1836. In the original, the uniforms of the two armies were reversed as to colour: the Americans were shown in red and the British in blue; the date of the battle was also wrongly given as 1813. These errors have been corrected.

TITLE PAGE: The Seal of Upper Canada.

This 'Seal of Our Province of Upper Canada', authorized by Royal Warrant of March 28, 1792, appears to have been designed by, or for, Lieutenant-Governor John Graves Simcoe. The motto has been translated as: 'The greatness of the Empire advanced through the supreme guardianship of a Caesar.'

BETWEEN PAGES 146 AND 147:

The Articles of Capitulation of Fort Detroit, August 16, 1812. *Courtesy of the Ontario Archives.*

A scene on Lake Ontario – preparing for action on September 28, 1813. *Courtesy of the Ontario Archives.*

The attack on Fort Oswego, May 6, 1814. From a drawing by L. Hewitt, engraved by R. Havell. *Courtesy of the Royal Ontario Museum, University of Toronto.*

A map of eastern Lake Ontario. From an unsigned, undated manuscript describing the fortifications of Sackets Harbor. *Courtesy of the Royal Ontario Museum.*

Preface

The one hundred and fiftieth anniversary of the War of 1812-14 is upon us, but little has been done to commemorate this most significant episode in the history of the province and of the Canadian people apart from purely local celebrations of battles and sieges. It is therefore fortunate that the Ontario Historical Society at its annual meeting in June 1962 decided to sponsor this collection of articles as its method of observing this anniversary. Such a volume, it was believed, would reach a much larger audience than could be rallied by a succession of local celebrations, and would impart something of the unhappy yet heroic events of those years to a wide circle of readers. Besides resurrecting worth-while studies buried in relatively inaccessible periodicals, it would give readers some idea of the scope and variety of the published literature on this epoch in the history of the Ontario region. Subsequently, the Society arranged for the Macmillan Company of Canada, through the good offices of its president, Mr. John M. Gray, to undertake publication. It thus became possible to improve the quality of the finished work by bringing the editorial, artistic, and typographical resources of this leading publishing house to the task.

The selection of articles for inclusion in the present volume reflect the book's origins. It was considered that the best work of the Ontario Historical Society and other local historical societies in the province should be used wherever possible before turning to other Canadian and foreign scholarly publications. Since most of the writing upon the subject of the present volume appeared in Ontario and Canadian historical journals and records, the best treatment in print of a particular topic usually has been chosen. In some cases, however, it was necessary to fall back upon studies of less than first rank or to omit certain important subjects entirely. Occasionally, these gaps and inferior pieces reflect the deficiency of scholarly research into certain aspects of the war. Often, however, omissions have a simpler explanation: the sheer impossibility of dealing with each and every phase of the War of 1812 in Upper Canada within a limited space. The uneven presentation helps to demonstrate the academic and emotional characteristics of historical writing over the past seventy-five years, particularly the unscholarly, even naive, approach of speakers and writers at the turn of the century – except a select few, like the late Brigadier-General Cruikshank, whose canons of scholarship were as strict as those of any modern student.

In editing so diverse a group of articles it was necessary to chart a careful course between the rights of an author, writing in another time, in a different medium, for another audience, and the interests of the present-day reader. Every effort was made to preserve the original work unaltered as long as no ambiguity or confusion resulted. Texts were not interfered with merely for the sake of uniformity or standardization. The authors (or the original editors) were indulged in whichever spelling of Sackets Harbor or Crysler's Farm they favoured, and military titles, names of units, the time of day, words ending in *-or* or *-our*, etc., follow the rules appropriate to the time, place, or medium of original publication.

On the other hand the present-day reader was also kept in mind. Obvious errors and misspellings (like 'Proctor' for Procter) were corrected, except when these occur in titles. Repetition, inevitable when so many articles treat of the same matters, has been reduced to a minimum. Digressions and trivia have been pruned to permit the publication of as many worth-while articles as space allows. Footnotes that only give source references have been deleted in the belief that most readers would derive no benefit from them, while the original can always be consulted by those who wish to investigate the references. To assist the general reader, biographical details and explanatory notes have been added in the form of footnotes enclosed within square brackets. Finally, there is included a select bibliography, listing the most important published source materials and pertinent studies.

Our thanks go to the many persons, societies, and publications whose generous assistance made this volume possible, and in particular to Mrs. E. A. Cruikshank, widow of Brigadier-General Cruikshank, from whose voluminous writings no fewer than seven pieces have been selected. At the head of every article are listed the persons or institutions that granted permission to republish their work. Credit should also be extended to the several local historical societies on which we depend for so much of the scholarly writing about this particular phase of Canadian history, and to the Ontario Historical Society for making this collection possible.

For the actual preparation of the present volume, thanks are due first and foremost to Mr. Wesley B. Turner of York Memorial Collegiate Institute, Toronto, who helped greatly with the selecting and editing of the material and was also responsible for the index. Mr. Turner and Professor John S. Moir of Carleton University, Ottawa, contributed generously to the plan of compiling this commemorative volume. As well as being a major contributor to the collection, Professor Charles P. Stacey, with his wide knowledge of Canadian military history, gave invaluable advice and assistance. Professor Maurice Careless, who wrote the introduction to this book, was equally helpful. The Toronto Public Library, the University of Toronto Library, the Ontario Archives, the Public Archives of Canada, the Military Institute, Toronto, and the Royal Military College of Canada, Kingston, all assisted with the compilation of the bibliography and provided answers to many vexing biographical and military problems. The Canadiana Gallery of the Royal Ontario Museum, the Ontario Archives, the Royal Military College, and the Toronto Public Library are responsible for the fine illustrations. Mr. Geoffrey Matthews, cartographer of the Department of Geography, University of Toronto, designed the maps.

June, 1964 Morris Zaslow

JAMES MAURICE STOCKFORD CARELESS is chairman of the Department of History, University of Toronto, co-chairman of the Archaeological and Historic Sites Board of Ontario, and a past president of the Ontario Historical Society. His publications include the two-volume biography, 'Brown of The Globe', and 'Canada: A Story of Challenge', the latter a recipient of the Governor General's award in 1954, the former in 1964. The following introduction was prepared especially for this volume.

Introduction

BY J. M. S. CARELESS

One hundred and fifty years ago, the lands of Upper Canada that now form part of the Province of Ontario were a major battleground in the War of 1812-14 between Great Britain and the United States. This volume marks the hundred and fiftieth anniversary of that conflict. Prepared under the auspices of the Ontario Historical Society, it is a collection of out-of-print papers and essays on Upper Canada and the war, many of which were originally published in the records of the Society itself. From its earliest beginnings in 1888, the Society has worked to conserve and develop a knowledge of Ontario's past. In that spirit it now seeks to commemorate one of the most striking and significant episodes in Ontario history. For the War of 1812 was of immense importance to the newly settled British province of Upper Canada, which had only been established in 1791. Its very survival was bound up in the struggle, and the effects of the war would stamp the Ontario community for generations to come.

In the campaigns of 1812, '13, and '14, this most exposed, inland British colony endured repeated American attacks: thrusts along its vital St. Lawrence lifeline and through the south-western country above Lake Erie, the sweep of invasion across its Niagara Peninsula, raids on its capital, York, and the burning of Niagara, St. Davids and Port Dover. There were counter-thrusts, raids, and reprisals on neighbouring American territory – at Michilimackinac, Detroit, Buffalo, or Sackets Harbor. There was crucial naval conflict on the Great Lakes, which on Lake Ontario produced a British warship more powerful than the *Victory*, Nelson's flagship at Trafalgar. In much of Upper Canada there were dangers of guerilla attack or fears of treason and conspiracy. In short, for the young province, this war was plainly no mere forest skirmish.

To Great Britain, whose regular troops still bore the brunt of the defence of Upper Canada, the fighting there might seem only a backwoods clash in a minor war, caught up as she was then in the giant struggle against Napoleon in Europe. For the United States, the inland western war was obviously of much more concern; although not the sole concern, because the American seaboard and the Atlantic were also scenes of battle. Upper Canada was not the only British North American colony to be touched by the conflict, but it was the most persistently involved. The chief American offensive effort was devoted to its conquest. Lower Canada was much less subjected to attack, while the Maritime provinces were largely shielded by British sea-power – not to mention a notable lack of enthusiasm for the war among their New England neighbours. Proportionately, Upper Canada was affected most of all.

Moreover, if the battles in Upper Canada were fought not by huge Napoleonic armies but by forces generally numbering a few thousands, and if the provincial militia actively engaged might usually be counted in hundreds, this scale of combat was still by no means small for a colony that then contained only eighty or ninety thousand inhabitants. Whatever the fight in Upper Canada might be to populous, powerful Britain, or the fast-expanding American republic, to the people of the little province this indeed was major war. It remains the only real war fought in English Canada in defence of its own soil. No wonder it left its mark. A too-easy tendency in Canada today to disparage the 'little' War of 1812, and its heroic glow in past tradition, ignores the fact that the very creation of heroes and legends out of the conflict reveals the impact that it made on popular consciousness. Has Canada since, after two world wars, found a military hero to equal General Brock?

The effects of the war are discussed in their particulars in articles below; but here one may spend a moment on its general impact on the minds of the colonial people. Above all, the experience of the War of 1812 gave Upper Canada a sense of itself as a distinct community, and that sense of community, that Upper Canadian outlook, would in the long run contribute to the shaping of both Ontario and Canada.

Before the war, Upper Canada had been little more than a loose string of settlements along the American border, largely populated from the United States and uncertain in their loyalties. Granted, there were United Empire Loyalists among them, whose own feelings had been sharply defined by their opposition to the American Revolution. Yet the Loyalists' allegiance had been to the British connection, or perhaps to the old colonies that were no more: they had not yet necessarily identified themselves with their new homeland. Furthermore, the largest single element in the province were those American pioneers who had come in the wake of the Loyalists seeking fertile, empty land. If they had no strong cause to dislike a provincial regime that offered free lands and little taxes, these sons of the republic had no reason either to feel firmly committed to the British colony. In fact, there was a widespread assumption among them that the spread of American settlement into Upper Canada would lead naturally and irresistibly to its incorporation into the United States. The province yet had no real definition or commitment. It was virtually an overflow of the American frontier, which seemed destined to absorb it.

The war changed things decisively. Successful armed defence showed that Upper Canada was not to be automatically absorbed, and gave a hard new meaning to the border. Attack and invasion pressed its people together as Upper Canadians in a common crisis, and compelled them to commit themselves. The loyally-minded took up active resistance. Would-be neutrals found that they had to choose sides, if only for self-protection – and it was manifestly the American invaders who had brought in a war that threatened their crops and farms and families. As for those who nevertheless chose openly to espouse the American cause, they had to leave the province as enemy aliens, depart with the retreating invaders they had supported, or in some cases face arrest and sentence for treason. The war acted as a screening process, straining out the most disaffected and leaving a community largely convinced of, or converted to, a vociferous provincial patriotism.

It is scarcely surprising that there should have been a problem of disaffection during the war. What is surprising is that it was not more influential, and that actual treason did not become more serious, considering the numbers of potential American sympathizers particularly in western Upper Canada. One answer seems to lie in the conduct and course of the fighting itself. Although later generations might glibly refer to 'Canadian' victories (and 'Canadian' leaders like the wholly British commander, Isaac Brock), the provincial militia generally played a subsidiary part in the struggle. It was far from an undistinguished or unimportant part; but the fate of the colony turned on the skill and efficiency of professional British soldiers. Hence disaffection – or merely lack of zeal among struggling farmers for lengthy military service – did not prevent initial successes by regular British forces, aided, of course, by elements of loyal militia.

These same early successes in 1812 won over the hesitant and made others feel it unsafe to renounce British allegiance. In the main, the lines were drawn, and the pattern gradually hardened, even though reverses to British arms followed later. Through two more years of fighting, during which many of American origin served in the militia, the problem of disaffection remained endemic and recurrent, but not critical. By the war's end,

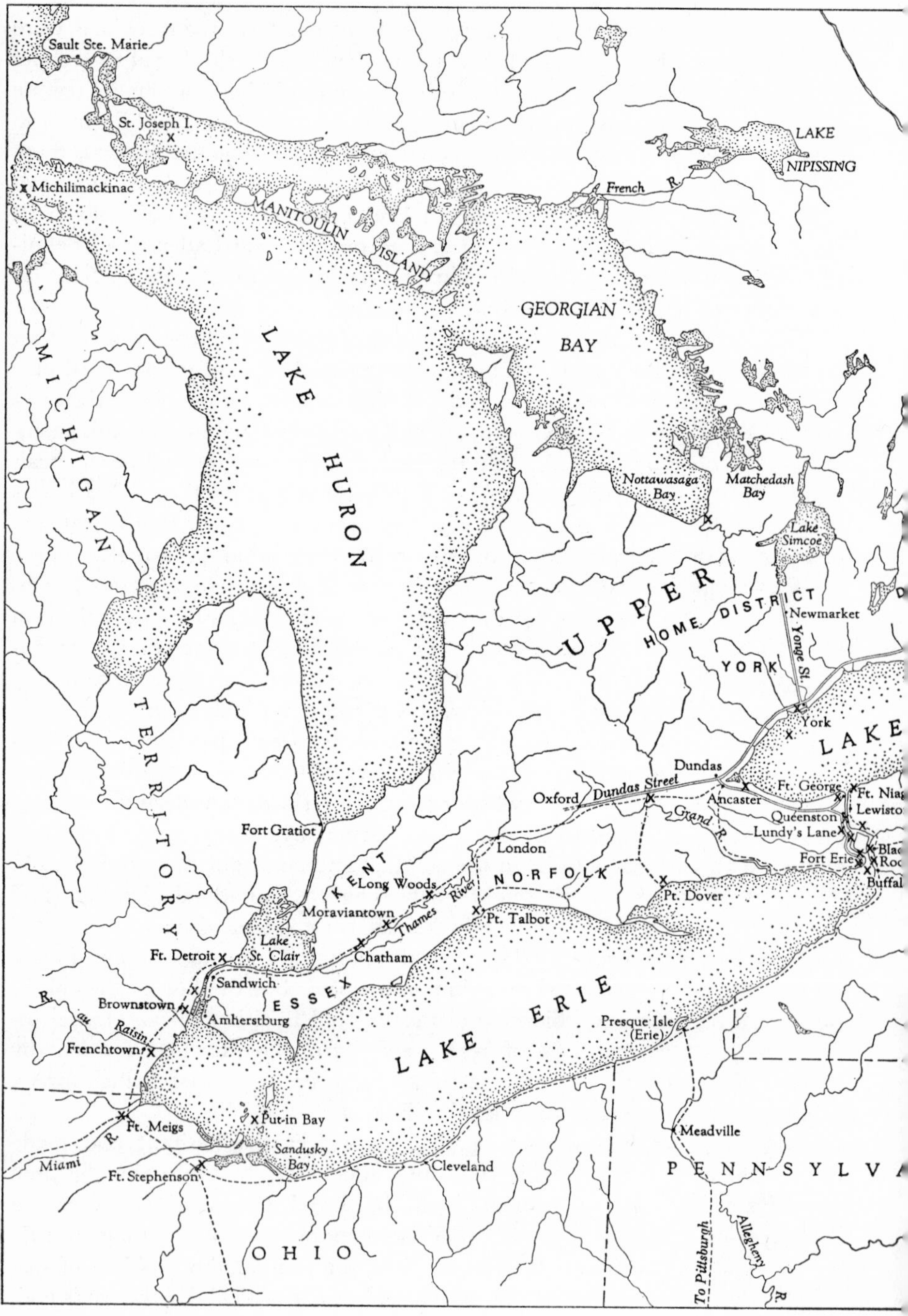
Sault Ste. Marie
St. Joseph I.
Michilimackinac
MANITOULIN
ISLAND
LAKE
NIPISSING
French R.
GEORGIAN
BAY
LAKE HURON
MICHIGAN
TERRITORY
Nottawasaga Bay
Matchedash Bay
Lake Simcoe
UPPER
HOME DISTRICT
Newmarket
Yonge St.
YORK
York
LAKE
Dundas
Oxford
Dundas Street
Ancaster
Ft. George
Grand R.
Queenston
Lundy's Lane
Fort Erie
Fort Gratiot
London
KENT
Long Woods
NORFOLK
Thames River
Moraviantown
Pt. Talbot
Pt. Dover
Lake St. Clair
Ft. Detroit
Chatham
Sandwich
ESSEX
Brownstown
R. au Raisin
Amherstburg
Frenchtown
LAKE ERIE
Presque Isle (Erie)
Put-in Bay
Ft. Meigs
Miami R.
Sandusky Bay
Ft. Stephenson
Cleveland
Meadville
OHIO
To Pittsburgh
Allegheny R.

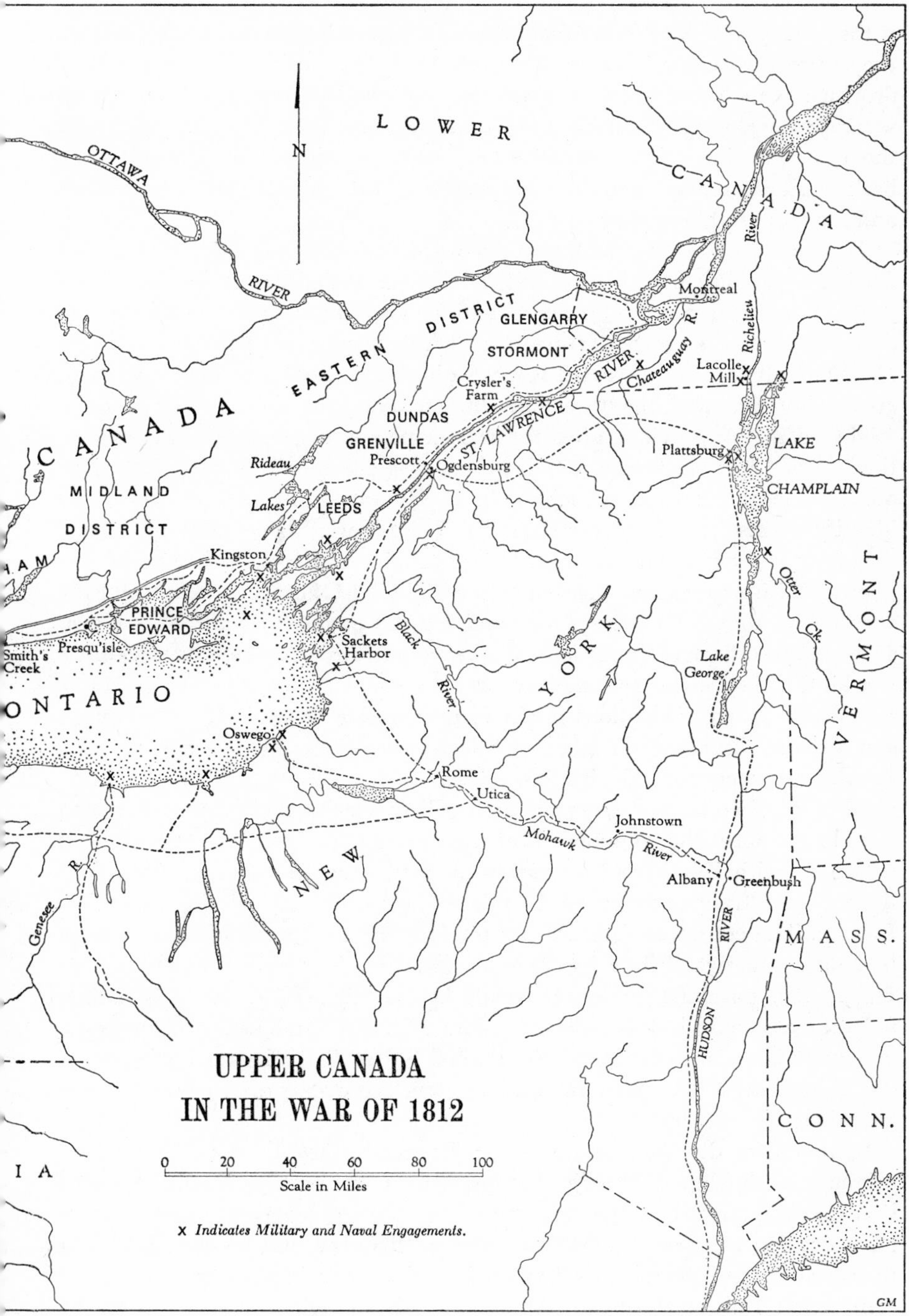

LOWER
N
OTTAWA
RIVER
CANADA
EASTERN DISTRICT
GLENGARRY
STORMONT
DUNDAS
GRENVILLE
LEEDS
MIDLAND DISTRICT
CANADA
Montreal
Richelieu River
Chateauguay R.
Lacolle Mill
Crysler's Farm
ST. LAWRENCE RIVER
Prescott
Ogdensburg
Rideau Lakes
Kingston
PRINCE EDWARD
Presqu'isle
Smith's Creek
ONTARIO
Sackets Harbor
Black River
Plattsburg
LAKE CHAMPLAIN
Otter Ck.
VERMONT
Lake George
YORK
NEW
Oswego
Rome
Utica
Johnstown
Mohawk River
Albany
Greenbush
HUDSON RIVER
Genesee R.
MASS.
CONN.
IA
UPPER CANADA IN THE WAR OF 1812
0 20 40 60 80 100
Scale in Miles
x Indicates Military and Naval Engagements.
GM

if the bulk of the American inhabitants of Upper Canada were not 'Britons', they were not 'United Statesers' either. They were British Americans, in a province whose continued allegiance to the British empire guaranteed its separate development outside the United States. Since both Loyalists and the post-war tide of immigrants from Great Britain could take this same basic position, it was clear that Upper Canada had been put on a definite and far more stable footing.

This does not mean that the war worked only to unify the province. Indeed, the prejudices and suspicions that it left behind intensified a growing internal political rivalry. As Tory and Reform factions developed in the post-war period, emotional appeals to British loyalty and vehement charges of American leanings revealed a more divisive consequence of the years of armed invasion and the threat of disaffection. Yet, whatever strife there might be in the province after the war, a new and generally-held assumption seemed no less apparent: that there was a community of Upper Canada, a community with which both Tories and Reformers could readily identify themselves. The very strength of the Tories' belief that their local oligarchy knew best how to manage the province (a feeling they could display to British governors, or even to the Colonial Office in Britain) and the very power of the Reformers' demand for the people to control their own affairs were different expressions of a newly assertive common consciousness – a kind of provincial nationalism.

Some of its manifestations might seem negative or strained: anti-American animus, distrust of 'Yankee' political innovations, effusively proclaimed devotion to everything British. However, there was as well pride in the survival of Upper Canada, determination still to survive and grow in America outside the spreading republic. If this was a colonial mentality that looked to the tie with Britain as a necessary support, it evinced an increasing confidence that Canadians could do things their own way within the British Empire. The course, in fact, was set towards the emergence of a new nation in North America. While its creation would obviously not be the work of Upper Canada alone, that work would be essential. The modern Canadian federal state could hardly have come into existence if the central community of Upper Canada had gone to the United States, if the keystone of a transcontinental arch had gone. In this way, too, the results of the War of 1812 have been far-reaching.

So much for the war's results. As for its causes, they did not on the whole originate with Upper Canada. The province was drawn as a British possession into a quarrel between Britain and the United States. It largely turned on issues far away on the Atlantic Ocean: Britain's insistence on her right to interfere with American shipping, in order to maintain her blockade of continental Europe during the life-and-death struggle with Napoleon; the

United States' insistence on the rights of her ships, as neutrals, on the high seas. When the mounting friction led the republic to declare war in June of 1812, Upper Canada was at once involved as adjacent British territory open to attack. From the American viewpoint, it was accessible and vulnerable, ripe to be taken in a 'mere matter of marching', and the best place to punish Britain and force her to terms.

Nevertheless, western questions also played a part in bringing on the War of 1812. With these Upper Canada had a closer connection. The province had long faced problems of becoming entangled in clashes between Indians and Americans in the territory beyond its western borders. This neighouring area of the Great Lakes basin, known to the Americans as the Northwest, had been ceded by Britain to the United States after the American Revolutionary War. But the Indians of the Northwest held that no one had the right to grant away their lands, and they had struggled to resist advancing American power. British authorities in Canada showed sympathy for Indian efforts, partly because of the importance of the fur trade in the area to Canadian merchants, partly because of a hope that a successful Indian confederacy might deflect the westward American expansion that threatened Upper Canada as well. Yet they did not really seek to arm and inflame the western tribes, if only because the latter might turn in bitter anger – especially if defeated by the Americans – against the thinly-settled British province itself. In any case, the Indians formed their own confederacies, under the urgings of leaders like the Prophet and his brother, the great Shawnee chief, Tecumseh.

Western Americans, however, were widely convinced that British machinations lay behind the Indian leagues that had resisted them. When they had crushed the Prophet and his followers in the battle of Tippecanoe in 1811, they hotly demanded that the British power behind the Indians be broken also, that its base in Upper Canada be dealt with once and for all. 'War Hawk' members of Congress with expansionist ambitions, also urged a war against Britain. Western issues combined with the turmoil over sailors' rights on the oceans to bring about a declaration of war in Washington.

In the West, Canadian fur traders, at least, could view the war as an opportunity to win back the fur empire below the Lakes that they had been losing to American rivals, while the tribes of the Northwest well might see in it the last chance of all to save their lands from the United States. Without doubt, the Indians would prove valuable allies to the British in Upper Canada during the War of 1812 – as several of the articles collected for this book make plain.

The collection that follows is arranged in three parts. The first and largest deals with the conduct of the war: strategic factors, major battles, and minor engagements; the second treats it in relation to the civilian populace;

and the third discusses its aftermath, its effects on the province, and its place in Ontario and Canadian tradition. It should be stressed, however, that this is a selection of material. Substantial as it is, it could have been far larger and still not have covered all the events of the War of 1812 in Upper Canada, nor all the significant papers that bear on it. Rather the aim has been to produce a representative and well-rounded collection of articles with a variety of attributes. They demonstrate both the approach of older generations to the war and the findings of contemporary scholarship. The authors include well-known local historians, Canadian professional authorities of the present day, like C. P. Stacey, and such a 'father' of Ontario history writing in an earlier era as the indefatigable E. A. Cruikshank. By its contents and bibliography the book should also help to indicate the range of materials available in regional historical publications in Canada. Admittedly, the work produced by local and often amateur historians may vary widely in approach, presentation, depth of research, and degree of judgment. Yet much sound writing has been done on local topics which is of enduring value to general Canadian history. Certainly, far too much has been done for anyone professing interest in the past of this country to be uninformed or supercilious about the importance of its local and regional history. But the final aim has been to provide a book recording the main themes and the outstanding episodes of the Upper Canadian war. It is with this purpose that the Ontario Historical Society now puts forth this present volume.

PART ONE

The War on Land and Water

The following comprehensive, concise examination of the military and morale factors in the crucial opening weeks of the war provides a most fitting beginning to this section. The elements of the situation Brock faced so courageously recur again and again, permitting the reader to observe how well, or how badly, other commanders recaptured those qualities of thought and action that made Brock's campaign a classic. ... From 1945 to 1959, C. P. STACEY *served as director of the Canadian Army Historical Section. He is a former member of the staff of Princeton University and at present is Professor of History at the University of Toronto. He has published numerous articles and half a dozen outstanding volumes in the field of Canadian military history, winning a Governor General's Award in 1948 and the Tyrrell Medal of the Royal Society of Canada in 1955. This study is taken, by permission of the author and of the Department of National Defence, from 'Introduction to the Study of Military History for Canadian Students' (1960 edition), which Colonel Stacey edited for the Directorate of Military Training, Army Headquarters, Ottawa.*

The Defence of Upper Canada, 1812

BY C. P. STACEY

The principles of war can be illustrated by small campaigns as well as great, and by old campaigns as well as those of our own times. It would be difficult to find a series of operations providing a much better object lesson than those of 1812 in which Major-General Sir Isaac Brock[1] defeated the attempt of superior United States forces to conquer the Province of Upper Canada. This campaign, fought nearly a century and a half ago against an adversary who is now our fast friend and essential ally, will repay study by anyone seeking enlightenment as to the qualities that make a great commander.

When the United States declared war in June 1812, General Brock was in command of the forces in Upper Canada and was also temporarily

[1] [Sir Isaac Brock (1769-1812) was born in Guernsey and entered the British army in 1785. He became lieutenant-colonel of the 49th Regiment in 1797 and commanded that regiment in campaigns in Holland (1799) and the Baltic (1801). He was sent to Quebec in 1802 and held the command of the troops in Canada in 1806 and 1807. In 1808 he became a brigadier-general and in 1811 a major-general. On September 14, 1811, he was appointed president and administrator of the province of Upper Canada, positions that he held until his death on October 13, 1812.]

administering the civil government of the province. The military problem that faced him was one of extreme difficulty, for the force at his disposal was very small and the boundary line to be defended was very long.

There was only one British regiment of the line in Upper Canada. This was the 41st (which is now the Welch Regiment). There was also a considerable detachment of the 10th Royal Veteran Battalion, another of the Royal Newfoundland Fencibles (chiefly used as marines on the Lakes) and one artillery company. Behind these regular forces stood the provincial militia, which was simply the men of military age organized in paper battalions on a basis of universal service, and at the outbreak of war virtually without training. A considerably larger British force, including five battalions of the line, was stationed in Lower Canada. All told, the two Canadas . . . were defended by roughly 7,000 troops fit to be considered regulars; of these, only a little over 1,600 were in the upper province.

The United States government had of course a relatively tremendous reservoir of manpower to draw upon, but its regular army was small. Though the establishment when war broke out was more than 35,000 all ranks, the actual strength was much less. The total number of regulars serving may have been in the vicinity of 13,000. Moreover, a large proportion of these were very recent recruits, and the effective force was certainly not superior to the British regulars in the Canadas alone. During the war, the United States called into service over 450,000 militiamen; but the average efficiency of these citizen soldiers, as events on the battlefield amply showed, was decidedly low.

The greater part of the British force had, however, to be retained in Lower Canada, for strategically this was the most important part of the country. Had the Americans followed a sound line of operations, they would have concentrated against Montreal, using the excellent communications available by Lake Champlain and the Richelieu River. The capture of Montreal would have severed the essential line of communication – that by the St. Lawrence – on which the defence of Upper Canada entirely depended, and the whole of that province would have fallen into their hands at an early date. The Americans, however, instead of acting in this manner, operated mainly against the frontier of Upper Canada, chopping at the upper branches of the tree rather than the trunk or the roots. In a long view this was fortunate, but it meant that the first shock of their attack had to be met by very inadequate British forces.

In the first months of the war, however, the defenders had one decided advantage: they possessed a distinct naval superiority on the Great Lakes. This was due to the existence of the force known as the Provincial Marine of Upper Canada. In a naval sense this force was very inefficient (it was primarily a transport service and was administered by the quartermaster-general's department of the army); but its armed vessels were superior to anything possessed by the Americans on the Lakes in the beginning, and it was in great part responsible for the preservation of Upper Canada in the first campaign. It must be noted that at this time the land communications of the province were extremely primitive, the roads being very few and very bad. Only by water could troops be moved with any speed.

Against this advantage we must balance a disadvantage. A large proportion of the population of Upper Canada were recent immigrants from the United States, people who could not be expected to come forward to repel an American invasion. Many other Upper Canadians, though loyal enough in a passive way, considered that the Americans' superiority in physical strength made defence useless. In view of the Canadian school-book legend of 1812, it may come as a surprise to some people to know that in July Brock wrote to the Adjutant-General at headquarters in Lower Canada as follows:

> My situation is most critical, not from anything the enemy can do, but from the disposition of the people – The population, believe me is essentially bad – A full belief possesses them all that this Province must inevitably succumb – This prepossession is fatal to every exertion – Legislators, Magistrates, Militia Officers, all, have imbibed the idea, and are so sluggish and indifferent in all their respective offices that the artful and active scoundrel is allowed to parade the Country without interruption, and commit all imaginable mischief. . . .
>
> What a change an additional regiment would make in this part of the Province![2] Most of the people have lost all confidence – I however speak loud and look big.

No commentary upon the campaign of 1812 should overlook this element in the situation. With greatly superior forces assembling on the frontier, and with the morale of the population (which was largely identical with the militia) at such a low ebb, many a commander would have adopted a supine defensive attitude. It was the greatness of Brock that, far from allowing these circumstances to discourage him, he realized that the best hope of carrying out his task successfully lay in assuming a vigorous local offensive.

A matter of great importance to the salvation of Canada was the attitude of the Indians on both sides of the border, particularly in the west. In view of the great disparity between the white populations of Canada and of the United States, and the thinness of the western population on both sides, the behaviour of the Indian tribes was likely to be decisive. If they were friendly to the Americans, or even neutral, Upper Canada would be much more difficult to defend. If their active aid could be enlisted for the British cause, the province's chances would be very much better.

[2] Another regiment, the 49th, was sent to Upper Canada in August.

All this was very clear to General Brock, and as early as December 1811 he emphasized it in a letter to Sir George Prevost,[3] the Governor-General and Commander of the Forces, remarking: 'Before we can expect an active co-operation on the part of the Indians, the reduction of Detroit and Michilimackinac, must convince that People . . . that we are earnestly engaged in the War.' He had thus formed, well in advance of the outbreak of war, the elements of a plan. Upper Canada was to be defended by a series of offensive strokes with limited objectives, which would have the special advantage of influencing the Indians to take the British side. On learning that the United States had declared war, Brock sent instructions to Capt. Charles Roberts, commanding the small British post at distant St. Joseph Island, near Sault Ste. Marie, giving him discretion as to whether to stand on the defensive or to attack the American garrison at Michilimackinac. Roberts decided to attack, and on 16 July, the day after he received these orders, he embarked his few regulars and a body of Canadian fur traders and Indians (a little over 500 men in all) and led them against Mackinac. The British seized the heights commanding the fort and dragged up a gun; and the American commander, who had had no information of his country's declaration of war, had no choice but to surrender. This early and bloodless success brought the neighbouring tribes flocking to the British standard, and it had a great influence, accordingly, on the subsequent events on the Detroit frontier.

On this frontier the Americans attempted their first offensive. Brigadier-General William Hull,[4] an old and inefficient officer, had advanced from the interior of Ohio before the declaration of war, with some 2,500 men; and on 11 July he crossed the Detroit River and invaded Canada. The small British force on that frontier did not resist his crossing – which considerably displeased Brock; but Hull took no active steps to dislodge it,

[3] [Sir George Prevost (1767-1816) joined the British army in 1784 and served in the West Indies. In 1801 he was appointed civil governor of St. Lucia and in the following year governor of Dominica. (For his successful defence of that island against the French in 1805 he was created a baronet.) In 1808 he became lieutenant-governor of Nova Scotia and in 1811 captain-general and governor-in-chief of British North America. His conciliatory ways endeared him to the French in Lower Canada but he was severely criticized for his cautious generalship, particularly in connection with the withdrawal from Sackets Harbor in 1813 and the defeat at Plattsburg in 1814. A court martial was convoked to investigate the latter episode, but Prevost died before it met.]

[4] [William Hull (1753-1825) served in the Revolutionary Army and attained the rank of lieutenant-colonel. A peace-time career in law and politics after 1783 led to his appointment as governor of Michigan Territory in 1805. When war began in 1812 he was in command of the north-western army. His surrender of Detroit brought him to trial before a court martial at Albany in January 1814. He was sentenced to be shot but was reprieved because of his age and his services during the Revolution.]

and it continued to hold the fort at Amherstburg and the territory around it – a constant threat on the American's flank.

The British naval superiority now made itself felt. The last sixty miles of Hull's line of communications running back to Ohio lay along the shores of Lake Erie and the Detroit River, and was always exposed to interruption by an enemy having control of the water. Hull twice sent detachments back to 'open the communication'; both were cut up, by British Indians under Tecumseh[5] and troops from Amherstburg, in engagements on 5 and 9 August. The Provincial Marine had previously captured a schooner carrying Hull's official correspondence. More mail was captured in the fight on the 5th. The American general was easily discouraged. He began to withdraw from Canada to Detroit on 7 August, and completed the withdrawal on the 11th.

General Brock with his small force could not take the offensive at any point on the frontier without leaving other points unguarded, and had the Americans been enterprising and efficient his situation would have been impossible. As it was, his own first move was to the Niagara frontier, where he contemplated an attack on Fort Niagara. However, he did not attempt this, arguing that it was more important to get on with training the militia; and the Americans made no immediate offensive move in this sector. Brock then returned to York (now Toronto), the provincial capital, for the session of the legislature. This gave him an opportunity, in his civil capacity, of addressing himself to the province and giving a strong lead to its people, so many of whom were uncertain and disheartened.

By the time the Assembly was prorogued, it was clear that for the moment the main threat to Upper Canada was on the Detroit frontier. Brock immediately launched a vigorous counter-offensive. Hull's invasion and a bombastic proclamation which he had issued had considerably discouraged the Canadian militia along the Detroit; but when Brock asked those assembled at York for volunteers to march against the invaders, more came forward than transport could be found for. The general had already ordered a small regular reinforcement to Amherstburg. He had tried to organize a force to operate on the Thames, but this had been largely frustrated by the unwillingness of the militia in the nearby districts. He now dispatched 100 militiamen from York to the Long Point district

[5] [Tecumseh (1768?-1813) was a celebrated Shawnee leader who attempted to organize the Indians against American encroachments upon their tribal lands and to persuade them to abandon their dependence upon the white man and return to primitive ways. This design was overthrown in 1811 with the defeat of the Indians by General W. H. Harrison at Tippecanoe in Tecumseh's absence. Tecumseh joined the British in 1812, took an active part in the capture of Detroit and subsequent campaigns on that front, and fell in the battle of the Thames (Moraviantown), October 5, 1813.]

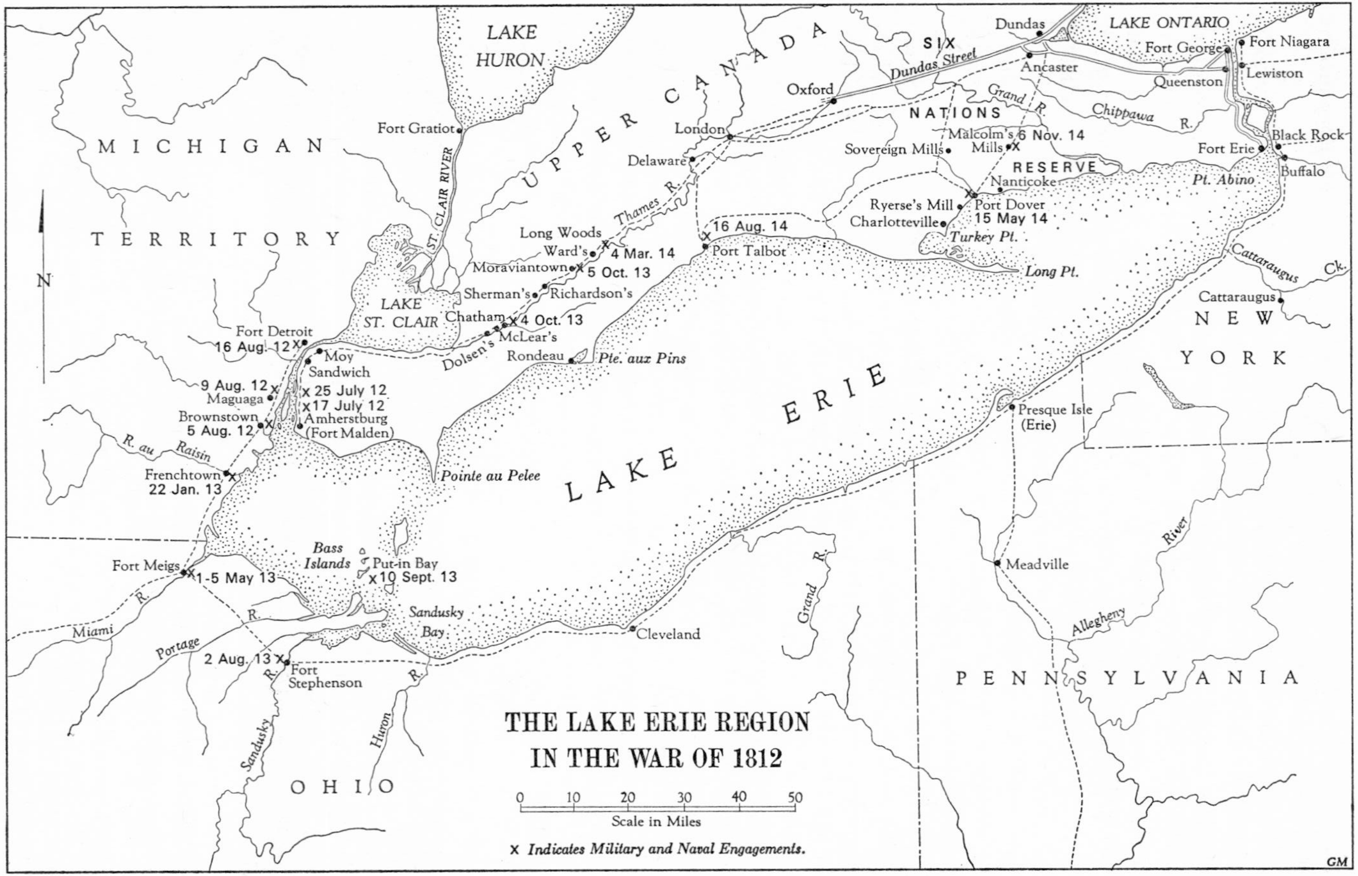
THE LAKE ERIE REGION
IN THE WAR OF 1812
0 10 20 30 40 50
Scale in Miles
x Indicates Military and Naval Engagements.
LAKE HURON
LAKE ONTARIO
LAKE ST. CLAIR
LAKE ERIE
UPPER CANADA
MICHIGAN TERRITORY
NEW YORK
PENNSYLVANIA
OHIO
SIX NATIONS RESERVE
N
Dundas
Dundas Street
Ancaster
Fort George
Fort Niagara
Lewiston
Queenston
Oxford
Grand R.
Chippawa R.
Black Rock
Fort Erie
Buffalo
London
Malcolm's Mills
6 Nov. 14
Sovereign Mills
Delaware
Nanticoke
Pt. Abino
Thames R.
Ryerse's Mill
Port Dover
15 May 14
Charlotteville
Turkey Pt.
Long Pt.
16 Aug. 14
Port Talbot
Long Woods
Ward's
4 Mar. 14
Moraviantown
5 Oct. 13
Sherman's
Richardson's
Chatham
4 Oct. 13
McLear's
Dolsen's
Rondeau
Pte. aux Pins
Fort Gratiot
ST. CLAIR RIVER
Fort Detroit
16 Aug. 12
Moy
Sandwich
9 Aug. 12
Maguaga
25 July 12
17 July 12
Amherstburg
(Fort Malden)
Brownstown
5 Aug. 12
R. au Raisin
Frenchtown
22 Jan. 13
Pointe au Pelee
Bass Islands
Put-in Bay
10 Sept. 13
Fort Meigs
1-5 May 13
Miami R.
Portage R.
Sandusky Bay
2 Aug. 13
Fort Stephenson
Sandusky R.
Huron R.
Cleveland
Grand R.
Cattaraugus Ck.
Cattaraugus
Presque Isle
(Erie)
Meadville
Allegheny River
GM

on Lake Erie. At that place, he wrote to Prevost on 29 July, 'I propose collecting a force for the relief of Amherstburg.'

On the night of 5 August, the same day on which he prorogued the Assembly, Brock himself sailed from York for the head of Lake Ontario. Pushing rapidly on overland to Port Dover, he found the relief force awaiting him there, along with boats to carry them up Lake Erie. (Colonel Thomas Talbot,[6] the redoubtable founder of the Talbot Settlement, had had considerable difficulty with the militia of the district, but had finally obtained a fair number of volunteers.) On the 8th, Brock embarked his tiny 'mass of manœuvre', which amounted in all to about 50 regulars and 250 militia with one 6-pounder, and, coasting along the lake shore, reached Amherstburg and made a junction with the British force there on the night of 13 August. Bad weather and bad boats had delayed the movement, which nevertheless seems very rapid in the existing circumstances.

The general immediately divided his whole force into three miniature 'brigades', two consisting of militia stiffened by small regular detachments and the third of the main body of the 41st Regiment. On 15 August orders were issued for crossing the Detroit and moving against the American army.

Few officers would care to cross a broad river with the prospect of attacking on the farther shore a force twice as strong as their own in a fortified position. Brock himself recorded afterwards that his colonels advised against it. The general, however, was taking a 'calculated risk'. The captured correspondence had told him how low was the Americans' morale and how discouraged their commander, and the very fact of their retreat from Canadian territory had further emphasized the poor state of their army. Even so, his decision remains a fine example of the offensive spirit which wins battles.[7]

On the evening of 15 August Brock opened fire upon Fort Detroit with five guns which had been emplaced on the Canadian shore. The bombardment inflicted some casualties and further discouraged the Americans;

[6] [Thomas Talbot (1771-1853) first came to Upper Canada as private secretary to Lieutenant-Governor Simcoe but did not settle permanently in the colony till 1803. He became celebrated as the colonizer of the Talbot Settlement, along the shore of Lake Erie in Dunwich Township. During the war he was in command of the 1st Middlesex militia regiment and of flank companies and embodied militia in the London district.]

[7] Brock's own account of his appreciation of the situation has been preserved: 'Some say that nothing could be more desperate than the measure, but I answer that the state of the Province admitted of nothing but desperate remedies. I got possession of the letters my antagonist addressed to the Secretary at War, and also of the sentiments which hundreds of his army uttered to their friends. Confidence in the General was gone, and evident despondency prevailed throughout. I have succeeded beyond expectation. I crossed the river contrary to the opinion of Cols. Procter, St. George, etc.; it is therefore no wonder that envy should attribute to good fortune what in justice to my own discernment, I must say, proceeded from a cool calculation of the *pours* and *contres*.' (Brock to his brothers, September 3, 1812.)

Brock had made a judicious contribution to the disintegration of poor Hull by sending him a demand for surrender which remarked that, while he did not intend to 'join in a war of extermination', the Indians would 'be beyond control the moment the contest commences'; and soon after daylight on the 16th the little British force crossed the river in boats and landed three miles below Detroit. The army consisted of some 700 white troops, of whom 400 were militia, and 600 Indians, with five small field guns. The battery opposite Detroit was served on this day by gunners landed from the Provincial Marine. Although Brock does not mention it, Hull in his apologia emphasizes that the British landed 'under cover of their ships of war', and it is clear that co-operation between the land forces and the Marine was close throughout.

Brock had planned to take up a strong position and trust to the effect of his artillery fire to compel Hull to come out and meet him in the open field. He now received information, however, that a detachment of 500 men had left Detroit three days before and that their cavalry were only three miles in rear of his own force. He accordingly took another bold decision – to make an immediate assault upon Detroit. The troops advanced upon the fort, but before the attack could begin the American commander sent forward a flag of truce and proposed a discussion of terms. The sequel was the surrender within an hour of Hull's whole army (including the detachment above referred to), with 35 guns and a great quantity of other arms and stores.

Thus General Brock had won a resounding victory and entirely removed the menace to the western frontier, almost without firing a shot. Well might he write to the Commander-in-Chief, 'When I detail my good fortune Your Excellency will be astonished.' There was, however, more than good fortune to thank for what had happened. The energy and boldness with which Brock himself had acted were the chief causes of this extraordinary result.

On Hull's own showing, it was the vulnerability of his communications (constantly exposed to interruption as a result of the British control of the water), and the fear of the Indians, that induced him to his ignominious surrender. As he put it, the loss of Mackinac had 'opened the northern hive of Indians' and the expectation of the upper tribes 'swarming down' upon his army went far to take the heart out of him. What the success at Mackinac had done in the case of the Indians, the capture of Detroit may be said to have done among the white population of Upper Canada. This brilliant victory silenced the croakers and encouraged loyal citizens. Canadians now realized that a successful defence of the country was quite possible. The militiamen whom so many had considered dupes suddenly became saviours and heroes, and before the year 1812 was over the Canadian legend that attributes the saving of the country primarily to the militia was already well on the way to establishment.

Having saved the situation in the west, Brock handed over the forces there to a subordinate and rushed back east; he arrived at Fort George on the Niagara eight days after Detroit surrendered. For a time operations were suspended as the result of an armistice negotiated by Prevost, and during this period the United States brought up additional strength to the Niagara frontier.

On 13 October the Americans collected here began to cross into Canada at Queenston. Brock, with characteristic energy and offensive spirit, galloped to the spot; and in leading the small force on the ground against the Americans, who had gained the summit of the escarpment, he fell in action. He never knew that the capture of Detroit had brought him a knighthood. His successor, General Sheaffe,[8] collected all available troops and destroyed the invading force later in the day, winning a victory which further raised the spirits of the people of Upper Canada. In November another incompetent American commander made a gesture at invasion on the Niagara above the Falls, but this came to nothing. The campaigning season ended with no part of Upper Canada held by the Americans, and with an important section of the Territory of Michigan in British occupation.

Although the war went on for two more years, the worst danger to Upper Canada had passed in 1812. In that year, when the British forces were so small and the morale of the population so low, the Americans had their great opportunity. That they failed to profit by it was due partly to their own unpreparedness, but to a large extent also it was due to Isaac Brock.

Although Canadian histories have rarely recognized this, the successful defence of Upper Canada was due in great part to the fact that the province was better prepared for war than the United States. The latter had a great superiority in numbers and physical power, but their power was not organized. The Mother Country had provided in Canada the elements of organized power which the Americans largely lacked: a naval force equal to controlling the Lakes and their connecting rivers; a small but efficient body of regular troops; and trained officers capable of skilful and energetic leadership. The forces were tiny, but in the circumstances they were enough.

[8] [Sir Roger Hale Sheaffe (1763-1851) joined the British army in 1778, became lieutenant-colonel of the 49th Regiment in 1798, and arrived in Canada with that regiment in 1802. In 1811 he was appointed a major-general and upon Brock's death succeeded to the civil and military commands in Upper Canada. For his part in the victory at Queenston Heights he was created a baronet. In June 1813, however, he was removed from his positions because of his weak conduct of the defence of York against the Americans. He became a general in 1838.]

There have been few campaigns in which the vision, energy, and decision of a commander have been more influential than in this one of 1812. The manner in which Brock rose superior to discouragements which a lesser man would have used as excuses for inactivity may serve as an object lesson to every officer who would learn the arts of command. . . .

The whole campaign exemplifies in a particularly striking manner the importance of *Maintenance of Morale*. It was in great part superior morale that enabled Brock's force to impose upon and overcome Hull's; and this superiority in morale was mainly the result of bold and effective leadership. In turn, the victory at Detroit itself gave a fillip to Canadian morale generally which made the continued defence of the country possible. There has never been a better illustration of Lord Montgomery's remark, 'High morale is a pearl of very great price. And the surest way to obtain it is by success in battle.'

It would be difficult also to adduce a better example of the dividends to be gained from *Offensive Action*. In spite of the odds against him, Brock saw the importance of seizing the initiative from the enemy and taking the offensive; and the results which he obtained should be an inspiration to every commander who is faced by superior forces.

Similarly, we see in this campaign a successful application of the principles of *Concentration of Force* and *Economy of Effort*. Brock could not concentrate *material* force superior to that of the enemy, but he did concentrate all the force he had the means to move. Of his superiority in *moral* force, there is no need to speak further. His resources were slender, but he employed them judiciously and produced at the decisive time and place a concentration which proved equal to the task. His operations also illustrate the principle of *Flexibility*. British naval superiority on the Lakes conferred upon him 'physical mobility of a high order', enabling him to use his limited resources to the best advantage. The manner in which he was able to shuttle his forces freely and rapidly back and forth along the long frontier they had to guard compensated, to a considerable extent, for the forces' smallness, and made a great contribution to the saving of Upper Canada in this campaign.

FURTHER READING: E. A. Cruikshank (ed.), *Documents relating to the invasion of Canada and the surrender of Detroit* (Ottawa, 1913); W. C. H. Wood (ed.), *Select British documents of the Canadian War of 1812* (Toronto, 1920-8), volume 1, pages 347-418, 455-579; W. H. Merritt, *Journal of events principally on the Detroit and Niagara frontiers, during the War of 1812* (St. Catharines, 1863, and later editions); E. A. Cruikshank, 'General Hull's invasion of Canada in 1812', *Royal Society of Canada*, third series, section 2, volume 1 (1907), pages 211-90; C. Oman, *Studies in the Napoleonic Wars* (London, 1929), pages 207-30.

Victory at Detroit gave Upper Canada a brief respite, but along the Niagara a more formidable invasion threatened. To this Brock next addressed himself, and the result was one of the decisive battles of the war, an action that secured the province until the following spring, tremendously enhanced the morale of the defenders, and immortalized the name of Sir Isaac Brock. . . . ERNEST A. CRUIKSHANK *(1853-1939), farmer, journalist, soldier, and civil servant, was a most assiduous amateur historian, whose researches, chiefly upon military subjects, extended over more than half a century. 'The Battle of Queenston Heights', one of his earliest writings, first appeared in 1888. Written in a more leisurely age than our own, and one more tolerant of minute details, it typifies the industry, meticulous care, and high concept of scholarship that characterized the work of this pioneer student of the Canadian War of 1812. The article presented below is from the second edition (1891) of a pamphlet of the same title published by the Lundy's Lane Historical Society; it appears through the courtesy of the Society and of Mrs. Matilda J. Cruikshank.*

The Battle of Queenston Heights

BY ERNEST A. CRUIKSHANK

It is unnecessary here to trace the march of events immediately succeeding the declaration of war by the United States, on the 18th of June, 1812; how Brock cheered up the despondent, decided the wavering, and overawed the disloyal among the inhabitants of the province by a settled policy, to use his own words, of 'speaking loud and looking big'; how, prevented by the express instructions of his superior from attacking the enemy beyond the Niagara, he assembled an enthusiastic body of volunteers and, taking with him almost every regular soldier at his disposal, flew to repel the invader at the Detroit; how he promptly determined to cross that river contrary to the opinion of his most trusted officers; and how his audacity was rewarded by a complete and bloodless victory, is sufficiently well known.

But, while conquering at Detroit, he could not fail to be apprehensive that disaster might have befallen the weakened garrisons on the Niagara, and scarcely twenty-four hours were permitted to elapse before he was on his way thither, carrying with him all the troops that had accompanied or preceded him to that quarter, fully alive to the truth of the Napoleonic maxim that 'in war, time is everything'. Brock then hoped to duplicate his exploit by the capture of Fort Niagara and the dispersal of the forces assembled on that frontier. That it would have been an easy task, there can now be no reasonable doubt, for, although superior in numbers, the American troops there were, it is admitted, in a very indifferent state of discipline, without any heavier ordnance than six-pounders, and but few of them, and without artillerists. A few days later, when the true extent of Brock's success was made known, their demoralization became complete. The most absurd rumors were believed and spread. Panic-stricken fugitives from Detroit, anxious to excuse their cowardice, gravely related that a hundred fresh scalps had been laid at Colonel Elliott's[1] feet, and that he had paid for them at the rate of six dollars each. Not only the Western Indians, but those residing in Michigan and Canada were reported to have taken the hatchet, and to be already on their way to devastate the border settlements of Ohio. The appearance of two British war vessels on the south shore of Lake Erie threw the inhabitants of Chautauqua county into a paroxysm of terror. Blood-curdling traditions of the slaughter of Cherry Valley and Wyoming were recalled, and a general flight began. The militia became clamorous for pay, and sought furloughs under every possible pretext. When refused, they feigned sickness or deserted.

The intensity of Brock's disappointment may be imagined when he learned, on his arrival at Fort Erie on the 22nd of August, that an armistice had been proclaimed five days before.[2] . . . The indefatigable Brock hurried on to Kingston, where he inspected the militia, examined the growing fortifications, and wrote to Sir George Prevost for permission to attack Sackett's Harbor, where the American shipping on Lake Ontario had taken refuge. With his present superiority upon the lake, he assured him that its capture would be an easy matter. A portion of the American troops at Niagara would be probably recalled for its relief, and while they were marching overland he would sail up the lake and throw his whole force against the posts they had left. But to the Governor-General this daring scheme of operation seemed far too hazardous, and in reply he enjoined Brock not to provoke the enemy by needless annoyance, but to remain

[1] [Matthew Elliott (1739-1814) was a member of the legislature for Essex (1801-12), colonel of the 1st Essex Regiment and deputy superintendent in the Indian Department from 1795 to 1799 and after 1808. He was present at the capture of Detroit and at the battles of Frenchtown, Miami, and Moraviantown, and died near Burlington Heights while still on active service.]

[2] [Sir George Prevost proposed an armistice as soon as he learned of the repeal of the orders-in-council, an ostensible cause for the American declaration of war. The American commander, General Henry Dearborn, gladly accepted the proposal in view of the weakness of his forces and the need for time to strengthen his defences. On the Niagara front the truce was negotiated between generals Sheaffe and Van Rensselaer.]

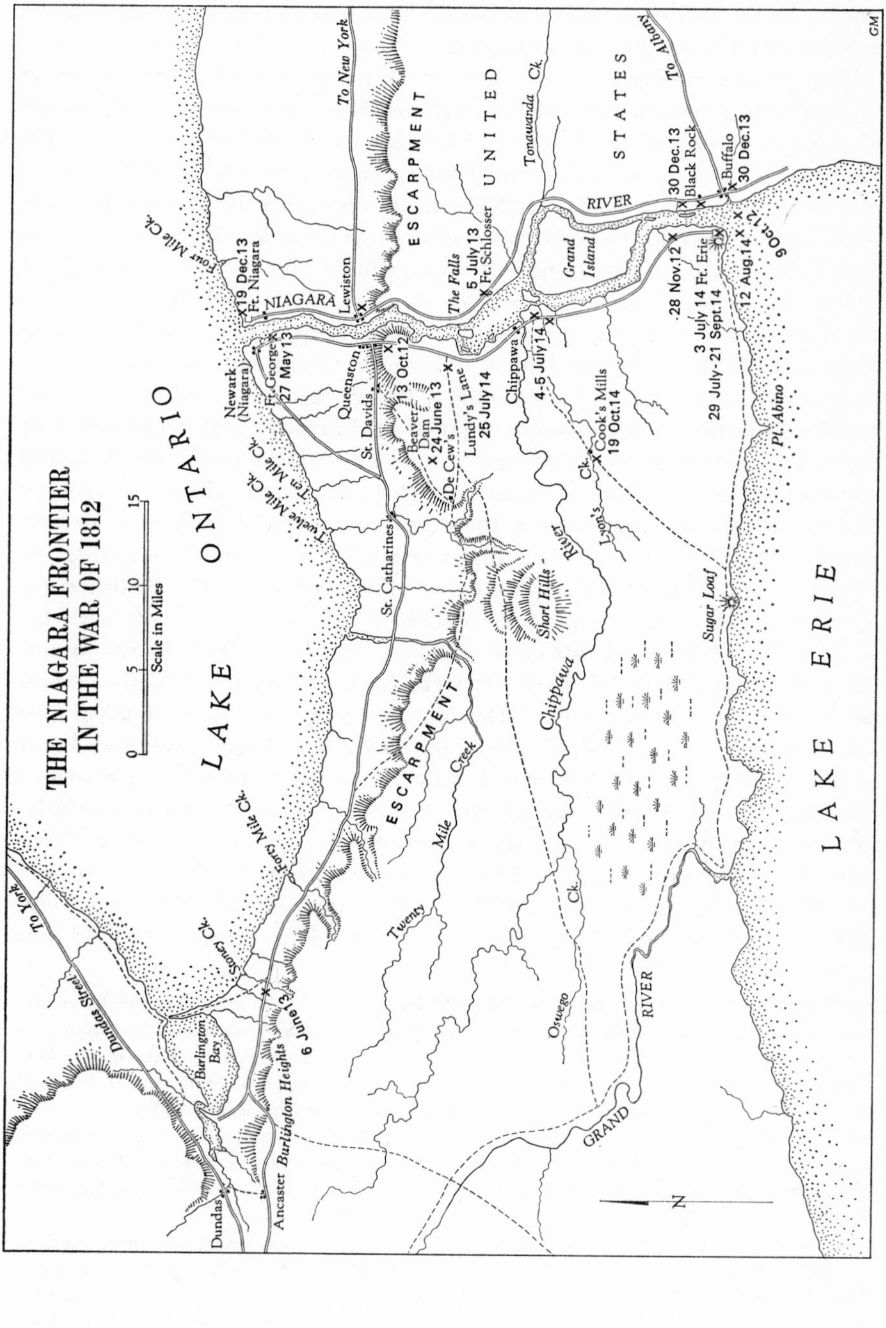
THE NIAGARA FRONTIER
IN THE WAR OF 1812
0 5 10 15
Scale in Miles
LAKE ONTARIO
LAKE ERIE
To York
Dundas Street
Dundas
Ancaster
Burlington Heights
6 June 13
Burlington Bay
Stoney Ck.
Forty Mile Ck.
Twelve Mile Ck.
Ten Mile Ck.
Four Mile Ck.
Newark (Niagara)
Ft. George
27 May 13
19 Dec.13
Ft. Niagara
NIAGARA
Lewiston
To New York
Queenston
13 Oct.12
St. Davids
St. Catharines
Beaver Dam
24 June 13
De Cew's
Lundy's Lane
25 July 14
The Falls
5 July 13
Ft. Schlosser
Chippawa
4-5 July 14
Cook's Mills
19 Oct.14
Lyon's Ck.
Chippawa River
Short Hills
ESCARPMENT
ESCARPMENT
Twenty Mile Creek
Oswego Ck.
GRAND RIVER
Sugar Loaf
Pt. Abino
Grand Island
RIVER
Tonawanda Ck.
UNITED STATES
28 Nov.12
3 July 14 Ft. Erie
29 July-21 Sept.14
12 Aug.14
9 Oct. 12
30 Dec.13
Black Rock
Buffalo
30 Dec.13
To Albany
N
GM

strictly on the defensive, and even hinted that he had risked too much when he ventured to cross the river at Detroit.

This project having been rejected, Brock returned to Niagara, where he learned that [General Stephen] Van Rensselaer[3] had already given notice of the termination of the armistice.[4] Lewiston Heights were whitened with the tents of a large encampment. Other camps were visible at Schlosser, Black Rock, and in rear of Fort Niagara. Batteries had been erected on the commanding ground opposite Fort George and at Lewiston, and armed with heavy guns. A large flotilla of boats, suitable for the transportation of troops, lay moored under the guns of the fort, at the mouth of the river, and others had been taken up to Lewiston. Forty bateaux, each capable of carrying thirty men, were known to have been built in Tonawanda creek. Every day large bodies of men could be seen exercising and marching to and fro, attended by a numerous train of field artillery and detachments of cavalry. Everything pointed to an immediate attack, while Brock found himself at once hampered by want of officers, men, and artillery, and wrote to Prevost that he must have a thousand more regular soldiers to defend that frontier. The latter replied that not another man could be spared for Upper Canada under any circumstances. Without delay the British commander set to work to supply the deficiency of men and means with his wonted energy. Detachments of troops were ordered up from Kingston and down from Amherstburg. Batteries were built and mounted with cannon taken from the fortifications of Detroit. An extensive system of telegraphs and beacons was established, stretching from the Sugar Loaf and Point Abino, along the lake and river to Lundy's Lane and Queenston, and thence inland to Pelham Heights, by which the movements of the enemy could be instantaneously signalled over the entire peninsula by day or night. Two thousand captured muskets, and the accoutrements of Hull's regular troops, were distributed among the militia of the province. His tireless activity and watchfulness excited the admiration even of his enemies. 'I send you

[3] [Stephen Van Rensselaer (1764-1839) inherited large estates in the upper Hudson River valley and had an active career in politics, including terms as state senator and lieutenant-governor of New York. As major-general of the state militia at the beginning of the war he held command over operations along the Niagara frontier. An amateur in military matters, he relied on a cousin, Colonel Solomon Van Rensselaer, a trained and experienced soldier. As a result of the battle at Queenston Heights, he was replaced by Brigadier-General Smyth. After the war he was prominent in the construction and management of the Erie Canal, served as chancellor of the University of the State of New York, and established the Rensselaer Polytechnic Institute at Troy.]

[4] [The armistice was repudiated by the United States government which was determined to proceed with the war notwithstanding the repeal of the orders-in-council. The respite was a great benefit to the Americans in the Lake Ontario sector as it permitted them to strengthen their forces along the Niagara front and to commence building a flotilla at Sackets Harbor.]

Brock's seal,' Lovett[5] wrote to a friend, 'with his appropriate motto, "He who guards never sleeps." ' Earthworks of some description were constructed on every commanding point along the river from Queenston to its mouth and at any menacing movement of the American troops alarm-guns were fired and horsemen rode off in every direction. . . .

A variety of motives absolutely forced General Van Rensselaer to assume the offensive. During September six regiments of regular infantry, five of New York militia, a battalion of rifles, and several companies of artillery joined his army. The Pennsylvania contingent had assembled at Meadville on the 20th, and was marching to Buffalo. Forage and provisions had already begun to grow scarce, and the autumn rains would undoubtedly increase the ravages of disease already frightfully prevalent among his militia. [General] Dearborn[6] strongly urged him to attempt the passage of the river, as he declared they must reckon upon obtaining possession of Upper Canada before the winter set in, assuring him at the same time that Harrison[7] would invade the province by way of Detroit with six or seven thousand men, while another strong body of troops were already assembled at Sackett's Harbor, where a squadron was fitting out to contest possession of Lake Ontario, and he, in person, promised to menace Montreal from Lake Champlain. The ultimate success of these operations he regarded as almost certain, but he warned Van Rensselaer that much would depend on his movements on the Niagara.[8] . . .

Early in October Van Rensselaer summoned a council of war, to which

[5] [John Lovett was private secretary to General Van Rensselaer.]

[6] [Henry Dearborn (1751-1829) was a captain of militia in the battle of Bunker Hill (1775) and commanded a regiment during later phases of the Revolutionary War. After a term in Congress he served as Secretary of War during the whole of Jefferson's presidency. In 1812 he was placed in command of the Lake Ontario and St. Lawrence sector of the front. In 1813 he led the expedition against York and succeeded in capturing Fort George. He resigned in June 1813 amid criticism of his failure to conquer the Niagara peninsula and his command was divided between generals James Wilkinson and J. P. Boyd.]

[7] [William Henry Harrison (1773-1841) was a member of a leading Virginia family who served in the Indian campaigns of 1793-5 under General Wayne. While he was governor of the Territory of Indiana (1800-12) he won the battle of Tippecanoe and broke up the Indian confederation organized by Tecumseh and the Prophet. At the outbreak of war he became a general and succeeded Hull in the command of the Detroit and Erie sectors. After the war he embarked upon a political and diplomatic career that culminated in his election in 1840 as ninth president of the United States. A month after his inauguration he died, the first president to fail to complete his term of office.]

[8] General Dearborn wrote to Mr. Eustis, Secretary of War, on September 1, 1812: 'When the regular troops you have ordered for Niagara arrive at that post, with the militia and other troops on the march, they will be able, I presume, to cross over into Canada, carry all the works at Niagara and proceed to the other posts in that province in triumph.'

he invited General Smyth,[9] who had just taken command of a brigade of regular troops at Buffalo; General Hall, of the New York militia; and the commandant of each regiment of United States troops. Smyth showed his contempt for the militia general under whom he was forced to serve by neglecting to attend or even to explain his absence. Van Rensselaer had intended to concentrate the whole of his regular troops near Fort Niagara and the militia at Lewiston, and attempt the passage of the river simultaneously at both places, but in consequence of Smyth's misconduct this scheme was abandoned and he determined to cross from the latter place only, as he felt satisfied that the forces he had already assembled there were amply sufficient for the purpose. Staff officers, under one pretext and another, had visited the British lines, and the result of their observations, coupled with information received from his spies, had made him pretty thoroughly acquainted with the numbers and composition of the forces opposed to him.

No doubt was entertained of at least partial success. He confidently anticipated being able to secure a foothold in Canada, where he could establish his army in winter quarters and prepare for an early campaign next year. The primary object of the invasion was simply described as being to expel the British from Queenston and obtain a shelter from the inclemency of the weather. More than eight thousand troops were assembled under his command, of whom about half were regulars. Three hundred artillery and eight hundred regular infantry of the 6th, 13th, and 23rd Regiments occupied Fort Niagara, and nine hundred regular soldiers and 2,270 New York militia were encamped near Lewiston. At Buffalo General Smyth had 1,650 regular troops, three hundred and eighty-six detached militia, two hundred and fifty sailors and four hundred Indians, besides the local militia. The advance guard of the Pennsylvania brigade of two thousand men had also arrived at Buffalo, and the remainder was within easy march of that place. Many bateaux and flat-bottomed boats were in readiness at Black Rock, Tonawanda, and Gill Creek above the Falls, and at Lewiston and Four Mile Creek below, and a sufficient number could be collected at any given point in a few hours to carry over a thousand men. His train of field artillery was large and well equipped.

To resist this formidable army Brock had fifteen companies of regular

[9] [Alexander Smyth (1765-1830) was born in Ireland and came to Virginia as a boy. He gave up a successful political and legal career in 1808 to join the United States army as colonel of a rifle regiment. In July 1812 he was promoted to brigadier and appointed inspector-general of the American forces. In September 1812 he was posted to the Niagara front to take command of a brigade under General Van Rensselaer. Following the battle at Queenston Heights he succeeded to Van Rensselaer's command, but he was removed from military employment in December 1812 for mismanaging the invasion of Upper Canada in the vicinity of Fort Erie. He returned to Virginia, took up his legal profession, and was elected to Congress from 1817 to 1825 and from 1827 till his death.]

infantry, which may have mustered sixty rank and file each; two officers and thirty men of the Royal artillery, with five field guns; a troop of militia drivers and a troop of Provincial cavalry, besides the flank companies[10] of the five Lincoln and two York Regiments of militia. The fourteen flank companies probably did not average more than thirty-five officers and men each, or less than five hundred in all. . . . To guard a frontier which practically extended from the Sugar Loaf on Lake Erie to Four Mile Creek on Lake Ontario, and to occupy the numerous posts and batteries between, and maintain communication over a line of sixty miles, he had actually less than a thousand regular troops and six hundred militia, with a reserve of possibly six hundred militia and Indians. Half of this force was scarcely adequate to garrison Fort George and the adjacent batteries, and a body of troops could hardly be marched from one end of his line to the other in less than two days. The concentration of large bodies of men near Fort Niagara and Buffalo, where great numbers of boats were collected, forced Brock to weaken his centre and strengthen his wings, anticipating that an attempt would be made to turn his flank, and land troops a few miles in rear of the works protecting it. Four companies of the 49th, two of the Royal Newfoundland Regiment, four of militia, and a small detachment of Royal Artillery occupied Fort Erie and a series of batteries extending as low as Frenchman's Creek; four companies of militia and the grenadier company of the 41st were posted along the river between that point and Chippawa; the flank companies of the 49th and two flank companies of the York militia held the batteries near Queenston; the earthworks at Brown's and Field's points were each guarded by a militia company; while four battalion companies of the 49th and the flank companies of the 1st and 4th Lincoln Regiments and the field guns were quartered in and about Fort George. A chain of outposts and patrols maintained constant communication between all these posts, and the Indians were held in reserve in small parties several miles in rear. . . .

The successful result of an attack upon two small armed vessels at Fort Erie[11] served to raise the spirits of Van Rensselaer's army in a remarkable degree, and was actually a serious blow to their opponents, owing to the extreme scarcity of provisions, apart from the loss of the vessels. This occurred early on the morning of the 9th October, and Brock arrived on the spot before sunset, but, having apparently satisfied himself that no im-

[10] [The flank companies, two from each militia regiment, were filled by volunteers who were to receive military training at least six times a month, as opposed to the remaining (or battalion) companies which were called out only four times a year in peace-time and monthly in time of war. The flank companies gave a good account of themselves in numerous actions in the War of 1812.]

[11] [See page 86.]

mediate attempt to cross the river was contemplated there, returned to Niagara next day. . . . This hurried journey had the effect of hastening Van Rensselaer's movements, for a spy returned to his camp with information that Brock had left Niagara in great haste and was supposed to have gone to Detroit. Encouraged by this report, and feeling, as he expressed it, 'that the national character is degraded and the disgrace will remain, corroding the public feeling and spirit until another campaign, unless it be instantly wiped away by a brilliant exploit in this', he determined to strike while the enthusiasm of his troops was yet at its heat over the recent exploit, and fixed the hour and place for crossing the river for three o'clock next morning at Queenston. The stream was there at its narrowest; a ferry had been established for years, and although the current was swift the navigation was well ascertained and an indifferent oarsman could pull across in less than ten minutes. His artillery, superior in numbers and calibre, could cover the landing from the high ground above Lewiston, where batteries had already been thrown up for it. The occupation of Queenston Heights and investment of Fort George by a sufficient force would, he believed, sever the British line of communication and drive their shipping from the mouth of the river, 'leaving them no rallying point in this part of the country, appalling the minds of the Canadians, and opening a wide and safe communication for our supplies'. 'The blow', he added, 'must be struck soon or all the toil and expense of the campaign will go for nothing, and more than nothing, for the whole will be tinged with dishonor.'

Accordingly, the regulars from Fort Niagara and strong detachments from Buffalo were ordered to join the main body at Lewiston before midnight, and boats sufficient to contain 500 men were secretly brought overland from Gill Creek. A furious storm of wind and rain swept over his camp while the troops were drawn up in readiness to enter the boats, and the pilot of the expedition deserted in the darkness. In consequence, the attack was indefinitely postponed. The rain continued with unabated violence for twenty-eight hours, until the roads became almost impassable. Van Rensselaer then desired to wait a few days in the hope of reverting to his original plan, but the impatience of his troops seemed to be rather increased than diminished by their recent failure, and the pressure brought to bear upon him was too great to be withstood. His force was now still further increased by the arrival of three hundred and fifty regular soldiers, under Lieut.-Col. Chrystie, at Four Mile Creek, east of Fort Niagara. The appearance of these boats and the detention of a large force near that place led Brock to believe that an attempt would be made to land to the westward of Niagara, and prevented him from reinforcing the detachments at Queenston, and though he had become aware of the attempt to cross the river there he regarded it simply as a feint to divert his attention from the true point of attack. The evident activity of the enemy near Buffalo at the same time restrained him from weakening the right of his extended line.

The river as it issues from the gorge at Queenston is barely two hundred yards in width, and flows at the rate of about four miles an hour. The cliffs which wall it in above are almost perpendicular, rising to the height of about 200 feet above the stream, yet on the Canadian side in many places were so overgrown by shrubs and trees, which struck their roots into the clefts and crannies of the rocks, as to make it possible for an ordinarily active man to climb up with little difficulty from the water's edge to the summit. A few hundred yards west of the landing stood the village, consisting of a stone barracks and about twenty scattered dwellings embosomed in gardens and peach orchards. The river-road leading from Niagara formed the principal street, and wound up the heights beyond. It was bordered by luxuriant orchards, grain fields, and meadows all the way to Niagara, forming, as a traveller wrote, 'a rare and interesting sight in Canada'. Another road, commencing at the landing and crossing this at right angles, led to St. Davids, throwing off a branch which ascended the heights about a mile to westward and finally united with the Portage Road above. In the angle formed by the intersection of these two roads, at the south-east corner of the village, stood the large stone house of the Honourable Robert Hamilton, with its walled courtyard and substantial out-buildings. The adjacent plain was dotted with many farm houses near the roads, and the fields were generally enclosed by ordinary rail fences, diversified near the foot of the heights by an occasional low stone wall. Half-way up the side of the mountain, in a natural fold of the ground, a small redan battery had been built, with its angle fronting the river and armed with an eighteen-pounder, and at Vrooman's, or Scott's Point, nearly a mile below, a twenty-four pound gun had been mounted *en barbette*[12] on a crescent-shaped earthwork commanding – although at very long range – both landings and the breadth of the river between. Captain Williams, with the light company of the 49th, was stationed at the redan, and the Grenadiers of the same regiment, under Captain Dennis,[13] and Captain George Chisholm's company of the 2nd York, were quartered in the village. Outposts and sentries

[12] [A gun mounted *en barbette* is one that fires over a low parapet instead of through an embrasure.]

[13] Afterwards Major-General Sir James B. Dennis, who commanded the Second Brigade of Infantry at the battle of Maharajpur on December 29, 1843. Born in 1778, he served for some time in the navy as a midshipman, but he entered the 49th Regiment as an ensign on September 2, 1796. In the action at Copenhagen in 1801 he served on board the *Monarch* and was wounded in both hands. At Stoney Creek on June 6, 1813, he was again wounded in two places by musket balls and much contused by having his horse killed under him. He was made a K. C. B. on October 30, 1844, and promoted to be a major-general on November 11, 1851. He died in London on January 14, 1855.

watched the river from the landing to Vrooman's Point, which was occupied by Captain Samuel Hatt's company of the 5th Lincoln and a small party of the Lincoln militia artillery under Lieut. John P. Ball. The entire force of regulars and militia distributed about Queenston did not exceed two hundred men. Cameron's and Heward's companies of York militia lay at Brown's Point, three miles distant, but there were no other regular troops nearer than Fort George. . . .

In a battery named Fort Gray, on the brow of the cliff, above the village of Lewiston, two eighteen-pounders were mounted with the intention of silencing the gun in the redan, and two mortars and two six-pounders were planted on the bank of the river below to cover the landing and drive the British out of Queenston. Chrystie's and Fenwick's regiments of regulars from Fort Niagara, and three militia battalions from Schlosser, were marched to Lewiston by inland roads after dark on the evening of the 12th, and long before the appointed hour of three o'clock more than 4,000 men were assembled there without exciting special attention. Twelve boats, each of which could carry thirty men, and two others having a capacity of eighty each, manned by veteran fishermen familiar with the river, were already moored at the landing. The night was intensely dark, rain was still falling gently, and the winds and the roaring of the river drowned the sound of their movements. Everything seemed to conspire to favor their enterprise.

Colonel [Solomon] Van Rensselaer had originally been selected to command the advance guard, but when Chrystie arrived he stubbornly refused to waive his rank and it was then agreed that the latter should lead a column of three hundred regular troops, while Van Rensselaer headed an equal number of militia. The militia composing this detachment were accordingly chosen with great care from among the best-drilled men, and, by their commander at least, were believed to be superior to the United States troops in point of discipline. Forty picked men of the regular artillery, conducted by Lieut. Gansevoort, all of whom had long been quartered at Fort Niagara and knew the river well, were selected to head the other column, and were followed by four companies of the 13th United States Infantry, which was regarded as one of the best-disciplined regiments of the regular army. Next in succession, Col. Fenwick and Major Mullany were to cross with five hundred and fifty regulars, then an equal number of militia was to follow, and so on, until the entire division, consisting of the 6th, 13th, and 23rd United States Infantry, detachments of three regular artillery regiments acting as infantry, a battalion of volunteer riflemen, and the 16th, 17th, 18th, 19th, and 20th Regiments of New York militia, were passed over. Some of the artillerymen were provided with matches and rammers to work the captured guns, and a detachment of engineers was detailed to fortify a position as soon as it was taken. The number of officers and men exceeded four thousand, of whom at least fifteen hundred were regulars,

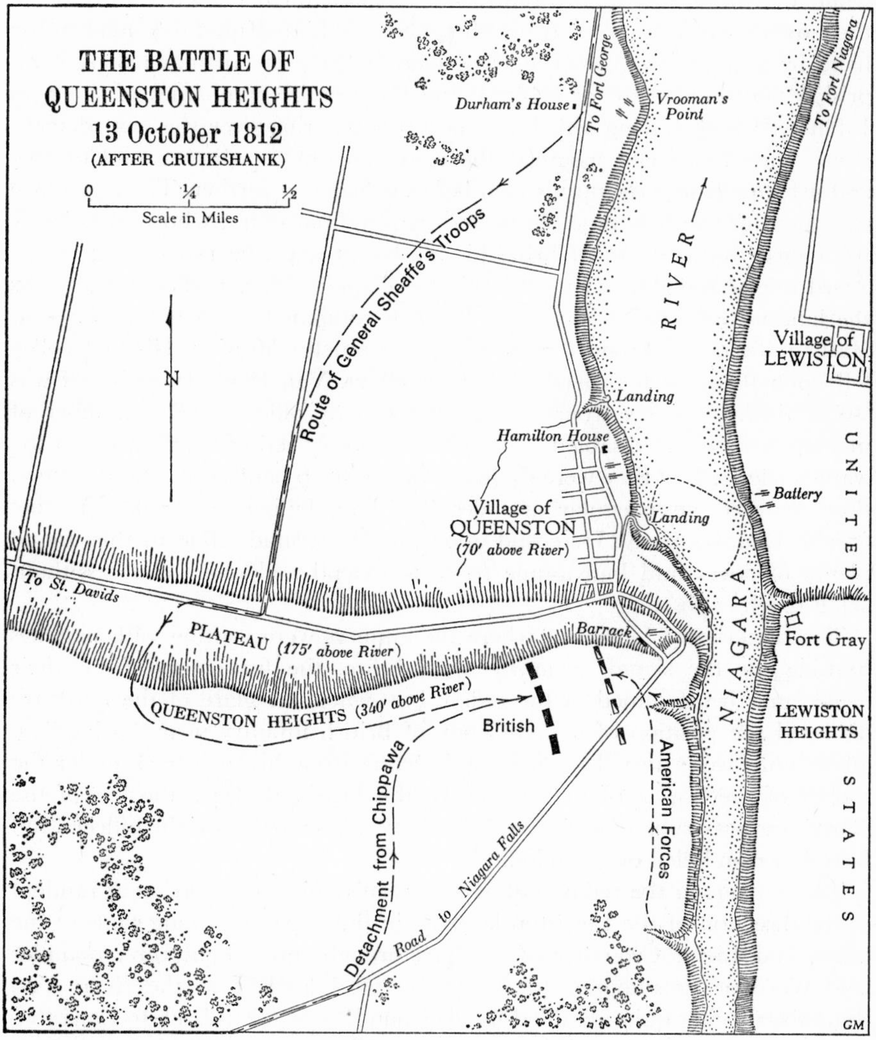

and, barring accidents, it was supposed that the whole force might be ferried over in seven trips. The two largest boats were also fitted with platforms on which a fieldpiece with its carriage could be loaded.

In less than a quarter of a hour from the time the boats pushed off, ten of them, conveying three hundred men, reached the opposite shore at the exact spot selected for effecting a landing, quite unperceived by the British sentries. Three, among them the two largest, were carried down by the current, and of these only the smaller one succeeded in landing below, while the other two finally returned by command of Colonel Chrystie to their own shore to make a fresh start. Chrystie himself was wounded in the hand by a grape shot. Most of those who landed were regular troops, comprising the detachment of artillery and three entire companies of the 13th Infantry,[14] and, having sent back the boats to bring over the next detachment, Van Rensselaer assumed the command in the absence of Chrystie, and attempted to form up his men before advancing further. Their presence was then for the first time discovered by a militia sentry, who was so badly frightened that, instead of firing his musket at once, he ran into the main guard to give the alarm. In a few minutes Captain Dennis advanced towards the landing with forty-six men of his own company and a few of Captain Hatt's militia, and found the enemy still in much confusion. His first volley fell upon them, as it proved, with fatal effect. Van Rensselaer himself was struck down with six wounds, several company officers and a number of men were killed or disabled, and the entire body retired in disorder to the water's edge where they were sheltered by the steep bank. From that position they returned an irregular and desultory fire, killing one and wounding four of Dennis's party. Here and upon the low ground adjacent they found plenty of cover and had ample room to extend and move about without being much exposed.

The batteries at Lewiston, where the gunners were waiting with matches burning for the signal, instantly opened fire, the first round from their heavy guns being aimed at the redan, but, when the glare of the musketry disclosed the position of a small body of British infantry near the landing, all six guns were turned upon it, and Dennis drew his men back under the shelter of the houses of the village. In this brief encounter the loss of the Americans was subsequently stated to have amounted to eight officers and forty-five men killed or wounded.

The gunners in the redan and at Vrooman's Point began firing at random in the direction of the Lewiston landing, in the hope of striking some of the boats, and Lieut. Crowther of the 41st brought up a light three-pounder field piece or grasshopper to sweep the road leading to the river. Van Rensselaer, being quite disabled by his wounds, was taken back to Lewiston, and the command devolved upon Capt. John E. Wool[15] of the 13th, a brave but very young and inexperienced officer, who for more than two hours seems to have been quite satisfied with retaining his foothold beside

[14] Wool's, Malcolm's, and Armstrong's.

[15] [John Ellis Wool (1784-1869), who fought so well at Queenston Heights, rose rapidly in the United States army after the war and was appointed inspector-general in 1821. During the Mexican War he organized volunteer forces and was a commander at the Battle of Buena Vista. He held Fortress Monroe, Virginia, for the Union in 1861. He became a brigadier-general in 1841 and a major-general in 1848, and retired in 1863.]

the river, while the batteries behind him were fast wrecking the village of Queenston. His men, however, maintained a brisk but harmless fire from the shelter of the bank. Reinforcements were steadily pushed over to his assistance, but misfortune still attended them. The boatmen had become frightened by the heavy firing and many of them had disappeared. Their places were supplied by soldiers who lacked skill and knowledge of the river. Of the second division of five or six boats, one was sunk by a roundshot from the hill and two, loaded with men, were swept far out of their course by the current. One of these, commanded by Lieut. Col. Fenwick of the artillery, struggled ashore in the cove below Queenston near Hamilton's wharf and attempted to ascend the bank there. They were at once briskly attacked; Fenwick himself received a pistol shot in the face which partially blinded him, besides two other wounds, and was taken prisoner with most of his men, Major Mullany and two others only escaping in the boat under a general fire, which damaged it so badly that it reached the American bank in a sinking condition. The other boat drifted fairly within range of Vrooman's battery and was captured there. The remaining boats returned to their own shore. The river being so narrow, many objects could be distinguished upon the opposite shore when lit up by the flashing of the artillery, and the shouts and shrieks of the combatants even were occasionally heard by thousands of interested spectators at Lewiston. Within half an hour of landing, Wool's force was doubled by the arrival of Ogilvie's and Lawrence's companies of the 13th, forty artillerymen under Lieut. Randolph, and a detachment of militia, and all the wounded men were removed, but no officer of superior rank came to assume command. . . .

Convinced by unmistakable signs that an attack was meditated within a day or two, Brock had been engaged till midnight in dispatching orders for the assembly of the militia. It was no surprise then for him to be aroused shortly after three o'clock by the distant booming of artillery up the river. He rose at once, but, still adhering to his opinion that the true attack would not be there, he remarked that it was only the war between the sentries. The steady cannonade and blazing beacons along the heights satisfied him at length that this was something more serious, and he mounted his horse and rode out of the gate just as a dragoon galloped up to announce that the enemy had landed at Queenston. As it was yet uncertain whether another landing was not intended in the vicinity of Niagara, the British general contented himself with giving instructions for Captain Holcroft, R. A.,[16]

[16] [William Holcroft (1777-1858) joined the Royal Artillery as a cadet in 1795, and fought in the Low Countries (1798-9) and at Copenhagen (1807). He became a captain in 1808 and was promoted to brevet-major for his part in the battle at Queenston. He commanded the artillery of the Centre Division in the battles of Fort George, Stoney Creek, and Fort Niagara in 1813 before returning to England on sick leave. He was 'a singularly gallant and capable officer'.]

to follow him with two guns and a party of Indians, while the remainder of the garrison remained under arms in readiness to act in any direction, until daylight more fully disclosed the designs of the enemy, and then set off at full speed, accompanied only by Captain Glegg of the 49th and Lieut.-Col. Macdonell,[17] his aides-de-camp. At Field's and Brown's Point he paused for an instant to direct the militia companies quartered there to follow him, leaving behind only a sufficient number of men to man the batteries at each place.

Day dawned grey and chill, with a thin fog rising from the river. Four boats filled with men were then seen to push off together from Lewiston, and at the same instant the head of a column of troops appeared again above the bank at the Queenston landing. Dennis hastily called down the light company by sound of the bugle from the heights to his support, and concentrated his fire on this force, which very soon retired again under cover of the bank, where their movements were almost entirely screened from view, although they had lost some men by the random fire of the light company during the morning.

Observing that the battery on the heights was now occupied only by a few men working the gun, Gansevoort pointed out to Wool a narrow fisherman's path leading around a rocky point and winding upwards to the summit, and suggested that a detachment might gain the rear of the British position unobserved by this route. Although already bleeding from more than one wound, Wool eagerly adopted the proposal, and, leaving a hundred men to occupy the landing and engage the attention of the British in that quarter, he instantly began the ascent at the head of the remainder, giving strict orders to an officer to shoot any man who attempted to turn back. They met no sentinel nor force of any kind, and gained the summit of the heights quite unopposed.

At this instant Brock rode into the village, splashed with mud from head to foot. He was at once recognized and welcomed with a hearty cheer by the men of the 49th, in which regiment he had served in every rank from subaltern to colonel. Reining in his horse for a moment to acknowledge their salute, he rode up the slope to the redan and there dismounted.

A striking scene presented itself to his gaze. A single glance showed him battalion upon battalion of troops drawn up in rear of the American batteries in readiness to embark; other detachments were entering their boats, some already upon the river, and an unknown number in possession of the Queenston landing. Their guns were throwing round and grape shot into the en-

[17][John Macdonell (1785-1812) was called to the bar of Upper Canada in 1808, was appointed attorney-general of the province, and was elected to the legislative assembly for Glengarry in 1812. He became provincial aide-de-camp to Brock, was present at the surrender of Detroit, and was killed at Queenston Heights.]

closures of the village, where Dennis still contrived to maintain a foothold, and an occasional shell from their mortar battery rose shrieking into the air. So far everything seemed to promise well. The party that had landed had not gained an inch of ground in three hours, and near a hundred prisoners had been taken with small loss.

Watching the flight of a shell from the gun beside him he observed that it burst prematurely, and turning to the gunner Brock advised him to try a longer fuse. The words were scarcely out of his mouth when a shout rose from the hillside above, followed by a volley of bullets whistling overhead, and a body of the enemy came charging down upon the rear of the battery. Resistance was out of the question, and there was no time even to mount, so leading their horses by the bridle the three officers ran hastily down the road to the village, followed by the dozen artillerymen working the gun, who fortunately had sufficient presence of mind to spike it before they came away.

All this was plainly visible to the troops at Lewiston, whose shouts could be heard amid the roar of the cannon as their flag rose over the battery, and they then pressed down eagerly to the boats. It was evident that the principal and probably the only attack was to be made here, and Brock despatched a message to Sheaffe at Fort George to turn every gun that would bear upon the American batteries opposite, and send forward the battalion companies of the 41st and flank companies of the militia. Then mounting his horse he rode at a gallop to the further end of village where the light company of the 49th was drawn up in line awaiting orders. Again he was received with a loud cheer, and wheeling his horse in the direction of the heights he exclaimed: 'Follow me, boys,' and led them at a run to the foot of the ascent. There he paused and dismounted, saying: 'Take breath, boys – you will need it in a few moments' – a significant announcement, which elicited another hearty shout.

The crest of the height was densely wooded in many places and its side dotted with clumps of small trees and shrubs richly spangled with the crimson, russet, and golden tints of autumn. These thickets, in combination with the natural inequalities of the ground, furnished excellent cover for the American riflemen. The redan was occupied by the main body of their troops, but they were unable to make any use of the captured gun. Freshly landed men were already ascending to their assistance, and the mortar battery had begun to throw shells in the direction of Brock's party in the hope of checking its advance.

Convinced of the great importance of regaining the lost position before the enemy was heavily reinforced, he ordered Dennis to join him with the 49th Grenadiers and Chisholm's company of York militia, leaving only a few men in the village to hold the Americans in check in that quarter. When these companies came up he detached Williams with a section of his own company and the whole of the militia, making about seventy men in all, by a roundabout route to turn the left of Wool's position. Observing this movement, the latter detached a party of 150 men to meet it, but after a brief interchange of shots the Americans fell into confusion and began to retire. Seizing the favorable moment, Brock sprang over the stone wall behind which he had directed his men to take shelter and led the way directly up the steep ascent towards the battery, waving his sword and shouting words of encouragement to the grenadiers, who followed him with a ready cheer.

The rain had ceased, and strong, slanting gleams of sunshine broke through the parting clouds. The ground was thickly strewn with fallen leaves, slippery with wet and yielding treacherously, and as the men stumbled and fell here and there the line was quickly broken. Wool sent a reinforcement to support his advance party, and their fire soon began to tell. 'This is the first time I have ever seen the 49th turn their backs!' Brock exclaimed angrily as he noticed unwounded men dropping to the rear, and at the rebuke the ranks promptly closed up. Macdonell brought up in support the companies of Cameron and Heward, which had just arrived from Brown's Point much exhausted, having run nearly all the way. The force then engaged in the direct assault of the heights, including the last-named companies, numbering about one hundred and ninety men. The militia flank companies were uniformed in scarlet and advanced with such steadiness that Wool was led to believe that he was being attacked by four companies of the 49th. His own command had been increased to about five hundred rank and file, two-thirds of whom were regular soldiers, yet notwithstanding their advantage in numbers and position, being at the same time pressed warmly on the flank by Williams's detachment, they began to shrink from the contest.

Seeing that the supports were lagging at the foot of the hill, Brock shouted to Macdonell to 'push on the York volunteers', and led his own party to the right with the evident intention of joining Williams. A bullet struck the wrist of his sword-arm, inflicting a slight wound to which he paid no attention, but continued to wave his sword and encourage his men. His tall, portly figure and energetic gestures, as well as his conspicuous uniform and position several yards in front of the line, naturally made him a special target for the bullets of the enemy, although he does not seem to have been personally recognized by them. At last a rifleman stepped out of a thicket less than fifty yards away and took deliberate aim at him. More than one man of the 49th observed this and fired hastily in the hope of anticipating his shot, but without effect. The fatal bullet struck their leader in the breast very near the heart and he sank slowly to the ground and expired, after murmuring a few broken sentences to those nearest him to conceal his death from the men and continue the fight.[18] A group of the 49th at once gathered about their prostrate leader and one of them was severely wounded by a cannon shot and fell across his body.

Macdonell spurred his horse sharply to the front and called upon the grenadiers to avenge their leader's death. Williams at the same moment led forward his detachment from the thickets on the right, and the combined force charged at once fiercely upon the front and flank of the enemy, who were already in disorder and huddled together about the battery, out of which they were quickly expelled and driven obliquely upwards towards the summit of the heights in the direction of the river. Being hotly pursued, an officer raised a handkerchief or a white cloth on the point of his sword as a flag of truce, but this was quickly snatched away from him by Wool, who by great exertions succeeded in persuading his men to make another stand on the very verge of the cliff. A body of fresh troops, including an entire company of the 6th U.S. Infantry, and another of volunteer riflemen, opportunely came to his assistance at this critical moment and enabled him to prolong his line until he outflanked his assailants in both directions. They had also fallen into much disorder through the haste and impetuosity of their advance. Williams, who was on the right of the line, was disabled by a ghastly wound in the head, which prostrated him upon the ground apparently dead, and a considerable number of men were killed or wounded. Dennis received a severe wound in the thigh but stopped the flow of blood with his hand and continued in the action to the last. Lieut. Archibald McLean, afterwards Chief Justice, was also severely wounded and carried from the field. Macdonell had as yet escaped unharmed, although, being the only mounted officer present, he naturally attracted the fire of the enemy by whom he was supposed at the time to be the General, and his hat and clothes were pierced in many places. But now, while attempting to restore order and form the men for a fresh attack, his horse was struck by a shot, and as the animal plunged in agony the rider also received a mortal wound and was thrown from the saddle. At this moment the main body of the enemy, who numbered three or four hundred, were assembled about thirty yards in front under cover of thickets and logs, keeping an incessant but desultory fire, but seemed to be in much confusion. In spite of the efforts of Dennis and other officers, the British then gave way in turn and retreated to the foot of the heights, carrying with them, however, the dead body of their General as well as

[18] [According to Major J. B. Glegg's letter to William Brock from Fort George on October 14, 1812: 'The ball entered his right breast and passed through on his left side. His sufferings were of very short duration, and were terminated in a few minutes, when he uttered in a feeble voice: "My fall must not be noticed or impede my brave companies from advancing to victory." ']

Lieut.-Colonel Macdonell and most of the wounded. They were not vigorously pursued and did not lose more than a score of prisoners, most of whom were too badly injured to be removed. Dennis refused to quit the field and succeeded in collecting most of his men at the farther end of the village, which was still occupied by Lieut. Crowther with a squad of militia artillerymen in charge of two small guns. He eventually retired to Durham's farm on the river-road about a mile distant and abreast of Vrooman's Point.

The result of this engagement had a highly inspiriting influence upon the troops at Lewiston, numbers of whom instantly professed great eagerness to cross the river and share the glory of the day. They still possessed a sufficient number of boats to carry over the remainder of the division before ten o'clock; the passage of the river was now for some time entirely unopposed, and why they did not make better use of their opportunities has never been satisfactorily explained. One officer of rank (Col. Chrystie) stated that he crossed the river three times, and that Major Mullany went from one side to the other no less than five times during the day. For five hours after Brock's death they were practically in unmolested possession of the landing and the heights as well, and Col. Van Rensselaer asserted that as long as the men showed any inclination to cross the boats were well managed. As it was, considerable bodies both of regular troops and militia were brought over with a six-pound field piece, its carriage and tumbril, as well as harness for horses and other equipment. Shortly after seven o'clock Colonel Chrystie came over and assumed the command, but, finding himself unable even to dislodge the garrison from the village, he recrossed the river to bring over reinforcements with artillery and intrenching tools. Upon hearing his report of the situation, General Van Rensselaer despatched an urgent order to General Smyth at Buffalo to move his brigade to his support, and sent over an engineer officer to lay out a fortified camp. About noon he crossed in person. General Van Rensselaer and Colonel Chrystie examined the position on the heights and gave directions for its immediate fortification. A party of engineers, under Lieut. J. G. Totten, was set at work and field works traced out. The gun in the redan was unspiked and brought to bear upon the village. Colonel Winfield Scott,[19] the future conqueror of Mexico and Commander-in-Chief of the United States army, having arrived from Buffalo during the morning

[19] [Winfield Scott (1786-1866) joined the United States army in 1808 and fought at Queenston Heights as lieutenant-colonel of the 2nd Artillery. In 1813 he was General Dearborn's chief of staff at York, Fort George, and Stoney Creek. He was made a brigadier-general in 1814 and distinguished himself at the capture of Fort Erie and at the battles of Lundy's Lane and Chippawa. Afterwards he commanded in campaigns against the Indians; during the Mexican War he led the main force from Vera Cruz to Mexico City; and he organized the defence of Washington during the early months of the Civil War. He was appointed general-in-chief of the army in 1841 and was the unsuccessful Whig candidate in the presidential election of 1852.]

with a battery of artillery, placed his guns in position at Lewiston and crossed the river to take command of the regular troops at Queenston, who were reinforced by detachments of the 6th and 23rd U.S. Infantry and 2nd and 3rd Artillery. About the same time Brigadier-General William Wadsworth assumed command of the militia brigade, consisting of portions of Allen's, Bloom's, Mead's, and Stranahan's regiments, and Moseley's battalion of riflemen. The precise number of men belonging to these corps that passed the river it is now impossible to ascertain. Estimates by their own officers ranged from one thousand to sixteen hundred. Some companies of militia were represented by officers without men, others by men without officers, while a few were almost or quite complete.

The sound of a heavy cannonade from the mouth of the river excited the worst apprehensions in the minds of the little band that had halted at Durham's house, until they were reassured by the arrival of Captain Derenzy with several companies of the 41st and militia, a detachment of Royal Artillery with two field guns under Captain Holcroft from Niagara, and a party of Indians led by Captain John Norton[20] and Lieut. John Brant.[21] Panic-stricken stragglers from the field, whom these reinforcements encountered on the road, reported that Dennis's entire command had been cut to pieces and that five thousand men had landed. Accordingly, they advanced much of the distance at the double, and when they reached Queenston they were out of breath and quite exhausted. Under these circumstances it would have been folly to attempt the recovery of the heights, where the numbers of the enemy could have been seen momentarily increasing, but Holcroft promptly planted his guns on the high ground below the village and endeavored to interrupt the passage of the river.

Small parties of the enemy had entered the upper part of the village, where they plundered some of the houses, but they made no effort to occupy it in force. After a few shots, finding that his pieces were too far away to reach their boats, Holcroft again limbered up, and, guided by Captain Archibald Hamilton, to whom every inch of ground was familiar from boyhood, dashed boldly across the ravine and through the village until he reached Hamilton's house, where he took up a position within the courtyard partly

[20] [John Norton (1771?-1831?) was born in Scotland and came to Canada as a private in the 65th Regiment. After leaving the army in 1788 he lived among the Six Nations and subsequently was appointed interpreter to the Mohawks. He was present at Detroit and led the Mohawks at the battle of Queenston Heights. He exerted considerable influence over Joseph Brant and following Brant's death he engaged in a lengthy, rancorous controversy with William Claus over their respective claims to be considered as the spokesman of the Six Nations. After the war he travelled in Georgia and the lower Mississippi country, finally returning to Scotland to live. See also pages 184-6.]

[21] [John Brant (1794-1832) was a son of Joseph Brant, born at the Mohawk village, Grand River. He led the Indian detachments at Beaver Dam and in other actions.]

sheltered by the ruins of the wall. Derenzy at once supported him with a company of the 41st, and his fire soon became effective, although he lost some of his best men. A few spherical case-shot drove away the enemy's riflemen and he then engaged the batteries opposite, firing also, when an opportunity offered, at boats on the river. The battery on Lewiston Heights was still out of range, but the guns at the landing were three times silenced and a scow and at least two other boats sunk in the act of crossing. Such was the precision of his fire that from that time forward very few men succeeded in passing the river.

In the meantime Scott had thrown out pickets to the edge of the woods on the left of his position, and the Indians were detached in that direction to drive them in and annoy their working parties. This was accomplished in fine style, as their approach through the woods and an orchard was undetected, and the American outposts were surprised and completely routed with considerable loss. A large body of infantry then advanced to repel them, and the Indians instantly ran to the woods again, whence they kept up an incessant fire accompanied with shrill whoops. The suddenness of the attack and the character of the assailants produced a genuine panic, which extended itself even to Lewiston, where a militia company on the point of entering the boats abruptly halted and refused to proceed. Norton continued to skirmish with and annoy their outposts, and although several times attacked always eluded his assailants by plunging into the woods, where they dared not follow, although one Indian was captured by a party of American riflemen. Norton himself was wounded and his party sustained considerable loss, but was never entirely driven out of action. Numbers of the American militia deserted their companies and attempted to regain their own shore, and thenceforth their force continued to diminish. In addition to the serious annoyance and loss inflicted upon the enemy by this movement, direct communication was again opened with the garrison at Chippawa.

Upon reaching Queenston, Derenzy had at once sent a message to General Sheaffe describing the situation of affairs, and the latter soon afterwards arrived and assumed command. He lost no time in ordering every man that could be spared from the garrisons of Fort George and Chippawa to join him without delay. By two o'clock the detachments from the former post had all arrived, leaving it occupied only by a few men of the Royal Artillery and Lincoln militia, and those from Chippawa were known to be rapidly approaching. The force already assembled consisted of Holcroft's detachment of Royal Artillery with two six-pounders, a squad of Swayze's Provincial Artillery with two three-pounders, under Lieut. Crowther, five companies of the 41st Regiment, Capt. James Crooks's and John McEwen's companies of the 1st Lincoln, William Crooks's and Abraham Nelles's companies of the 4th Lincoln, commanded on this occasion by Lieut. Thomas Butler and Ensign

James Dittrick, Hatt's and Durand's companies of the 5th Lincoln, Applegarth's company of the 2nd York, a small company of negroes from Niagara, under Capt. James Cooper, a few troopers of Merritt's Provincial dragoons, and the remnants of the two companies of the 49th and three of the York militia engaged in the morning, probably numbering in all rather more than 800 of all ranks, exclusive of the Indians, who certainly did not exceed two hundred.

As the enemy's forces appeared to be still considerably more numerous than his own, and they were busily engaged in fortifying their position in evident anticipation of another direct attack from below, the British commander determined to leave Holcroft's two guns, supported by a detachment of infantry, to occupy the village and prevent the passage of reinforcements, while with the remainder of his troops he moved around their flank, ascending the heights by a path in rear of the woods already occupied by the Indians, and formed a junction with the column advancing from Chippawa, which would increase his numerical strength by 150 men. Although this manœuvre would compel him to make a detour of nearly three miles before engaging, he would at once escape the enfilading fire of the batteries at Lewiston, avoid the steep ascent in the face of the enemy, render their field works useless, and place his men on an equal footing with them on the open and level ground above, supported by the fire of the two light guns under Lieut. Crowther.

The Indians redoubled their activity as the column approached, keeping, however, well under cover, and thoroughly succeeded in baffling any attempt to harass its advance. In a couple of hours Sheaffe gained the cleared ground on the right of the woods occupied by them, extending as far as the Portage Road, where he remained until he saw Captain Richard Bullock[22] advancing from Chippawa with part of the grenadier company of the 41st, and Captain Robert Hamilton's and John Rowe's companies of the 2nd Lincoln, strengthened for the occasion, like most of the others, by a number of volunteers from the ranks of the sedentary militia. . . .

[22] [There were two Richard Bullocks, presumably father and son, serving as officers in the 41st Regiment at this time. Captain Richard Bullock, here referred to, became a lieutenant in 1796 and later a captain in the 41st, in which capacity he was present at the capture of Detroit, the battle at Queenston Heights, and the forays into Michigan and Ohio in the early months of 1813. By September 1813 he was in command at Michilimackinac and he held this position during the early months of 1814. The second Richard Bullock, a lieutenant, also served in the same operations but continued with the 41st Regiment and was present in the battle of the Thames in October 1813. At the end of the year he took part in the capture of Fort Niagara and the burning of Black Rock. In 1814 he was promoted to captain and he participated in the unsuccessful night assault upon Fort Erie. After the war he became sheriff of the Midland district and as adjutant-general of militia was responsible for organizing the defences of Upper Canada during the Rebellion of 1837. He died some time after 1857.]

The combined force, numbering about 930 officers and men, including Indians, was formed for the attack with the light company of the 41st, under Lieut. McIntyre, and the two companies of the 49th, still commanded by the dauntless Dennis, on the left of the line next the Indians, supported by the flank companies of the 1st and 4th Lincoln Regiments, under Lieut.-Col. Johnson Butler of the 4th Lincoln Regiment. The centre and right wing were composed of the five remaining companies of the 41st, having in support the rest of the militia under Lieut.-Col. Thomas Clark of the 2nd Lincoln. The two small field pieces, drawn by men with drag ropes, preceded the advance of the line, which was necessarily deliberate.

The number of combatants actually arrayed against them at that moment cannot be exactly stated, but could hardly have been less than seven hundred, of whom more than half were regulars. Like the British, this force was made up of detachments from many corps. Its ranks had been much diminished by desertions since the Indians had renewed the fight, numbers of men stealing down to the river and lurking there in the hope of finding means of escape. Perceiving that Sheaffe was preparing for a decisive attack upon his position, and probably having no desire to grace his triumph as a prisoner, General Van Rensselaer determined to return to Lewiston, with the lingering hope of enlisting a reinforcement from the large body of militia still congregated there. He had scarcely entered his boat when the skulkers at the landing crowded into it in such numbers that it was in actual danger of being swamped by their weight, and pushed off heedless alike of his threats and entreaties.

His departure left Colonel Scott in command, having under him Colonel Chrystie and Brigadier-General Wadsworth, who had waived his right to command. Sheaffe's movement obliged him to abandon his uncompleted fieldworks and take up a new position on the crown of the heights, where a slight barricade was hastily extemporized with fence rails, logs, and brushwood, with the left flank resting on the edge of the cliff and the riflemen on the other facing the Indians from among the brush huts formerly occupied by the 49th light company. The gun in the redan could not be made to bear in this direction, and his solitary field piece was therefore planted in front of the centre of the line, near the site of the present monument, where it was partly masked by the underbrush. General Wadsworth, who certainly did not lack courage, passed rapidly through the ranks of the militia without hat or coat, encouraging them and explaining the plan of defence. While waiting the attack, Scott received a message from Van Rensselaer stating that he had been unable to induce a single regiment, or even a company, to advance to his relief, but forwarding a supply of ammunition and assuring him that if he felt unable to maintain his position boats would be sent to remove the troops and the artillery would cover his retreat. . . .

The contest was begun by the advance of the light company of the 41st, supported by about thirty-five militia and a party of Indians, who fired a single volley and then charged with fixed bayonets upon the riflemen on the right of the American line, which, being unprovided with weapons to resist this form of attack, gave way in great confusion, leaving that flank exposed. On witnessing the success of this movement, Sheaffe gave the signal for a general advance. The entire line, after firing a volley, raised the Indian war-whoop and charged with great fury under cover of the smoke. The gun was taken and the position carried almost without resistance, and the entire body of American troops forced swiftly back upon the river, the British line by the advance of the wings gradually assuming the form of a crescent, and overlapping them on both flanks. Some of the fugitives, braving the fire of the guns in the village, ran down the hill towards the landing; a few took shelter in a house where they were taken; Scott, himself, and a number of others, scrambled down the steep bank to the water's edge, in the hope of finding the promised boats; Wadsworth and Chrystie, with more than three hundred officers and men, surrendered on the verge of the cliff.

Meanwhile the fire of Holcroft's artillery had rendered the passage of the river so dangerous that the remaining boatmen positively refused to undertake it and dispersed. As no boats were waiting to receive them, a few desperate men plunged into the river and attempted to swim across, of whom some perished; the remainder tried to secrete themselves among the rocks and thickets along the shore. The Indians lined the cliffs above, or perched themselves in the trees, whooping incessantly and firing at the fugitives whenever an opportunity offered. Under these circumstances Scott was glad to raise a white flag in the hope of preserving the lives of the rest of his command. For a few minutes, even after this was done, the Indians continued to shoot down or tomahawk the unresisting crowd, either not observing or disregarding this token of submission, until it is said that Sheaffe grew so indignant at their misconduct that he dashed his hat and sword on the ground. When they were finally restrained, 390 officers and men surrendered there. Some yet evaded discovery, and forty were brought in next day, swelling the number of prisoners taken to 925, according to official account, among whom were one general, five lieutenant-colonels, four majors, nineteen captains, and forty-four other officers.

Stragglers continued to surrender for several days, eventually increasing the aggregate to 958, of whom about 450 belonged to the United States regular army and the remainder to the militia of the State of New York.

The total British loss, exclusive of Indians, amounted to fourteen killed, seventy-seven wounded, and twenty-one missing, several of whom were taken prisoners. The flank companies of the 49th Regiment suffered most, losing eight killed, thirty-three wounded, and six missing. The York militia came next with two killed, seventeen wounded, and five missing. The Lincoln militia reported fifteen wounded and ten missing. Two Cayuga chiefs and three warriors, whose names have been preserved, were killed, and Norton and eight others wounded. Although this loss was insignificant in point of numbers, the death of General Brock was felt to be an almost irreparable blow, and by many of his opponents was considered to have fully compensated for their defeat. Lieut.-Col. Macdonell was the only other British officer killed. . . .

There can be no doubt that the loss of the vanquished was severe. A single company of the 13th lost thirty men in killed or wounded, and four out of the five captains of that regiment engaged were disabled by wounds. Three captains and three subalterns were killed, and, besides those who were taken prisoners, two colonels, four captains, and five subalterns were wounded. There were 120 wounded officers and men among the prisoners, thirty of whom died. The hospital at Niagara was filled, and the remainder sheltered in the court house and churches. One hundred and forty others had been removed before the surrender to Lewiston, and of these, not less than 100 are reported to have been buried within a month, many of them dying from flesh wounds through insufficient care.

Van Rensselaer's failure was complete and disastrous. He had lost all his best officers, and the flower of his troops, and the entire division engaged was practically rendered incapable of resuming operations in the field. Its organic efficiency was irretrievably destroyed. Ten days afterwards, he abandoned the struggle in despair by throwing up the command.[23]

General Sheaffe on the other hand did not escape censure in Canada for not following up his victory by an attack upon Fort Niagara, which had been practically evacuated by its garrison in consequence of a hot and effective bombardment from the British batteries that afternoon.

FURTHER READING: E. A. Cruikshank (ed.), *Documentary history of the campaign upon the Niagara frontier, 1812-14* (Welland, Ontario, 1896-1908), parts III and IV; W. C. H. Wood (ed.), *Select British documents . . .* , volume I, pages 580-639; F. H. Severance, 'The case of Brig.-Gen. Alexander Smyth, as shown by his own writings . . .', *Buffalo Historical Society*, volume 18 (1914), pages 213-55.

[23] 'Van Rensselaer's Campaign did not, like that of Hull's, cost a Province, but it sacrificed nearly as many effective troops as were surrendered by Hull.' – Henry Adams, *History of the United States*, vol. VI, page 353.

By the autumn of 1812 the American and British flotillas had begun to contend for supremacy upon Lake Ontario, the key to the conquest of Upper Canada. In an attempt to win control, Commodore Chauncey launched an attack, which proved inconclusive, upon Kingston harbour in November 1812. Then the onset of winter forced both fleets to take shelter at Sackets Harbor and Kingston, where each was equally exposed to the possibility of destruction at the hands of enemy raiders. Both sides began building ships to take command of the lake in the coming summer and both stood on the defensive while giving out the impression they contemplated launching attacks themselves. The war on Lake Ontario assumed a cautious, indecisive character that persisted to the end. . . . J. MACKAY HITSMAN, *a member of the Canadian Army's Historical Section, has published a number of articles, chiefly on military subjects, and is preparing a history of the War of 1812. This article first appeared in 'Military Affairs' (volume 23, 1959) and is presented with the consent of the editor of that journal, and of the author.*

Alarum On Lake Ontario, Winter 1812-13

BY J. MACKAY HITSMAN

The war of nerves that developed on both sides of Lake Ontario during the winter months of 1812-13 is an excellent example of how a relatively simple situation can get out of hand when commanders have time to ponder unduly about the courses open to both the enemy and themselves. Particularly when, in fact, the necessary men and munitions are not immediately available for offensive operations. The problem was control of Lake Ontario during the course of the coming campaign. The means were the opposing naval squadrons, which had to be kept safe during the months the lake would be frozen over and augmented by additional and larger ships then under construction.

As a consequence of the surrender at Detroit of the American army which was to have swept across Upper Canada during the summer of 1812, and Major-General Henry Dearborn's listless behaviour as commander of the northern theatre of operations, Captain Isaac Chauncey[1] had been ordered

[1] [Isaac Chauncey (1772-1840) continued in command of American naval operations on Lake Ontario throughout the war. He subsequently commanded the Mediterranean squadron (1816-18) and was Commissioner of the Navy between 1821 and 1824 and from 1832 until his death.]

forward from the New York navy yard, of which he had been in charge for four years, 'to assume command of the naval force on lakes Erie and Ontario, and to use every exertion to obtain control of them this fall'. Considered to be one of the most efficient officers in the United States navy, Chauncey had just passed his fortieth birthday. His service at sea included the closing stages of the undeclared naval war with France (1798-1800) and the conflict with the pirates of Tripoli (1801-5). Although he did not reach Sackets Harbor until 6 October, about 170 seamen and marines, 140 ship's carpenters, more than 100 cannon and other stores had gone forward earlier. In less than a month Commodore Chauncey was cruising the eastern end of Lake Ontario with a make-shift squadron consisting of the 18-gun brig *Oneida* and six converted schooners.

On 10 November Chauncey chased into Kingston the *Royal George*, a 22-gun corvette which was then the largest warship on the Great Lakes. After an exchange of shots which lasted upwards of an hour and forty-five minutes, the American vessels withdrew. Damage was slight and casualties were only one killed and a few wounded on each side. But there could be no gainsaying the fact that Chauncey had wrested command of Lake Ontario from the British army's badly officered and generally incompetent Provincial Marine. Until the approach of winter put an end to further navigation, his vessels were able to cruise unmolested off Kingston.

Chauncey's brief glance at the Kingston defences was, however, to result in the beginning of considerable excitement over nothing. In addition to crediting the Provincial Marine's vessels with 108 guns and crews totalling 890 officers and men, Chauncey reported that 'the enemy had more than 30 guns mounted at Kingston and from 1,000 to 1,500 men'. Actually, the Canadian vessels mounted only 52 guns and were manned by a mere 230 officers and men; while the harbour defences consisted only of two batteries mounting half a dozen small ship's guns and a blockhouse under construction on Point Henry to carry a six- and nine-pounder. Apart from the local militia, many of whom had sprung to arms only when the alarm had been sounded, Colonel John Vincent's[2] garrison consisted of 458 regulars, about half of whom belonged to his own 49th Regiment of Foot.

Although Colonel Vincent's experience of active warfare had been limited, he had 31 years of commissioned service behind him and seems to have been better suited to the artifices of war than Commodore Chauncey. Thus the

[2] [John Vincent (1765-1848) entered the British army in 1781, became a captain in the 49th Regiment in 1786, and eventually followed Sheaffe in command of that regiment. Before coming to Canada he served in the West Indies, Holland, and Denmark. He attained the rank of lieutenant-colonel in 1813, major-general in 1813, lieutenant-general in 1825, and general in 1841. He commanded at Kingston in 1812, at Fort George in 1813, and at Montreal in 1814 until he returned to England on sick leave.]

bearers of his flag of truce despatched to Sackets Harbor on 16 November managed to create the impression that Chauncey's attack had caused considerable damage and had crippled both the *Royal George* and a converted schooner. They also brought back word to Kingston of the 24-gun corvette *Madison*, which Chauncey was to launch on 26 November, after a phenomenally short construction period of 45 days, and the plan to lay down a sister ship immediately.

It might be noted here that New York's military-minded Governor Daniel Tompkins,[3] who earlier had accompanied Chauncey to Sackets Harbor, had warned Brigadier-General Jacob Brown,[4] then commanding the state militia there, 'against Flags of truce and the introduction of deserters to your encampment. The former are often sent for insidious purposes and the latter are seldom to be trusted or relied upon.'

On 1 December Commodore Chauncey wrote the Secretary of the Navy in Washington that the season was now so far advanced, and the weather so intensely cold, that it was unsafe to navigate Lake Ontario. Therefore, he planned to lay up his vessels in a couple of days and then visit Buffalo and Presqu'ile to make arrangements for the spring campaign. But Chauncey was worried about the 'exposed position' of his little navy during the coming winter months: 'Altho' I think the Vessels with their crews are fully competent to protect themselves against any attacks of musketry, yet if the Enemy by any desperate effort should succeed in obtaining possession of the Forts in this Town, the vessels must fall of course, as they could not be moved for the ice.'

> Viewing the immense importance of the command of this Lake to the Enemy [this letter continued] no one can doubt but that he will make a desperate effort to regain the ascendancy that he has lost, and really the accomplishment of the object is not a difficult Task to an Enterprising officer. Closed up as we shall be within about 30 miles of Kingston where the enemy can (and most likely will) collect a force of from 3 to 4,000 men for the express purpose of destroying our naval ascendancy on this Lake, he can with great ease (after

[3] [Daniel Tompkins (1774-1825) was admitted to the New York bar in 1795 and soon entered public life. He was a member of the state legislature, of the state Constitutional Convention of 1801, and of the state supreme court. As governor of New York from 1807 to 1817 he actively supported the war against Britain. He was vice president of the United States between 1817 and 1825.]

[4] [Jacob Jennings Brown (1775-1828) was a county judge and brigadier-general of militia in New York state, and upon the outbreak of the war was given charge of the Oswego–Lake St. Francis sector of the front. In 1813 he directed the defence of Sackets Harbor against Prevost's attack. The next year he was commissioned a major-general in the regular army and led the American forces at the capture of Fort Erie and in the battles of Chippawa and Lundy's Lane. Because of severe wounds received at the latter engagement, he handed over his command to General Izard in October 1814.]

this month) cross from Kingston to Long or Grand Island [now Wolfe Island] on the Ice, from thence to Gravelly Point [now Cape Vincent], so along the shore to Chaumont Bay, across that Bay to this Harbor in about 12 hours as all their Troops are exercised to walk with Snow Shoes. Now, Sir, suppose 2 or 3,000 men cross in the way pointed out, what can save us here? Nothing but a re-enforcement of Regular Troops sufficient to repel any attack that may be made upon us, and so preserve our little Fleet from otherwise certain destruction.

At the moment, Colonel Alexander Macomb's[5] military garrison consisted of 500 regulars and about 1,000 militia. But not more than 600 of the latter were fit for duty and even this number was being reduced daily by desertions, discharges, and furloughs. Moreover, the three months' tour of service for most of the remainder would expire at the end of the year. Macomb was co-operating in the construction of blockhouses to guard against any surprise, but Chauncey estimated that a further 500 to 1,000 regulars were needed. The previous day he had written General Dearborn at Albany to this effect. Chauncey was ready to counter any argument that reinforcements would be required elsewhere for operations in the spring: the fleet could then transport them anywhere 'with more facility than they can march'.

In an effort to verify his suppositions and obtain first-hand intelligence, Chauncey sent a flag of truce across to Kingston on 5 December with the late owner of the sloop *Elizabeth*, a Mr. Vaughan who was well acquainted with Kingston from pre-war days. The latter discovered from an old acquaintance, now an officer on the *Royal George*, that the garrison consisted of only 600 regulars and 1,000 militia, although a further 2,000 militia might be assembled from the surrounding country within 24 hours. The Provincial Marine's vessels had been unloaded and laid up for the winter. As Chauncey reported to Washington, however, 'Mr. Vaughan could not learn that the enemy contemplated an attack upon this place this winter: on the contrary, they appeared to apprehend one from us.'

Actually, however, consideration was being given at Kingston to the possibility of launching an attack against Sackets Harbor, in much the manner envisaged by Chauncey. On 3 December Captain Andrew Gray had despatched an outline plan for such an operation to Sir George Prevost, Captain-General and Governor-in-Chief in British North America, with headquarters at Quebec. A member of the Quartermaster-General's staff, which was charged with the supervision of the Provincial Marine, Captain Gray had

[5] [Alexander Macomb (1782-1841) entered the American army in 1799 and by 1812 was lieutenant-colonel of engineers and adjutant-general. In 1814 he was put in command of the frontier bordering on Lake Champlain, with the rank of brigadier-general. For his successful defence of Plattsburg against Sir George Prevost he was made a major-general and in 1835 he became commander-in-chief of the United States army.]

been advised, following his arrival at Kingston, that Sackets Harbor was but weakly defended by two batteries and that there were no blockhouses or other enclosed works. His suggestion called for only one battalion being sent forward from Montreal during January, after having been trained in the use of snowshoes, to augment the local troops. 'The principal thing to be apprehended,' his letter concluded, 'would be the intelligence of our movements reaching the enemy; but if the enterprize is conducted with dispatch the blow would be struck before he could avail himself of any information he might receive. We would require 3 or 4 pieces of Artillery, on sleighs, to destroy any Block houses or Temporary works they may in the meantime run up.'

Unfortunately, however, an attack on Sackets Harbor ran counter to the purely defensive policy which a naturally cautious Sir George Prevost was endeavouring to follow. Prevost hesitated to attempt any operation that might result in heavy casualties to his already inadequate forces. Moreover, a purely local success would be worse than useless should it tend to unite the American people behind a war which was particularly unpopular with the Federalist voters of New England and northern New York. Yet Lieutenant-Colonel R. H. Bruyeres, Commanding Royal Engineer in the Canadas, was directed to look into the matter during his forthcoming trip to report upon the defences of the upper province.

When Lieutenant-Colonel Bruyeres reached Kingston on Saturday, 16 January 1813, he met Captain Gray who had returned there from York. He also appears to have gone into the question thoroughly with Colonel Vincent. But, as he wrote to Sir George Prevost, it was 'now so long since any information has been obtained from that Post (being previous to the closing of the Navigation) that it is indispensably necessary first to procure a correct knowledge of the force at present there, and whether they have fortified and strengthened their position with the Ship guns, for it is ascertained they have nearly 100 pieces of Artillery in that Harbor for Naval purposes. Much will therefore depend to what use they have applied these Guns during the Winter.' Colonel Vincent intended to take advantage of a recent incident at Prescott to send a flag of truce to Sackets Harbor. An attempt would also be made to employ spies.

Actually there had been very little change at Sackets Harbor. Before leaving for Buffalo on 13 December 1812, Chauncey had written the Secretary of the Navy that his vessels were laid up for the winter and that the bay was frozen 'quite across'. The squadron was moored in a line, flanked by two of the vessels, which would help protect the remainder against any sudden attack. When Colonel Macomb was transferred to Plattsburg, military command devolved upon Brigadier-General Richard Dodge of the New York militia. This officer must have seen through Colonel Vincent's subterfuge, for the bearer of the flag of truce failed to bring back to Kingston any useful intelligence.

Once again at Kingston, on his return trip from visiting the more westerly posts, Lieutenant-Colonel Bruyeres wrote Sir George Prevost on 13 February that no intelligence had as yet been obtained concerning the situation at Sackets Harbor. But he would delay his departure for two or three days in the hope that the 'two persons . . . now employed for that purpose' might return. From what had been learned during his trip, however, he concluded that 'the Enemy are extremely active, and using the greatest executions to strengthen the whole line of Frontier both on the St. Lawrence and Niagara Rivers with Troops, and will be prepared with a formidable Marine Force to act on this Lake very early in the Spring.'

Chauncey must have arrived back at Sackets Harbor shortly after the British flag of truce had come and gone on 19 January. On the following day he sent a rather querulous despatch to Washington, complaining that he had found everything much as when he had left: no additional regular troops had arrived and the blockhouses had not yet been completed.

The letter also mentioned four deserters having arrived from Kingston, but Chauncey seems to have taken at face value their exaggerated story that its garrison now numbered 1,000 regulars – because it corroborated information received from other sources. These other sources were farmers, who had crossed into Canada to sell flour and pork for higher prices and then had had their sleighs commandeered to transport troops and stores to Kingston, and the detachments of militia scattered between Salmon River and Ogdensburg on the American side of the St. Lawrence. In consequence, there was a fairly widespread belief in northern New York that the British were planning an attack on Sackets Harbor. For instance, on 22 January the *New York Evening Post* carried the following despatch from Canandaigua, dated 10 days earlier:

> *Look Out:* – From information we have received, we think it highly probable, that the British are preparing to make a descent on Sacket's Harbor with a view of destroying the American vessels which are hauled up there for the winter. – Their destruction, would be important to the British, as thereby they may retain the command of Lake Ontario, which they cannot do, if our little fleet is *well* found in the spring. A great number of sleighs, loaded with British troops, have been seen to pass up on the other side of the St. Lawrence, and as soon as the river is frozen over, it is apprehended they will cross.

On 5 February, the day before he set out for Albany to discuss the conduct of the coming spring campaign with General Dearborn, Chauncey wrote Washington that he had 22 guns mounted upon *Madison* and had her well manned.

We keep the Ice cut from around her and have everything in a state of preparation to repel an attack at a moment's notice either night or day. All the other Vessels are so arranged that they are calculated to protect each other, and as no officer or man is permitted to leave his Vessel after 8 o'clock, I think that we can protect our fleet against any force that will be brought against us by the Enemy, provided the Army will keep the Forts and prevent the assailants from turning our own guns upon the Vessels. Two Block houses are nearly completed and I have 8 guns prepared, with their ammunition, ready to mount upon them the moment they are ready. These houses will add much to the means of protecting the Fleet and Forts against any sudden attack.

The plan approved in Washington for operations against Upper Canada called for the capture of Prescott and Kingston as the first objective of the spring campaign, the capture of York as the second, and the reduction of Forts George and Erie on the Niagara River as the third. As Mahan was later to state in his two-volume study of the War of 1812, the capture of Kingston would have solved 'at a single stroke every difficulty' in the inland theatre of operations: 'No other harbor was tenable as a naval station; with its fall and the destruction of shipping and forts, would go the control of the lake, even if the place itself were not permanently held. Deprived thus of the water communications, the enemy could retain no position to the westward, because neither re-enforcements nor supplies could reach them.'

Heartened by the news of the successful surprise attack launched by Major Forsyth's[6] riflemen from Ogdensburg against the Canadian militia garrisoning the village of Brockville, however, Secretary of War Armstrong[7] now began to develop more daring tactical concepts and saw no need to wait for spring. On 24 February he wrote General Dearborn, suggesting that Colonel Zebulon Pike's[8] two brigades at Plattsburg be despatched in sleighs up the

[6] [Benjamin Forsyth (d. 1814), commanded a company of U. S. Rifles in raids upon Gananoque (September 1812) and Elizabethtown (Brockville) and in the defence of Ogdensburg (both in February 1813). In 1813 the unit participated in the first attack upon York and the capture of Fort George and in 1814 was engaged along the Lake Champlain sector in the battle of Lacolle Mill. Late in June Forsyth, now a brevet lieutenant-colonel, was killed in a skirmish at Odelltown.]

[7] [John Armstrong (1758-1843) served throughout the Revolutionary War and reached the rank of major. Afterwards he became secretary of state and attorney general of Pennsylvania. Between 1800 and 1809 he was a member of the United States Senate for New York, then minister to France and to Spain. In 1812 he was assigned command at New York city with the rank of brigadier-general and in the following year became secretary of war in succession to William Eustis. The capture of Washington in 1814 led to his disgrace and resignation on September 3, 1814.]

[8] [Zebulon Montgomery Pike (1779-1813) became a lieutenant in the American army in 1799, explored the upper Mississippi River in 1805-6 and the headwaters of the Red and Arkansas rivers in 1806-7, in the course of which he examined the locale of Pike's Peak, Colorado. He published an account of these expeditions in 1810. He afterwards became a brigadier-general, and he was killed while leading the attack on York on April 27, 1813.]

St. Lawrence to attack Kingston, where Dearborn could join him with the balance of his troops.

Three days earlier, however, Commodore Chauncey had written the Secretary of the Navy throwing cold water on a proposal made by a subordinate (Lieutenant Wolcott Chauncey) to lead 50 volunteers across the ice to Kingston and destroy the Provincial Marine's vessels there. According to the Commodore's information, the ice was kept broken around these for a distance of 12 feet and such a tiny assault force would be shot down, before it could negotiate this obstacle, by the ship's guns and those in the batteries and blockhouse. Chauncey wrote that he had deemed it unwise to attempt anything unless he could send a sufficiently large force to take the forts and blockhouses; in which case the vessels would necessarily be captured. 'You must be aware', this letter emphasized, 'that a defeat would be attended with disastrous consequences and perhaps put us back a whole summer.'

Although Dearborn had fought through most of the Revolutionary War as a regimental officer and had had a tour on Washington's staff during the Yorktown campaign, he had had no command experience. Later a politician and Secretary of War for eight years under President Jefferson, he had been serving as Collector for the Port of Boston when Madison appointed him senior major-general of the United States army in 1812. Albeit no fool, he had just passed his 62nd birthday and was too old and set in his ways to react properly to the sudden activity now evidenced by Sir George Prevost.

Sir George Prevost had perfectly good reasons to visit Upper Canada, as soon as the legislature of the lower province could be prorogued and before the spring thaw should render the roads impassable. There had been rather alarming reports of increased activity by the Americans; shipbuilding at York was progressing slowly; while the continued ill-health of Major-General Sir Roger Sheaffe, administering that province, had prevented the transaction of any public or military business for several weeks. Prevost began his long and tedious journey by sleigh from Quebec on 17 February, travelling continuously and with as much speed as the depth of snow would permit. When he arrived at Prescott on the evening of 21 February he found that two of the four companies of the 8th (or King's) Regiment of Foot, which had been despatched to reinforce the troops in Upper Canada, had got that far only a few hours earlier. Following Prevost's departure for Kingston on the following morning, his reluctant consent to a conditional attack upon Ogdensburg was immediately turned into the real thing. The temporarily augmented garrison of Prescott charged across the ice and quickly routed the Americans, who retreated inland.

As soon as the news reached Albany on 25 February, General Dearborn began to draw the wrong conclusions, which were reinforced during succeeding days by a succession of rumors. Colonel Pike was ordered to reinforce Sackets

Harbor with 400 of his regulars, travelling across country by sleigh from Plattsburg, while Brigadier-General Brown was directed to call out 300 to 400 of his militia brigade to act as a screening force in northern New York. Dearborn concluded a hasty despatch to the Secretary of War with the information that Commodore Chauncey had not yet returned from New York: 'I am satisfied that, *if he had returned as soon as I had expected him, we might have made a stroke at Kingston on the ice*; but his presence was necessary for having the aid of the seamen and marines . . . .' In a further despatch on the following day, Dearborn relayed a report that Prevost was moving to Upper Canada with a considerable force. As a consequence, Dearborn had ordered 400 more of Pike's command to follow the first detachment from Plattsburg. The troops at Greenbush also were put in motion for Sackets Harbor, while Major Forsyth and his riflemen were moved there instead of returning to Ogdensburg.

Chauncey's immediate reaction to this news, which greeted his arrival at Albany on the evening of 27 February, was somewhat different. After writing to the Secretary of the Navy on the following morning that General Dearborn had left for Sackets Harbor and that he would follow later in the day, Chauncey expressed the opinion that Prevost was in Kingston 'more for the purpose of superintending the defense of that post than for any attack upon us'. Following his own arrival at Sackets Harbor on 3 March, Chauncey immediately reported that he had found his 'vessels in a perfect state of preparation to meet the enemy'. He did not believe, however, that Sir George Prevost was prepared to accept the large number of casualties that an assault was certain to entail. Moreover, should an attack fail, as Chauncey was confident it would, Kingston and its naval squadron would then be at the mercy of a strong counter-attacking force.

On the other hand, Dearborn's despatch to the Secretary of War was an alarming document. He was convinced that 6,000 to 8,000 troops had been collected at Kingston, including 3,000 British regulars, and that an attack might be expected within 48 hours. Even counting the local militia who had been called in, his miscellaneous garrison totalled only 3,000. Should Prevost attack before the regulars arrived from Plattsburg and Greenbush, the result would 'at least be doubtful'.

Dearborn's gloom seems to have been contagious, for two days later (5 March) Chauncey was writing his own superior in similar vein: 'We are still safe but hourly expect a visit from the other side. The enemy is obviously collecting a large Force at Kingston and by every account that we can collect from deserters and others a visit is contemplated. Sir George Prevost is to command in person and has assured his friends that he will destroy our little Fleet here or perish in the attempt. The latter I have no objection to, but the former I shall endeavour to prevent.'

As the days passed, however, Commodore Chauncey adopted a more optimistic view. But, since the British commander at Prescott had refused to receive a flag of truce and no further deserters appeared, Chauncey felt that something was in the wind. His guess that the activity reported at Kingston was intended to mask an early offensive against General Harrison's troops on the Detroit frontier was, however, just as faulty an appreciation as that of General Dearborn. On 9 March Dearborn reported that the 400 troops had arrived from Greenbush. But he had heard nothing from Colonel Pike:

> I have sent three expresses to meet him; neither has returned. I have suspicions of the express employed by the Quartermaster General to convey the orders to Pike; the earliest measures were taken for conveying a duplicate of his orders. I hope to hear from him today. His arrival, with eight hundred good troops, would be very important at this time.
>
> I begin to entertain some doubts whether Sir George Prevost will venture to attack us, but will not relax in being prepared to give him a decent reception. . . . The ice will not probably be passable more than from six to ten days longer; it is not usually passable after the 15th of March. This unexpected movement of the enemy will effectually oppose the movements contemplated on our part.

In his anxiety, General Dearborn had overlooked the practical difficulties facing Colonel Pike. According to a letter written by a resident of Hopkinton, in the Federalist stronghold of St. Lawrence County: 'Although they hire and press all the horses and sleighs they can to expedite their march, yet Col. Pike's detachment was five days *riding* from Plattsburg to this place a distance of 75 miles – Three soldiers were frozen so that they died in coming from Plattsburg, and many more were badly frozen.'

Chauncey reported, on 12 March, that he was

> . . . more and more convinced that the Enemy does not intend an attack upon this place, but keeps up the appearance of it, for the purpose of covering his Designs upon Genl. Harrison. . . . Genl. Dearborn thinks differently from myself upon this subject and is in hourly expectation of an attack. We have accounts that 6,000 men passed up on Sunday last. This cannot be true, for taking all the accounts together they would make out more than 20,000 men at Kingston. This force we know that they cannot raise in so short a time. I presume that the truth is that people on the other side are as credulous as our own countrymen, and that they magnify a few Sleighs loaded with stores and accompanied by guards into a Brigade of Regular Troops.

After mentioning that Colonel Pike had arrived that morning with about 600 men and another officer with about the same number was expected in a day or two, Chauncey's letter continued: 'We are well prepared to meet the enemy whenever he may think proper to pay us a visit. I have stationed an officer and thirty Seamen in each Block House to manage the carriage guns. Exclusive of these men there will be stationed at each House from 50 to 75 Soldiers with Muskets. With this force they ought to be well defended and I have no doubt will be.'

General Dearborn never did renounce his belief that the danger of attack had been real, even though finally satisfied that no attempt would be made from Kingston. His letter of 14 March merely advised the Secretary of War that Sir George Prevost, after visiting York and Niagara, had returned to Montreal, since it was now too late in the season to risk launching an attack across the ice.

Two days later, Commodore Chauncey wrote the Secretary of the Navy: 'I think it would not be presumptuous in me to say that I consider the Fleet here as perfectly safe from any attacks from the Enemy.'

Independently, and for somewhat different reasons, however, Chauncey and Dearborn now decided against mounting an attack against Kingston as soon as navigation should open. Instead, they both recommended a rearrangement of the plan of operations earlier approved by President Madison. York should be the first objective. Only after the British forts on the Niagara frontier had been seized should they direct all their resources against Kingston.

York was captured on 27 April and partially burned, following the accidental explosion of a magazine which killed Brigadier-General Pike. A month later Chauncey's fleet assisted Dearborn's army to dislodge Brigadier-General Vincent from Fort George and, temporarily, from the whole Niagara peninsula. But in Chauncey's absence the garrison of Kingston crossed the lake, protected by its own squadron which was now manned by the Royal Navy, and attacked Sackets Harbor on 29 May. That the attack failed, however, was due as much to the poor judgment shown by Sir George Prevost as to the spirited resistance offered by Brigadier-General Brown with the few American regulars and militia available. As it was, the new ship under construction and a captured schooner were set on fire and a large quantity of naval stores destroyed by Lieutenant Chauncey to prevent the possibility of their falling into British hands. Captain Gray was killed while leading an assault against one of the blockhouses. Neither Kingston nor Sackets Harbor were ever again threatened, each squadron took care to avoid battle under conditions favorable to the other, and the struggle for naval supremacy on Lake Ontario degenerated into a mere shipbuilding competition.

FURTHER READING: W. C. H. Wood (ed.), *Select British documents . . .* , volume 2, pages 55-134, 186-227; E. A. Cruikshank, 'The contest for the command of Lake Ontario in 1812 and 1813', *Royal Society of Canada*, third series, section 2, volume 10 (1916), pages 161-223; C. P. Stacey, 'Commodore Chauncey's attack on Kingston Harbour, November 10, 1812', *Canadian Historical Review,* volume 32 (1951), pages 126-38; C. P. Stacey, 'Naval power on the Lakes', in *After Tippecanoe*, edited by P. P. Mason, pages 49-59; A. Pound, *Lake Ontario* (Indianapolis, 1945).

During 1813 the Americans planned to overwhelm Upper Canada by assaults from Detroit, Niagara, and along the St. Lawrence and Richelieu rivers. Supported by Chauncey's squadron American troops crossed the Niagara River, seized Fort George, and advanced inland in pursuit of the British, who retreated towards Burlington Heights. The brilliant, surprise night attack at Stoney Creek interrupted the American advance and permitted the defenders to re-establish their positions upon the Niagara peninsula. The Americans retired to Fort George and, eventually, back across the river. Though Stoney Creek was a brief, small-scale affair, it was one of the most decisive operations of the war. . . . LIEUTENANT-COLONEL WOOD *is deputy director of the Historical Section, Army Headquarters, Ottawa. This study is made available through the courtesy of the author and of the editor of the 'Canadian Geographical Journal', where it first appeared (volume 64, March 1962).*

The Many Battles of Stoney Creek

BY HERBERT FAIRLIE WOOD

In the early hours of Sunday, the 6th of June, 1813, in a clearing in the woods a few miles east of the present city of Hamilton, some 2,000 Americans, invading Canada, were surprised by about 700 British soldiers and put to flight. Their two generals managed to get themselves captured; the British general became lost in the woods, and when he rejoined his army the next day he was found to have lost his hat, his sword, and his horse. The British, having won, retired from the field; the Americans, having lost, reoccupied it. This was the battle of Stoney Creek, celebrated in song and story, and it was typical of the sort of thing that went on during the War of 1812.

A. R. M. Lower has had the last word on this three-year conflict.

> The war itself was satisfactory to all parties in that both sides won it; the American tradition is one of glorious victories and so is the Canadian. The British, who did most of the fighting . . . have no tradition at all and there are few English people who have ever heard of it. . . . It produced no Marlboroughs or Nelsons. It was a succession of timorous advances and hasty retreats, of muddle-headed planning and incompetent generalship, interspersed with a few sharp actions and adroit manoeuvres which reflected credit on a few individuals.

In the narrow view, the battle of Stoney Creek fits neatly into the picture drawn above, but in perspective it was one of the very few decisive encounters of the war, and could almost come under Professor Lower's heading of 'adroit manoeuvre'.

The end of the War of 1812 did not terminate hostilities. The regional historians and the autobiographers took over, and waged battles no less ferocious than the actual engagements of the war. Since, as usual, each side had exaggerated the casualties of the enemy while minimizing its own, and the public pronouncements of the respective governments had contained more propaganda than veracity, contending historians found a fertile field. When the private letters were uncovered, and the secret dispatches released, the field was further enriched, until there was enough material to support the preconceived views of almost every shade of opinion. The battles continue, intermittently, to this day, as fresh snippets of information are uncovered in old attics.

The first battle of Stoney Creek was precipitated by the British in a desperate attempt to avoid a conventional action with a numerically larger invading force. On 27 May, Major-General Henry Dearborn, an aged American hero of the Revolution, had landed some 6,000 men on the Canadian shore of the Niagara river. Supported by the guns of Fort Niagara and Commodore Isaac Chauncey's fleet, he had driven the British from Fort George and inflicted considerable losses.

Brigadier-General John Vincent, a professional soldier, retreated with the remnants of his small force of British regulars along the Queenston heights, pulling in his outposts and his garrison at Fort Erie and leaving the peninsula undefended. By the time the lethargic Dearborn had organized a pursuit, Vincent had gathered together about 1,600 infantry and a handful of cavalry and Indians. So low was his opinion of the Canadian militia, however, that when numbers of them joined him he made it clear that he wanted none of them. The settlers, though much disturbed at being left to the mercy of the Americans, nevertheless dispersed to their homes. They were to play their part later.

General Dearborn entrusted the pursuit to Brigadier-General William Henry Winder, a successful lawyer. His advance-guard soon brought him word that his force was inadequate to deal decisively with Vincent, so he decided to stop at Forty-mile Creek and call for reinforcements. On the 3rd of June these arrived, commanded by the 53-year-old political appointee Brigadier-General John Chandler, who, being senior, took command. Their combined forces totalled about 3,400. General Chandler ordered the advance to continue, and on the 5th of June, driving Vincent's outposts before them, the Americans came to Stoney Creek. There, aware that Vincent was digging in some seven miles away on Burlington Heights, Chandler decided to camp for the night.

Vincent reacted to this forward movement by sending his senior staff officer, Lt.-Col. John Harvey,[1] to reconnoitre the enemy position. Harvey was one day to become, in turn, Lieutenant-Governor of New Brunswick, Governor of Newfoundland, Lieutenant-Governor of Nova Scotia, a Knight Commander of the Bath, and a Lieutenant-General. In 1813 he was an able, courageous, and imaginative officer of thirty-five. He saw that the enemy had encamped astride the Fort George–Burlington road, in a small field surrounded by dense forest. A sunken farm track, running across the front of the position, made an ideal forming-up place. In his own words, 'the enemy's guards were few and negligent; his line of encampment was long and broken; his artillery was feebly supported; several of his corps were placed too far to the rear to aid in repelling a blow which might be rapidly struck in front'. He returned to Vincent on Burlington Heights and recommended a night attack.

General Vincent was no Wellington, but he had energy and determination. Harvey's plan offered a priceless opportunity to delay the enemy until reinforcements could arrive from Kingston. The General decided to act.

At this time, one of those rare incidents occurred that brighten the lives of generals and influence battles; the British learned the American countersign. Authorities have differed as to how this happened, but recently-uncovered evidence bears out the truth of an old legend that a young settler named 'Billy' Green learned of the countersign from a paroled prisoner and went directly to Vincent's camp with the information.[2] Elements of two British regiments, the 49th and the 8th, numbering in all some 700 muskets, were formed up just before midnight and started towards the enemy lines.

Meanwhile the Americans settled down in their field near Stoney Creek. Camp-fires were lit along the farm track to their front, and a meal was prepared and eaten. Siting four light guns on a rise in ground so as to command the road to Burlington and ordering his men to sleep on their arms, Chandler stationed an outpost in a log church to his front, ringed his position with a line of pickets, and joined Winder and the staff in the grounds of James Gage's farm-house, which overlooked the position. It was pitch black, with a mist rising from the low-lying ground.

The British force arrived in the area at about two in the morning. Vincent accompanied the column, although he had placed Harvey in command. To ensure surprise, the latter had ordered all flints removed from muskets and

[1] [John Harvey (1778-1852), one of the ablest soldiers in the war, joined the British army in 1794 and fought in Europe, Cape of Good Hope, Egypt, and India before coming to Canada. In 1812 he was appointed deputy adjutant-general of the forces in British North America. He was mentioned in dispatches for his part in the actions of Stoney Creek, Crysler's Farm, Fort Niagara, Black Rock, Oswego, Lundy's Lane, and Fort Erie. The dates of his governorships are: New Brunswick, 1837-41; Newfoundland, 1841-6; and Nova Scotia (where he introduced the principle of responsible government) 1846-52.]

[2] ['Billy' Green (1794-1877), who lived at Stoney Creek, also guided the British force to the American encampment and took part in the ensuing battle.]

had stressed the importance of silence. Some of his company commanders took his words so seriously that they insisted on unloaded muskets as well.

Using the countersign, the British advance-guard quickly surprised and bayoneted the pickets they encountered, surrounded and captured the outpost in the church, and began to debouch from the woods on to the cart track that defined the forward edge of the enemy position. At this point, things began to go wrong. The leading files, finding themselves among the camp-fires of the enemy, broke into battle cries and alerted the Americans. Sporadic firing broke out and the enemy were treated to the astonishing spectacle of the British force, illuminated by the camp-fires, attempting to form line and load and prime their weapons within a few yards of the position.

As the American firing increased, the British rushed forward to close with the enemy and the officers began to lose control of their men. The most distinguished action, and the most helpful, was carried out by Major Charles Plenderleath, commanding the 49th Regiment, who, seeing the enemy guns above him coming into action, gathered together about forty men and stormed forward. The gunners got away two rounds at point-blank range, but the shot passed overhead and Plenderleath's men routed the American gunners and captured the guns. Believing their line to have been penetrated, the Americans began to fall back to the cover of the woods. The battle quickly degenerated into confused fighting in the dark. Friendly troops fought each other, the two American generals were captured, and General Vincent, his horse shot under him, got hopelessly lost in the woods.

As dawn broke, Colonel Harvey, realizing the necessity of concentrating his scattered force, began to pull his men back into the cover of the forest. But the Americans, deprived of their senior officers, had lost their enthusiasm for the fight. After reoccupying the position long enough to destroy the stores accumulated there, they turned about and marched back to Forty-mile Creek. The night attack had achieved its object – the interruption of the American pursuit.

Events on the lake now influenced affairs. Chauncey, having learned of an attack on his base, sailed away to intercept the British naval forces. But Commodore Sir James Yeo,[3] commanding the Royal naval squadron, evaded him and came sailing down the coast with reinforcements for Vincent. Yeo's appearance off the river, and the setback at Stoney Creek, so alarmed Dearborn that he recalled all his forces to the shelter of Fort George. This was the

[3] [James Lucas Yeo (1782-1818) entered the Royal Navy in 1793 and served during the whole of the French Revolutionary and Napoleonic wars. He won rapid promotion, becoming a captain in 1807 and commodore in charge of the naval forces on the Great Lakes in 1813 under the authority of Prevost. In the next year he was appointed to the full, independent command on the Lakes and in 1815 he was made a Knight Commander of the Bath in recognition of his services. After the war he was commander-in-chief off the west coast of Africa, but he died during the return voyage to England.]

signal for the Canadian militia. Gathering from miles around in loosely-organized groups, they hung on the flanks and rear of the retreating columns, screaming Indian war-cries and harassing the invaders. Thus the hapless Americans, so recently victorious, were hustled back into the ruins of the fort they had stormed so confidently such a short time before. The peninsula was safe again and, except for the foray in the following month that ended in the humiliation of Beaver Dam,[4] the Americans remained in their beleaguered bridgehead until they abandoned it in November.

The battle of Stoney Creek has been fought many times since. There was even a minor skirmish on one occasion over the spelling of the name, which was only resolved when it was proved beyond doubt that the creek was named after an early settler and did not refer to the condition of the streambed. The last battle has probably not yet been fought. . . .

The years have altered the battlefield of Stoney Creek. The creek itself still trickles down to Lake Ontario, but most of James Gage's land is now a bustling sub-division. The old plank road has disappeared, the forest has long since been cut down, and the visitor can find little in the appearance of the countryside to help him reconstruct the battle. There is the Monument, of course, a tribute to the energy of local citizens as much as to the victors, and the Gage house has been rescued from decay and made into a museum.

It is, in fact, the local historical societies that we must thank for preserving the rich heritage of the Niagara Peninsula. These small groups have always vociferously defended the ancient landmarks, colourful old buildings, and undisturbed countryside that form priceless links with the past. Every Canadian should wish them well and cheer them on, as they fight again and again the historic old battles – among them, Stoney Creek.

FURTHER READING: E. A. Cruikshank (ed.), *Documentary history . . .*, parts VI, X; H. Corman, 'An account of the battle of Stoney Creek derived from the recollections of Abraham Corman', *Wentworth Historical Society*, volume 7 (1916), pages 26-34; E. A. Cruikshank, 'The battle of Stoney Creek and the blockade of Fort George, 1813', *Niagara Historical Society*, no. 3 (1898); C. M. Johnston, *The head of the lake: a history of Wentworth County* (Hamilton, 1958).

[4] [Early in June 1813, Brigadier-General Vincent established an outpost of some fifty men of the 49th Regiment under Lieutenant James FitzGibbon at a stone house near Beaver Dam, on the road from Queenston and St. Davids to Burlington. A similar post under Major de Haren of the 104th Regiment was stationed nearer the lake on the main road from Fort George. The Americans occupying Fort George, harassed by these detachments and by Indians, decided to drive the British from these positions. On June 24, Colonel C. G. Boerstler with nearly 600 men set out for Beaver Dam, but his advance was slowed by a series of Indian ambuscades. FitzGibbon, informed of the Americans' predicament, brought up his men and moved to cut off their retreat. He summoned Boerstler to surrender, and the latter, believing himself surrounded, complied. In order to give his demand more authority, FitzGibbon used the name of Major de Haren, who in fact came up with some 200 men just in time to sign the surrender document. The victory, however, as FitzGibbon acknowledged, really belonged to the Indians.]

The most dangerous attack during 1813 was aimed against Montreal from Sackets Harbor and from Plattsburg, for the St. Lawrence River was the life-line of Upper Canada, the interruption of which would isolate the province and expose it to inevitable conquest. Yet despite the almost overwhelming superiority of numbers, the invasion failed. Crysler's Farm, fought in open, undulating country, revealed the superior discipline and coolness under fire of the British and Canadian regulars and left them in possession of the field. The American commanders, disheartened by the defeat (which paralleled that of the eastern wing of their invasion at Chateauguay), abandoned the advance, and Upper Canada was saved for another year. . . . RONALD WAY *has supervised the restoration of Fort George, Fort Erie, Old Fort Henry, and Upper Canada Village. He is director of historic sites for the Ontario–St. Lawrence Development Commission. This article, from the 'Canadian Geographical Journal' (volume 62, June 1961), appears by permission of the author, of the Royal Canadian Geographical Society, and of the Ontario–St. Lawrence Development Commission.*

The Day of Crysler's Farm

BY RONALD L. WAY

The battle of Crysler's Farm occurred on Thursday, the 11th of November, 1813. It was a contest of some eight hundred British and Canadians against more than four times their number of Americans. The scene was set on the northern shore of the St. Lawrence, twenty miles to the west of Cornwall and seven miles east of present-day Morrisburg. It was fought upon the open fields of a farm owned by one John Crysler. This was the first occasion in the War of 1812 when British drill, discipline, and the *thin red line* were fairly tested against an enemy whose talent and preference was for 'bush fighting'. Crysler's Farm was one of the decisive battles of that war . . . .

Secretary Armstrong's cherished plan for the 'Grand Invasion', for the execution of which [major-generals] Wilkinson[1] and Hampton[2] had become

[1] [James Wilkinson (1757-1825) became a captain in the American army in 1775, accompanied Arnold on the expedition against Quebec, and served under Gates at Saratoga. After the Revolution he settled in Kentucky where he became a secret agent and pensioner of the Spanish

the chosen instruments, now took the form of a pincer movement against Montreal. Wilkinson with a force of approximately 9,000 men was to launch a major offensive from Sackett's Harbour, its initial objective the reduction of Kingston, to be at once followed by a swift descent of the St. Lawrence to Montreal. In the move down-river, Wilkinson was to effect a junction with Hampton, who was to advance his division of 7,000 men from Plattsburg to the St. Lawrence. In Armstrong's opinion, the combined forces would be more than sufficient to capture Montreal and end the war.

When, on September 5th, the Secretary of War himself arrived at Sackett's to give personal direction to the offensive, Commodore Chauncey, who had so easily persuaded Dearborn that Kingston was too strong to be attacked, lost no time in advocating to both Armstrong and Wilkinson that the British stronghold could be safely by-passed. The American high command debated the pros and cons of ignoring Kingston, while the concentration of troops went on, in Armstrong's words, 'at a snail-like pace'. Finally, by the middle of October, there was assembled at Sackett's Harbour a truly formidable force for the times. Wilkinson had no less than fourteen regiments of infantry, Forsyth's riflemen, three regiments of artillery, and two regiments of dragoons – a total of some 8,000 men. For transportation down-river there were better than 300 bateaux, scows, and small craft, with an escort of twelve gunboats. At Plattsburg, on Lake Champlain, the uncooperative Hampton had assembled 7,000 troops. After diversions, delays, and debates, the proponents of 'manifest destiny' were poised for the attack – the lateness of the season meant that it could not be long delayed.

Meanwhile, what of the British? Both Sir George Prevost, the supreme

governor of Louisiana. He fought in Wayne's campaign against the northern Indians and took over Detroit from the British in 1796. He was made a brigadier-general in 1792 and succeeded Wayne as commander-in-chief in 1796. In 1805 he was appointed governor of Louisiana Territory, but he became implicated in the Burr conspiracy of 1806-7. Eventually in 1811 he was acquitted by a court martial on charges arising from his relationships with the Spaniards and with Burr. In 1813 he was appointed to command the forces along the St. Lawrence River with the rank of major-general. The failure of his campaign against Montreal led to another court of inquiry upon charges of neglect of duty and drunkenness, but he was acquitted and received an honourable discharge from the army. He became a speculator in Texas lands and died in Mexico City.]

[2] [Wade Hampton (1751?-1835) fought in the American Revolution, afterwards represented South Carolina in Congress, and became a brigadier-general in 1809 in command at New Orleans. During the War of 1812 he was given charge of Norfolk, Virginia, from whence he was sent to direct the attack against Montreal from the south. Blocked at Odelltown in his northward advance from Plattsburg, he attempted another move against Montreal by way of the Chateauguay River. Here, on October 26, 1813, his army was rebuffed by a much smaller force of Canadian Voltigeurs and Canadian Fencibles. Taken together with Wilkinson's reverse at Crysler's Farm, the two defeats spelled the end of the American campaign of 1813 against Montreal. Hampton was exonerated by the War Department but returned to private life in April 1814.]

commander, and his subordinate, Major-General de Rottenburg,[3] charged with the defence of the Upper Province, had their sources of information. Colonel Pearson,[4] at Prescott, from his contact with the over-friendly people of Ogdensburg, reported to Prevost on October 15th that 'no one believes Kingston to be the point of attack, but all agree that Prescott or Montreal, or both, are the desired objects'. On the other hand, de Rottenburg had intelligence from one Samuel Casey, a 'respectable inhabitant of Kingston', who had crossed secretly to the American side and, with the assistance of Quaker friends, had reconnoitred Sackett's Harbour. Returning on October 17th, this trusted spy reported: 'They [the Americans] gave out that they were going to Prescott but merely to draw reinforcements from this place. Kingston has always been their real object and no other.' De Rottenburg dutifully relayed this information to Prevost, along with his own curious opinion that the enemy, frustrated in his designs against Kingston, and never having seriously intended anything against Lower Canada or even Prescott, would likely attack York. Despite all that his detractors were one day to say of him, Sir George was a level-headed soldier and had determined on a policy of wait and see. As early as October 12th he had cautioned de Rottenburg and Sir James Yeo to keep a close watch on Wilkinson's troop concentration and ordered that, the instant there was evidence of Montreal being the objective, part of the Kingston garrison must be dispatched to Montreal. For commander of this corps, he suggested Lieutenant-Colonel Joseph Morrison of the 2nd Battalion of the 89th Regiment whom he described as an 'active and intelligent officer'.

That the British commanders were perplexed as to American intentions was not surprising, for the enemy did not finally settle on a plan of action until October 17th. Then, at last, the decision was reached to by-pass Kingston and concentrate upon the descent of the river and the taking of Montreal. Orders were at once dispatched to Hampton to advance to the St. Lawrence by way of the Chateauguay River, and that very evening the command was given for the immediate embarkation of all Wilkinson's troops. It was not an auspicious beginning: the night turned stormy and no less than

[3] [Francis, Baron de Rottenburg (1757-1832) was born in Danzig and served in the French and Polish armies, before joining the British army in 1794. He was sent to Canada in 1810 with the rank of major-general, was appointed commander of the forces in Lower Canada in 1811, and in 1813 replaced Sheaffe as commander and administrator of Upper Canada. At the end of the year he retired from these positions to become commander of the Left (i.e. eastern) Division. He returned to England in 1815, was knighted in 1818, and became a lieutenant-general in 1819.]

[4] [Thomas Pearson (d.1847) became a lieutenant-colonel in 1811 and inspecting field officer for Upper Canada in February 1812. In 1813 he was in command at Fort Wellington and he participated in the battles of Crysler's Farm, Oswego, Chippawa, Lundy's Lane, and Fort Erie. He was knighted in 1835 and became a lieutenant-general in 1841.]

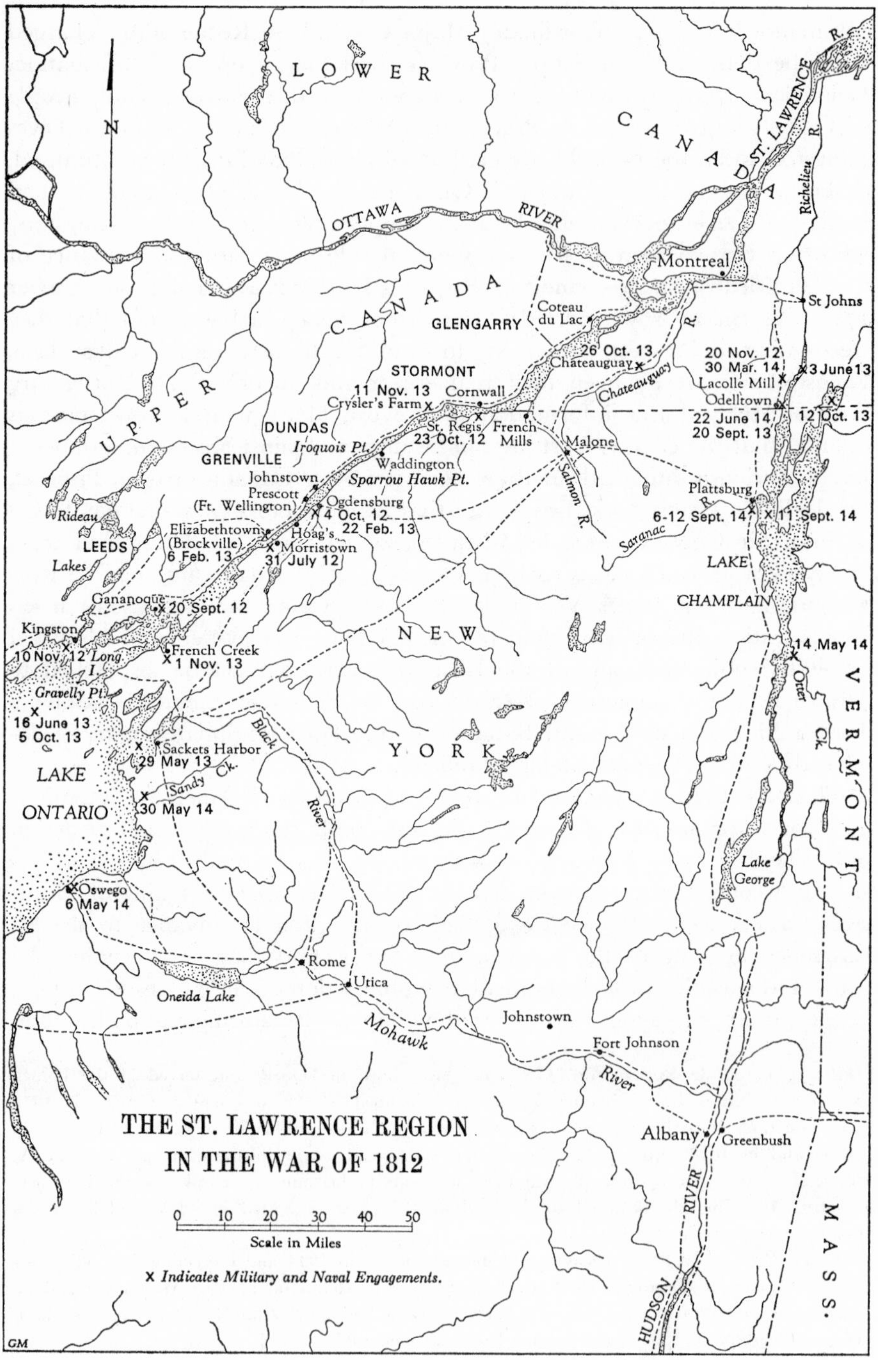

LOWER CANADA
UPPER CANADA
OTTAWA RIVER
ST. LAWRENCE R.
Richelieu R.
Montreal
St Johns
Coteau du Lac
GLENGARRY
26 Oct. 13
Chateauguay
Chateauguay R.
20 Nov. 12
30 Mar. 14
3 June 13
Lacolle Mill
Odelltown
12 Oct. 13
22 June 14
20 Sept. 13
STORMONT
11 Nov. 13
Crysler's Farm
Cornwall
St. Regis
23 Oct. 12
French Mills
Malone
Salmon R.
DUNDAS
Iroquois Pt.
GRENVILLE
Waddington
Sparrow Hawk Pt.
Johnstown
Prescott
(Ft. Wellington)
Ogdensburg
4 Oct. 12
22 Feb. 13
Hoag's
Morristown
31 July 12
Elizabethtown
(Brockville)
6 Feb. 13
Rideau
LEEDS
Lakes
Plattsburg
6-12 Sept. 14
11 Sept. 14
Saranac R.
LAKE CHAMPLAIN
Gananoque
20 Sept. 12
Kingston
10 Nov. 12
Long I.
French Creek
1 Nov. 13
NEW YORK
14 May 14
Otter Ck.
VERMONT
Gravelly Pt.
16 June 13
5 Oct. 13
Sackets Harbor
29 May 13
Black River
Sandy Ck.
LAKE ONTARIO
30 May 14
Lake George
Oswego
6 May 14
Rome
Utica
Oneida Lake
Mohawk River
Johnstown
Fort Johnson
Albany
Greenbush
HUDSON RIVER
MASS.
THE ST. LAWRENCE REGION
IN THE WAR OF 1812
0 10 20 30 40 50
Scale in Miles
x Indicates Military and Naval Engagements.
GM

fifteen boats were lost with valuable stores before they reached the rendezvous at Grenadier Island. For more than a week, gale-like winds and unseasonable blizzards pinned the freezing Americans down on their island and it was not until November 1st that they were able to complete their move down-river to French Creek.[5] . . . Intermittently under attack by the British gunboats and held back by unfavourable weather, Wilkinson's army remained at French Creek until the morning of the 5th, when they moved to Morristown.[6]

The British high command had not been sure of the significance of the move to French Creek. It might very well be a feint which did not preclude a move across the river towards Kingston. Not until [Captain W. H.] Mulcaster[7] brought his flotilla back post-haste on the 5th with the positive word that Wilkinson was moving down-stream from French Creek were the enemy's intentions certain.

At Kingston the news was received with both relief and apprehension. Because the fall of Montreal must inevitably lead to the loss of everything to the westward, including Kingston, it only substituted the indirect for the direct attack. In Wilkinson's path the only man-made obstacles were the small fort at Prescott, where Colonel Pearson had a few hundred men, and the equally weak defences at the Coteau du Lac. Beyond lay Montreal with no fortifications and a pathetic garrison of four hundred marines and two hundred sailors, supported by the loyal, but generally untried, militia of Lower Canada. De Rottenburg now lost no time in implementing Prevost's explicit instructions of the 12th of October and Saturday November 6th was a day of feverish preparation.

The detachment from the Kingston garrison consisted of nine companies of the second battalion of the 89th Regiment, totalling some 450 men, the remains of the eight companies of the 49th Regiment, reduced by casualties to approximately 160 men, and a small complement of Royal Artillery gunners and drivers with two 6 pdr. field-guns – the whole amounting to some 630 rank and file. At ten o'clock that same Saturday night they were hurriedly embarked on board the *Lord Beresford* and *Sir Sidney Smith* schooners, seven gunboats, and a number of bateaux. The naval escort was commanded by William Howe Mulcaster, an aggressive 32-year-old Royal Navy Captain, and was manned by sailors of the fleet. In over-all command

[5] Now Clayton.

[6] Morristown is approximately twelve miles above Ogdensburg.

[7] [William Howe Mulcaster (1785-1837) served with distinction in the Royal Navy under Yeo in the West Indies and attained the rank of commander in 1809. He was posted to North America in 1810 and transferred to the Great Lakes in 1813. He was very active in campaigns on Lake Ontario and the upper St. Lawrence and was wounded while leading a body of seamen in the attack on Oswego in May 1814. He was knighted in 1831 and became aide-de-camp to King William IV.]

of the expedition – officially described as a 'corps of observation' with instructions to make contact with the enemy, and impede and hinder their progress in every way possible – was Lt.-Col. Joseph Wanton Morrison of the 89th Foot.

Lt.-Col. Harvey of Stoney Creek fame was Morrison's second-in-command; Lt.-Col. Charles Plenderleath, Brock's old friend, led the 49th. Both these officers were more experienced than Morrison, who had never seen action in Canada and had never handled a battalion – let alone a corps – in battle. His choice as commander was due to nothing but Prevost's personal judgment of his potential and ability. At the time, Morrison, who had joined the army as an ensign in 1793, was just thirty years old. His only previous active service had been as a lieutenant in the campaign in Holland in 1799, where he had been severely wounded. Sir George Prevost was not, however, the first senior officer to note Colonel Morrison's worth. As early as 1809, Sir John Doyle, in writing an inspection return on the 2/89th Regiment, had said: 'This battalion is commanded by Major Morrison, a most attentive, zealous, clear officer.' Morrison was more than a competent soldier; he was a man of high integrity and strong religious principles, united with a constant concern for the welfare of the troops under his command. Of him, a junior officer was to write in after years: 'There is not one amongst us who would not go with him to the world's end.' Such was the man who, late at night, on November 7th, 1813, embarked with his troops upon the dark St. Lawrence, to brave the blockade of Chauncey's powerful fleet and the hazards of night-time navigation amidst the Thousand Islands. It was the beginning of an incredible pursuit, for at this point the pursued outnumbered the pursuers fifteen to one.

The five days, November 6th to November the 10th, saw the American armada slowly descend the river, while the energetic British pursuers gradually closed the gap. Since the guns of Fort Wellington effectively commanded the 1,800-yard breadth of the St. Lawrence at Prescott, Wilkinson sagely determined that his craft should run the gauntlet of their fire under cover of darkness. Consequently, on the 6th, he moved from Morristown only as far as Hoag's – three miles above Ogdensburg. Here was landed his ammunition and all the men not required for the handling of the boats. That night the unloaded flotilla ran past Fort Wellington with negligible damage, to re-embark the detoured army the next morning at the 'Red Mill', four miles below Ogdensburg. While at Hoag's, Wilkinson had received the news from hard-riding Colonel King that General Hampton had been ignominiously checked at Chateauguay on October 26th by a tiny force of Canadians. Apparently unperturbed, because Hampton's large army was barely scratched, Wilkinson sent back word by the same officer that Hampton was to meet him at a new junction-point – St. Regis near Cornwall.

So far, the ailing Wilkinson had not had a pleasant journey, but things were due to get much worse. His cumbersome convoy had been plagued by inclement weather, a shortage of competent pilots, and the fire of persistent British gunboats. Now, a more serious factor was to make itself evident. While still above Ogdensburg, Wilkinson had addressed a proclamation to the inhabitants of the Canadas stating, in essence, that he had invaded to conquer, not to destroy, 'to subdue the forces of His Britannic Majesty not to war against his unoffending subjects'. He promised protection to the persons and property of those who would remain quietly at home, but treatment as avowed enemies to those found in arms. The proclamation closed with these grandiloquent words: 'To menace is unmanly – to seduce is dishonourable – yet it is just and humane to place these alternatives before you.' Wilkinson's information was that the Canadian militia were responding so badly that the call-out of a regiment produced but fifteen men, of whom fourteen had deserted during their first night of service. Now came disillusionment. With war at their doorstep, the roused Canadians, from Leeds to Glengarry, swarmed to the defence of their beloved valley, and the northern shore of the St. Lawrence buzzed like a hive of angry bees. Canadian militiamen turned every narrow stretch of the river into a shooting gallery and from behind trees and boulders maintained a galling fire upon the hapless Americans – a guerilla warfare in which the lack of formal military training was no handicap. Forcibly impressed with 'the active universal hostility of the male inhabitants of the country', Wilkinson retaliated. On Sunday the 7th he detached colonels Alexander Macomb and Winfield Scott with 1,200 élite troops, followed by the reckless Forsyth and his riflemen, to land on the Canadian shore and clear out the pestiferous militia from Iroquois Point, where the river narrowed to a dangerous 500 yards. Here, Macomb and Scott forced the withdrawal of some 200 Dundas militia led by Captain John Munroe and proceeded down the Canadian shore.

The main force of Americans arrived on November 8th at Sparrow Hawk Point, approximately opposite Iroquois Point and eighteen miles below Ogdensburg. Wilkinson called a council of his senior officers – generals Lewis, Boyd,[8] Brown, Porter,[9] Covington, and Swartwout – to determine future

[8] [John Parker Boyd (1764-1830) joined the United States army in 1786 but resigned in 1789 to become a soldier of fortune in India in the armies of various native rulers. He rejoined the American army in 1808 as a colonel, fought under General Harrison at Tippecanoe in 1811, and was appointed a brigadier-general. He was present at the taking of Fort George in May 1813 and commanded a brigade in the campaign against Montreal that terminated at Crysler's Farm.]

[9] [Peter Buell Porter (1778-1849) was a congressman from New York from 1809 to 1813 and a leader of the War Hawks. As chairman of the Committee on Foreign Relations he prepared the report of December 1811 recommending war with Great Britain. He led a body of Pennsylvania and New York volunteers and Indians at the battles of Chippawa and Lundy's Lane

strategy in the light of newly-received advice as to the strength and activity of the enemy. The decision to press on towards Montreal was emphatically reaffirmed. At the same time, General Brown was ordered to cross the river with the second brigade, two companies of artillery, and detachments of dragoons – some 2,500 men. Combining with Macomb's advance-guard, Brown was to march overland to Cornwall, sweeping from his path the Canadian militia occupying the shore at the treacherous Long Sault Rapids, which the lightened American flotilla had still to shoot. That same day, Wilkinson was apprised of the rapid approach of his pursuers from Kingston; Morrison and Mulcaster had lost no time and on the evening of the 8th were already at Prescott. On the 9th, General Brown's land force was on the march. At the same time, Brigadier-General Boyd was landed 'with all the well men of the other brigades excepting a sufficient number to navigate the boats' to form a rear-guard against the advancing Morrison. Should the British attack, Boyd's orders were 'to turn about and beat them'. The following day, the main American flotilla dropped down-stream and encamped that night on the Canadian shore at Cook's Point, to await General Brown's word that he had cleared the way for a safe passage of the Long Sault.

Meanwhile, Colonel Morrison had left Prescott on the morning of the 9th, his corps of observation augmented by a detachment from Fort Wellington commanded by Lt.-Col. Pearson and consisting of the two flank companies of the 49th Regiment, three companies of the Canadian Voltigeurs, a detachment of the Canadian Fencible Regiment, some militia artillery with a 6 pdr. gun, and a half-dozen Provincial Dragoons. The two schooners, drawing too much water, were perforce left behind at Prescott and the troops they carried transferred to bateaux. With the 240 men he had picked up at Fort Wellington, Morrison's little army now numbered 800 rank and file – one-tenth of Wilkinson's available force.

Pressing on, Morrison landed a short distance above Point Iroquois on the evening of the 9th. Here, he was close on the heels of the Americans, and a reconnoitring party was sent out to check the enemy's strength and position. On the 10th, the chase was on again. There was a slight skirmish with some troops from Boyd's rear-guard, who retired after a few rounds from the British field-guns. Pausing only to dispatch a gunboat to Waddington on the American shore, to recover previously lost stores, Captain Mulcaster skilfully got within range of the American armed craft, chased six of them behind a point, and was only driven off when the Americans landed a battery of two eighteen-pounders. The small British army, now ashore, pushed along the King's Highway to reach Munroe Bay, two miles

and the siege of Fort Erie. From 1816 to 1822 he served as one of the commissioners charged with determining the boundary between the United States and Canada. He was Secretary of War during the presidency of John Quincy Adams.]

above Cook's Point on the night of November 10th. Colonel Morrison set up headquarters at the home of John Crysler[10] – a scant mile from General Wilkinson's command post at the tavern of Michael Cook.

It was the eve of the decisive battle of Crysler's Farm. Militia Captain John Crysler, who was to lend his name to that action, was a prosperous Loyalist land-owner, with valuable interests in the lumbering trade and a well-earned reputation for open-handed hospitality. In Crysler's well-appointed home, Colonel Morrison convened that night a conference of all his commissioned officers. Their decision was to stand and fight, providing the enemy could be inveigled into an attack on ground favourable to the British. Morrison, calm and judicious, had carefully assessed the possibilities of the terrain about Crysler's and wisely concluded that it was ideal for his purposes.

From the Crysler farm-house a road led at right-angles from the river to a swampy, impassable wood about half a mile distant. The forty-foot road allowance was lined by heavy five-foot log fences – excellent potential cover for Morrison's troops. Eastward from the farm buildings stretched for nearly a quarter of a mile a flat and level field, luxuriantly green with a crop of fall wheat and unbroken by tree, fence, or ditch. Beyond lay even, ploughed ground, intersected by two gullies and terminating in the steep banks of a sizeable ravine. This ground was, in effect, a plateau parallel to the river's bank, here twenty-five feet high. It was bounded by the King's Highway, which ran along the high shore. In the centre of the swiftly-flowing river was a tree-covered island, the bay at its eastern end being beyond small-arms range from Cook's Point, where the Americans were encamped.

Morrison's tactical evaluation of the open fields of Crysler's Farm was based upon a clear perception of the strengths and weaknesses of the opposing forces. His British soldiers were specifically trained for warfare upon the cultivated plains of Europe, but so far, during the War of 1812, the densely-wooded Canadas of that time had not afforded such a battlefield. The strength of the redcoat lay in his marionette-like drill and an iron discipline, acquired through years of rigid training. The heavy infantry of the line were literally what the name implied – the men intended to fight in line, standing, marching, and manoeuvring shoulder to shoulder in two ranks, each soldier occupying a prescribed space of twenty-two inches. This close-order drill was based on the 'touch' system, which precluded any swinging of the arms since every man had to maintain constant contact with those on either side of him. Unlike drill of today, which is taught mainly to instil habits of discipline, drill in 1812 was primarily designed to facilitate the precise manoeuvring of masses of men in the face of the enemy, often under heavy fire.

[10] Spelled variously – Chrystler, Christler, etc. Crysler signed his name as shown.

Movements back and forth from column to the classic thin red line or to the square for the repulse of cavalry, the complicated wheels involved in a change of front or echelon movements necessitated a cadence in marching far slower than that of today. The standard infantry weapon was the flint-lock muzzle-loading musket which, in the hands of well-trained troops, had a rate of fire of approximately three rounds a minute and an effective range of 100 yards, providing the target was no smaller than a barn door. Equipped with neither fore-sight nor rear-sight, it was not intended to be aimed, but, rather, presented in the general direction of the enemy. When discharged, the loose-fitting musket-ball rattled along the smooth-bored barrel to be unpredictably deflected by whatever lip of the muzzle it last happened to touch. Due to the limitations of firepower, the British soldier's primary weapon, upon which he was taught to depend, was the triangular socket bayonet, jammed firmly on the barrel at the commencement of an action. Prerequisite to the successful application of British drill and battle tactics was open ground.

In the American army, on the other hand, even the professional soldier had little understanding or appreciation of the principles of European warfare. Those battles of the Revolutionary War for which the Americans could claim a victory had been almost invariably a form of bush-fighting in which their frontiersmen were truly formidable. Subsequent experience of United States forces in the Indian Wars had involved the same type of combat. In contrast with the British soldier, who could seldom trace his acquaintance with fire-arms beyond the day of his enlistment, most Americans were, from childhood, proficient in the use of a rifle. No poaching laws prohibited them from furnishing their tables with the plentiful game of the surrounding forest. While the American soldier was by tradition and temperament less amenable to discipline than his British counterpart, his independent attitude had not been a serious handicap in forest fighting. . . . It should be pointed out that the Americans' aptitude for bush-fighting was shared by those other North Americans – the Canadians.

Morrison, in his calculated risk to hazard a battle upon favourable ground should the Americans attack, was banking on drill and discipline to offset heavy numerical odds. The hard core of the British force lay in the remains of the 49th Regiment under Colonel Plenderleath and Morrison's own battalion, the 2/89th. The 49th Foot from Hertfordshire had been in Canada since 1803 when Brock, their former Colonel, had brought them out.[11] Although reduced by casualties to less than one quarter their authorized

[11] In 1881, the 49th (Hertfordshire) Regiment of Foot was amalgamated with the 66th Foot and became the 1st Battalion of the Princess Charlotte of Wales's (Royal Berkshire) Regiment. In 1960, the Royal Berkshire Regiment was amalgamated with the Wiltshire Regiment and is now The Duke of Edinburgh's Royal Regiment (Berkshire and Wiltshire).

strength, they were tough, battle-seasoned soldiers, veterans of such actions as Queenston Heights, Salmon River, Frenchman's Creek, York, Fort George, Stoney Creek, Beaver Dams, and Black Rock. The enemy, who knew them well, had dubbed them the 'Green Tigers' from the facing colour of their 'madder-red' coatees and the fierceness of their fighting. In contrast, the second battalion of the 89th Regiment were Irish troops recently arrived from Britain.[12] Under Morrison's command, they had earned favourable inspection reports, but had yet to be tested under fire. The Canadian Fencible Regiment, of which a small detachment had joined Morrison's corps at Prescott, were not – as has often been erroneously stated – a militia unit, but a regiment of the British army. Raised in the Lower Province in 1803 for service in the Canadas, their personnel was mainly French-Canadian. At Prescott, Morrison had also acquired three companies of the Provincial Corps of Light Infantry (Canadian Voltigeurs), an incorporated militia battalion[13] from Lower Canada. Officered by sons of French-Canada's proudest families, they had been specifically trained as skirmishing troops, and wore grey uniforms with black facings and accoutrements. With their light infantry muskets they were excellent shots. Morrison's artillery consisted of three 6 pdr. field-guns, in charge of Captain Jackson of the Royal Artillery. Thirty Mohawk warriors, led by Lt. Anderson[14] of the Indian Department, and six militia dispatch riders from the Provincial Dragoons rounded out his little army.

Against Morrison's eight hundred, General Boyd's rear-guard alone could field four thousand troops. They consisted of Boyd's own brigade, the first, which included the 12th and 13th Regiments; Brigadier-General Covington's third brigade of the 9th, 16th and 25th Regiments and the fourth brigade under Brigadier-General Swartwout with the 11th, 14th and 21st Regiments. He had twice the number of field-guns available to the British and in his cavalry, a squadron of the 2nd Regiment of Dragoons, he possessed a weapon which Morrison could not match.

Throughout the night of November 10th to 11th, a cold rain, laced with sleet, fell incessantly. The troops, both British and American, with the exception of ranking officers, sought cover where they could, but most slept on the cold wet ground, their firelocks between their legs. Towards morning, the rain tapered off as the day dawned bleak and grey with a cold east wind

[12] In 1881 the 89th Foot was amalgamated with the 87th Foot to form the Princess Victoria's (Royal Irish Fusiliers).

[13] [Incorporated militia battalions consisted of volunteers who were embodied for the duration of the war, rather than a period of weeks or months. They were raised under, and were subject to, the militia laws.]

[14] [Charles Anderson (1785-1844), interpreter with the Indian Department, was promoted lieutenant in June 1813 and captain in November 1813 for distinguished service at Sackets Harbor and Crysler's Farm. He settled in Otonabee Township and became trader at Rice Lake.]

and the threat of a further storm. About eight o'clock in the morning as Lt. John Sewell of the 49th was toasting a piece of pork on the point of his sword, the senior officer of his company, Captain Nairne, called to him, 'Jack, drop cooking, the enemy is advancing.'

Upon the alarm, the battalion companies of Sewell's regiment were hastily formed in close column behind the fences of the road leading northwards from Crysler's house to the woods, seven hundred yards away. Six companies of the 89th simultaneously formed a second column to the left of the 49th, the two formations equally spaced in the distance between the farm buildings and the woods. Totalling some 460 men they constituted Morrison's main body and reserve. According to Lt. James FitzGibbon,[15] the 89th appeared in their scarlet uniforms but the knowledgeable 49th wore their grey great-coats. As the men of the 49th and 89th waited in column[16] ready to deploy into line or march against the as-yet-unconfirmed attack, sporadic musketry was heard from the east towards the American encampment at Cook's Point. Lt.-Col. Pearson, commanding the detachment from Fort Wellington, was considerably closer to the firing, Morrison having directed him to take up a strong advanced position upon the Montreal road more than half a mile forward of the main body. He had with him the Grenadier and Light Companies of the 49th Regiment, less than fifty men of the Canadian Fencibles and one of the three British field-guns. His front was somewhat protected by one of the smaller ravines; his right flank rested upon the steep river bank; his left was covered by three companies of the 2/89th under Captain Barnes, arranged in echelon[17] from the right and supported by a second 6 pdr. Considerably in advance of Pearson and a good mile from the main British force were the three companies of the Canadian Voltigeurs. Extended as skirmishers in the vicinity of the large ravine from the river to the woods, they had skilfully utilized the cover of rocks, stumps and fences and in their drab uniforms were almost invisible. In the woods to their left were Lt. Anderson's thirty Indians.

Major Heriot commanded the skirmishers and with his men were three troopers of the Provincial Dragoons. John Loucks was one of these militia cavalrymen and, as he watched, he had observed the approach of a party of Americans from the trees at Cook's Point. When they were not quite

[15][James FitzGibbon (1780-1863) was born in Ireland and came to Canada in 1802. As a lieutenant in the 49th Regiment he fought in the battle of Stoney Creek and afterwards brought about the surrender of Colonel Boerstler at Beaver Dam. He also took part in the raid on Black Rock in December 1813. In 1822 he was appointed assistant adjutant-general and he helped organize the defence of Toronto during the Rebellion of 1837. He returned to England in 1846 and was appointed a military knight of Windsor in 1850.]

[16]Technically speaking, they were in column of close companies.

[17]Echelon is a military formation in which components are arranged in the form of steps or parallel lines, each with its front clear of that in advance.

within range, one of the British Indians had suddenly discharged his musket in the direction of the enemy. This was the first shot fired.

The startled Americans, a reconnoitring party, had replied with a volley which, in spite of the long range, ploughed up the sand about the feet of the troopers' horses. Alarmed in turn, the Canadian dragoons had spurred their mounts at break-neck speed for Morrison's headquarters with word that the enemy was attacking in force. This was the alarm that had interrupted Lt. Sewell's breakfast. That it was premature was not immediately evident or young Loucks might have received more than a gentle chiding from the British officer who told him that while 'It was all right to fall back, . . . it was not good form to ride so fast in the face of the enemy.'

While Morrison's land forces were preparing for the anticipated attack, Captain Mulcaster had made the best of a bad situation in positioning his gunboats both to support the right flank of the army and to resume his shelling of the American flotilla. The river's high bank made desirable an anchorage in mid-stream for a maximum field of fire but, unfortunately, this was not feasible due to the rapid current and a great depth of water. One of the gunboats was directed to anchor in the bay at the foot of the island; another was positioned directly opposite Crysler's house, while the third was stationed at the head of a rush-bed some distance up-river. The first two were each armed with a brass 6 pdr., but the third and largest, the *Nelson*, mounted a 32 pdr. carronade[18] and a 24 pdr. long gun, which had been borrowed from the armament of Fort Henry at Kingston. Her long gun had already done considerable damage to the Americans and was in position to do so again.

Meanwhile, in the American camp at Cook's Point, General Wilkinson was still awaiting word that Brown was safe in Cornwall before committing his flotilla to the Long Sault. Not only was Wilkinson sick and confined to bed, but Major-General Lewis, his second-in-command, was equally indisposed and doctoring himself with blackberry brandy. Ill as he was Wilkinson did not relinquish his authority. What followed is best explained in his own words:

> At half-past ten o'clock a.m. an officer of the dragoons arrived with a letter in which the general [Brown] informed me that he had forced the enemy[19] and

[18][The carronade was a short, large-calibre gun, usually used on naval vessels, developed by the Carron Ironworks in Scotland in 1779. Its low-velocity, heavy ball was capable of inflicting greater tearing and splintering damage at medium ranges than was a shot fired from a long gun, which was likelier to make a clean hole through its target.]

[19]Late on November 10 a skirmish took place between Brown's advance-guard and some 300 Dundas and Glengarry Militia commanded by Major Dennis of the 49th. The badly-outnumbered Canadians destroyed the bridge across Hoople's Creek and retired without loss after inflicting some casualties upon the Americans.

> would reach the foot of the Saut [sic] early in the day. Orders were immediately given for the flotilla to sail, at which instant the enemy's gunboats appeared and began to throw shot among us. Information was brought to me at the same time from Brigadier-General Boyd that the enemy's troops were advancing in column. I immediately sent orders to attack them. This report was soon contradicted. Their gunboats, however, continued to scratch us and a variety of reports of their movements and counter-movements were brought to me in succession, which convinced me of their determination to hazard an attack when it could be done to greatest advantage, and I therefore determined to anticipate them. Directions were accordingly sent to Brigadier-General Boyd, to throw the detachments of his command, assigned to him in the order of the preceding day, and composed of men of his own, Covington's and Swartwout's brigades, into three columns, to march upon the enemy, outflank them, if possible, and take their artillery.

For the attack, General John Boyd, upon whose shoulders the Elijah's mantle of command had descended, possessed eight regiments of infantry, a half-dozen 6 pdr. field-pieces and the dragoons of the 2nd Regiment – a minimum of 4,000 men. He made the opening move in the battle. These are his words:

> While the rear division of the Army, consisting of detachments from the 1st, 3rd, and 4th Brigades and placed under my command to protect the flotilla from the enemy that hung on our rear, was under arms in order to move . . . down the St. Lawrence, a report was brought to me from the rear-guard that a body of about two hundred British and Indians had advanced into the woods that skirted our rear. General Swartwout with the 4th Brigade was immediately ordered to dislodge them. General Covington with the 3rd Brigade being directed to be within supporting distance. General Swartwout dashed into the woods and with the 21st Infantry [a part of his brigade] after a short skirmish drove them back to the position of the main body. Here he was joined by General Covington. The enemy had judiciously chosen his ground among the deep ravines which everywhere intersected the extensive plain and discharged a heavy and galling fire upon our advancing columns. No opposition or obstacle, however, checked their ardor. The enemy retired more than a mile before their resolute and repeated charges. During this time the detachment of the 1st Brigade under Colonel Coles, whose greater distance from the scene of action retarded its arrival, rapidly entered the field.

After this glorifield account of how several thousand Americans forced the retirement, and only after hard fighting, of less than 200 Canadian skirmishers, look at the scene through British eyes – those of Lt.-Col. Harvey, Morrison's second-in-command:

> At two o'clock . . . the enemy suddenly showed his columns in the woods in our front, consisting of three heavy ones (apparently brigades), of infantry, a considerable amount of cavalry on the road on his left, and riflemen on his

right and in his front. . . . I was convinced we had, with 800 men, to meet, in the open field, a force of not less than 4,000 and strong in an arm of which we were wholly destitute – cavalry. Our light troops – Voltigeurs – were thrown forward and showed a good countenance, but were, of course, immediately driven back; and the enemy advanced at the *pas de charge à la Française*, which was quickly changed by a well-directed fire from our field-pieces, to one more comporting with the dignity of the American nation.

Lt. John Sewell from his position in the ranks of the 49th saw it this way:

We moved up a small eminence that commanded a view of the enemy. Our column was deployed [into line]; the enemy was performing the same evolution within range of our fire and that of the two field-pieces commanded by Capt. Jackson R.A., posted in our rear on a small elevation which enabled them to fire over our bayonets. The combined fire of our regiment and that of the two field-pieces with shrapnel hastened the enemy in the forming of his line and returning our fire.

Now followed immediately the second phase of Boyd's attack. An American medical officer, Amasa Trowbridge, after describing the retreat of the British skirmishers saw the main body of the British 'advancing in columns on the west extremity of Chrysler's field'. He observed:

They opened a fire of musketry, and from a six-pounder, which was heavy and galling upon our troops, composed of the 21st Regiment and a detachment from the 1st brigade, commanded by Colonel Coles. This body was now ordered to flank the enemy's left. This was promptly done under a heavy fire from the enemy. General Covington, having been ordered up, now took the position just left by [Colonel] Ripley[20] and Coles, nearly in front of the enemy and within rifle-shot distance.

Came now the tidal waves of the American attack. While Swartwout's brigade, consisting of the 11th, 14th, and 21st Regiments, with the 12th and 13th Regiments from the 1st Brigade under Colonel Coles marched to turn the British left, simultaneously General Covington led the 9th, 16th, and 25th Regiments of the 3rd Brigade in an advance which not only engaged the much narrower front of Morrison's main body, but threatened to turn its right. Covington, misled by the grey great-coats of the 49th, was heard to call to his men: 'Come lads, let me see how you will deal with these militia men.' He soon discovered his mistake.

Ripley who, with his 21st Regiment, participated in the effort to turn the British left, had this to say:

[20] [Eleazar Wheelock Ripley (1782-1839) served a term in the Massachusetts state legislature and was given command of a regiment in the war. After Crysler's Farm he saw action at Chippawa, Lundy's Lane, and Fort Erie and he was promoted to brigadier-general in 1814. Afterwards he settled in Louisiana where he was elected to the state senate and then to Congress.]

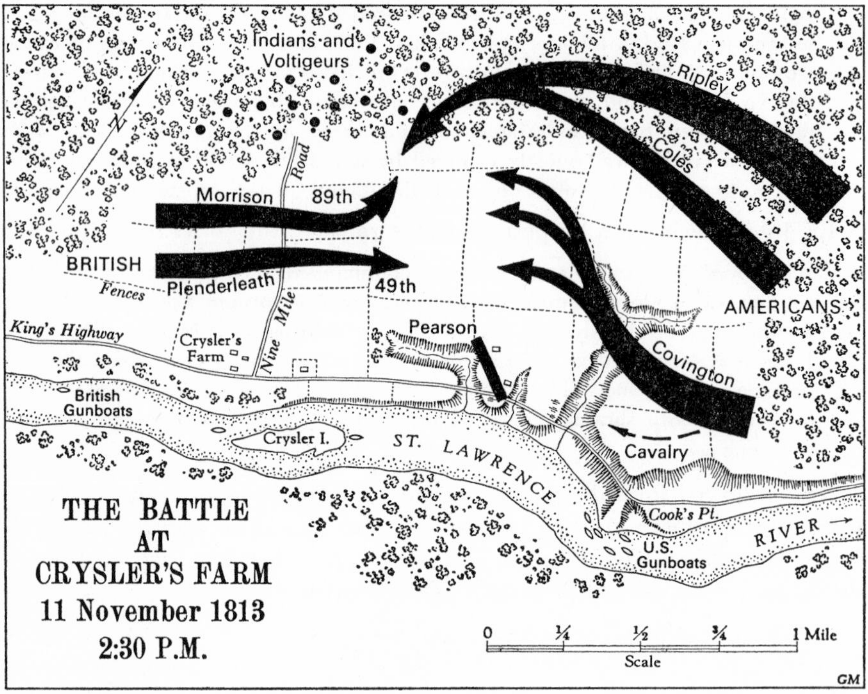

THE BATTLE AT CRYSLER'S FARM 11 November 1813 2:30 P.M.

> I advanced against the left of the enemy. After a slow and hard march across muddy fields for half a mile, I passed a creek in boggy ground and saw the enemy at long musket shot. I advanced to attack. Suddenly at short musket shot a line of the enemy got up from concealment and delivered two volleys. My men, disregarding my officers, dodged behind stumps and opened individual fire. The confusion was so strong that I could not stop the shooting until their ammunition was exhausted, whereupon they could not be prevented from retiring. I was able to rally at the creek as the other two regiments approached. After ammunition was replenished, I joined the 11th and 14th in a new attack.

The two volleys from concealed troops referred to by Ripley were from the Voltigeurs and Indians now covering Morrison's left flank at the edge of the woods. How the main body of the British, the thin red line of the 49th and 89th Regiments, dealt with the combination of Ripley, Cole, and Covington is described by Sewell:

> We had then been engaged for some time, line to line, when I observed the Voltigeurs bolting out of the woods on the left of our line like greyhounds and simultaneously I saw the enemy debouch from the same wood threatening the left of the 89th Regiment at about 50 yards from my old gallant corps.

> To meet this movement Colonel Morrison changed front, placing his battalion at right angles to the 49th and facing the enemy who being in close column received the fire of the 89th, and at the same time that from Jackson's two guns. This was too much for the American column and it fell back under cover of the woods. On this the 89th resumed its position on the left of the 49th and the British line advanced in direct echelon from the right.

In the combat, line to line, British drill and disciplined fire power had, so far, outmatched numerical superiority. Harvey makes a point of it: 'On arriving within musket distance the enemy's columns halted, and commenced a heavy but irregular fire, which our battalions returned with infinitely more effect by regular firing of platoons and wings.[21] The superiority of this fire, aided by that of our three field-pieces, which were admirably served, gave, after a severe contest, the first check and repulse to the enemy . . . .'

How the Americans suffered is tersely told by Amasa Trowbridge:

> General Covington soon received a mortal wound by a rifle shot. Colonel Preston, next in command, was soon after wounded in the thigh by a ball, fracturing the bone. Major Comins was next wounded, and was obliged to retire. Many platoon officers were wounded or killed, and within twenty minutes after, the whole brigade was in confusion and left the field. A few minutes previous two six-pounders were brought up by Lieutenant Smith and posted near some houses occupied by the enemy.

Four additional American field-pieces arrived soon afterwards. Boyd in his official report to Wilkinson wrote: 'It should be remarked that the artillery, excepting two pieces, under Captain Irvine attached to the rear division . . . did not reach the ground until the line, for want of ammunition, had already begun to fall back. When they were arranged, in doing which I was assisted by the skill of Colonel Swift of the engineers, their fire was sure and destructive.'

With this last statement the British would not have disagreed. Harvey wrote:

> I perceived that it would be impossible in our advanced position, to stand long against the grape from his field-pieces, which it was accordingly determined to charge. The 49th was moved on against the field-guns opposite them, the 89th in echelon supporting; and though this charge was not executed as

[21] A battalion consisted of eight regular companies, to which one grenadier company and a light or skirmishing company were added. Apart from the two specialist detachments, a company was an administrative, not a tactical, unit. When the battalion was formed for action, the regular companies were divided into eight equal parts, then sub-divided into sixteen. Hence the terms 'division' and 'sub-division'. The fire of a division was referred to as 'platoon fire' and each platoon or division fired in turn so as to avoid a pause in the fire while reloading. From this came the expressions 'rolling platoon fire' or 'rolling volleys'. When in line, the half of a battalion to right or left of its centre was called a 'wing'.

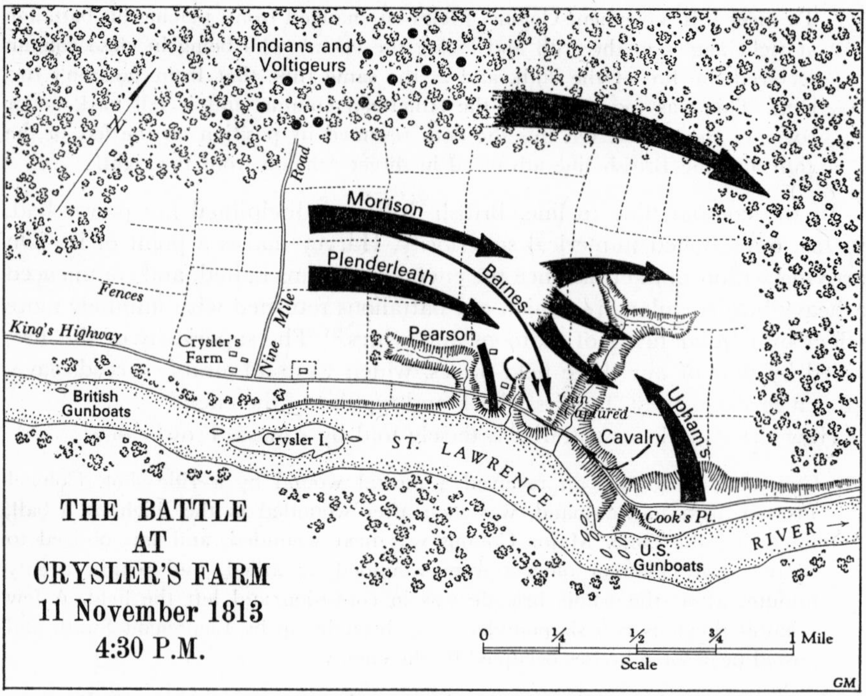

> intended, nor as far as the proposed point, it nevertheless decided the fate of the day, as the enemy immediately fell back, leaving in the possession of the three companies of the 89th regiment, on the right, one of his six-pounders, with its tumbril, etc., which they had spiritedly charged, after having repulsed a treble charge of the enemy's cavalry.

To Morrison and Harvey it was the turning of the tide; to the men of the 49th who had entered the action as the 'remnant' of a battalion it meant punishing casualties amounting to their dissolution as an effective fighting force. Understandable bitterness and pride creeps into the account of Sewell, the young lieutenant:

> As the line consisting of the 89th and 49th was advancing in echelon, Colonel Harvey ordered Lieut. Colonel Plenderleath to charge the enemy. At the time this order was given we were distant from the enemy about 120 yards of ploughed, wet, heavy ground intersected by two parallel snake fences that we had to pull down. As we advanced over the heavy ground our progress was much retarded by the intervening fences. Not a shot was fired to cover our advance, consequently there being nothing to disconcert the enemy's fire it was directed on us from riflemen and artillery and in the short space of 10 minutes we lost eleven officers out of eighteen and men in proportion.

> Such a movement so unskilfully directed could not but end in disaster. Between officers and men more than one half were killed or wounded; the old and bold 'Green Tigers' were helpless under a deadly and unreturned fire. To have closed with the enemy under these circumstances would have been more unjustifiable temerity but the intuitive faculty of the gallant Col. Plenderleath redeemed the error of an imperative order founded on ignorance and issued by a red tape Staff Adjutant General who was very inexperienced in field movements. The commands 'Pass to the rear files from the right of companies', 'Halt', 'Front', 'Pivot', 'Cover', 'Left wheel into line', 'Fire by platoons from the centre to the flanks' our chief gave with the sangfroid of an ordinary parade and they were executed with the coolness of a review notwithstanding being under grape and canister from the enemy's guns to which we were in close proximity. About this time my Captain was killed. I assumed command of the company and I could see the enemy and more of the field than in the supernumerary rank, and to my no small anxiety I saw a squadron of cavalry galloping up the high road towards our right front. Ellis who commanded the right company wheeled it four paces[22] and poured in a volley and so did our flank companies that were posted on the other side of the road. I think that Jackson's guns had one round at them. Be that as it may many saddles were emptied ere they went right about. Their leader was a gallant fellow, he leaped over the fence and was riding toward our right but alone: some of our men rushed out to attack him with their bayonets fixed. But observing that he was alone he took the fence again in good hunting style and followed his men who were in full retreat.

It appears that the charge of the 49th was, in the manner of its execution, one of those mistakes in the interpretation of orders so common in the history of battles. Harvey apparently took for granted that Plenderleath would reform line from echelon before delivering the charge. The Colonel of the 49th, however, taking his orders literally, began the movement with his companies separated in the successive parallel lines of the direct echelon formation, with his most advanced company on the right. As the American cavalry threatened to ride down and envelop the 49th's disconnected companies, Plenderleath had no alternative but to halt the charge and reform line upon his left and rear-most company, where the main body of the 89th supported his left flank. The commands reported by Sewell substantiate such a movement which, to the Americans, appeared as a withdrawal of a few rods. With the line hurriedly reformed, the backwards wheeling of the right flank company under Captain Ellis was sufficient to prevent its right flank being turned by the charging dragoons. To one American it seemed that the wheel exposed 'a masked battery, which played on us with great effect, mowing down our ranks both horse and foot . . .'.

Disastrous as was the charge to the American cavalry it was not com-

[22] The company was backwards wheeled on the left.

pletely in vain. According to Trowbridge: 'The enemy's attention was so much diverted from Ripley and Cole's retreating detachment that, by passing, partly covered by the forest they made good their retreat. The guard left at the boats was ordered up, commanded by Colonel Upham. They occupied a position a few minutes in front of the enemy, who remained stationary . . . keeping up a steady fire from two six-pounders upon every thing that appeared on the field to annoy them.'

Now Upham's 600 men covered the rout of the whole of Boyd's forces. As Harvey put it: 'Some efforts were still kept up, but the fire of our platoons and guns, and above all, the steady countenance of the troops, finally drove the enemy out of the field; and about half-past four o'clock he gave up the contest and retreated rapidly through the woods, covered by his light troops.'

Morrison also summed up the battle's climax and finale:

> The 49th was then directed to charge the gun posted opposite to ours, but it became necessary when within a short distance of it to check the forward movement in consequence of a charge from the cavalry on the right, lest they [the cavalry] should wheel about and fall upon their [the 49th's] rear but they [the cavalry] were received in so gallant a manner by the companies of the 89th under Captain Barnes and the well-directed fire of the artillery that they quickly retreated, and by an immediate charge of those companies one gun was gained.
>
> The enemy immediately concentrated their force to check our advance, but such was the steady countenance and well-directed fire of the troops and artillery, that about half-past four they gave way at all points from an exceeding strong position, endeavouring by their light infantry to cover their retreat, who were soon driven away by a judicious movement made by Lieut.-Colonel Pearson. The detachment for the night occupied the ground from which the enemy had been driven . . . .

The fighting was now over. Darkness, hastened by the returning storm, soon halted the British pursuit. While upwards of one hundred American prisoners were taken, there is no doubt that had cavalry been available to Morrison many more would have been rounded up. In the unequal contest the Americans, by their own admission, lost 102 killed and 237 wounded, of whom Brig.-Gen. Leonard Covington and Col. James P. Preston subsequently died. Against this we have Col. Harvey's statement that nearly 180 of their dead were counted on the field. Morrison's losses, on the other hand – according to his official casualty return, dated November 14, 1813 – amounted to 22 killed, 148 wounded, and 9 missing. Of the battered 49th, Captain Nairne was dead, Colonel Plenderleath among the wounded. True to this regiment's grim tradition that the officer who carried the unit colour in battle was always hit, young Ensign Richmond, who bore it at Crysler's

Farm, was among the casualties. Both Col. Pearson and Capt. Davis of the commissariat had had close calls when their horses were killed under them.

While Morrison's official report to his superior, General de Rottenburg, was a masterpiece of conciseness, Boyd and Wilkinson poured forth a veritable torrent of words in an effort to convince the American Secretary of War that they had not really been soundly trounced by a force which they outnumbered four to one – apparently on the grounds that the real victor is he who 'lives to fight another day'. One American, however, under no compunction to vindicate his fellow countrymen, lamented in a private letter on November 13th:

> Our troops retreated with great precipitation to the boats, and crossed the river, leaving the British on the field. . . . We lost several boats by fire of the British Gun-boats. What appears most extraordinary in this affair is that nearly 1000 of our troops crossed to the American side during the engagement! This misfortune has greatly chagrined the officers, and disheartened our troops. The taking of Montreal is no longer thought to be a work of ease; and many wish themselves honourably out of the expedition.

An undeniable fact is that when Wilkinson, fearful that the British would claim a victory, asked Boyd if he could maintain himself on the Canadian shore, Boyd's reply was that 'he could not'. His army, in confusion and panic, was hastily embarked under cover of darkness and the American flotilla proceeded some four miles down-stream to take refuge on the American side. The cavalry and light artillery, secure in the knowledge that infantry could not overtake them, retreated down the Canadian shore towards General Brown and Cornwall. On the following morning, Wilkinson's main force was re-embarked, the armada ran the Long Sault, and, that same day, Macomb, Brown, Wilkinson and company were all together at Barnhart's, three miles above Cornwall. At that place, a perhaps not unwelcome message reached Wilkinson. Colonel Atkinson, Hampton's Inspector-General, arrived with a letter from his commander in which he declined to join Wilkinson at St. Regis and announced his intention of retreating to Plattsburg.

Wilkinson now had his excuse. Officially he could never admit that a drubbing by an inferior British force had broken his morale and that of his army. Nor would his ill-health, the inclement weather or the late start of his campaign figure in his explanations of withdrawal. All the blame could now be placed on Hampton's defection. Hastily, a council of Wilkinson's ill-starred generals was called at Barnhart's. Solemnly, and with rage at scapegoat Hampton, they agreed to abandon the attack on Montreal. Speeded by the news that Colonel Morrison's corps of observation was again close at hand, the armada was re-embarked to proceed, impotent, to winter quarters at French Mills.[23] As one American contemporary put it, 'The St. Lawrence

[23] On the Salmon River in New York State below Cornwall.

campaign is at an end, and this is their "Grand Plans" that would confound every European. What stupid asses they are.'

The people of Williamsburg Township in Dundas County would remember the day of Crysler's Farm. Anxiety over loved ones serving with the militia or the commissariat, concern about the safety of their homes and possessions mingled with that nervous exhilaration which grips innocent bystanders enmeshed in the pages of history. For them, the War of 1812 could no longer be viewed objectively. It had been brought to their very doorsteps. They, and their descendants, would never forget.

For the British and Canadian soldiers who fought at Crysler's Farm, official recognition of their victory did not come before many of them were dead. Not until 1847 were medals granted by Queen Victoria to the rank and file, the decoration authorized being the British General Service Medal with a bar reading 'Christler's Farm'. Many of the survivors did not bother to make application for the honour – as they were required to do – with the result that the official list of Canadian recipients published in the *Canada Gazette* records the issue of only twelve Crysler's Farm medals. The ranking officers had been granted a corresponding medal in gold.

For Major-General James Wilkinson, Crysler's Farm meant open disgrace and the beginning of the end. Relieved of his command early in 1814, he faced a court martial in January 1815 on four separate charges: (1) neglect of duty and un-officer-like conduct, (2) drunkenness on duty, (3) conduct unbecoming an officer and gentleman, (4) countenancing and encouraging disobedience to orders. The trial was protracted. Its verdict for defeated Wilkinson: severe censure and dismissal from the service.

To 'clear and concise' Lt.-Col. Morrison, Crysler's Farm brought honour and glory in this, his first field command. His promising career was soon to be given a severe check, for at Lundy's Lane in July 1814 the young colonel was so badly wounded in the arm that he was placed on half pay until 1821. His abilities had not gone unnoticed, however, and in the latter year he was recalled to active service as Colonel of the 44th Foot. Placed in command of the campaign against the Burmese in 1824, Morrison was promoted to Brigadier-General and conducted his expedition with a skill which brought him unstinted praise. In common with hundreds of his men, General Morrison fell victim to a tropical fever. Invalided home, he failed to reach England and died at sea on February 15, 1826. Thus ended the life and career of Joseph Wanton Morrison, C.B., warmly praised in published General Orders, recipient of a formal vote of gratitude from the Assembly of Lower Canada, and described as 'pre-eminent and next to . . . the gallant and immortal Brock, for the glory of his achievement at Crysler's Farm'.

The Canadian press, represented by the *Quebec Mercury*, editorialized:

When we consider the nature and extent of the Enemy's preparations . . . the number of the troops employed . . . we cannot sufficiently admire the gallant efforts of the handful of brave men who have so successfully defeated it. To the determined valour and steady discipline of the small band of heroes, under Lt. Col. Morrison, we owe it, that this formidable force of the enemy has been checked in its career before it had even approached the frontier of our Province, and that an enterprise for which so much had been expected by them has terminated in their compleat discomfiture and disgrace. . . .

FURTHER READING: W. C. H. Wood (ed.), *Select British documents . . .*, volume 2, pages 429-67; F. B. Hough, *A history of St. Lawrence and Franklin counties, New York . . .* (Albany, 1853); R. Sellar, *The U. S. campaign of 1813 to capture Montreal: Crysler, the decisive battle of the War of 1812* (Huntingdon, Quebec, 1913).

On Lake Erie each commander followed the same strategy as on Lake Ontario – to outbuild his opponent, to blockade him, to attack his bases from the land, to assist in the movement of men and supplies along the waterway, and to aid military operations. Battle was to be sought by the stronger fleet and avoided by the weaker flotilla, for defeat could bring irretrievable ruin on the land as well as on the water. Such was the outcome when the weaker British squadron was destroyed on September 10, 1813, in a fierce engagement off Put-in Bay. At one stroke the westernmost sector of Upper Canada came under the control of the American forces and the British withdrew to the Niagara front. The battle of Lake Erie demonstrated the vital role of naval power in preserving Upper Canada and by implication justified the avoidance of a contest by the British fleet on Lake Ontario. . . . This article is reprinted from the transactions of the Royal Canadian Institute, volume 6 (1899), with the permission of Mrs. E. A. Cruikshank and of the Institute.

The Contest for the Command of Lake Erie in 1812-13

BY ERNEST A. CRUIKSHANK

Long before the actual declaration of war took place Major-General Brock had foreseen and pointed out that the defence of Upper Canada would be largely dependent on the command of the lakes and that a successful invasion of that province was scarcely possible as long as this remained with the British. In a letter to the Governor-General dated December 2nd, 1811, he remarked:

> From Amherstburg to Fort Erie my chief dependence must rest on a naval force for the protection of that extensive coast. But considering the state to which it is reduced, extraordinary exertions and great expense will be required before it can be rendered efficient. At present it only consists of a ship and a small schooner, the latter of a bad construction, old, and in want of many repairs yet she is the only King's vessel able to navigate Lake Huron, whilst the Americans have a sloop and a fine brig capable of carrying twelve guns and in perfect readiness for any service.

In merchant shipping the Americans possessed an undoubted superiority. They had three stout schooners and a sloop of between sixty and ninety tons burden besides five or six smaller vessels, while only five small schooners or sloops were the property of Canadian owners. The construction of a schooner to carry twelve guns which was named the *Lady Prevost* was at once authorized. Brock then urged the superannuation of Commodore Alexander Grant, who was eighty-five years of age and had been in command a full half-century, and that two companies of the Royal Newfoundland Regiment should be sent forward to act as seamen and marines. These precautions, trifling as they were, gave him the temporary control of Lake Erie, for the American government was strangely negligent in utilizing its extensive resources in that quarter until disaster convinced them of the necessity.

The services of the only two British ships afloat when hostilities began were by no means inconsiderable although they were weakly manned and not efficiently officered. Captain Hall, who had succeeded Grant in the command, blockaded the United States brig *Adams* at the shipyard in the mouth of the River Rouge below Detroit, where she had been lately rebuilt. On July 3rd, Lieut. Frederick Rolette, a young French-Canadian officer in command of the *Hunter*, captured the *Cayahoga Packet* with General Hull's baggage and many official documents of value. He then cruised along the south shore of the lake taking several boats and small craft loaded with provisions and effectually cutting off Hull's communication by water with the coast below from which he expected to draw most of his supplies, and finally, on August 7th, he captured a convoy of eleven bateaux having on board the baggage and fifty-six wounded men belonging to a column sent to reopen the communication with Ohio by land.

At the same time the *Queen Charlotte* by her presence in the river alone had delayed Hull's operations and prevented the advance of his siege artillery against Amherstburg while Brock was enabled to send forward reinforcements by water from Long Point and Fort Erie in perfect safety, gaining several days' time and avoiding the fatigue of the overland march. On August 16th that ship covered the landing of the British troops in Michigan while part of her crew manned the batteries opposite Detroit. On the surrender of the garrison the only two armed vessels possessed by the American government on the upper lakes, the *Adams* and a worn-out sloop, were taken.

Although only a few merchant schooners and a sloop still remained uncaptured and these had been collected at the shipyard of Black Rock in the mouth of Niagara River where they were blockaded by batteries on the opposite bank, Sir George Prevost still felt far from secure in that quarter. . . .

The *Lady Prevost* had been launched at Amherstburg about the middle of July and, as soon as she could be made ready to sail, was sent to Fort Erie to protect that flank of the line of defence on the Niagara while the greater part of the regular troops were withdrawn for the relief of Amherstburg.[1] The *Adams* was put in commission as the *Detroit* soon after her capture and for the remainder of the year all the vessels were chiefly employed in transporting troops and stores, the *Hunter* on Lake Huron and the others on Lake Erie, although there were scarcely seamen enough to navigate them in fair weather.

A return of October 2nd, 1812, shows that there were only six officers, eleven petty officers, eight able seamen, and nineteen ordinary seamen distributed among these four vessels, while their regular complement was twelve officers, thirty-six petty officers, forty-four able seamen, and forty-four ordinary seamen. An attempt was made to supply this serious deficiency by putting on board an additional number of the Royal Newfoundland Regiment to act as marines or sailors as circumstances might dictate. . . .

Vessels so weakly manned were scarcely capable of defence when boldly attacked, even by rowboats, and the *Detroit* in company with the merchant brig *Caledonia,* while lying at anchor off Fort Erie, was actually surprised and taken on the morning of October 9th, by a party of 124 American seamen and soldiers, in three boats which silently approached under cover of an intensely dark night. The *Detroit* was subsequently destroyed to prevent her recapture, but the *Caledonia* was triumphantly carried off to the Black Rock navy yard, where she was added to the other vessels lying there, which were already being converted into gunboats.

This was, however, the only loss sustained by the British on Lake Erie during 1812, while the advantages secured from the control of the lake cannot easily be overestimated. While the armies of generals Hull and Harrison were painfully struggling through the swamps and thickets of Ohio and Michigan, with their pack-horses dying by hundreds along the road, their opponents were enabled to transport troops and artillery from place to place with comparative ease and rapidity. The British commanders were accordingly enabled to strengthen the garrison of Amherstburg by troops from the Niagara River, and, when danger had passed in that quarter, to take them back in time to repel an attack on the latter line. A part of the 41st Regiment was sent in this way from Niagara to Amherstburg, and was present at the surrender of Detroit. This detachment then returned and took part in the battle of Queenston. During the winter it marched overland to Amherstburg, and participated in the seige of Fort Meigs and the battle of Miami, in May 1813.[2] The ruinous fortifications of Amherstburg on General Hull's approach were hastily armed with cannon from Fort George at

[1] [Brock withdrew the troops from the Niagara frontier and York in order to counter General Hull's invasion from Detroit. Amherstburg, however, was not taken by the Americans and its retention by the British was a factor in Hull's decision to abandon the invasion of Upper Canada.]

Niagara, and a few weeks later the batteries along the Niagara River were mounted with the artillery captured at Detroit. The command of the lake alone made this practicable. The movements of British armed vessels along the south shore of the lake, and the occasional landing of small foraging parties, created indescribable alarm, and considerable bodies of militia were called out from time to time, and maintained under arms at Sandusky, Cleveland, Erie, Chautauqua, and Cattaraugus. The time for defensive preparations gained by the British was invaluable.

The necessity of securing the control of the lakes for the accomplishment of their plans of conquest had, in fact, been forcibly pointed out to Dr. Eustis, the American Secretary of War, as early as January 2nd, 1812, by General John Armstrong, who was destined to succeed him in office before the year was out. 'Resting, as the line of Canadian defence does, in its whole extent, on navigable lakes and rivers, no time should be lost in getting a naval ascendency on both, for *caeteris paribus,* the belligerent who is the first to obtain this advantage will (miracles excepted) win the game.' . . .

But the boastful declarations of the advocates of war, both in and out of Congress, that the militia of Kentucky or Ohio, alone, could and would take Canada, seem to have impressed their government so strongly that it preferred to put its trust for the time in its land forces alone, which promised at least a superiority in numbers that seemed overwhelming. General Hull's discomfiture, succeeded by other disasters, convinced the President and his advisers of their mistake, and several hundred seamen, accompanied by a large body of shipwrights, were despatched to the lakes.

At the Black Rock shipyard they found the merchant schooners *Catharine* and *Amelia,* and sloop *Contractor,* to which was soon added the prize brig *Caledonia.* These vessels were rapidly fitted out as gunboats, and armed with those heavy long guns which had already proved so effective at sea.

These preparations soon became known to Sir George Prevost, and caused him much uneasiness, as his correspondence with Lord Bathurst[3] shows. On

[2] [This campaign of the 41st Regiment was directed by Colonel Henry Procter for the purpose of maintaining the British hold upon Detroit and thus securing the westernmost part of Upper Canada against invasion from that quarter. In January 1813 Procter attacked and defeated an American force under General Winchester at Frenchtown, or River au Raisin. But he lacked the troops to follow up his victory and General Harrison proceeded to build Fort Meigs at the rapids of the Miami (or Maumee) to protect the forces being assembled for the recovery of Detroit. In April and May 1813 Procter directed a raid against the new fort and besieged it without success. Procter made a final foray into Ohio in July 1813 but failed to capture either Fort Meigs, or Fort Stephenson on the Sandusky River. See pages 123-4.]

[3] [Henry Bathurst, third earl of Bathurst (1762-1834), was an M.P. for Cirencester from 1783 to 1794 when he succeeded to the peerage. He occupied a succession of ministerial posts after 1783 in the governments of William Pitt and his successors, becoming secretary for war and the colonies in June 1812. He held this position until 1827 when he became lord president of the council in the government of the Duke of Wellington, 1828-30.]

October 26th he asked for the appointment of a captain in the Royal Navy to superintend the 'naval establishment' on the lakes. On November 5th he wrote that the Government of the United States had sent the crew of the frigate *John Adams* to man its vessels, and begged for officers and crews for the British ships. . . . Fearing that assistance from Great Britain might arrive too late, Prevost applied to Sir John B. Warren, commanding on the Halifax station, for at least a sufficient number of officers and men to navigate the ships on the lakes. In January 1813 Captain Hall went to Quebec to enlist seamen for Lake Erie. He met with little success, owing largely to the high rate of wages then being paid in the merchant service, and the men he obtained were generally of an unsatisfactory description, being incompetent and dissipated. At the same time instructions were given to General Procter[4] to build at Amherstburg a ship intended to carry fourteen twelve-pound carronades, and four long nines in bridle ports, in the bow and stern, and two decked gunboats, to be armed each with a long eighteen. With the exception of timber, which could be procured close at hand, the principal part of the materials – nails, bolts, pulleys, deadeyes, lead, copper, glass, paint, resin, cordage and sails – would have to be sent up from Montreal or Quebec with the shipwrights.

'There are not shipwrights in this province to do half the work,' Captain Gray reported on December 3rd, 1812. 'It might, under those circumstances, be advisable to engage all the master shipwrights in Lower Canada with their men, and send them up to work by contract or otherwise.'

There was even greater difficulty in providing guns and ordnance stores. Six carronades destined for the *Queen Charlotte* had been taken to arm gunboats on the Sorel and St. Lawrence. There were none in the arsenals at Quebec or Halifax. Prevost quite unexpectedly succeeded in purchasing eighteen old carronades from a Quebec merchant, but these were appropriated forthwith for the armament of the ships at Kingston, and those needed for Lake Erie had then to be requisitioned from England. By the middle of March only eighty seamen of the most wretched quality had entered for service on both lakes, and the Governor-General was obliged to forward a most urgent requisition to the Colonial Office for 445 seamen for Lake Ontario and 170 for Lake Erie. But, even had the full number been sent out, a return showed that the Lake Erie squadron would still be far short of its complement.[5] The result of his repeated appeals may be traced in Lord

[4] [Henry Procter (1787-1822) came to Canada as commanding officer of the 41st Regiment. He served under Brock in the Detroit campaign and afterwards commanded the Western District, carrying the war into Michigan and Ohio. He was appointed a major-general in June 1813, but following his defeat at Moraviantown he was court-martialled, publicly reprimanded, and suspended from his rank and pay for a period of six months. See also pages 114-29.]

[5] Returns by Captain P. L. Chambers, D.A.Q.M.G., dated at Amherstburg, March, 1813. Total complement required 479 officers and men. Present, 108 – short 379.

Bathurst's despatches. On December 9th, 1812, he announced that 200 seamen had been ordered to proceed to Quebec for service on the lakes, chiefly composed of those who had lately manned the flotilla at Riga and were supposed, in consequence, to be already acclimated. On January 13th, 1813, he wrote that the number had been increased to 300, and on March 12th to 450. Finally, on August 14th, when of course it was too late to avert disaster on Lake Erie, he informed Prevost that 300 additional seamen would be sent from England and that Admiral Warren would be instructed to lend him 300 more to be employed on the lakes.

Meanwhile the Government of the United States was making determined efforts to equip a squadron competent to gain possession of Lake Erie as a preliminary to the recovery of Detroit. Presque Isle (lately renamed Erie) was selected as the best place for building vessels of war as having a spacious and landlocked harbour, with 'a sufficiency of water on the bar to let them into the lake, but not a sufficiency to let heavy armed vessels of the enemy into the bay to destroy them.' A large body of militia could also be easily assembled from the adjacent country for their protection. In the beginning of January 1813, Commodore Chauncey, with Eckford, his naval constructor, visited the place and approved of the work already done on two gunboats and gave instructions for the construction of two large flush-decked brigs or corvettes of the class of the *Wasp* and *Hornet*, which had won such notable victories on the ocean. A considerable body of ship-carpenters and axemen had already been at work for some time, and these were reinforced about March 1st by another party sent for the purpose from New York. Chauncey designated for the command Captain Oliver Hazard Perry,[6] lately in command of a flotilla of gunboats at Newport, R.I., an energetic young officer who had seen some active service in the war with Tripoli ten years before as a midshipman but was not otherwise distinguished. He brought with him to Erie one hundred of his best seamen, about the end of March, and found that, besides the two brig corvettes, a clipper schooner and three gunboats had been already laid down. The difficulties of building, although great, were decidedly less there than on the Canadian shore. There was no lack of skilled labour as the private shipyards of the United States were absolutely idle. Pittsburgh, his base of supplies, was much nearer than Montreal and conveyance by water was practicable nearly all the way. Large boats loaded with artillery and naval stores ascended the Allegheny river, French, Deadwater, and Muddy creeks to the site of Fort Le Boeuf, now Waterford.

[6] [After the Battle of Lake Erie, Captain Perry (1785-1819) commanded the warship *Java* in the Mediterranean. In 1819 he led a small fleet on an expedition to South America where he contracted yellow fever and died. The action on Lake Erie touched off an extremely acrimonious and unedifying controversy between Perry and his second-in-command, Captain J. D. Elliott, that continued for years after Perry's death.]

Thence there was a passable wagon road to Erie. The work of construction accordingly proceeded rapidly. . . . Redoubts were thrown up and guns mounted to command the harbour's mouth. A body of two thousand volunteers and militia was assembled for the protection of the place.

Early in May the schooners *Ariel, Porcupine, Scorpion,* and *Tigress* were launched, and on the 24th of the same month the two brigs were put afloat. In addition to these vessels, the prize brig *Caledonia* and five merchant schooners lying at the Black Rock shipyard had been purchased and equipped for war, but were prevented from entering the lake by the batteries opposite. On May 28th, however, Fort Erie was evacuated and the whole line of the Niagara abandoned by the British forces. No time was then lost in removing the blockaded vessels but six days were consumed in towing them up the river and it was not until June 13th that they were enabled to sail from Buffalo, heavily freighted with naval stores.

The two small gunboats whose construction had been authorized by the Governor-General were built on the Thames near Chatham and launched early in April, but small progress was made on the new ship at Amherstburg owing both to the lack of workmen and materials. . . .

On April 23rd a flotilla composed of the *Lady Prevost*, *General Hunter*, *Chippawa*, the new gunboats *Eliza* and *Colonel Myers*, and transports *Mary*, *Nancy*, and *Miamis*, under the command of Captain Hall, conveyed General Procter's division to the mouth of the Miami River where the troops were landed. The gunboats ascended the river until within easy range of Fort Meigs. Part of the seamen were landed to assist in manning the siege batteries, and were said by Procter to have rendered the most essential service, although they suffered no loss in action.

After the siege was raised, the *Hunter* was despatched with provisions and stores to Mackinac where the garrison was almost starving, and the *Queen Charlotte* was sent for supplies to Fort Erie as Procter's whole division was then in great distress for lack of both food and clothing. The want of seamen absolutely prohibited any offensive operation.

'Our gunboats are now idle,' Procter wrote on May 23rd, 'for want of hands. We are endeavouring to man one. They might have been made good use of if we had had sailors since we left Miami in intercepting supplies for Mr. Harrison, which, as Colonel Nichol[7] observes, he can now receive by the lake only.' . . .

[7] [Robert Nichol (1774?-1824) came to Canada as a young man, clerked in the store of his cousin, Robert Hamilton, then opened his own business at Port Dover. He rose in wealth and influence and represented Norfolk County in the legislative assembly from 1812 until 1821, when he was appointed a judge. During the war he was quartermaster-general of the militia and he participated in the actions at Detroit, Frenchman's Creek, Stoney Creek, Black Rock, and Fort Erie. His property in Norfolk county was greatly damaged and when he died suddenly as the result of an accident his family was left in financial difficulties.]

Sir John Warren had responded to the Governor-General's appeal for officers by sending him captains Robert Heriot Barclay,[8] Robert Finnis, and Daniel Pring and four lieutenants of the Royal Navy. Captain Barclay . . . had lost his left arm in the service but had not particularly distinguished himself, although undoubtedly brave and skilful. None of the other officers were in any way known to fame. Barclay arrived at Kingston early in May and took charge of the ships lying there without crews. A few days later he was superseded by Sir James Lucas Yeo who came directly from England with thirty-six officers and 450 seamen to assume the command on both lakes. Yeo offered the command of the Lake Erie squadron to Captain William Howe Mulcaster, with whom he had been closely associated for many years. Mulcaster declined, chiefly, it is hinted, in consequence of the miserable equipment of the vessels and deficiency of seamen. It was then tendered to Barclay who accepted without hesitation, possibly from reluctance to serve under Yeo who was several years younger than himself.

The American fleet was in possession of Lake Ontario, and as it was understood to be considerably superior in guns and men, and as the result of the contest there was justly felt to be of supreme importance, Yeo absolutely refused to part with any of the officers or seamen who had come with him from England. Barclay was accordingly obliged to proceed to his post accompanied only by three lieutenants, a surgeon, a master's mate and nineteen seamen, twelve of whom were French Canadians. At York they overtook a detachment of the 8th on its way in boats to join General Vincent at Niagara. On May 27th, when within twenty miles of Fort George, they learned that Vincent had been driven from his position, and marched overland to join him at De Cew's Falls. Next day it was ascertained that the *Queen Charlotte*, which had been lying under Point Abino, had gone up the lake to avoid an attack, and they were obliged to undertake the toilsome overland journey to Amherstburg, where they arrived about June 10th.

The ship on the stocks at that place was still in a very backward state from want of the most necessary stores, as nearly everything intended for her equipment had been either taken or destroyed when the Americans captured York. But on June 16th he succeeded in manning the *Queen Charlotte* and *Lady Prevost* and sailed down the south shore to reconnoitre the harbour of Erie. He ascertained that it was well protected by batteries and blockhouses garrisoned by about 2,000 men, and that the two brigs had their lower masts in.

'The only thing I can hope for', he wrote despairingly, 'is that reinforcements will be sent to Brigadier General Procter to enable me to destroy the

[8] [Barclay (1785-1837) had lost an arm at Trafalgar. Following the battle off Put-in Bay he faced a court martial but was honourably acquitted. He was promoted to commander in November 1813 and to post captain in 1824.]

American vessels before they are ready. . . . I expected to find four companies of the 41st at Long Point, and found only one.' As Barclay cruised down the lake from Long Point towards Buffalo, Perry with his five vessels was moving slowly upwards, hugging the south shore. Off the mouth of Cattaraugus Creek the ships of both were distinctly seen, when about fourteen miles apart, by the crew of a small boat midway between them. The day was hazy and Barclay passed on without observing the American flotilla. Perry considered this a very fortunate escape for him, but it is doubtful whether the two British vessels were sufficiently manned to have risked an attack. On June 19th and 20th Perry took his ships across the bar into the harbour of Erie where they were out of danger. He had received a letter from the Secretary of the Navy directing him to name one of his new brigs the *Lawrence* in honour of the dead captain of the *Chesapeake*, and the other *Niagara*, to commemorate their recent success on that frontier.

On the 28th Barclay again reconnoitred the harbour and ascertained that the two new brigs were still in the inner harbour, apparently in a forward state but not yet rigged. Besides these he noted two smaller brigs and seven schooners, all of which appeared to be armed, manned, and ready for sea. Next day he wrote from Long Point to the Governor-General, complaining warmly of the want of seamen and stores. 'The ships', he said, 'are manned with crews, part of whom cannot even speak English, and none of them seamen and very few in numbers.'

In fact, nearly every letter written by Procter or Barclay at this time contained an anxious appeal for seamen and soldiers to carry out the proposed attack upon the harbour of Erie before the American squadron could put to sea. . . .

But the promised troops did not come and nothing could be done without them. On July 4th General Procter wrote to Captain McDouall[9] that the detention of 'the force ordered here by the commander of the forces has prevented this district from being in a state of security, which the destruction of the enemy's vessels at Presque Isle would have effected, a service that might very easily have been completely effected a very short time since, but which, I apprehend, may now be attended with much difficulty.'. . .

General de Rottenburg who commanded the division engaged in blockading the American army at Fort George positively declined to co-operate in the proposed expedition against Erie and on July 11th Procter wrote again.

> By my brigade major I also was informed that the Major General could not act with me and Captain Barclay at present; that he must first secure the com-

[9] [Robert McDouall (d.1848) was appointed an aide-de-camp to Governor Prevost in 1812 and was promoted to major in 1813. He was mentioned in dispatches for his part in the battle at Stoney Creek but his principal success was his defence of Michilimackinac against the Americans in 1814. He became a major-general in 1841.]

mand of the lower lake after which there will be no difficulty in recovering the command of the upper one? With all due deference I beg leave to dissent from the above. If means had been afforded me which were no more than your Excellency has repeatedly directed should be sent me, I could in all probability have effected the destruction of the enemy's vessels at Presque Isle and have secured the superiority of this lake and also in so doing have made a powerful diversion in favour of the Centre Division. I am further of opinion if we lose the superiority of this lake it will not be recovered without much difficulty. . . . Captain Barclay with all his resources goes to Long Point to bring Lieut. Col. Evans and in the hope of finding naval stores there, and sailors. If the enemy's vessels should be out an engagement cannot be avoided and if they are not yet ready he will endeavour to keep them in the harbour. Besides the detachment of the Royal Newfoundland Regiment, I have been obliged to send fifty men on board the vessels from the 41st Regiment and some of the detachment under Lieut. Col. Evans will also be detained from necessity.

Nor was Captain Barclay less plainspoken and insistent in his demands for aid. Writing after his arrival at Long Point on July 16th, he said:

I enclose a statement of the force of the rival squadrons and if prompt assistance is not sent, although my officers and crews will do everything that zeal and intrepidity can do, the great superiority of the enemy may prove fatal. . . . The *Detroit* will be ready to launch on the 20th inst but there is neither a sufficient quantity of ordnance ammunition or other stores and not a man to put in her. If that vessel was on the lake I would feel confident as to any action they might choose to risk for the present although for the good of His Majesty's Province I must attack, I cannot help saying that it is possible they may have an advantage, though I trust not a decided one.

I have communicated with Sir J. Yeo on the same subject and if the exigencies of the service on Lake Ontario will not admit of his sending many seamen, even 50 would be of the greatest service at present but it will require at least 250 or 300 seamen to render His Majesty's squadron perfectly effective. . . .

Whatever hopes they may have still entertained of effective assistance must have been dispelled by the Governor-General's very unsatisfactory replies. On June 20th, writing from Kingston, he announced to Procter that he had given directions to General de Rottenburg to push on the remainder of the 41st Regiment and advised him to 'encourage as much as possible the exertions of the navy; bring forward the united power to both services to crush the enemy's endeavours to obtain the ascendency on Lake Erie when a favourable opportunity presents itself'. But on July 11th he rather curtly informed him that the 'ordnance and ordnance stores you require must be taken from the enemy whose resources on Lake Erie must become yours. I am much mistaken if you do not find Captain Barclay well disposed to play that game.'

Perry's squadron was fully armed and equipped by July 10th, but he wisely refused to take the lake until provided with a sufficient complement of able seamen. The number then at his disposal is not stated but must have been at least thrice as many as Barclay had, though he was no doubt unaware of his opponent's weakness in this essential respect. He is said to have brought 152 from Newport but of these one-third were detained for service at Sackett's Harbour. Fifty-five were detailed to his assistance by Chauncey on May 29th and there must have been some at the navy yards at Black Rock and Erie before he took command. A recruiting station had been established at Erie and over one hundred ordinary seamen and landsmen besides forty marines had been enlisted. His command is said to have suffered much from disease but he must have had nearly three hundred seamen of all descriptions when Barclay appeared off the port on July 19th. His crews could no doubt have been easily completed with boatmen, soldiers, and militia but Perry would not consent to do this and risk defeat. The British squadron passed and repassed the harbour's mouth and in the afternoon disappeared in the direction of Long Point. On the 21st it returned and ran in close enough to exchange shots with the gunboats inside. . . .

On the 28th Barclay was obliged to abandon the blockade by stress of weather and lack of provisions, although he had perceived that the Americans had 'everything near ready for hauling their vessels over the bar. When this is done,' he admitted, 'we must retire to Amherstburg.' The frequently repeated tale that he stated that he expected to find the enemy fast on the bar on his return must be dismissed as purely fictitious. On the contrary, he appears to have abandoned all hope of detaining them in that port, and informed General de Rottenburg that as soon as the sailors he still expected should arrive he would proceed to join General Procter, whom he hoped to find at Sandusky Bay, where he intended to land his soldiers, and then go on to Amherstburg to equip the *Detroit*. Finding that no seamen were on the march to join him, he again stood across the lake towards Erie on August 5th, and, discovering that the American squadron was out of the harbour, bore away for Amherstburg.

On the following day Perry crossed the lake to Long Point with eight vessels and returned to Erie, where he was joined on the 9th by Captain J. D. Elliott with eight officers and a hundred seamen from Lake Ontario. Chauncey, it appears, was able to supply Perry from time to time with drafts of men without weakening his force materially, while Yeo was unable to do anything for Barclay without risking the loss of his squadron.

Writing to Prevost on August 9th, Procter announced his repulse at Sandusky, and added,

> The enemy's vessels are out of Presqu'Isle harbour, and so decidedly stronger than ours that Captain Barclay has been necessitated to return to Amherstburg with all haste to get the new vessel ready for sea, which she will be in eight

or ten days, and then only want hands. Whatever may happen to be regretted may be fairly attributed to the delays in sending here the force your Excellency directed should be sent. Had it been sent at once, it could have been used to the greatest advantage, but it arrived in such small portions, and with such delays, that the opportunities have been lost. . . . You will probably hear of the enemy's landing shortly at Long Point, whence they may gain the rear of the Centre Division, and also affect my supplies. An hundred and fifty sailors would have effectually obviated this evil. . . .

As he had not yet received any reply to his letter of June 24th from Sir J. B. Warren, Prevost had by that time determined, as a last resort, to lay up the troop-ship *Dover* at Quebec, and send most of her crew to the lakes. This decision was made known to Procter in a letter dated at St. David's on August 22nd.

I have the satisfaction [he wrote] to inform you, that the first lieutenant of that ship, with 50 or 60 seamen, are now at Kingston, from whence they will be forwarded, without delay, to Amherstburg. You will make this circumstance known to Captain Barclay. You will not fail in forwarding frequent and very particular details of the state of public affairs in the Western District, as the movement I have made to this from the centre of operations has arisen, in a great measure, from my anxiety respecting your situation, and altho' it may be one of some difficulty, you cannot fail in honourably surmounting it, notwithstanding the numerical superiority of the enemy's force, which I cannot but consider as overbalanced by the excellent description of your troops and seamen valourous and well disciplined.

The experience obtained by Sir James Yeo's conduct towards a fleet infinitely superior to the one under his command will satisfy Captain Barclay that he has only to dare, and the enemy is discomfited.

Such a letter could not fail to wound the feelings of both Barclay and Procter, when they had begged for assistance in vain for months, and we accordingly find the latter replying on the 26th:

Your Excellency speaks of seamen valourous and well disciplined. Except, I believe, the 25 Captain Barclay brought with him, there are none of that description on this lake – at least on board His Majesty's vessels. There are scarcely enough, and of a miserable description, to work the vessels, some of which cannot be used for want of hands, such even as we have. I have the highest opinion of Captain Barclay, and have afforded him every aid I possibly could. . . . Captain Barclay has, besides the Royal Newf'dland, one hundred and fifty of the 41st Regt., better soldiers they cannot be, but they are only landsmen. . . . I will venture to offer my opinion to Your Excellency, that as long as Captain Barclay, without seamen, can avoid the enemy, he should do so. All my ordnance is on board, except the field, and in the event of any disaster to the fleet, the arrival of any body of seamen would be of no use whatever. Seamen should be pushed on even by dozens.

The day before, Perry's squadron had left its anchorage among the Bass Islands, where great numbers of boats were being collected for the transportation of troops, and after reconnoitring Amherstburg dropped down the lake about twenty miles to a settlement on the Canadian side, where they seemed to contemplate landing. But two or three days later it again disappeared, and was supposed to have gone to Long Point. . . .

On [September 1st] Yeo had landed two lieutenants, two gunners, and forty-five seamen at Burlington, for the Lake Erie squadron, with twelve 24-pounder carronades, intended for the armament of the *Detroit*. The guns went no further, but the seamen, commanded by Lieut. George Bignall, late of the *Dover*, arrived at Amherstburg on the 6th, much fatigued by the journey. In this detachment there were no less than sixteen boys, and probably none of the seamen were very efficient in gunnery. Barclay wrote at once to say that the number was 'totally inadequate' to make his squadron effective, but, 'deplorably manned as it was', unless he received certain information that more seamen were on their way to join him, he would be obliged to give battle to the enemy. Bignall was put in command of the *Hunter*, and his men distributed among all the vessels, so as to give a few of the best seamen to each.

Having waited in vain until the evening of the 9th, when there was no longer a single day's flour in store, and both troops and seamen had already been placed on half allowance of other articles, with the exception of spirits, of which there was so little that it was entirely reserved for the day of battle, after consulting with General Procter and obtaining his consent, Barclay entered the lake with six vessels. His flagship, the *Detroit*, was armed with two long twenty-four-pounders, one eighteen on a pivot, six twelves, eight nines, a twenty-four, and an eighteen-pound carronade. Most of this strange medley of guns had been taken from the ramparts of Fort Amherstburg, and the only means of discharging them was by snapping pistols over the touch-hole. Sails, cables, blocks, and anchors were also borrowed from the other vessels to enable the *Detroit* to take the lake. The *Queen Charlotte*, Capt. Robert Finnis, carried one long twelve on a pivot, one nine, and fourteen twenty-pound carronades. The *Lady Prevost*, Lieut. Edward Buchan, had one long nine mounted on a pivot, two sixes, and ten twelve-pound carronades. The *Hunter*, Lieut. George Bignall, mounted four sixes, two fours, and two two-pounders, besides two twelve-pound carronades. The *Little Belt* carried one long twelve on a pivot, and two sixes; and the *Chippawa* a single nine-pounder on a pivot. The armament of the three latter vessels was so contemptible that it scarcely deserves to be taken into consideration. Like Lord Cochrane, when he sailed in the *Speedy*, the commander of any one of them might have paced the deck with an entire broadside of shot in his pockets.

The broadside force of the squadron accordingly consisted of twenty long guns, ranging in calibre from two- to twenty-four-pounders, throwing in the aggregate 195 pounds of shot, and fourteen carronades throwing 264 pounds.

At daybreak on the morning of the 10th the American squadron was discovered in motion among the Bass Islands, near Put-in Bay. When last seen it had been reported to consist of twelve vessels, but only nine could then be distinguished, and it was afterwards learned that the schooner *Ohio* and two tenders had been detached to obtain provisions. The brig-corvettes *Lawrence* and *Niagara* each carried two long twelves and eighteen thirty-two-pound carronades, and were undoubtedly more than a match in close action for the whole British squadron. Perry had, besides these vessels, the brig *Caledonia*, of two long twenty-fours and one twenty-four-pound carronade; and the schooners *Ariel*, of four long twelves, *Scorpion*, one long thirty-two, and a thirty-two-pound carronade; *Somers*, one long twenty-four, and a thirty-two-pound carronade; *Porcupine* and *Tigress*, each a long thirty-two, and *Trippe*, a long twenty-four. All of these guns were mounted on circles, and could be fought on either side. The total broadside force of the American squadron consisted, therefore, of thirteen long guns, throwing 264 pounds of shot, and twenty-one carronades throwing 664 pounds. In the early part of the action, it is stated that the *Lawrence* and *Niagara* used both of their long guns on the engaged side. . . .

[The author then presents figures, based upon William James for the British side, Theodore Roosevelt for the American side, and upon other authorities, to support his contention that the American naval force 'was actually much superior' to the British in terms of ship tonnages, weight of broadsides, and numbers of seamen.]

The British squadron was foredoomed to defeat because of its unpreparedness. Fugitives and deserters from Canada had kept Perry well informed of the state of the British vessels, and he was, perhaps, over-confident, while Barclay knew that the odds against him were so great that scarcely anything short of a miracle could save him.

When the American squadron was first seen the wind blew gently from the southwest giving Barclay the weather gage. He at once bore up with the intention of coming to an action among the islands but the wind very soon shifted to southeast, bringing the enemy directly to windward. All that could then be done was to heave to and form line of battle heading to the southwest, 'according to a given plan so that each ship might be supported against the superior force of the two brigs opposed to them'. This was in the following order, *Chippawa, Detroit, Hunter, Queen Charlotte, Lady Prevost, Little Belt.*

The American squadron approached slowly with a wind that was sometimes scarcely perceptible and sometimes rose to a four- or five-knot breeze. A light shower of rain came on, passed over, and left the sky perfectly cloudless. It was quite ten o'clock before Perry cleared the islands, and an hour later, when about three miles distant, he formed his vessels into the conventional closehauled column of attack a cable's length apart with the *Ariel* leading followed by the *Scorpion, Lawrence, Caledonia, Niagara, Somers, Porcupine, Tigress*, and *Trippe*. The distance from front to rear of his column was accordingly about a mile when all the ships preserved their proper distance, and the attack was delivered obliquely at an angle of nearly fifteen degrees, by which he avoided being raked fore and aft as he approached and could return the fire from the British squadron with his broadside guns trained sharply forward. He then hoisted on his flagship a blue banner bearing in large white letters the words ascribed to the dying Lawrence: 'Don't give up the ship!'

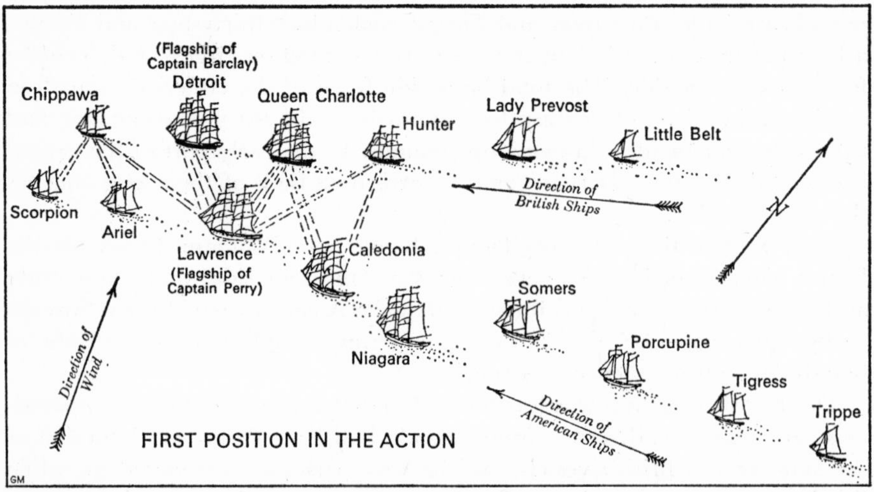

At fifteen minutes before noon a bugle sounded on board the *Detroit* which became the signal for three hearty cheers from the crews of the squadron. Then the flagship fired her long twenty-four at the *Lawrence*, but the shot fell short. Five minutes later she found the range with the same gun and struck Perry's ship fair on the bow. *Scorpion* hove to at once and replied with her long gun but the *Lawrence* kept silently on her course until five minutes to twelve when both her twelve-pounders were fired simultaneously from the two forward starboard ports. Then at noon precisely several shots were fired from her carronades which fell far short. The *Detroit* and *Chippawa* continued to direct their fire solely upon her but owing to the want of even the rude appliances for discharging the guns generally in use at that time it was necessarily slow, and only the three heaviest guns on the first-named vessel could have had any material effect although the smoothness of the water favoured precision in gunnery. In fifteen minutes the *Lawrence* gained a position within canister distance, that is to say about three hundred yards from the *Detroit*, where she hove to and fired her entire broadside. By that time the *Caledonia*, *Niagara*, and *Somers* had engaged the *Hunter* and *Queen Charlotte*, at first opposing a long thirty-two, two twenty-fours and two twelves to a single twelve, two nines, and two sixes, and later on the *Niagara* firing all her broadside guns at such a distance that they did little or no damage.

After continuing this rather unequal contest for about a quarter of an hour and observing that his assailants displayed no inclination to come any nearer until they had disabled his ship, Captain Finnis directed the master's mate to bear up, pass the *Hunter*, and lay the *Queen Charlotte* on the quarter of *Lawrence* where his carronades would become effective. But just as this change of position was on the point of being successfully accomplished and before a man had been hurt on the *Queen Charlotte*, a round shot from one of the American schooners instantly killed both Capt. Finnis and Lieut. S. J. Garden of the Newfoundland Regiment who commanded the troops. This was an irreparable loss and Sir James Yeo did not hesitate to say that if Finnis had lived the result of the battle would have been different; a few minutes later the first lieutenant, Thomas Stokoe, was struck senseless by a splinter. The command then fell to Lieut. Robert Irvine of the Provincial Marine, a gallant young officer, who as Barclay reported 'behaved with great courage but his experience was much too limited to supply the place of such an officer as Captain Finnis'. The only officers then remaining to assist him were a master's mate of the Royal Navy, two boy midshipmen of the Provincial Marine, a gunner, and a boatswain. Of ten seamen belonging to the *Dover* who had been assigned to this ship one had been killed and four wounded. The remainder of the crew had suffered in proportion and nearly all this loss had been inflicted by the raking fire of the *Caledonia* and two other schooners which were absolutely out of range of the *Queen Charlotte*'s guns. This ship consequently soon fell out of her new station and henceforth failed to render any material assistance to the *Detroit*. But the duel between that vessel and the *Lawrence* continued at close range for more than two hours. In their eagerness to disable their principal antagonist quickly the American gunners are believed to have overloaded their carronades with shot, and, either from this cause or some other, their fire was not nearly as effective as had been expected, while the British ship although so greatly overmatched in weight of metal and other respects certainly succeeded in inflicting far more injury than she received from this particular opponent, but the long guns of the *Ariel*, the *Porcupine*, and even the *Caledonia* had done her much damage. Gun after gun ceased firing as they were disabled or had their crews swept away until about half-past two the *Lawrence* was entirely silenced and dropped astern while the remaining vessels continued to drift slowly ahead and to leeward with the rising wind. The destruction on board of her had been terrible. Two officers and twenty men were killed and six officers and fifty-five men wounded. Her masts were standing, but every brace and bowline had been shot away. Her hull was dreadfully shattered. Most of the guns on the engaged side were dismounted, their breechings having been torn away or their carriages knocked in pieces until but one could be discharged.

At the rear of the line things were going badly with the British. Lieut. Bignall, commander of the *Hunter,* finding that the American schooners were rapidly disabling his vessel while the shot from his light guns were falling short, made sail to the front in the hope of assisting the *Chippawa.* The *Lady Prevost* and *Little Belt* were then attacked by the *Somers, Tigress, Porcupine,* and *Trippe* which remained at long range and battered them deliberately to pieces with entire impunity. The *Lady Prevost* lost men rapidly and her commander, Lieut. Buchan, was disabled by a wound in the head which rendered him temporarily insane. The command then devolved upon Lieut. Rolette of the Provincial Marine who was soon afterwards severely injured in the side and badly burned by an explosion which disabled several of his crew. Finally the rudder was cut away by a round shot and the *Lady Prevost* drifted helplessly out of action to leeward. The *Little Belt* lost her commander and escaped destruction only by running to the head of the line where she was entirely out of the fight.

All this time the *Niagara* had remained in her original station, a cable's length astern of the *Caledonia* which had avoided coming within carronade distance, and consequently had effected little, although firing her two long guns and occasionally a broadside. When finally the *Detroit* drifted astern silent and disabled, the *Caledonia* passed her to leeward and the *Niagara* coming forward with the freshening wind went to windward of her and sent a boat on board for a supply of round shot. At this Captain Perry determined to abandon his ship and transfer his flag to the *Niagara,* which was then nearly abreast of her at a distance which was variously estimated from thirty yards to half a mile, but probably did not exceed three or four hundred yards. Telling his wounded first lieutenant, Mr. Yarnall, that he would leave him to surrender the ship, he entered a boat and reached the *Niagara* in safety. When he came on deck he informed Captain Elliott that his own vessel was quite disabled, complained that he had been sacrificed and that the conduct of the schooners in keeping so far away had lost the battle. He does not appear to have accused Elliott at that time of any misconduct and the latter cordially volunteered to carry orders to the laggard vessels. The motto flag of the *Lawrence* had been either shot away or hauled down and dropped overboard, where it was found floating by Purser McGrath who commanded the boat from the *Niagara*, and her colours were struck soon after Perry's departure, when it is said by one account only nine, and by others fourteen or eighteen, unwounded men remained on board.

Finding that the *Niagara* had received comparatively little injury, Perry hoisted the signal for close action and bore down directly for the centre of the British squadron, which was then huddled in a disorderly group about

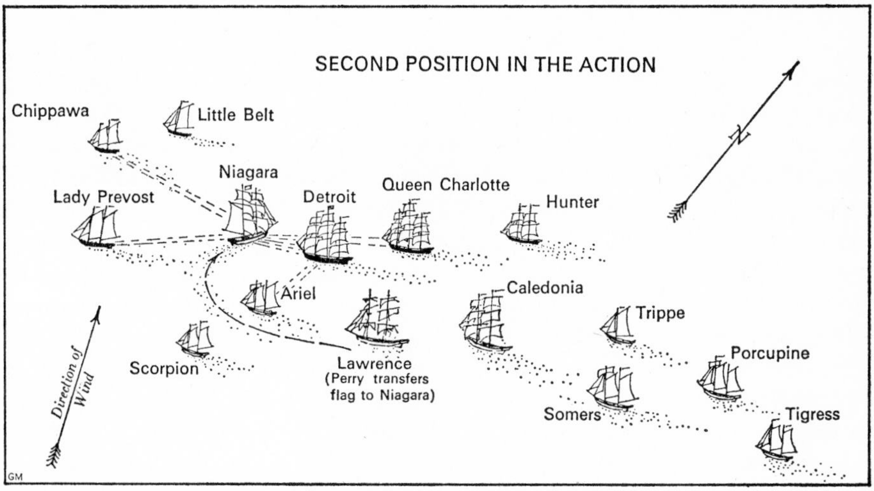

their flagship. When his ship gained the weather bow of the *Detroit,* he fired a broadside, and Captain Barclay, who had already received a severe contusion on the hip, was stretched senseless on the deck by a shot which tore away his remaining arm and part of his shoulder-blade. His hurt was supposed to be mortal and he was carried below. First-Lieutenant Garland had been mortally wounded early in the day, and Second-Lieutenant George Inglis took Barclay's place on the quarterdeck. As most of the larboard guns were disabled he tried to wear ship to avoid being raked and to bring the other broadside to bear, but, the *Queen Charlotte* running up to leeward at that moment, the two ships fell foul and remained for some time unable to reply to the raking fire of the *Niagara* with a single gun. Perry's ship then passed through the British squadron, firing her port broadside into the *Chippawa, Little Belt,* and *Lady Prevost,* and her starboard guns into the entangled *Detroit* and *Queen Charlotte,* which she then engaged close to leeward within pistol shot. These two ships were cut off and practically surrounded by the American squadron. The *Scorpion* on their weather bow, the *Ariel* nearly abeam, the *Caledonia* on their weather quarter, the *Somers,*

Tigress, and *Porcupine* nearly astern, the *Trippe* on their lee quarter, and the *Niagara* on their lee bow concentrated all their fire on these hapless vessels. They are said to have suffered still more from the deliberate gunnery of the schooners than from the more hurried broadsides of the *Niagara.* 'The efficiency of the gunboats was fully proved in this action,' writes an eyewitness, 'and the sterns of all the prizes bear ample testimony of the fact. They took raking positions and galled the enemy severely. The *Lady Prevost* lost twelve men before either of the brigs fired on her.'

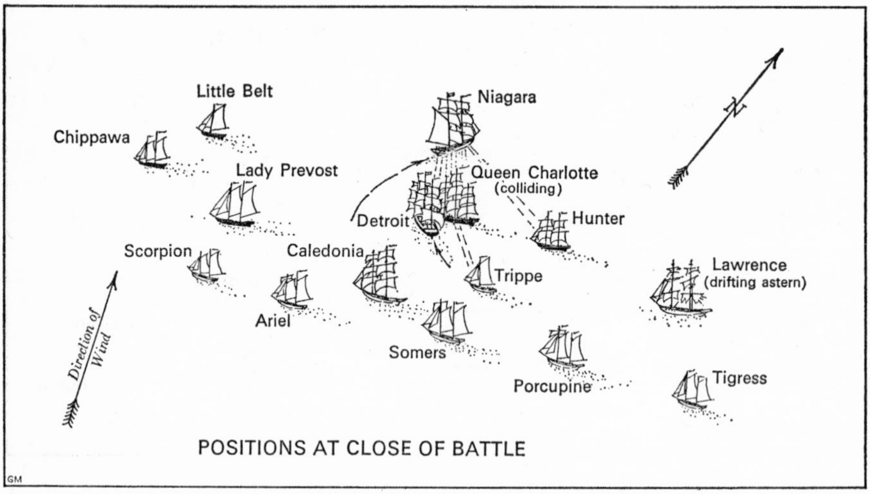

POSITIONS AT CLOSE OF BATTLE

When at length the *Detroit* got clear, Inglis directed the *Queen Charlotte* to shoot ahead if possible, and attempted to back the foretopsail to get astern when he found his ship completely unmanageable. A few minutes later the *Queen Charlotte* hauled down her colours. The *Detroit* was then exposed to the whole fire of all the American vessels, raking her ahead and astern. The mizentopmast and gaff had fallen, the other masts were badly wounded, most of the stays and braces were cut away, the hull was much shattered and many guns had been disabled. Seven or eight of the ten experienced seamen were killed or wounded, and more than half of the entire crew had fallen at their stations. In this situation, on being hailed from the *Niagara,* Inglis replied that he would surrender and the other vessels rapidly followed his example.

The beaten squadron had been fought to the last extremity beyond a doubt. 'The sides of the *Detroit* and *Queen Charlotte*', said an eyewitness, 'were shattered from bow to stern; there was scarcely room to place one's hand on their larboard sides without touching the impression of a shot, a great many shot cannister and grape were found lodged in their bulwarks, which were too thick to be penetrated by our carronades unless within pistol shot distance. Their masts were so much shattered that they fell overboard soon after they got into the bay.'

Every commanding officer and second-in-command of the British vessels had fallen. In all, forty-one officers and men had been killed and ninety-four wounded. The loss of the American squadron was officially stated at twenty-seven killed and ninety-six wounded, of whom two killed and twenty-seven wounded were reported on board the *Niagara*. . . .

The chances of war had throughout favoured the American squadron. There was first the sudden change of wind which gave it the weather gage, then the death of Captain Finnis, and finally the fouling of the *Detroit* and *Queen Charlotte*. Even Mr. Roosevelt feels bound to admit that 'if the victory had not been so complete it might have been said that the length of the combat and the trifling disparity in loss reflected more credit on the British.'

The results of the battle were of the highest importance. The control of the upper lakes passed over to the victors. General Procter was forced to retreat from Amherstburg and owing to his indecision and unpardonable negligence was overtaken and routed.

But, considerable as these advantages were, much greater were confidently expected.

> Mackinac passes into our hands of course [said a writer in *Niles' Weekly Register*]. St. Joseph's, too remote for intelligence or succour from the enemy, is given into our possession. All the places of deposit for Indian supplies will be broken up, and the savages employed in the *business* of the British during the summer and cut off at this critical season from their accustomed resources must perish by thousands for want of food and clothing. The trade of the North-West Company, a mighty mercantile establishment of vital importance to Canada and of great consideration to the Mother Country, is done. In less than four weeks we may have the reality of the things here anticipated.

But these expectations were all doomed to remain unfulfilled. Most of the Indians with Procter joined the Centre Division of the British army at Burlington and took part in General Drummond's[10] winter campaign. Others having already returned westward arrayed themselves again under Dickson's leadership next year. On the lakes misfortune attended every movement of the Americans. Four of their vessels, the *Ariel*, *Chippawa*, *Trippe*, and *Little Belt* were destroyed at the capture of Buffalo (December 30th, 1813). An expedition against Mackinac was repulsed with severe loss (August 4th, 1814). Two schooners, the *Porcupine* and *Somers*, were

[10] [For Sir Gordon Drummond (1771-1854), see pages 315-20.]

captured, by boats off Fort Erie (August 12th, 1814), and two others, the *Scorpion* and *Tigress*, left to blockade Mackinac, were taken in a similar manner on September 3rd and 4th. Practically the only service of much consequence performed by the American squadron was the conveyance of a body of troops to Long Point (May 14th, 1814), and covering the landing of a division of their army at Fort Erie (July 3rd, 1814).

FURTHER READING: C. O. Paullin (ed.), *The battle of Lake Erie, a collection of documents, chiefly by Commodore Perry . . .* (Cleveland, 1918); 'Perry's Victory Centennial Number', *Journal of American History*, volume 8, no. 1 (January-March 1914); W. W. Dobbins, *History of the battle of Lake Erie (September 10, 1813) and reminiscences of the flagships 'Lawrence' and 'Niagara'* (Erie, Pennsylvania, 1913).

In contrast to the previous study, this article looks not so much at the battle itself as at the reasons for the disparity between the two squadrons that faced each other on September 10, 1813. The author finds his explanation – and with it the explanation for the outcome – principally in the different logistical situations of the two contending fleets, the one at the end of a long, difficult supply route from the British Isles via Montreal, Kingston and Niagara, the other in close proximity to youthful, growing industrial resources in the trans-Allegheny west. The article appeared in the 'Canadian Historical Review', volume 39 (March 1958), and is presented here through the kindness of the editor of that journal, and of the author.

Another Look at the Battle of Lake Erie

BY C. P. STACEY

The history of the War of 1812 has to a considerable extent been written in purely tactical terms. Historians, particularly the authors of general histories, have dwelt upon what happened on the battlefield and have paid less attention to strategic considerations and still less to administrative considerations ('logistics') ; though these things often, and indeed usually, determined the outcome of the individual engagements. The Battle of Lake Erie is a case in point.

In warfare on the Great Lakes the British, though far superior in naval strength at the outset, were at a serious administrative disadvantage. The lakes' Canadian shores afforded few of the resources necessary to the support of a naval establishment. A town like Kingston or Amherstburg, where vessels had been built and troops stationed for a considerable time, was likely to have small stocks of naval and military equipment in store, but such equipment was not produced in Canada to any extent. Guns and heavy anchors were not cast in Canada,[1] nor apparently were heavy cables produced, although some cordage was made at Amherstburg, the British naval station on Lake Erie,[2] and doubtless elsewhere.

[1] Peter Kalm reported about 1749 that 'cannon and mortars' were cast at the St. Maurice Forges, but there seems to have been no such activity early in the nineteenth century.

[2] 'To purchase all the Cordage from Captn. Mills at Amherstburg as this tends greatly to promote the growth of hemp' (Memorandum by General Brock, c. February 1812).

That heavy equipment had to cross the Atlantic from Britain was not in itself an extremely serious disadvantage, for in spite of occasional losses to American or French privateers ocean transport for the British was relatively easy and reliable. The worst feature of the British situation was the extraordinary difficulty of the transport problem between tidewater and the theatre of operations on the lakes, and within that theatre itself. Just what the effect of the St. Lawrence rapids was appears in an account written from Kingston in 1814 by an officer who had lately made the trip up the river:

> The travelling from Quebec to Montreal is either performed in the steam boat or by land either of which methods is expeditious the time being but two days, large vessels come up to Montreal which is situated at the head of the Navigation of the St. Lawrence, here the rapids commence and the only water carriage is in batteaux which are towed along shore where the current is strong, but generally rowed, three of the worst rapids are avoided by means of Canals with locks – if the rope breaks in passing these rapids the boat is lost and those on board perish, such accidents sometimes happen; a batteau is generally eight days in going from Montreal to Kingston, a distance of 200 miles, but if the wind blows fresh ahead they are much longer. All the Guns and Stores for the Ships of War must be brought up in these batteaux it is not an unusual thing for an hundred to arrive here together as they wait for a Convoy of Gun boats to protect them from the enemy.

In the winter, of course, land transport had to be resorted to; and although this was the season when the roads of Canada were most passable, Sir George Prevost reported that he had paid £1,000 for sending one large cable from Sorel to Kingston by land.

The St. Lawrence was only the first leg of the British inland line of communication. It supported the naval squadron on Lake Ontario, but the establishments on the upper lakes were dependent on the precarious extension of it west of Kingston. The farther west a British garrison or a British warship, the longer and shakier was its line of supply. In Upper Canada roads were either non-existent or vile. Only by water could heavy stores be moved with any ease, and even troops on foot found movement by land difficult. General Drummond wrote from Niagara Falls in the autumn of 1814: 'The disappointment I experienced at finding that half the 90th Regiment had been left to Struggle through the dreadful Roads betwixt Kingston and York at such a season, and at *such a Crisis*, was greater than I can express.' The British could not afford to lose control of the lakes, for those waters were not only their frontier and their fighting front, but also their essential line of communication. From Montreal westwards they were, strategically, 'formed to a flank'.

Because of its position on this communication, Ontario was the most important of the lakes; and on it, by tremendous efforts, the British managed to hold their own. The control of the lake changed hands repeatedly as one side or the other commissioned new and more powerful ships. At the end of hostilities the British held it, thanks to their great new three-decker H.M.S. *St. Lawrence*. But they had lost Lake Erie once and for all on September 10, 1813, when their squadron under Commander R. H. Barclay was defeated and captured by a superior American squadron commanded by Master Commandant Oliver Hazard Perry. Much ink has been spilled about this bloody little battle, and particularly about the unedifying later controversy between Perry and his second in command, Elliott, the commander of the U.S.S. *Niagara*. But comparatively little has been written about a more important matter – the logistical process by which that superior American squadron was created and the victory made possible.

At the time when the United States declared war, in June 1812, the British enjoyed complete naval control of Lake Erie, thanks to the Canadian force known as the Provincial Marine. They had there the *Queen Charlotte* of sixteen guns and the *General Hunter* of six; and during the summer of 1812 they added to their force the 10-gun schooner *Lady Prevost*.[3] It is true that the Provincial Marine was not a real fighting navy. It was primarily a military transport service and was administered by the Army. Nevertheless, its armed vessels were capable of controlling the Great Lakes, and the control they exercised largely explains the British successes during the 1812 campaign, including General Brock's capture of Detroit. The only actual American naval vessel on the lakes at the outset was the brig *Oneida* on Lake Ontario, built in 1809. The brig *Adams* on Erie apparently belonged to the War Department, and though the Navy took her over she was still unarmed when captured by Brock's army at Detroit. Although Captain Isaac Chauncey, U.S.N., who had been appointed to command the American forces on the Great Lakes, succeeded in seizing control of Lake Ontario – with the *Oneida* and a group of converted merchant schooners – at the very end of the 1812 season of navigation, the contest for Erie began seriously only in 1813. Perry arrived at Presqu'Isle (Erie, Pennsylvania), to which the American base was transferred from Black Rock, near Buffalo; Barclay arrived at Amherstburg; and shipbuilding was pressed at both bases. When the rival commanders reached their stations, the Americans were already building two 20-gun brigs, the *Niagara* and *Lawrence*, the British a 19-gun ship, the *Detroit*. These were the largest units engaged in the subsequent battle. Let us examine the process of fitting them for action.

At Amherstburg Barclay found 'a general want of stores of every description'. And to get stores from outside was next to impossible, for he was close to the extremity of that long and exposed line of communication that has

[3] A statement signed by Barclay, accompanying a letter of July 16, 1813, gives *Queen Charlotte* eighteen guns, *Lady Prevost* twelve, and *Hunter* six.

been described. The normal communication with Amherstburg was by Lake Ontario and the Niagara River, stores being portaged around the gorge and the falls to Fort Erie, whence they were taken on again by water up Lake Erie. But the initial American operations of 1813 cut this line: Fort George, at the mouth of the Niagara, was captured on May 27. This threw the British back on the less satisfactory line overland from the head of Lake Ontario to Long Point on Lake Erie, the Grand River sometimes being used for the final stage.[4] The American raid on York in April had had an even worse effect on Barclay's fortunes. Prevost wrote on July 20:

> The Ordnance Ammunition and other Stores for the Service on Lake Erie had been deposited at York for the purpose of being transported to Amherstburg, but unfortunately were either destroyed or fell into the Enemy's hands when York was taken by them; & the subsequent interruption to the communication by their occupation of Fort George has rendered it extremely difficult to afford the supplies Capt^{tn}. Barclay requires, which are however in readiness to forward to him, whenever circumstances will admit of its being done with safety.

Commodore Chauncey reported gleefully from York that the Americans had found there twenty cannon from 6-pounders to 32s, and much shot and other munitions, 'a great deal of which was put up in boxes and marked for Niagara and Malden [Amherstburg]':

> The store which the enemy burned was filled with cables, cordage, canvas, tools, and stores of every kind for the use of this Lake and Lake Erie, supposed to be worth $50,000. The loss of stores at this place will be an irreparable one to the enemy, for independent of the difficulty of transportation, the articles cannot be replaced in this country. . . . In fact I believe he has received a blow that he cannot recover.

So far as Lake Erie was concerned, this was scarcely an overstatement. The raid on York has usually been regarded as a rather nugatory operation; but though Chauncey's letter describing his intention of making it does not indicate that he knew the stores so urgently needed by Barclay were in the town, the raid's effect upon the situation on Lake Erie was so considerable as to give it very real significance. Barclay never did receive the guns for his flagship;[5] and the *Detroit* went into action on September 10 armed with the cannon from the ramparts of Amherstburg's Fort Malden ('a more curiously composite battery', writes Admiral Mahan, 'probably never was mounted'). Nor was this all. At Barclay's court martial testimony was given that 'sails and other articles' had to be taken from the *Queen Charlotte* to render the

[4] If the worst came to the worst the whole journey to Amherstburg could be made overland.

[5] 'Do you wish the 10. 24 p^{rs}. carronades intended for the Detroit to be sent on and to what Place?' (Harvey from Four Mile Creek to Procter, Sept. 17, 1813). These were weak weapons even if they had arrived in time.

Detroit fit to take the lake; and that the matches and tubes provided at Amherstburg were so bad that throughout the action it was necessary to 'fire pistols at the Guns to set them off'.

So much, very briefly, for British 'logistical support'. It is evident that Barclay's squadron had to be fitted out on the basis of the resources available at Amherstburg, and that these were very inadequate. Let us turn to the American side, where the picture was rather different.

One advantage which the British enjoyed at the beginning of the war was the fact that there were no American naval bases on the Great Lakes. Bases had to be created before there could be squadrons. So far as the resources for the purpose existed ready-made, they were to be found at the U.S. navy yards on the Atlantic seaboard; and the means of getting ordnance and stores from those yards to the chosen sites on the lakes became a matter of great importance. When Chauncey was appointed to the lake command, he sent the raw materials of his enterprise on from the New York navy yard, which he had lately commanded. He catalogued them for the Secretary of the Navy: 'one hundred and forty ship-carpenters, seven hundred seamen and marines, more than one hundred pieces of cannon, the greater part of large caliber, with muskets, shot, carriages, etc. The carriages have nearly all been made, and the shot cast, in that time [three weeks]. Nay, I may say that nearly every article that has been sent forward has been made.' Admiral Mahan, whose book on this war remains after half a century the best ever written about it, remarks that these words reflect the United States' lack of preparation for war. This is true; but the fact that these articles could be manufactured locally, and so rapidly, also reflects an American advantage over Canada. No such manufacture was possible in the British provinces.

It is fair to say that the New York area, with its navy yard and primitive yet considerable industrial resources, was a good source of the war material required by the U.S. Navy on Lake Ontario. Nor were the communications between New York and Sackets Harbor, the U.S. base on that lake, particularly difficult. There was water transport by the Hudson and Mohawk rivers as far as Rome, the only serious obstacle being overcome by a portage road. The roads from Rome to Sackets were so bad that they could not be used with any convenience in winter; but there was also the water route by a canal connecting with Wood Creek, which flowed into Oneida Lake, and on by the Oswego River into Lake Ontario. This had the disadvantage that the final leg of the communication, across the corner of Lake Ontario, was exposed to interruption by the British when they controlled the lake. They did attempt to cut it on several occasions, but never with very marked success.

As long as the American base for Lake Erie was at Black Rock, it too was dependent for logistical support upon New York and its navy yard, and upon the line of communication by the Hudson and the Mohawk, supplemented by a long land haul from the head of navigation on the Mohawk to the Niagara. Thirteen miles of this road was 'intolerably bad'. But the whole picture was changed when Chauncey moved the base from Black Rock to Erie in the winter of 1812-13. Erie had relatively good communications with Philadelphia through Pittsburgh. Now the Philadelphia navy yard, and the industrial resources of the Philadelphia area, could be applied to the support of the establishment on Lake Erie; and New York could concentrate on supporting those on lakes Ontario and Champlain. By 1812 there were good roads between Philadelphia and Pittsburgh; and from Pittsburgh the Allegheny River and its tributary French Creek provided water transport to within fifteen miles of Erie. That last fifteen miles had to be covered by road. Five years before the war a traveller reported the road was bad, but subsequently it seems to have improved. Obviously this was not an ideal line of communication; but it was far superior to Barclay's from Amherstburg to Montreal – shorter, simpler, and less difficult. And it had the special advantage of not being exposed to interruption by the enemy at any point.

What today seems the most surprising of Perry's logistical advantages remains to be described. It has attracted little attention from historians, and is scarcely mentioned by Mahan. Many of the heaviest of Perry's vessels' fittings did not have to come from the seaboard: they were manufactured in Pittsburgh. The iron industry was already developing in western Pennsylvania. Pittsburgh's first foundry was erected in 1804, its first steamboat launched in 1811.[6] The town was ready to grasp the opportunity offered by the war. The *Pittsburgh Directory for 1815* tells the story. Pittsburgh's population has increased from 4,740 to 'upwards of 9,000' since 1810. 'This great increase is to be attributed to the late war with Great Britain, which converted a great portion of the capital of the seaboard into manufactures, much of which was concentrated in this place.' Among the town's industries is 'an anvil and anchor factory, Capable of furnishing anvils and anchors of the largest size. Many of the anchors for Commodore Perry's squadron on lake Erie, were made at this Factory.' Pittsburgh also possesses 'three large and extensive Rope Walks, which make all kinds of ropes, twine and cordage. The principal part of the cordage for Perry's Fleet was made here. Two cables weighed each, about 4,000 lbs. and were 4½ inches in diameter.' There were 'three Foundries in Pittsburg and one in Birmingham', and one of them was equipped for boring cannon. There were no such facilities as these in Upper Canada in 1813.

On April 10 Perry reported to Chauncey from Erie:

> I have the honor to inform you, I have just now returned from Pittsburg. Most of the articles, we shall want can be procured there, such as anchors, rigging

[6] The fact that at Erie 'Iron and cordage may be procured with facility from Pittsburg' was a factor in Chauncey's decision to move the Lake Erie base from Black Rock.

&c and cambooses[7] by sending to Phila.[a]. for a pattern to cast by. . . . The canvass must come from Phila.[a]. I have written M[r]. Thompson on the subject and for such other things as cannot be had at Pittsburg.

Most of the carpenters have at length arrived *without* their tools, which will probably be here in ten days. The *two* blacksmiths from Philadelphia have arrived. M[r]. Brown does not expect much from them. . . . Many are the difficulties we have to encounter but we *will* surmount them all.

The guns that won the battle of Lake Erie, however, were not cast at Pittsburgh. As early as September 26, 1812, Chauncey had asked Secretary of the Navy Paul Hamilton to have forty-four 32-pounders 'cast immediately' and sent on to Black Rock during the winter. Whether this request was actually the origin of the armament of the *Lawrence* and *Niagara* seems rather doubtful, as it was not until January 27 that the Secretary (now William Jones) told Chauncey that he would immediately contract at Washington for 32-pounder carronades to arm the two brigs which by then had been authorized for construction at Erie. Apparently, however, the carronades did not have to be cast, for early in February there are references to twenty of them lying, still unproved, at Henry Foxall's foundry near Georgetown in the District of Columbia, and fourteen others being at the Washington Navy Yard. During the next few weeks these were sent on by wagon to Pittsburgh en route to Erie. The few long guns required were obtained, it appears, wherever they could be found – from Lake Ontario and possibly from New York; the Secretary of the Navy undertook to obtain a couple of guns belonging to the War Department which were at Pittsburgh.

Perry, it may be noted, had nothing to do with planning the squadron or initiating the work on it; construction was well under way when he reached the Lakes. But his driving energy clearly had much to do with pushing the work to completion. Incidentally, he was no admirer of the men of Pittsburgh, for the optimistic promises made to him during his visit in April were not carried out. He complained to Chauncey on June 13 that although the anchors for the brigs had been promised by May 1 he now heard that they would not be finished before July 20. His comment was, 'I make no comments on this abominable deception.' But in due course all the essential stores and equipment reached Erie, and on July 23 Perry wrote the Secretary of the Navy that both 'sloops' were ready to go over the bar, 'and the shot – the only thing that could have detained both of them – is now constantly arriving in considerable quantities'. The shot had been cast at Pittsburgh, under the superintendence of Captain Abraham R. Woolley, Deputy Commissioner of Ordnance at Fort Fayette, the army post there, whose help Perry gratefully acknowledged. The superior local resources of the United States had now done their work.

[7] Cambooses (cabooses) signify cooking places, galley stoves.

Of the manning of the rival squadrons only a word need be said here. Both were under-manned on the day of battle, but Perry's was evidently better off than Barclay's. The British commander described his crews as consisting of 'not more than fifty British Seamen, the rest a mixt Crew of Canadians, and Soldiers, and who were totally unacquainted with such Service'. This may have exaggerated his disadvantages, but the casualty list shows that of 135 officers and men killed and wounded 69 were soldiers of the 41st and Royal Newfoundland Regiments. Thirteen were 'landsmen'. The rest held naval ranks, and doubtless a proportion of them were men of the Provincial Marine. Theodore Roosevelt in his *Naval War of 1812* suggested that Canadian 'lake sailors, frontiersmen' were 'the very best possible material'. A modern Canadian may perhaps be permitted to share Barclay's prejudice in favour of trained fighting men. As for Perry, he too had soldiers and landsmen among his crews; but letters written by him before the action refer to the arrival of three drafts of seamen totalling nearly 230 all ranks and ratings, and it would seem that he had a rather larger proportion of naval personnel in his ships than his antagonist. Incidentally, both Barclay and Perry accused their superiors on Lake Ontario of sending them inferior men.

Why did the Americans win the Battle of Lake Erie? Because they had managed to create on the lake a stronger squadron than their opponents'. The heavy metal won the day in an action which was as valiantly and as bitterly contested as any ever fought on fresh water or salt. Roosevelt computes the actual American broadside in the battle as 896 pounds against 459 for the British. (Mahan points out, however, that the precise weight of the British broadside is not known; a sailor as competent as Barclay would certainly have contrived to employ more than half of the *Detroit*'s metal on the engaged side.) Barclay lost his one real chance of victory when, by relinquishing his blockade of Erie for a short time – a lapse on his part which has never been satisfactorily explained – he allowed Perry to get his brigs over the bar into the lake. In a stand-up fight between two squadrons so unevenly matched, nothing but mismanagement by the Americans could have given success to the British. In fact, the gallant Barclay very nearly did win – simply because the Americans attacked him in detail. But once the American commander shifted his flag from the shattered *Lawrence* and brought into close action the brig *Niagara*, hitherto merely on the fringe of the engagement, the game was up.

Roosevelt, relating these facts, remarks, 'Captain Perry showed indomitable pluck, and readiness to adapt himself to circumstances; but his claim to fame rests much less on his actual victory than on the way in which he prepared the fleet that was to win it.' This is less than just to Perry. Actually, the preparation of the fleet was far from being all his work, as we have seen;

much of the credit is due to Commodore Chauncey and Secretary Jones, and certainly that remarkable shipbuilder Noah Brown should not be forgotten. On the other hand, at the crisis of the fight, when an engagement which ought never to have been in doubt was close to being lost through no fault of his, it was the young commander's energy and resolution that saved the day; but for him the outcome would have been different. There are good grounds, indeed, for Henry Adams' opinion, so different from Roosevelt's: 'More than any other battle of the time, the victory on Lake Erie was won by the courage and obstinacy of a single man.'

This is a salutary reminder that there is more to warfare than heavy metal and big battalions; that wars after all are fought by men, and that mere physical power is useless unless directed with judgment and determination. Nevertheless, the Battle of Lake Erie was more a logistical than a tactical victory. Perry merely made good use of the superior weapon that was in his hands. If it had not been a superior weapon he would not have won.

The American squadron on Lake Erie, built 'from scratch', was stronger than its British rival (which had in part existed before the war) because its builders were served by a line of communication which, though neither short nor easy, was shorter and easier than the British communication with Montreal and Quebec. Still more important, Perry's communications with the seaboard, as we have seen, were secure from interruption; whereas Barclay's were exposed to enemy action and were in fact interrupted in the spring of 1813 with dire effect. At the same time, the Americans were far superior in local resources. Canada produced almost nothing required for the outfitting of naval vessels except timber. The immediate source of armament and equipment for the British lake squadrons was the depots in the St. Lawrence ports; the ultimate source was Britain. But the United States, though in 1813 still industrially a child as compared with the British giant, was capable of casting its own guns, shot, and anchors, and making its own cables. What is more, it was becoming capable of doing these things not only on the seaboard but also in the rising west, within comparatively easy reach of the theatre of operations on the upper lakes. However unappreciated by Perry, the lusty infant industries of Pittsburgh played a considerable part in his success. The growing industrial resources of the United States at large, combined with relatively energetic naval administration in Washington and on the lakes, were the unseen but solid foundations of the American victory on Lake Erie.

FURTHER READING: W. C. H. Wood (ed.), *Selected British documents . . .*, volume 1, pages 240-6, 253-8, volume 2, pages 243-319; A. T. Mahan, *Sea power in its relations to the War of 1812*, volume 2 (London, 1905); Theodore Roosevelt, *The naval War of 1812* (New York, 1883).

The military consequence of Perry's victory over Barclay was General Harrison's advance and Procter's withdrawal from the western part of Upper Canada. But neither the site of the battle, Moraviantown, nor the outcome was inevitable. Despite the flowery language and the dependence upon unreliable sources all too prevalent in the writing of local history half a century ago, the story of the disastrous retreat is told with fair accuracy. But the essential question is left unanswered: why did Procter change so abruptly from an aggressive role carrying the fight into the United States, to one of precipitate, headlong, seemingly cowardly flight from Amherstburg to the safety of Burlington Heights? . . . This article is taken with permission from volume 9 (1908) of the 'Papers and Records' of the Ontario Historical Society.

Thamesville and the Battle of the Thames

BY KATHERINE B. COUTTS

On the outbreak of the war of 1812 General Brock, upon whom the duty of defending Upper Canada had devolved, saw the importance of securing its western frontier. Thither therefore he went; and, with a good fortune which probably exceeded his utmost expectations, he found himself by the middle of August, without a blow struck or a life lost, master of the Fort of Detroit with its supplies of ammunition and ordnance, including some interesting revolutionary trophies, and of the vast territory of Michigan, out of which five sovereign states have since been formed. It was at this time that took place the first and only meeting between Brock and Tecumseh, the two most heroic figures of the war. For Tecumseh, smarting under a sense of wrongs endured by his people at the hands of the Americans, had hastened at the first rumor of war to proffer his aid to the British. Brock soon returned to the Centre Division, leaving in command at the West General Henry Procter, with a small number of regular troops, mostly of the Forty-first Regiment, and some companies of Kent and Essex Militia. Though all that could be spared, Procter's force was confessedly inadequate. But he had as allies a body of Indians varying in number from time to time. He complained that these Indians were 'not a disposable force' and that their zeal was too apt to be in inverse proportion to his need. These are the well-known characteristics of Indian warriors. Yet there was one amongst them – Tecumseh his name – whose zeal and constancy were afterwards to form a standard by which Procter should be tried and found wanting.

During the thirteen months that followed, the gallant Right Division and their allies gave a good account of themselves. Richardson,[1] who was with them the whole time, says that Procter gained from their gallantry and success a reputation that no act of his own deserved. Indeed it is borne in upon the most casual reader of his narrative that, though Procter was at the head of the defence, Tecumseh was its soul.

After the disastrous Battle of Lake Erie – September 10th, 1813 – which left Procter denuded of his great guns and cut off from his source of supply, he held a council at which it was resolved to destroy the forts of Detroit and Amherstburg and retire via the Thames route upon the Centre Division.

The decision was bitterly opposed by Tecumseh, the mouthpiece of the Indian contingent. He accused Procter of direct breach of trust with his people and demanded that, if the British must retreat, the forts and ammunition should be given to the Indians, who would themselves oppose the landing of the Americans. He compared Procter to a 'fat animal which slinks away, its tail between its legs', and finally hurled at him that ultimate epithet of scorn – an old squaw.

Harrison said afterwards that Procter must have been infatuated not to make a stand as Tecumseh advised. It is certain that situations as desperate as his have been retrieved, and, had there been a leader who

> When the right arm's shattered waves
> The good flag with the left,

history might have a different story to tell. Such a leader, however, Procter was not; and I believe that his resolve to retreat has never been assailed as a normal measure. A compromise was finally arrived at which Tecumseh accepted, though unwillingly. It was to destroy the forts and retire, with such ammunition and stores as they could carry, to Moraviantown, the farthest point on the Thames to which bateaux could ascend; to fortify this village and there await the enemy. Moraviantown had been built, so far as it *was* built, by a company of Delaware Indians who, led by their missionaries, had migrated thither from the Ohio in 1792. The Moravian church abandoned its work there only about five years ago. Procter called it half way to the Centre Division, though it is but a bare third to Ancaster – the Centre Division's outpost. Did Procter make this promise in good faith? I think not. He

[1] [John Richardson (1796-1852) was born in Queenston and raised at Detroit and Amherstburg. He was a cadet during the early part of the war and was taken prisoner at Moraviantown, an experience that made him a bitter critic of General Procter. He secured a commission in the British army and embarked upon a precarious literary career in England, Canada and the United States. He died in poverty but has won posthumous fame as one of Canada's foremost early writers.]

made it to escape a present perplexity. He seems to have persuaded himself that Harrison would be content with the possession of the forts and would not pursue. At all events, the way he conducted his retreat shows no intention of fighting; and he did not fight. He took much pains to save the great quantity of unnecessary and forbidden personal baggage he had carried off. The safety of his little army, his honor, his reputation – these things he lost sight of. He left Sandwich September 27th and marched at the leisurely rate of nine miles a day for five days. The roads were shockingly bad, for it had been a rainy season.

Having reached Dolsen's, four miles below Chatham, he left his little army there, and, with his personal staff and baggage and the women and children, went forward to Moraviantown. He took all the guns but one, and his only officer of engineers, as if to arrange for fortifying. But he left no orders to guide Colonel Warburton, the second-in-command; and at Moraviantown he took not a step towards his promised fortifications, though the place is said to have afforded facilities. Abattis[2] could have been constructed, the houses occupied, etc.

Whilst thus tarrying by the way and knowing nothing of the general's plans, Warburton got word of the approach of the enemy. Harrison had left Sandwich on the second of October and was already, on the third, close behind them. The British retired to Chatham; and the Indians seeing what they thought a good place to make a stand where now Tecumseh Park is, clamored to fight there. Warburton was in much perplexity and consulted anxiously with the other officers. All were indignant at the general's conduct and a proposal was seriously made to deprive him of the command and confer it upon Warburton, who declined, as he very well might, so perilous an honor. However, by the arguments of Elliott, the commissioner, the Indians consented to go on, a few remaining behind and actually disputing the progress of the Americans. A further march of six or seven miles brought the little army to Richardson's, where Procter joined them. Leaving a rear-guard here, he led the half-fed troops to Sherman's, where the night of October fourth was spent, Tecumseh, according to local tradition, having spent this, his last night on earth, in Sherman's barn. The Sherman of the day – Lemuel by name – was a member of Captain Shaw's company of Kent Militia which in May 1813 applied for, and seems to have got, leave to go home and till their farms. At all events it was not in the battle of the Thames, though it was in that of the Longwoods the following March, where two of Captain Shaw's sons were wounded – one mortally. The Sherman house was the first built within the limits of the present Thamesville, and probably the only one then standing. It was built on the knoll above the river now occupied by the Sherman cemetery.

[2] [An abattis is a form of defencework fashioned by placing felled trees with their tops to the front so as to obstruct an attacking force.]

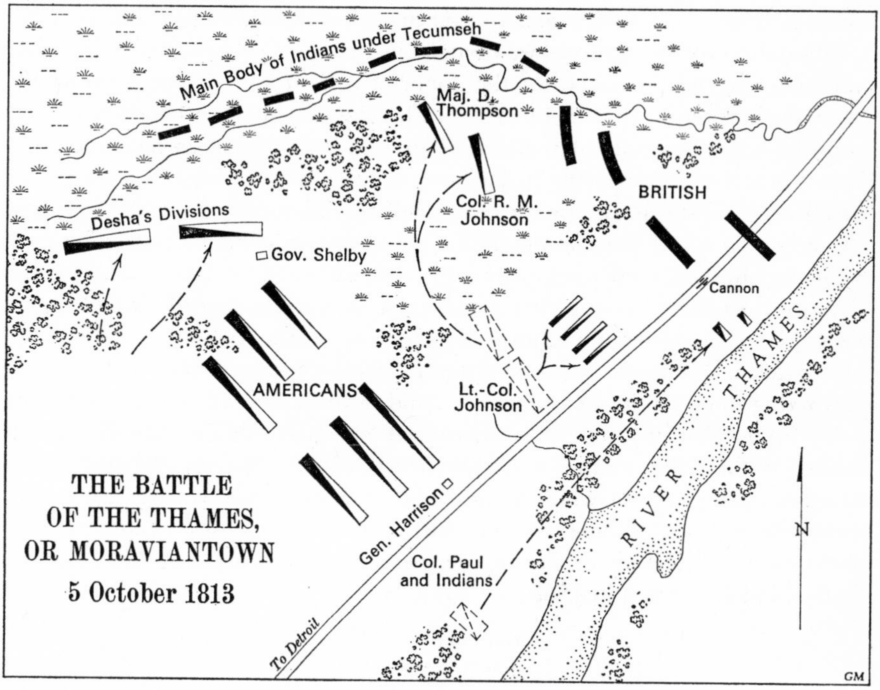

THE BATTLE OF THE THAMES, OR MORAVIANTOWN
5 October 1813

On the morning of the fifth the rear-guard joined the rest of the army at Sherman's, with the disheartening news that all their supplies of food and ammunition had fallen into the enemy's hands through the night, the guard as well as the sick and wounded being made prisoners. Raw meat was served for breakfast, but before that luxurious meal could be despatched news of the proximity of the enemy caused a further tramp of two muddy miles, this time to the scene of the battle. They were formed in two lines, the British in an irregular group in the woods which, having no underbrush, offered little obstacle to cavalry. The solitary gun, for which there was not a single round of ammunition, was at the left of the road. In a black ash swamp to the right, Tecumseh and his men were drawn up, and here alone, according to local authority, were abattis constructed. David Sherman, the fifteen-year-old son of the militia man referred to, was looking for his cows that afternoon in company with a boy named Ward. Naturally they looked in the direction where something unusual was going on. An Indian, sitting on a newly-felled tree, called the boys, questioned them a little, and advised them to get their cows and hurry home. He wore a scarf wound round his head in which was stuck a large white ostrich plume. When forty years later David Sherman surveyed a portion of his patrimony into village lots, he named the village after that Indian – Tecumseh. But, there being already a post office of that name in Essex, our village had to find another and was called Thamesville.

The battle of the Thames was fought in the Gore of Zone,[3] and lots 2, 4, 5, and 6 have been entered for the honor of being the site. Lots 5 and 6, the farm until recently owned by Mr. G. J. Watts, who inherited it from his grandfather, whose patent is dated 1849, was long known as the Tecumseh Farm, as it was supposed to be the actual battleground. But I am assured by Mr. John McDowell, the present owner of the Tecumseh farm, as well as of the adjoining land west, that all the relics known to have been found, – bayonets, muskets, and human remains, and skeletons of horses – have been found on the latter – lot 4. Mr. McDowell has a collection of bullets of two sizes, picked up himself within the past seven years. When the little army was arrayed, Tecumseh rode along the lines, shaking the officers by the hand and trying to cheer the weary, hungry, and dispirited men about to encounter a foe outnumbering them at least three to one. (The British had 367 of all ranks and their Indian allies were about 800, whereas Harrison's troops numbered at least 3,000 of which almost half were cavalry.) He was dressed in a close-fitting suit of buckskin and his favorite white ostrich plume waved above his head. How it recalls another hero – him whose commission Samuel de Champlain carried in 1608:

> The King hath come to marshal us
> In all his armor dressed,
> And he hath bound a snow white plume
> Above *his gallant crest.*

Procter with his staff took his stand behind the rear line. He may well have been ashamed to face the men whose confidence he knew he had lost and whom he was flinging to the enemy as the wicked man in the children's story flung the child from his arms to the wolves. I have no technical terms at my command but this is what happened: Harrison's advancing cavalry was met by a fire from the front rank who then retired. The second, attempting to fire, were borne down by the horsemen and in two minutes or less all was over. The Indians held out the longest; but when Tecumseh fell they also broke and fled. Of the British only about fifty men under Lieutenant Bullock escaped.

Where was Procter? Two minutes after the first volley was fired he was galloping east to Moraviantown, where his treasures were, and onward through the forest towards Burlington. The enemy pursued him fifteen miles, plundered the baggage which he was compelled to abandon – and which included his carriage – and returned, burning Moraviantown en route. Procter was court-martialed at Montreal in December 1814 and sentenced to a

[3] [A gore is a wedge-shaped tract of land lying between two or more townships and named after one of them.]

suspension from rank and pay for six months and a public reprimand. In his defence he had the meanness to throw the blame upon his little army. The Prince Regent was dissatisfied with the sentence, complaining that he was treated with inexcusable leniency; and one finds oneself for once agreeing with His Royal Highness.

The morning after the battle, Lemuel Sherman and his son David were amongst those who went down to bury the dead. The bodies were thrown into a pit from which relic-hunters have since carried off many a trophy. Mr. William Sherman assures me that he knows where Tecumseh was buried – that his father (then the boy David) had witnessed the burial and showed *him* the spot when a boy. There is a strong opinion, however, amongst historians 'that no man knows that sepulchre, and no man saw it e'er' – no white man at least.

Harrison left the sick and wounded at Sherman's and many of them spent the winter there, using the barn already mentioned as their hospital. The names of some of them cut into the boards are still to be seen. One of the Kentucky troops remained behind altogether. When David Sherman married he took up his abode with him, died in his house in 1857 and is buried in the family plot on the spot where Lemuel Sherman's house stood in 1813.

I have left for the last the few words I wish to say on Tecumseh. That great Shawnee Chief was born in 1768 in the valley of the Mad River within the present State of Ohio. Like his brother the prophet, he was believed to be of supernatural birth, being thus a hero to his own people in the classic sense, as he is a hero to us according to the better meaning of the word – not the one that came in about the time of the Boer War. From his earliest years he nourished wrath against the Americans from the belief that his people had been unjustly treated concerning their lands. He was, of course, a warrior. But a warrior of the best type known to our military age – wise in council, fertile in resource, magnanimous and fearless. If we may believe the story that he fled on the occasion of his first battle, it is interesting as indicatory that his courage had a moral rather than a physical origin. When war was declared in 1812 it was natural that he should come forward in aid of the British. Richardson says that he had nothing of the savage about him save the color and the garb. Kipling calls the savage people of today 'half devil and half child', and the description suits our own red men well enough. They were children for instability and devils for cruelty. Yet from the day Tecumseh took his stand beside Brock at Detroit till that on which Johnson's bullet stilled forever his noble heart[4] he never wavered in his determination and

[4] [Tecumseh was commonly believed to have been killed at Moraviantown by Richard M. Johnson (1780-1850), Kentucky politician, organizer of a body of Kentucky mounted riflemen that played a large part in the Americans' victory at that battle, United States senator, and vice president from 1837 to 1841.]

loyalty. And he had learned from civilization her noblest lesson that mercy 'which becomes the throned monarch better than his crown', and which shines with even greater lustre from the untutored savage. Richardson, who knew him well, speaks of him with affectionate enthusiasm. Harrison, against whom he fought, respected him while living and lamented his death. In the story of the war he towers above the short-sighted, selfish, and unready Procter. He stands, an equal, beside the heroic Brock.

Such he was; and of his great gifts he gave all in the Canadian cause. 'Green leaves of his labor,' he gave, 'white flower of his thought, and red fruit of his death.' Should we not then honor him 'as we honor our bravest who fall'?

In five years will come round the one hundredth anniversary of the battle of the Thames. How fittingly on that day would the Canadian people unveil a monument to the memory of the brave, the noble Shawnee who died in battle against the Invaders of Canadian Soil!

FURTHER READING: C. O. Z. Ermatinger, 'The retreat of Proctor and Tecumseh', *Ontario Historical Society*, volume 17 (1919), pages 11-21; D. A. N. Lomax, *A history of the services of the 41st (the Welch) Regiment . . . from its formation, in 1719, to 1895* (Devonport, England, 1899); B. H. Young, *The battle of the Thames, in which Kentuckians defeated the British, French, and Indians . . .*, Filson Club Publications, no. 18 (Louisville, Kentucky, 1903).

General Procter has found few defenders. Contemporary and later opinion has condemned him without reservation. Yet the widely differing conclusions of this article and the previous one indicate the permissiveness latent in the interpretation of historical evidence. The two contrasting views of Procter may be irreconcilable, but the two presentations enable the reader to achieve a more balanced judgment of Procter. . . . VICTOR LAURISTON, *novelist and writer on business and historical subjects, has had a long and distinguished career in journalism and civic affairs in Chatham, Ontario. This article is from the Kent Historical Society's 'Papers and Records' (volume 7, 1951), by permission of the author and of the Society.*

The Case for General Procter

BY VICTOR LAURISTON

This discourse need not lack a text. Any work, historical or fictional, dealing with the War of 1812 will furnish at least one reference, usually condemnatory, to Major General Henry Procter.

The French-Canadian Garneau blames him for abandoning the defensive, and a translator's footnote adds that 'Tecumseh, who fought like a lion against desperate odds, became a victim of Procter's ineptitude.' Miss McIlwraith's novel, *Kinsmen at War,* refers to Tecumseh as 'striving to stiffen the weak knees of General Procter, an adept at lying only'. My own immature verdict in 1913 was that Procter 'seems to seek excuses for failure rather than opportunities for success'. Such was still my view a few years ago when work upon a novel dealing with this scene and period compelled a closer study of documentary records.

On June 30, 1812, word reached Amherstburg that the United States had declared war. Colonel St. George got himself to strengthen the neglected fort. When, a week later, the American General Hull crossed to Canadian soil, the British garrison consisted of 100 men of the 41st Regiment and a handful of artillery, with 300 militia in two minds whether to fight or not – these to oppose an American force of at least 2,500.

There was, though, another important military factor – the Indian tribes, represented at the moment by a scant 150 braves camped on Bois Blanc. The Indians hated the Americans, yet shrewdly waited for some hint as to which side was likeliest to win. The capture of Michilimackinac decided them; the warriors swarmed to Bois Blanc, eager for presents, ammunition, and rations from the Great White Father, represented by old Matthew Elliott.

These Indians loomed large in every decision, every movement, on the Detroit frontier. In scouting and irregular warfare they could be very useful. In siege work, or the open field, they were valueless. They knew no discipline and little restraint, and came and went as they pleased. Outnumbering the British regulars, they were a tacit menace. The danger was ever present that they might turn to the Americans. To the British commander on the Detroit frontier, whoever he might be, these Indians were unpleasant and undependable allies, who must be humoured and bribed lest they become dangerous enemies.

To take permanent command on this difficult frontier, Sir Isaac Brock despatched the senior officer of the 41st Regiment, Colonel Henry Procter. This was Procter's first independent command. He was in his early fifties, and had seen more than thirty years' service. Significance might be attached to the circumstance that Brock, knowing the situation and the desperate odds, knowing also the man and his record, chose Procter for the most difficult post in his entire thin line of defence.

Procter, arriving late in July, read the situation with the swift comprehension of the trained officer. Instead of maintaining a cautious defensive, or attempting a frontal attack on Hull's position at Sandwich, Procter struck swiftly at Hull's weakest point – his long line of communication through an almost unpeopled wilderness. For this task he used the force best fitted – the Indians. They ambushed and slaughtered an American convoy at Brownston, and, stiffened by a few British regulars, halted a stronger detachment sent to Maguaga to re-establish Hull's communications. This pressure, as Procter had anticipated, compelled Hull to withdraw from Canadian soil; and his captured despatches, disclosing utter panic, emboldened Brock on his arrival to demand the surrender of Detroit, with what results we know.

Procter's skilful dispositions had prepared the ground for this achievement. We may imagine the earnest conferences between Brock and Procter in their few days together. Procter has been criticized for not maintaining a strict defensive. He had, in fact, argued against an attack on Detroit; but hereafter he made Brock's daring strategy his own. We have a right to surmise that this general strategy – involving the principle laid down by Marshal Foch more than a century later that 'the best defence is to attack' – was mapped in these unrecorded conferences between Brock and his subordinate.

One decision reached was that adequate defence of the Detroit frontier required at least 2,000 regulars. Brock might have found these; but Brock fell at Queenston, and the general directions of the war passed on to men unfamiliar with Procter's situation. Official records show that in December

1812 the two garrisons at Detroit and Malden comprised 377 officers and men – this to overawe disaffected Detroit, to hold the restless Indians in line, and to oppose the inevitable American advance.

Procter had established a small Michigan outpost on the River Raisin near Frenchtown. Early in January, General James Winchester,[1] eager for glory, snatched the opportunity afforded by General Harrison's absence to attack this outpost as a preliminary to a swift advance on Detroit.

Word reached Procter at 2 a.m. on January 19. At dawn on the 20th, leaving a bare handful of men to hold the two forts, Procter marched with 500 regulars and militia and some Indians. Before daylight on the 22nd he attacked Winchester.

Richardson, writing many years later, criticized Procter for opening with a cannonade instead of making a surprise attack. The fact is that, where the enemy occupied a fortified position of unknown strength, sound tactics called for artillery preparation.

Frenchtown was in many respects the most complete British victory of the entire war. By a forced march, striking deep into enemy territory, Procter not merely defeated but utterly annihilated a superior force strongly posted on its own ground; and, with prisoners more numerous than his own effective force, swiftly withdrew before Harrison's main army could come up.

Judge Woodward, who later gave his name to Woodward Avenue, was then a leading citizen of Detroit. He hated Procter. Yet he wrote thus to Secretary Monroe at Washington: 'The operations of the British commander are marked with the same minute correctness of judgment in this instance, and the same boldness of conception and execution which distinguished, in the former instance, his illustrious predecessor, General Brock. It is a military movement of equal, and, in fact, of greater splendour.'

American writers accuse Procter of permitting the massacre of Americans wounded by the Indians. This was Procter's first closeup of actual Indian warfare. Detroit had made no resistance, and there Tecumseh's potent influence had held the savages in check. Procter seemingly expected the Indians to keep their solemn promises to Brock and to himself to spare the prisoners. Unfortunately, Tecumseh was not at Frenchtown. Procter, by threats, persuasion, and actual bribes, rescued many of the Americans; and Winchester has left written testimony to the humanity and kindness with which the British general treated the prisoners. But Procter's outspoken disapproval of

[1] [James Winchester (1752-1826) served in the Revolutionary War, commanded the North Carolina militia against the Indians, and became a state senator when Tennessee became a state in 1796. He was appointed a brigadier-general under Harrison in 1812. Following his surrender to Procter on January 22, 1813, he was exchanged and given charge of the Mobile district in 1814. In 1819 he was appointed to determine the boundary between Tennessee and Mississippi.]

the savages and his efforts to restrain them marked the beginning of a steady, widening rift between the British commander and the Indians.

The cry for vengeance for their slaughtered brothers of the River Raisin roused the Americans to fresh efforts. His Frenchtown casualties had left Procter with less than 300 effectives. Supplies, alike of food, clothing, and ammunition, were precarious, and the men were paid irregularly or not at all. But as soon as some small reinforcements actually reached him, Procter again forestalled a threatened advance by swift attack, this time at Fort Meigs on the Maumee.

His entire available force consisted of 456 regulars and 461 militia, with about 1,200 Indians. Procter's bombardment had not yet effected a breach when, on the 5th of May, General Clay's relieving army, descending the river in boats, landed on both banks of the Maumee. Dudley's detachment captured the main British battery. A counterattack promptly drove them out. Of Clay's 1,300 men, barely 500 succeeded in entering the fort.

The Canadian militia, anxious regarding their spring planting, had gradually drifted home; the Indians, sated with scalps and plunder, vanished overnight. Procter found himself with less than 400 effectives to besiege a strong position garrisoned by 1,700 men. He had no alternative but to raise the siege.

Procter had for a third time broken the spearhead of an American thrust at the frontier; but through the spring and summer of 1813 the tragic story of official neglect went on. It is told with damnatory clearness in a long succession of despatches. Supplies were lacking; the men were half-fed, ill-clad, unpaid. Brock had estimated 2,000 regulars as needed to hold the frontier; but reinforcements dribbled westward in scant companies and platoons.

Meanwhile, new American armies were massing, and at Presque Isle, energetic Perry was building ships to dispute the control of Lake Erie. In despatch after despatch, Procter plainly urged the desperateness of his situation. Had he a few men to spare, he would re-establish that needed outpost on the River Raisin. He did try to establish the friendly Indians in the wild country between the River Raisin and Detroit – a shrewd move that, given time, would have created a potential buffer state. But time rushed mercilessly on, unlike the dawdling authorities at Quebec, Kingston, and York who hardly moved at all.

They did make promises. The 6th Company and staff would be sent; later, the remainder of the 41st Regiment. Sailors, pork, powder, Indian presents, all things needful were promised. Procter sent the *Queen Charlotte* to Fort Erie to bring the men and supplies; but at the crucial moment the American Chauncey secured command of Lake Ontario, Fort George was taken, communication was cut, and the ship returned empty.

On June 20th Prevost writes that he has instructed the new commander in Upper Canada, General de Rottenburg, to push on reinforcements and supplies – the remainder of the 41st Regiment, £1,000 *in specie*, £2,000 in army bills, salt pork, clothing, shoes, trenching tools, equipment for the naval department – all these are to go forward. 'Bring forward the united power of both services to crush the enemy's endeavors to obtain the ascendancy of Lake Erie,' writes Prevost. But, weeks later, nothing has reached Procter except this exhortation.

Procter sees the situation with tragic clearness, urges explicitly and with a reiteration that becomes monotonous the right move to make. Strengthen the land force, properly man and outfit Barclay's ships, and a joint military and naval attack on Presque Isle will yet make Perry's diligent efforts useless. Had that shrewd stroke been made possible, the entire story of the western campaign must have been far different.

Barclay himself pleads for sailors, for naval ordnance. 'Indeed,' he writes, 'the whole line under General Procter must lay open to the enemy in the event of their being able to make his Majesty's squadron retire', and he warns that, though he must attack the enemy fleet, unless reinforced he will fight at disadvantage.

Prevost repeatedly promises reinforcements; but they do not come. One wonders why. The man between, in that fateful summer of 1813 when Procter and his little army stood with their backs to the wall, was Major General Francis de Rottenburg, commander of the forces in Upper Canada. . . . General Vincent, a good soldier, singularly patient and generous, who out of his own scant resources sent Procter what help he could, shows bitterness toward but one fellow officer – de Rottenburg. When, by the victories of Stoney Creek and Beaver Dam, Vincent, Harvey, and FitzGibbon had made the Niagara frontier safe, de Rottenburg hastened to take command there; when Barclay's defeat threatened trouble, de Rottenburg just as quickly discovered he was needed at Kingston, and to strengthen that position took Vincent's three best regiments, sorely needed for the defence of Burlington Heights. The evidence may not be sufficient to prove that de Rottenburg deliberately kept for himself the supports intended for Procter; but the suspicion lingers.

Meanwhile Procter's Indian allies, grown restive, demanded not merely ammunition and presents but scalps and plunder. A stratagem, suggested by Tecumseh, to lure the garrison from Fort Meigs, was unsuccessful. The Indian Department officials then demanded an assault on Fort Stephenson, declaring that unless the fort was stormed the Indians would desert. Procter regarded the fort as too strong. Yet it was part of his task, and an important part, to keep the Indians in good humour. Reluctantly he ordered the assault. The regulars were repulsed with heavy loss; the Indians, who had promised to co-operate, fled ignominiously. Harrison, by a swift withdrawal, skilfully extricated his shattered force.

He returned to Amherstburg to find that, too late, additional men of the 41st Regiment had at last arrived. Seamen, fifty of them, and naval guns for the warship *Detroit*, now ready for launching, were to follow. But Perry's ships were over the bar; and on September 10th Barclay sailed to meet them, his vessels manned by landlubbers from the 41st Regiment and equipped with guns from the forts.

Few people realize how close the battle of Lake Erie came to being a British victory. Impetuous Perry's headlong attack permitted Barclay's weaker squadron to crush the van of the American line before the lagging rear could come into action. The *Lawrence* struck her flag; and the victory was virtually won when the *Detroit* and *Queen Charlotte* of the British fleet fouled each other's rigging, and, helpless to manoeuvre, were pounded into wreckage. The fifty seamen who would have averted that catastrophe were still east of Burlington where the promised naval guns waited under tarpaulin.

With Barclay defeated, the whole Detroit frontier now lay open to the invader.

Till September 12, Procter clung doggedly to the hope that Barclay had won and pushed on to bombard Presque Isle. That day he realized the truth. 'It is my opinion that I should retire to the Thames without delay,' he writes. Already he had prudently notified Colonel Talbot to provide food depots and prepare the roads for retreat. But de Rottenburg replied that he 'did not clearly see the necessity or expediency of immediate retirement'.

What de Rottenburg, hundreds of miles away, could not see, Procter saw with perfect clearness. Yet, as at every stage of the defence, the Indians had to be considered. But for the Indians, Procter could have commenced the retreat at once. He lingered solely to persuade them to accompany him.

Much has been written of that dramatic council at Malden where Tecumseh challenged Procter to hand over the arms and munitions to the Indians and leave them to defend the frontier alone. Had every Indian been a Tecumseh, that proposal might not have been preposterous. But where Tecumseh's loyalty was sure, that of his followers was uncertain. Already many were leaving for their homes, or deserting to the Americans. Acceptance of Tecumseh's proposal would have been equivalent to handing over the munitions to Harrison.

Despite his impassioned outburst, Tecumseh could not ignore the necessity for retreat. The forts had been denuded of their guns, to equip the fleet. Even with belated reinforcements, Procter in his own words had hundreds where Harrison had thousands. His entire regular force was less than 900 officers and men – not fresh soldiers, well equipped, in the pink of efficiency, but men weary from ten years and more of absence from their English homes. Half-starved, ill-equipped, ragged, consistently neglected through more than a year of warfare in a dismal wilderness where the only men not down with the fever were up with the fever, the relics of the 41st Regiment turned their backs on the frontier they had held so long. Over trails rendered almost impassable by the early autumn rains, they trudged, day after weary day, till they reached Dolsen's on the Thames. Some small unarmed sailing craft and bateaux carried the wounded, the women, and the scant provisions and supplies.

Procter had ordered Dolsen's to be fortified; but officers and men, worn by privations and sickness, had utterly lost heart, and his orders were simply ignored. The place, in any event, was unsuited for defence. While the men rested there, Procter with his captain of engineers rode upstream to seek a better position.

Tradition has it that he promised Tecumseh to make a stand at Chatham. The question is asked, why not? The British on the north bank of the river, the Indians east of McGregor's Creek, were well posted to repel the Americans advancing on the south bank of the Thames. The answer is simple. Perry's smaller ships now lay at Dolsen's; they could readily ascend beyond Chatham, and, enfilading both positions, would instantly render them untenable. They could, just as readily, transfer the land forces to the north bank, to outflank the British.

So, on the morning of the 4th of October, the Indians merely fought a delaying action behind the line of McGregor's Creek, and the retreat went on. That night the British camped east of Arnold's Mills, the Americans a few miles downstream. Next morning the last of the British craft grounded; and the disheartened soldiers manning them surrendered the supplies without firing a shot. Fugitives brought to Procter the tragic realization that his men had no ammunition except the few rounds they carried.

The ultimate stand took place a couple of miles east of the modern Thamesville. Procter's dispositions were skilful. To the left the British position was protected by the Thames, to the right by a large swamp; and a smaller swamp between narrowed the attacking front. One cannon was posted to enfilade the American advance; in the rear five more guns guarded a ford against a turning movement and promised protection for a possible retreat. In the larger swamp to the British right, Tecumseh's force, dwindled to about 500 warriors, was posted. Procter's calculation plainly was that the fire of the cannon and the volleys of the regulars would throw the advancing Americans into confusion, and the Indians, attacking from the swamp, would convert that confusion into defeat.

But the two thin red lines drawn across the road and through the beech woods that October afternoon numbered less than 400 men passably fit to fight. Procter, rising doggedly above all the harassment of neglect, distrust, and defeat, trusted implicitly to the proven courage of the 41st in the shock of actual battle; nor does he seem to have realized the utter demoralization of his shadow army. The gamble was desperate, more desperate than he knew, but he faced it in the intrepid spirit of Brock.

Those thin red lines had to face, not infantry, but hard-riding Kentuckians who shattered all military precedent by charging on horseback through the beech woods. The lone cannon was never even fired; the infantry fired two wavering volleys; then the line crumpled.

Tradition that Procter fled at the first volley is inferred from Richardson's narrative, supported by Lieutenant Bullock. These men were far to the right of the line, so far that Bullock escaped through the woods with his entire grenadier company, and Richardson almost escaped – too far, consequently, to see the actual fighting on the British left. Richardson, embittered by Procter's strictures on the 41st, wrote more than a quarter of a century after the battle. But, that same night, Captain John Hall, Procter's aide, writing from Delaware with the actual happenings of the afternoon fresh in his memory, simply said: 'One of the guns being deserted early in the action, the troops near it gave way and the consequence was a complete rout – notwithstanding the exertions of the general to rally them, so much so that I thought it impossible he could escape being taken.' Hall's story, the only contemporary eyewitness story, is confirmed by the fact that early in Procter's flight his pursuers were close on his heels; which would not have been the case had he fled at once instead of trying to rally his men.

To say that Procter should have stood his ground and shared the fate of his soldiers is to confuse the function of the soldier with that of the knight. Procter was a soldier; and in defeat his one duty was still to help win the war. The next day he was at the Grand River, collecting his scattered army.

Procter is depicted by most writers as thrown into utter panic. As to that, his subsequent course furnishes the clearest evidence. On the morrow of his defeat, he began like a good soldier to reassemble and reorganize his little force. He insisted on waiting at the Grand River till Bullock could collect the last of the fugitives; and on keeping his promise to Colonel Elliott to wait for the Indians who were scouting Harrison's movements. Colonel Young at Burlington had ordered a precipitate withdrawal of all outposts. Procter countermanded the order, and sent Colonel Hamilton back to the outpost at Turkey Point. A few days after the battle, Procter had assembled at Ancaster 246 out of the 397 regulars who had actually stood in the battle line at Moraviantown.

On the news of Moraviantown, Vincent had fallen back to the strong position at Burlington Heights. De Rottenburg ordered the abandonment of all Upper Canada west of Kingston. Vincent was reluctant to obey this order. He submitted the question of further retreat to a commission of five regular officers. Procter headed that commission. The commission unanimously reported that they saw no reason for further retreat; and Vincent, in defiance of de Rottenburg's orders, held Burlington. Procter's advice was amply vindicated. Within three short months the British regained all the

Niagara Peninsula, captured the American Fort Niagara and swept the American side of the river with fire and sword.

That recommendation, to hold Burlington against whatever odds, was Procter's last great service to the British cause; but he had still a service to perform for his superiors.

On the Detroit frontier, the obvious causes had brought the inevitable consequences. A brave officer with a forlorn hope had been left to hold a weak position against overwhelming odds. At every opportunity he had warned his superiors of the dangers of his position and the modest steps needed to make the frontier safe. His warnings had been disregarded, the needed reinforcements had been sent grudgingly or not at all. Despite this neglect he had been instrumental, partially at Detroit and wholly at Frenchtown and on the Maumee, in shattering on their own ground three enemy forces, each superior to his own. The reward had been neglect, starvation, hardship, and eloquent exhortations to carry on in the true spirit of the British soldier.

All that remained was for the superiors whose blind neglect had compassed the loss of the Detroit frontier to safeguard themselves by finding a scapegoat. Procter was court-martialed at Montreal in December 1814. The court acquitted him of any neglect and reproach in his personal conduct, but found him negligent and deficient in his handling of the retreat. He was sentenced to be publicly reprimanded and suspended from pay and rank for six months. . . .

The erroneous judgment of posterity is based, not on that court martial, but on Richardson's hot resentment of Procter's perfectly accurate statement that the conduct of the 41st Regiment at Moraviantown 'was not upon this unfortunate occasion such as I have on every other witnessed with pride and satisfaction. The inclination to retreat was too strong, nor did I receive that cordial aid I sought and was entitled to.' Procter, with his exacting standards of courage and endurance and his proud esteem of the British soldier, did not realize that he asked, just as his superiors asked, more than men could give.

No other commander and no other men in the War of 1812 were so utterly neglected, or in the face of utter neglect, achieved so much. The time has come to tell Canada the true story of their defence of this forgotten frontier, its sufferings, its hardships, its triumphs, and its ultimate tragedy.

FURTHER READING: W. C. H. Wood (ed.), *Selected British documents . . .*, volume 2, pages 3-12, 27-51, 319-41; E. A. Cruikshank (ed.), *Documentary history . . .*, part VI, pages 160-4, 241-2, 254-8; J. Richardson, *The War of 1812 . . .* (Toronto, 1902); E. A. Cruikshank, 'Harrison and Proctor; the River Raisin', *Royal Society of Canada*, third series, section 2, volume 4 (1910), pages 119-67.

Though the western portion of Upper Canada lay open to the invader after Moraviantown, the Americans did not occupy it in force. Instead, the war in this sector degenerated into a series of destructive marauding expeditions by American troops and at times by renegade Canadians. The British and the local militia were too weak to hold a regular front and contented themselves with ranging about the country. Pitched battles were rare; the present article recounts one of the most memorable of these, known also as the battle of Long Woods. It may be taken as an example of the sort of warfare waged in 1813 and 1814 in the no-man's-land west of Burlington Heights. . . . 'The Fight at Battle Hill' is reprinted with the permission of the London and Middlesex Historical Society from that society's 'Transactions' for 1911-12.

The Fight at Battle Hill

BY J. I. POOLE

. . . Shortly before the 1st of January, 1814, Lieut-Gen. Sir Gordon Drummond established a small outpost of the Centre Division at Delaware, a little village upon the Thames, about thirty-four miles east of Moravian Town, and about twelve miles west of the site of the present City of London. This village then consisted of only a few straggling houses, and a saw mill close by. This force was stationed at this place for the purpose of acting as a corps of observation over and keeping in check the straggling bands of American Militia who were constantly harassing the peaceful inhabitants of the London District. It comprised the Flank Companies of the Royal Scots, and a light company of the 89th Regiment, a detachment of Canadian (Kent) Militia, and a small body of Rangers, the whole being under the command of Captain Stewart, the full strength of which amounted to 196 men. Stewart was frequently obliged during the months of January and February to send out reconnoitring expeditions down the Thames, and even into the vicinity of Sandwich for the purpose of checking the desultory incursions of the enemy above referred to.

In order to act as a counterpoise to, and neutralize as far as possible the effect of the establishment of the British post at Delaware, Lieut.-Col. Butler,[1] who still held command at Detroit, established a similar post at

[1] [Anthony Butler of the 28th Regiment, United States army, was in command at Detroit from December 1813 to March 1814 and directed operations in the western sector of Upper Canada

McLear's, near Dolsen's Farm, on the banks of the Thames about two miles below where the city of Chatham now stands, at which station was placed a company of thirty-nine American regulars under Lieut. Larwell. The British having been apprised of the situation of this corps, Lieut. Medcalf with thirty-three regulars and militia marched through the woods from the Rond Eau and surprised it in the silent watches of the night (Dec. 23rd, 1813) capturing the whole party without loss of killed on either side, and only five Americans wounded.

Butler did not think proper to re-establish this post, but contented himself with sending out foraging expeditions from Detroit as before. In one of these incursions Captain Lee with a company of Michigan Rangers captured and carried off as prisoners Col. Baby, Capt. Springer, and several others of the Canadian Militia, who were most active in the defence of their country. . . .

Butler, however, finding his hold upon the south-western portion of the province rather uncertain, determined to make an attack upon some one or other of the British posts in the interior, and by its capture and destruction rid himself of the repeated onsets from which his wild and turbulent foragers suffered at the hands of their stubborn and resolute foe. Accordingly on Feb. 21st, 1814, he resolved upon despatching Captain Andrew Hunter Holmes[2] of the 24th U. S. (Tennessee) Infantry with a detachment from this regiment and also from those of the 26th Vermont, the 27th New York and the 28th Kentucky, together with two pieces of artillery. Holmes was directed to march against either Port Talbot or Delaware, as circumstances would permit or the exigencies of the situation might require. At this time a period of comparative tranquility seemed to prevail, and since in consequence thereof Captain Stewart was not molested in his little post at Delaware and as the militia was no longer considered necessary to aid in its maintenance, he concluded to order it home.

However, as the sequel will show, this short season of apparent peace was more imaginary than real. Holmes, immediately upon receiving his instructions from his superior officer, set out from Amherstburg, and having reached Pointe au Pelee found the roads between that place and the Rond Eau to be so much obstructed by fallen timber, deep snow, thickets, and wet swamps that he was obliged to abandon his guns at Pointe au Pelee, and trust to his small arms for the reduction of the British post at Port Talbot. The climate of this part of the country being less severe in winter than in the more north-

during that period. In February 1814 he was promoted to colonel of the 2nd Rifle Regiment. After the war he supervised the evacuation by the British of positions held in American territory, notably Michilimackinac.]

[2] [Andrew Hunter Holmes (d.1814) was a friend of Thomas Jefferson's and younger brother of David Holmes, first governor and United States senator from Mississippi. After the action at Battle Hill he took part in the American campaign to gain control of the upper Great Lakes and was killed during the assault on Michilimackinac on August 1, 1814. See pages 146-8.]

erly sections, the soil in the woods rarely freezes to such an extent as to allow the passage therein of such a relatively heavy load as a six pounder (the calibre of Holmes' guns) and in fact often makes insecure footing for a horse of ordinary weight.

Captain Gill with his company of Michigan Rangers, and Captain Lee with a troop of Michigan Militia Dragoons, having pursued some Canadian (Kent) Militia up the Thames under Lieut. McGregor, affected a junction with Holmes, at the Rond Eau, without serious obstruction, so that Holmes's total strength now numbered 180 men. He at once resumed his march for Port Talbot, but soon changed his determination upon hearing that his advance guard had fallen in with some Canadian militia, who he imagined would carry to Port Talbot the news of his coming, and then concluded to make an attempt to surprise Delaware. The settled conviction on the part of the British appeared to him to be that he intended to avoid Delaware and proceed to Port Talbot, which would in that event leave his rear open to attack, so that for this reason, also, he concluded to abandon his intended expedition to the latter place, and make a sudden rush upon the former, as indeed by his instructions from Butler he was authorized to do. He therefore altered his route and directed his march towards Delaware. Having crossed the Thames a short distance below Moravian Town, he proceeded rapidly along the forest highway leading through the 'Long Woods', a huge natural park extending from the site of the present village of Thamesville to Delaware, a distance of about thirty-seven miles and embracing within its woody domains an area of about 190,000 acres.

Almost in the very heart of this dreary solitude, at that time, lived with his family a quaint and lonely individual named George Ward, whose dwelling was known as 'Ward's Station', and whose memory is practically immortalized in the designation of the present village of Wardsville. . . .

Holmes's force, being nearly all mounted, traversed the sloughs of this unmitigated wilderness with wonderful celerity. The troops of which the invaders force was composed, and styled by American writers as 'Mounted Infantry', were for the most part hunters, trappers, and sportsmen, and says Coffin, 'inured to the wilderness, and between whom and the Indians there existed a constant warfare and deadly hatred'. As we might expect in men leading wild and reckless lives, there existed among them confused and unconventional ideas as to the right of personal property, combined with a marvellous tendency towards violating them. Supple and athletic, fearless, daring, sometimes vindictive, and frequently chivalrous towards a conquered foe, arrayed in a hunting frock and leathern trousers fringed with tassels, they were trained to cover their bodies behind trees from which they fired, without exposing themselves to any greater extent than was really necessary. They were not cavalry as we understand the term, as not a man among them carried a sword, but simply a rifle, and for fighting at close quarters there were fastened to their belt the cruel knife and awful tomahawk. Thus the hardy pioneers of Kentucky and Tennessee presented an appearance at once formidable as well as picturesque. Their usual tactics were to follow up the enemy on horseback, and then, dismounting from their docile steeds, step behind trees, and ply the unerring rifle. In the case of the roads being difficult for travel to footmen, they often each took up one of them, behind, on the backs of their trusty horses, and thus the march of the foot was greatly accelerated and a large stretch of country was in this way covered in a brief period of time.

These statements will now explain the rapid march of Holmes from Amherstburg to within fifteen miles of Delaware, and back to Fort Detroit. When Holmes reached a point in the woody and snow-covered bridle path 'only fifteen miles from Delaware, on the 3rd inst., we received intelligence', he says in his report, 'that the enemy had left Delaware with the intention of descending the river, and that we should probably meet him in one hour, that his force consisted of a light company from the Royal Scots, mustering for duty one hundred and twenty men, a light company from the 89th Regiment of foot (efficiency not known), Caldwell's Indians, and McGregor's militia, amounting in all to about 300 men'. This information was evidently not given to Holmes by any of his own scouts, since, had this been the case, he would have thus informed his superior officer, as he was always quite anxious that his skill should be exhibited to the best advantage, when making his report to Butler. . . . Holmes seems therefore to have procured his information (which was nearly correct) respecting his opponents' force from a renegade Canadian. This person seems to have met Holmes in advance of the British, since, according to his own report, the American officer was told that the British force was probably within one hour's march of him. Not knowing the ground, he at once retreated to what was then known as 'Twenty Mile Creek', so called from its being about twenty miles west of Delaware, this stream being also about three miles east of Ward's Station, and, having re-crossed it on a bridge, took up an excellent position on its western bank, now known as 'Battle Hill'.

Captain Gill, with about twenty Michigan Rangers, was left by Holmes to cover the retreat and watch the movements of the pursuing Canadian Rangers, under Caldwell. Holmes's command had originally amounted to 180 men, but hunger, cold, and fatigue had brought on illness, and, although none had died, yet all were much disheartened, and sixteen were sent home since they were unable to withstand the hardships connected with this wearisome march, so that his total strength now numbered 164 men. The main body of the Americans had barely encamped before it was joined by Gill with his American Rangers who had been driven in after exchanging a few shots with the Canadian Rangers who had vainly attempted to reconnoitre, although he was able to give the main body sufficient time to make good its retreat to Twenty Mile Creek. The remaining portion of the day and also the night were turned to good account by the American commandant. Disaffection had crept into the ranks of the invaders, and both officers and men loudly demanded that a retreat should be made still further, since many of them had suffered severely from fatigue and exposure, and alleged that others had been permitted to return home for these very same reasons. Holmes therefore was obliged to call a council of his officers to determine whether they should endeavor to maintain their present position, or retreat, and on this question there was considerable diversity of opinion. The Captain and his Adjutant, Ensign Heard, however, were strongly opposed to the latter alternative, and the impression finally prevailed that they should 'conquer the British or perish in the attempt'.

The strengthening of his position was then proceeded with, which was fortified by an abattis on three sides formed of logs, piled upon each other breast-high, and faced on the outerside with brushwood. The portion of the hills looking immediately to the east, and over which the road crossed, was also slightly strengthened in the same way. These hills, besides being very steep, were covered with water, which was brought up from the creek during the night in no stinted draughts, and being quickly frozen into ice, owing to the intense cold, was then concealed by snow being thrown thereon, so that the American position, previously naturally strong, was now practically unassailable.

The Canadian Rangers spent the night of the 3rd on the plain to the rear of the eastern hills, between which and the American camp lay a rather deep valley through which from north to south flows the creek which finally empties itself into the Thames about a mile south from where the road, now known as the Longwoods Road, crosses the hills. Although the ground is now cleared away, and the forest trees no longer wave their massive branches over the hills, the creek, and the ravine, still the western bank is yet an admirable location for defensive purposes, as against an enemy advancing from the east, and the American position was therefore well selected.

Stewart having received notification, late on the night of the third, from Captain William Caldwell that he had met with a party of Americans on that very day, sent Captain James Lewis Basden[3] at daylight on the morning of the fourth with the Regulars consisting of the companies previously

[3] [James L. Basden (1785-1856) joined the British army in 1800 as an ensign, served in India between 1803 and 1806, and became a captain in the 89th Foot. He came to Canada in 1813 and took part in the raid on Black Rock. After the engagement at Long Woods he fought at Lundy's Lane and in the siege of Fort Erie. He was a major during the First Burmese War 1824-5) and retired with the rank of lieutenant-colonel in 1843.]

mentioned, together with the company of the Kent Militia, under Lieut. McGregor, and about forty Indians, Wyandots and Pottawattomies, acting as scouts, under Captain 'Billy' Caldwell, a half-breed, to the support of the Rangers. Stewart himself was detained for several hours at Delaware, upon urgent business, with Col. Elliott, one of the survivors of Moravian Town, and not really expecting an action immediately, much to his subsequent regret was not present at the fight that followed. Being all on foot their march was necessarily laborious over the lightly crusted snow, through which they broke at every step. On the right hand and on the left, as they passed along, rose the primeval woods in which were great beech and maple trees, mantled in dazzling sheets of snow, and Nature herself was enshrouded in funereal white, and, except for the steady tramp of the troops, while they proceeded on their way the forest was as silent as the grave. At Twenty Mile Creek all was quiet, until the first dim redness tinged the eastern sky, and the hills and the woods grew visible in the morning light, when suddenly, the sound of arms was heard.

The Canadian Rangers, having risen from their wintry bed, were all alert, and after exchanging a few scattered, ineffective shots with the enemy, on the western hills, hastily retreated with the object of drawing the invaders from their strong position. This stratagem of inducing the Americans to leave their position on the opposite heights was well contrived, and had it been skilfully followed up could hardly have failed to effect the entire destruction of the enemy's force. Holmes, on discovering that the company of Canadian Rangers had disappeared, waited some time for their return, and then despatched Lieut. Knox with the Michigan Rangers to reconnoitre, and upon his return he reported that the Canadians had retreated with the utmost precipitation, leaving articles of baggage and camp furniture scattered about, and that judging from the number of fires, and the appearance of the trail, the strength of the enemy did not exceed sixty or seventy men.

The American commandant, displeased at the thought of his having retreated on the previous day from such a slender force, and, assuming that he had been previously wrongly informed as to the real strength of his opponents, now abandoned his position on the western hills and commenced a close pursuit of the flying Canadians, intending to endeavor to capture Delaware before the end of the day. He, however, had not proceeded more than five miles when Captain Lee of the Michigan Militia Dragoons, who was in advance of the main body, reported to him that the British and Canadians in considerable force were now arranging themselves in order of battle on ground of their own choosing; Caldwell, in the meantime, having been joined by the main body under Basden.

At this time the golden opportunity of making a flank movement through the woods, and thus cutting off the Americans from a retreat to Twenty

Mile Creek, presented itself to Basden. In fact he was strongly urged to do this by those of his men who were familiar with the physical features of the locality, and particularly by the two Caldwells. But, as he was by no means a strategist, he neglected doing so, and consequently lost his move in this game of military tactics. Had this been done, Holmes, in all probability, would have been driven towards Delaware or Port Talbot, and, without forage or other supplies, placed between two fires, in which case his entire command would have been either ultimately destroyed or compelled to surrender. Having taken advantage of Basden's blunder, he rapidly retreated and was thus finally enabled to resume his former position on the western bank of the creek, and at once began preparations for the struggle, notwithstanding the complaints of many of his men, who again strongly pressed him to retreat farther. Nor was this rapid retreat without its effect upon the mind of Basden, who only saw in Holmes's swift movements, the effects of fear and a settled design on the part of his foeman to avoid a conflict.

The American troops, being indifferently drilled, were formed in a hollow square, with the baggage and horses in the centre, in order to avoid the necessity of attempting military evolutions in action, which they were unable to perform. The brow of the west hill overhanging the creek, across which elevation stretched the road, was occupied by the detachment of the 24th Tennessee and 28th Kentucky, while those of the 26th Vermont and 27th New York defended the hills and the breastwork on the north side of the American position, the ravine here making a slight bend in a north-westerly direction, a very short distance beyond the north side of the road. The Michigan Rangers occupied a position on the west side of the square, while the Michigan Militia Dragoons stood on the south side of the American camp, the ravine here making another bend almost due south, as the waters of the creek rush onward and mingle with those of the Thames. These hills are all quite steep, and besides forming commanding eminences, about fifteen or twenty feet high, were fortified by long breastworks as above described.

Basden, then a young man of only twenty-nine years of age, like many others of the old school of British officers, believed that almost anything could be accomplished by dash and spirit, and that the enemy's entrenchments could be taken by storm, confidently expecting that he would thus be able to teach the Americans such a lesson that in the future they would positively desist from making any further foraging raids into Upper Canada. Had he been governed by prudence and judgment he would in all probability have succeeded in doing so, but, being as indiscreet as he was brave, he recklessly ordered a direct front attack instead of, in the first instance, endeavoring to turn the enemy's flank, thus repeating and accentuating the mistake made by himself during the previous part of the day. The desultory skirmishes with the enemy, occurring in connection with the advance and retreat of the Americans previously alluded to, in conjunction with the great depth of snow, for it was fully fifteen inches deep, tended greatly to retard the advance of the British and Canadians, so that it was about five o'clock in the afternoon of Friday, the 4th day of March, 1814, when they arrived on the eastern heights of the wide and deep ravine, through which Twenty Mile Creek discharges its waters. The company of Kent Militia under McGregor and the company of Canadian Rangers under Caldwell were instructed to make a flank movement up the valley, above the north side of the road, and upon the enemy's left where the detachments of the 26th and 27th were posted, and the Indians under Captain 'Billy' Caldwell were despatched to turn his right, where were stationed the Michigan Militia Dragoons and Rangers, while the British Regulars were to make an attack upon the centre of the American position defended by the detachments from the 24th and 28th.

Comparatively deadly work soon began. A more efficient corps for the flanking service to the left of the American position could scarcely have been selected from the whole irregular force in Upper Canada than this handful of men, fifty in number, led by McGregor and Caldwell, sheltering themselves behind trees as they noiselessly proceeded until they had passed up the ravine, under a heavy fire, to turn that portion of the invader's entrenchments, held by the soldiers of Vermont and New York, and then sounded their bugles, according to previous orders. The Indians, uttering their shrill war-cries, and also fighting from behind trees at a more respectful distance, engaged the right of the enemy, but owing to the fact that the latter had the advantage of an entrenched post, while the former fought from behind trees only, they were thus comparatively easily kept at bay.

It was, however, in the centre of the enemy's position where the struggle of the day took place. While the flanking movements were being made, the British Regulars commenced firing heavily upon the position held by the troops of Tennessee and Kentucky, these being the detachments from the 24th and 28th American Regulars. The foe, to the accompaniment of loud cries from the 28th of 'Hurrah for Kentucky!' 'Hurrah for Kentucky!' from their sheltered positions returned the fire with equal spirit and determination. Basden, putting himself at the head of the Royal Scots detachment, determined to try to carry by storm the main portion of the enemy's position, and for this purpose an advance was made from the eastern hills in double quick time, down a tongue of land sloping towards the western eminence, occupied by the 24th and 28th, and along which projection the road at that time ran, and being almost parallel with the southern limit of the modern highway. The road being exceedingly narrow, the detachment was formed 'into an open column of sections right in front', in which order it proceeded down the slope and over the bridge, which crossed the creek, being met at every step by a fire from the enemy posted on the heights above, which decimated their ranks but failed to dampen their glowing ardour. The hill upon which the 24th and 28th detachments had taken their position, 'actually at this moment', says Thompson, 'presented the appearance of a volcano belching forth cataracts of streaming fire, and dense columns of smoke; the air was filled with one continued roar of musketry, resembling the roar of a thousand drums, and as if to add a more terrific grandeur to the scene, the sun shot forth a few partial rays through the dense forest upon the conflicting parties', several of whom beheld this grand fountain of light, that afternoon, for the last time upon earth.

The detachment, having passed the bridge which spanned the creek, advanced to the foot of the western hills and within fifteen or twenty paces of the enemy posted behind the breastwork on the brow of the hill, from which was still poured into their ranks a most destructive fire. Here another occurrence of greater moment and of much more appalling nature presented itself to the minds of the brave Regulars and filled them with apprehension, altogether unprepared as they were for such an event. The face of the western hill, covered with ice, almost as slippery as glass and concealed by a slight covering of snow, was found to be extremely difficult if not impossible to climb. The enemy, screened behind the brow of the hill, discharging their fatal rifles with such startling effect as to practically destroy the front section of their opponents' advance, and those who followed, says Holmes, 'were much thinned and wounded', as the men of the 24th and 28th detachments, from their almost impregnable situation from above, fired volley after volley into the surging mass below.

Many were the brave attempts to overcome this unexpected natural obstacle, and reach the enemy's lines above. Basden himself, at the head of the foremost section, reached a point within three yards of the position held by the adversary, when a bullet, fired with fatal precision, laid him low, dangerously wounded in the upper part of the right thigh. As the invaders fought behind cover, few, if any, of them were struck during this vain but brave attempt of the British Regulars to carry the hill. The troops were therefore reluctantly obliged to abandon the charge and take refuge in diffused order behind trees at the bottom of the ravine, and at from twenty to thirty paces from the American line, and place their sole dependence upon the rifle.

This change of tactics, nevertheless, was largely neutralized from the fact that the enemy's regulars were now ordered to kneel upon the ground, so that the brow of the heights might protect them as far as possible from their opponents' view. The firing on both sides was still carried on with great vivacity. The cover afforded the British by the trees, however, proved in many cases to be quite insufficient, by reason of their frequently standing in squads behind the same tree, while the enemy discharged their rifles upon them from an extended front. The crisis of the day, at all events, was now over. From the close and rapid firing of the enemy stationed upon the heights, and also from the favored nature of their situation, the British dared not uncover, and under the circumstances a second charge up the hill was entirely out of the question. On the right flank of the enemy, the Indian attack was from the beginning necessarily weak, although they fought from behind trees, yet owing to the protected character of their antagonists' position, and the inherent inability of the red man to make any such attack as the circumstances of this particular case required, the American lines were at this point also incapable of being carried. On the enemy's left flank, however, the Canadian Rangers and Militia were on the point of scaling the invaders' works, when, through the failure of the front attack by the Regulars, and not being properly supported in consequence thereof, they were also repulsed.

Unable to sustain the unequal conflict, and favored also by the fast approaching shades of night, the British, amid repeated shouts of 'Hurrah for Kentucky!' from the detachment of the 28th still ringing in their ears, withdrew, after a close and gallant contest extending over a period of an hour and a half.

Ensign Mills of the 89th, upon whom the command devolved after the fall of Basden, wrote from the field just after the conclusion of the fight to Captain Stewart and handed his letter giving a few details of the fight to him. It will be remembered that Stewart was detained at Delaware and only arrived at the field near the conclusion of the action. In his letter, among other things, Mills says, 'I have the satisfaction to assure you that every man did his duty, and that we retired in perfectly good order.' On the day following the engagement (March 5th) Stewart wrote to Maj.-Gen. Riall,[4] who was afterwards taken prisoner at the battle of Lundy's Lane, July 25th, 1814, a brief account of this action, and enclosed Ensign Mills's letter. After having concluded his business at Delaware, Stewart hurried through the forest towards Twenty Mile Creek, and reached Battle Hill just previous to the close of the action, and on the following morning wrote Riall to the above effect. . . .

The losses of the British in this action were considerable, taking into account the number of men engaged, and amounted in all to 14 killed, 52

[4] [Phineas Riall (1775-1850) became a captain in 1794 and by 1811 was a lieutenant-colonel in the 69th Regiment. Following his arrival in Canada in November 1813 he led the destructive raids upon Lewiston and Black Rock. He was in charge of the Niagara frontier at the time of the American invasion of June 1814 and commanded at the battle of Chippawa and made the stand at Lundy's Lane. He was wounded and taken prisoner in the battle that followed. In 1831 he received a knighthood and he was made a general in 1841.]

wounded (six of whom died within one week after the action) and one missing. Volunteer Piggett, who had joined the detachment of the 89th only a few days before this action, besides being wounded was also taken prisoner. . . . No account seems to have been taken of any killed or wounded among the Indians.

The losses of the invaders, owing to their having fought from a sheltered position, only amounted to four killed and three wounded, including a non-commissioned officer. Says Kingsford, 'Although great gallantry was shown in the attack, it was most ill-judged, and led to the serious casualties already narrated, with no prospect of success.' The American Commandant forbore to pursue the British when they retired from the fatal ravines and over the eastern hills, as he was well aware that should he do so the same advantage of position would then accrue to them which had that afternoon been so highly beneficial to himself. Had he advanced into the ravine from his position on the western hills he would in all probability have been caught by the British in the identical trap in which they themselves had such hurtful experience only an hour or so previously, and of which they would in that event be very likely to make good use, especially as the creek could only be crossed by means of the same bridge over which the gallant Regulars had passed so lately, were he to commence a pursuit by means of mounted troops. Moreover, his soldiers being greatly fatigued and frost-bitten, and their shoes cut to pieces by the frozen ground, he was unable on this account also to follow up his foes on foot. The above reasons given by this clever officer for not pursuing the British and taking advantage of his victory seem at first sight to savor rather of the nature of excuses than reasons, yet taking into consideration all the circumstances of the case there is much to be said in favor of his conclusions. The British force engaged in this action amounted to 240 men, composed of the following corps:

Royal Scots Flank Company	101 men
89th Regiment Light Company	45 men
Militia and Rangers	50 men
Indians	44 men
Total	240 men

The whole American strength engaged in this conflict numbered one hundred and sixty-four men, computed as follows:

Regulars	94 men
Rangers and Militia Dragoons	70 men
Total	164 men

The latter had, however, the inestimable advantage of a superior location, together with an excellent knowledge of bush fighting, which threw the possibilities as well as the probabilities of success into their hands from the very beginning of the action. The great inequality of loss in this fight is therefore to be attributed to the judicious position chosen by Holmes (or rather chosen by the renegade Canadian who, according to tradition, selected it for him and also suggested pouring water on the face of the hill to make ice), who compelled Basden to attack him at a very great disadvantage; and this very event of itself, we are assured by one writer, more than his bravery deserves the reward of success. . . .

Holmes was, however, well aware that, notwithstanding his success at 'Battle Hill', his prospects for the capture of either Delaware or Port Talbot were now more remote than ever, since a superior force – although a lately beaten one – lay between him and either of these places, and he could not hope for a blunder like Basden's to be repeated. He therefore began a rapid march from the field at Twenty Mile Creek at nine o'clock on the evening of this action of Friday, March 4th, 1814, and reached Detroit, a distance of about ninety miles from the scene of his late conflict, in time to allow Butler to make a short report of the fight to Major-General Harrison, under date of March 7th, which report was transmitted to headquarters through Lieut. Shannon of the 27th New York.

The ground upon which this conflict took place is now known as south half of lot seven, in the first range north of the Longwoods Road, in the Township of Mosa, and County of Middlesex, and the north half of lot seven, in the first range south of Longwoods Road in the same township. The former lands were granted by the Crown to the late David Conradt by patent bearing date the 3rd day of November, 1830, and the latter were also granted by Crown patent to the late Jeremiah Grey on the 22nd day of July, 1831.

Formerly pieces of old muskets, rifles, military buttons, bullets, and other reminders of an age of strife were from time to time picked up on the scene of this forest conflict at Battle Hill. These finds, however, became rarer and rarer as time passed on, until now they have, to all intents and purposes, ceased to have existence, notwithstanding the efforts of the modern relic-hunter. The late Jeremiah Grey, of whom mention has just been made, ploughed up at the edge of the creek in the ravine, about the year 1870, the skeleton of some poor long-forgotten victim of Basden's wild charge up the western heights. Some time previous to this discovery, the bones of another soldier (evidently an American) were disinterred in the sandfield, just in the rear of the position occupied by the 24th and 28th detachments of the invader's force on that bleak afternoon of Friday, the 4th day of March, 1814. . . .

The muse of history has time and again sung the praises of the courageous and unsuccessful assault made by the soldiers of Pickett's Brigade of the Confederate army upon Cemetery Hill, the key to the Federal position, on the last day of the fierce battle of Gettysburg, July 3rd, 1863. She has been equally loud in her commendations of the gallant charge of the British troops upon the rocky precipices of Spion Kop during the late war in South Africa, and which has become familiar to nearly every person living throughout the length and breadth of our land. But it may be said, and in fact repeated, that within the limits of the County of Middlesex today there are not perhaps a dozen individuals familiar with the correct official accounts of this equally brave and daring attack upon the icy snow-clad heights at Battle Hill on the cold winter's afternoon of Friday, the 4th day of March, 1814.

Canadians, as a rule, make no boast of their loyalty any more than they do of the other manly virtues which they quite properly claim to be their national characteristics. The hillsides overshadowing the ravine at Twenty Mile Creek are the monuments of the gallant dead reposing beneath their shades; their names and the heroic efforts which they made at this place and set forth in the pages of history are the inscriptions recorded thereon. Even at this date can we not, by copying the lessons set so admirably before us by other sister societies, place a simple memorial here, commemorating the heroic death at Battle Hill of Captain Johnston and Lieutenant Graeme, as well as the other brave and unnamed regulars who died that Canada might live and our glorious heritage of freedom be preserved to us throughout the succeeding ages. The hand would surely wither which could desecrate that stone.

FURTHER READING: E. A. Cruikshank (ed.), *Documentary history . . .*, part IX, pages 204-5, 218-19, 223-6, 230-1, 292; W. C. H. Wood (ed.), *Select British documents . . .*, volume 2, pages 347-56; E. L. Jones, 'The Long Woods', *Canadian Army Journal*, volume 12 (1958), pages 64-76.

This article follows the war into the region of the upper Great Lakes, where the British held Michilimackinac and controlled the upper Mississippi region. The little schooner 'Nancy', driven north by the American victory on Lake Erie, became part of the new system established for supplying these positions. It was placed in service transporting cargo brought to Georgian Bay over a new route opened from York across the Nottawasaga portage. In 1814 an American flotilla ascended Lake Huron and the 'Nancy' was destroyed during an attack upon the new harbour. . . . The following account provides useful insights into a remote, little-known combat theatre of the war, and into the first steps in the development of Toronto's hinterland in Georgian Bay and beyond. It appeared originally in the 'Papers and Records' of the Ontario Historical Society (volume 9, 1908) and is reprinted with the approval of the Society and of Mrs. Cruikshank.

An Episode of the War of 1812: The Story of the Schooner *Nancy*

BY ERNEST A. CRUIKSHANK

In the summer of 1789, the firm of Forsyth, Richardson & Co., fur merchants of Montreal, undertook the construction of a schooner for the navigation of the upper lakes. . . . John Richardson, one of the partners, went to Detroit to superintend the work, in which he was deeply interested.

'The schooner', he wrote on the 23rd September, 1789, 'will be a perfect masterpiece of workmanship and beauty. The expense to us will be great, but there will be the satisfaction of her being strong and very durable. Her floor timbers, keel, keelson, stem, and lower uttock are oak. The transom, stern-post, upper uttocks, top timbers, beams, and knees are all red cedar. She will carry 350 barrels.'

He ordered a suitable figure-head of 'a lady dressed in the present fashion with a hat and feather' from the carver Skelling of New York. The schooner was launched on the 24th September, 1789, 'a most beautiful and substantial vessel', and in the spring following made her first voyage from Detroit to Fort Erie, whence she sailed upwards in June with a full cargo, bound for the Grand Portage at Sault Ste. Marie, with the intention of visiting Mackinac on her way back.

'She is spoken of here', Richardson wrote from Niagara, 'in such a high strain of encomium as to beauty, stowage, and sailing, that she almost exceeds my expectations.'

By 1793, the *Nancy* had become the property of George Leith Co., and is described as being of sixty-seven tons burden. Some time before the end of the century, she passed into the possession of the Northwest Fur Company, by whom she was employed in the transportation of furs and merchandise on lakes Erie, Huron, and Michigan. In 1805 she was navigated by Capt. Wm. Mills, who had some years before owned her in connection with Forsyth, Richardson, and Sir Alexander Mackenzie of Montreal. In a list of merchant vessels prepared early in 1812 by Colonel Matthew Elliott for the information of Major-General Brock, the *Nancy* is described as a schooner of about one hundred tons, lying at McIntosh's wharf, at Moy, opposite Detroit.

On July 1st, 1812, when the declaration of war by the United States became known to Lieutenant-Colonel St. George, the commandant of the British Garrison at Amherstburg, she was still lying at Moy waiting for a favorable wind to carry her into Lake Huron, and he at once ordered her to be brought down under the guns of that post to secure her from capture. Some light brass guns with which she had been armed were mounted in row-boats to patrol the river, and the schooner was impressed into the government service as a transport. On July 30th she sailed for Fort Erie under convoy of the Provincial schooner, *Lady Prevost.* Five days later she left Fort Erie on her return voyage, in company with the armed brig *General Hunter,* having on board sixty soldiers of the 41st Regiment and a quantity of military stores. The timely arrival of this small reinforcement had considerable weight among the reasons which induced General Hull to evacuate Canada.

During the summer and autumn of that year the *Nancy* was constantly employed in the important service of transporting troops, stores, and provisions between Detroit and Fort Erie. On April 23rd, 1813, she was included in the small squadron assembled to transport General Procter's division from Amherstburg to Miami Bay, to undertake the siege of Fort Meigs. . . .

[Shortly after the defeat of the British fleet on Lake Erie the *Nancy* was nearly captured at the head of the St. Clair River. On October 4, 1813, while the vessel was entering the river on a voyage from St. Joseph's down to Amherstburg, a demand was made that the ship surrender. When Captain McIntosh refused, the *Nancy* was fired upon, but it succeeded in escaping unharmed back into Lake Huron.]

As early as the 3rd of October, Captain Bullock had received information of the disastrous result of the battle on Lake Erie from Major-General Procter, who informed him that he had already recommended that supplies for his garrison should be forwarded from York to Matchedash Bay. His stock of provisions was then nearly exhausted, but by purchasing everything that could be obtained in the small settlements on the mainland he succeeded in laying in enough to keep his men until February. The *Nancy* arrived on the 18th with her sails and cables so badly damaged as to render her unfit to navigate the lake during the storms of autumn, and Captain McIntosh determined to take her to the Northwest Company's post, at Sault Ste. Marie, in the hope of procuring the necessary materials to refit her during the winter. Before he sailed, Robert Dickson,[1] Agent for the Western Indians, arrived from Matchedash on his way to Prairie du Chien.[2] After consulting with him, Bullock proposed that six gun-boats should be built at Matchedash to keep open the communication and protect supplies on their way to Mackinac, and requested that the garrison should be reinforced early in the spring by twenty artillerymen and two hundred infantry with four field guns. An officer and twenty-seven men of the Michigan Fencibles[3] were at once detached with Mr. Dickson to establish a post at Green Bay and the remainder of the garrison was put on short rations.

Continued stormy weather made it impossible to send forward any supplies from Matchedash before navigation closed, but it also prevented the American squadron from entering Lake Huron to undertake the reduction of Mackinac as had been at first intended.

The Governor-General was, however, fully impressed with the great importance of maintaining possession of that place, and lost no time in preparing a small force for its relief as soon as the lake again became navigable. . . .

Lieutenant-Colonel Robert McDouall of the Glengarry Light Infantry,

[1] [Robert Dickson (1767?-1823) was an important fur trader on the upper Mississippi and deputy superintendent in the Indian department with the rank of lieutenant-colonel. He was largely instrumental in bringing the western Indians into the war on the side of the British and commanded at the capture of Michilimackinac by Roberts on July 17, 1812. He was afterwards associated with Lord Selkirk in the founding of the Red River Colony and died at Drummond Island.]

[2] [Prairie du Chien, a trading post on the Upper Mississippi River, was held for Britain early in the war but was taken by an American expedition from St. Louis under General William Clark, the explorer and Governor of Northwest Territory, early in 1814. Although it meant dangerously weakening his garrison at Michilimackinac, Lieutenant-Colonel McDouall sent an expedition under Major William McKay to recover the post because of the potential effect of the American success upon the Indians of that region. McKay reached Prairie du Chien on July 17, 1814, with a force of some 120 white men and over 400 Indians. The American garrison surrendered after a two-day siege. A later attempt by Major Zachary Taylor to recover the position was repulsed in September 1814.]

[3] [A volunteer unit raised at Michilimackinac by William Bailey and commanded by Captain William McKay from January 1814 until it was disbanded on July 24, 1815. During the summer of 1814 it took part in the engagements at Prairie du Chien and Michilimackinac.]

an officer of tried courage and discretion, was selected for the command of this expedition. About the end of February 1814, McDouall crossed Lake Simcoe on the ice, following the Nine Mile Portage from Kempenfeldt Bay to the head waters of the Nottawasaga River, where he was directed to select a suitable place for building the necessary boats for the conveyance of troops and stores across Lake Huron. He was accompanied by a party of shipwrights, twenty-one seamen, eleven artillerymen in charge of four field guns, and two companies of the Royal Newfoundland Regiment, many of whom were expert boatmen. Although this route had the merit of being shorter than that by way of Matchedash yet it was less known and much obstructed by rocks and shoals which in many places rendered the channel so narrow that nothing larger than bateaux could pass. Favored by the unusual mildness of the season, McDouall began the descent of the river on the 19th of April, with thirty bateaux of the largest class, heavily loaded with provision and military stores. Six days later, he sailed from its mouth, and after an extremely hazardous and stormy voyage arrived at Mackinac, on May 18th, with the loss of but a single boat, the crew and cargo of which were saved. . . .

Dickson arrived at Mackinac a few days later, bringing with him two hundred picked warriors, and every effort was made to strengthen the defences of the island. It was proposed that the *Nancy* should be cut down to the dimensions of a gunboat and armed with the guns brought from the Nottawasaga, but as it was evident that she could not keep the lake in the face of the overwhelming force which the enemy could bring up from Lake Erie, McDouall became satisfied that he could make better use of these guns on shore and she was accordingly retained in service as a transport and sent away for a cargo of supplies. . . .

Meanwhile, a formidable expedition for the recovery of Mackinac had been organized at Detroit. The land force consisted of a detachment of United States Artillery, with several guns and howitzers, a battalion of regular infantry, composed of picked companies from the 17th, 19th, and 24th regiments, and a battalion of Ohio Volunteers, numbering in all nearly a thousand men. Lieutenant-Colonel George Croghan,[4] who had gained much reputation among his countrymen by his successful defence of Fort Stephenson, was selected for the command of these troops, and Major A. H. Holmes, who had lately conducted a vigorous raid from Detroit up the Thames as far as Delaware, was given the second place as commandant of the regulars. Six of the largest vessels of the Lake Erie squadron, mounting sixty guns and manned by more than five hundred seamen and marines under

[4] [George Croghan (1791-1849) entered the United States army in 1810 and was promoted to the rank of lieutenant-colonel for his defence of Fort Stephenson against Procter in 1813. He resigned from the army in 1817, served as postmaster at New Orleans in 1824, then re-enlisted as inspector-general. He was a colonel in the Mexican War, serving under General Taylor.]

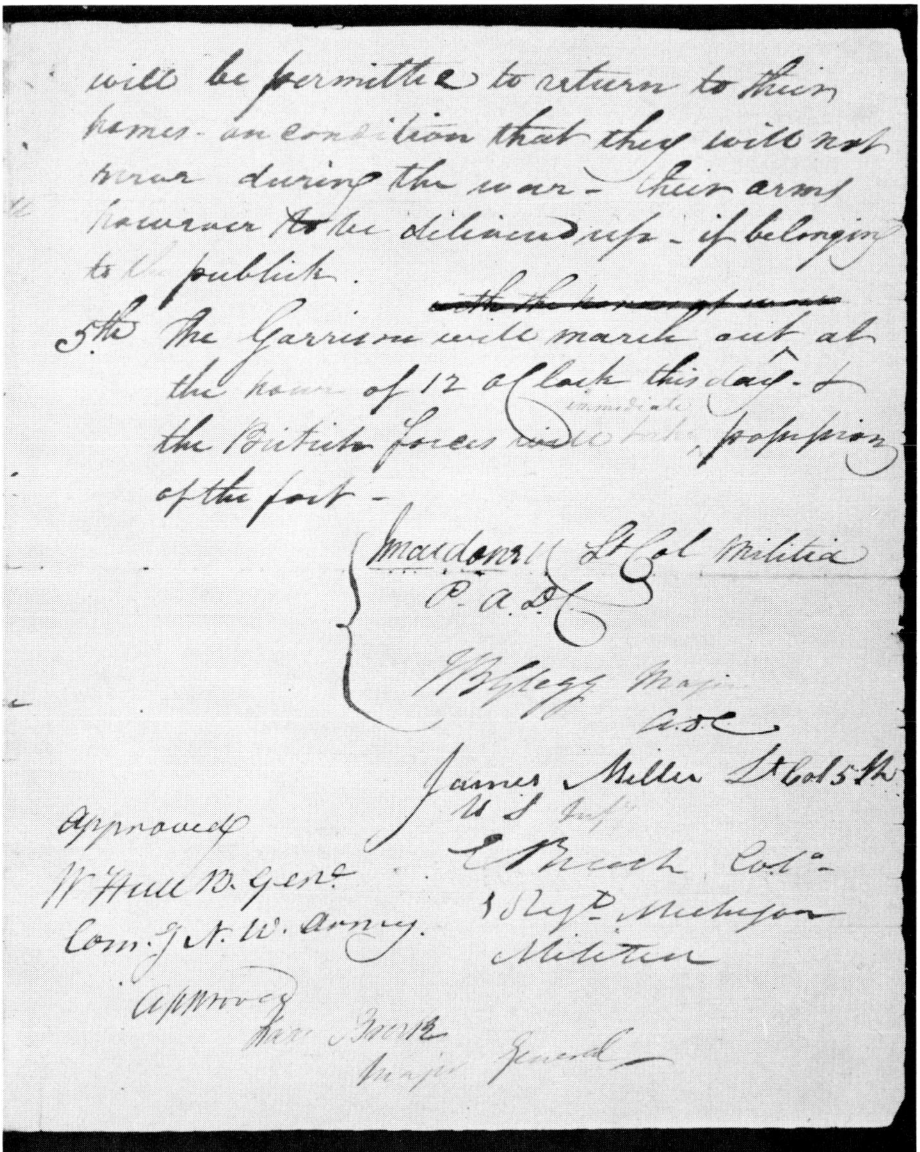
will be permitted to return to their homes - on condition that they will not serve during the war - their arms however to be delivered up - if belonging to the publick.

5th The Garrison will march out at the hour of 12 o'clock this day - & the British forces will take immediate possession of the fort -

J. Macdonell Lt Col Militia
P. A. D. C.

J. B. Glegg Major
A. D. C.

James Miller Lt Col 5th
U S Infy

E Brush Col
1 Regt Michigan
Militia

Approved
W Hull B. Genl
Comg N. W. Army.

Approved
Isaac Brock
Major General

Last page of the Articles of Capitulation of Brigadier-General Hull's force at Fort Detroit, August 16, 1812.

'A scene on Lake Ontario – United States sloop of war *Gen. Pike,* Commodore Chauncey, and the British sloop of war *Wolfe,* Sir James Yeo, preparing for action, September 28, 1813.'

The attack on Fort Oswego, Lake Ontario, May 6, 1814. The vessels in the foreground are the *Prince Regent* and the *Princess Charlotte,* with the *Charwell* and the *Star* covering the landing. On the right, in Oswego Bay, are the *Montreal,* the *Niagara,* and the *Magnet.*

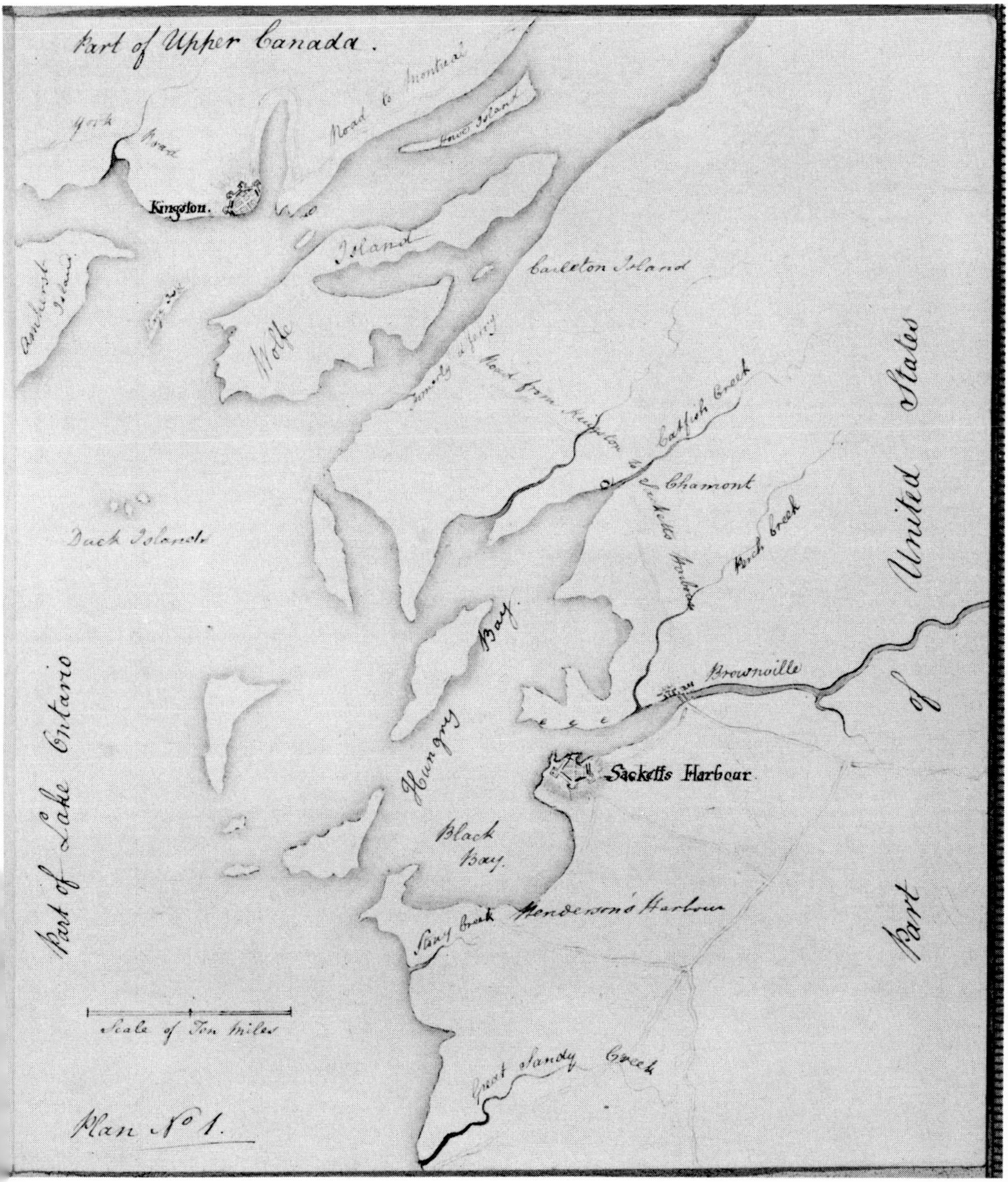

The Kingston–Sackets Harbor area of Lake Ontario, from an unsigned, undated manuscript presumably prepared in 1814 or 1815, listing and describing the fortifications of Sackets Harbor.

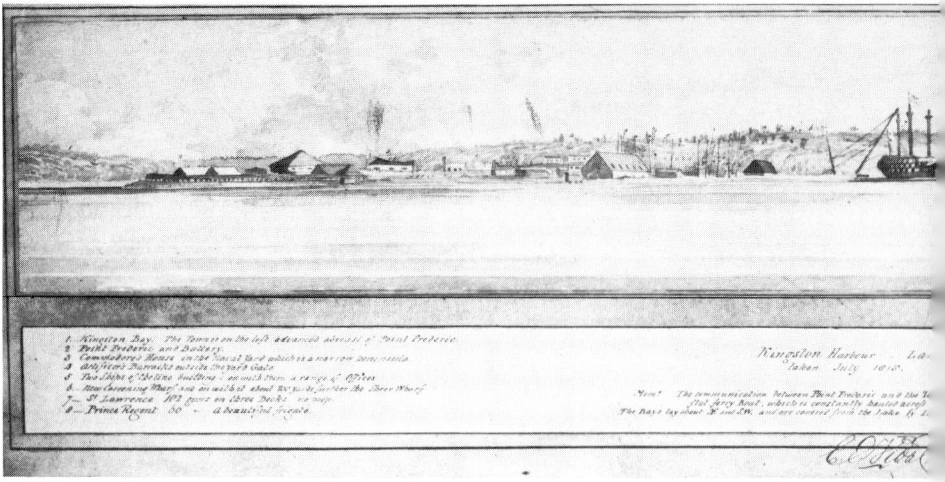

BRITISH COMMANDERS ON THE LAKES

Sir James Lucas Yeo
1782-1818

Robert Heriot Barclay
1785-1837

AMERICAN COMMANDERS ON THE LAKES

Oliver Hazard Perry
1785-1819

Isaac Chauncey
1772-1840

BRITISH MILITARY COMMANDERS AND ADMINISTRATORS

Sir Isaac Brock
1769-1812

Sir George Prevost, Bart.
1767-1816

Sir Roger Hale Sheaffe, Bart.
1763-1851

Sir Gordon Drummond
1771-1854

AMERICAN COMMANDERS IN THE CAMPAIGNS ON THE CANADIAN FRONTIER

William Hull
1753-1825

Henry Dearborn
1751-1829

William Henry Harrison
1773-1841

Winfield Scott
1786-1866

This fanciful engraving, some twenty-five years after the event, bears the inscription: 'Battle of the Thames, 5th Octr. 1813, Respectfully dedicated to the Real Hero Col. Richard M. Johnson, Vice-President of the United States.'

'Fort Erie – Defence of the blockhouse' – 1814

Commodore Sinclair,[5] provided with launches for landing artillery, were detailed to convey these troops to their destination. Sinclair sailed from Detroit on the 3rd of July but did not succeed in entering Lake Huron until the 12th, when he shaped his course for Matchedash Bay where he had been informed that the British had established a depot of supplies and were building gunboats, but having no pilot familiar with those waters and being enveloped for several days in a dense fog in a perfect maze of islets and sunken rocks the attempt was abandoned and he steered for the Island of St. Joseph. Arriving there on the 20th July, he learned that the military post had been abandoned a few weeks before and the garrison withdrawn to Mackinac. While his squadron lay windbound near this place, the Northwest Company's schooner *Mink*, on her way from Mackinac to Sault Ste. Marie, was intercepted and taken by his boats, which were then despatched to destroy the trading station at the latter place. This was accomplished without opposition, but much of the property deposited there had been removed before their arrival.

On July 26th the American squadron came in sight of Mackinac. Its presence in the lake had been known to the garrison for some time, and every possible precaution had been taken in anticipation of an attack. A strong redoubt had been completed on the summit of the cliff overlooking the former works which so greatly increased their strength that McDouall considered his position one of the strongest in Canada. 'We are in a very fine state of defence here,' he wrote, 'the garrison and Indians are in the highest spirits and all ready for the attack of the enemy. We apprehend nothing for the island but from want of provisions.'

The *Nancy* had already made two successful trips to the Nottawasaga and sailed again for that place a few days before. A message to her commander, warning him of the appearance of the American squadron off Mackinac and advising him to take his vessel as far up the river as possible and remain there until the blockade of the island was at an end, was entrusted to Lieutenant Robert Livingston,[6] a daring and adventurous officer of the Indian Department, who volunteered to deliver it. . . .

[5] [Arthur Sinclair joined the American navy as a midshipman in 1798, served in the undeclared war with France and against the Barbary pirates, and became a lieutenant in 1807 and a captain in 1813. He succeeded O. H. Perry as commander on Lake Erie.]

[6] [Robert Livingstone served in the British navy and the Royal Canadian Volunteers, became a fur trader and was living on St. Joseph's island in 1812. During the early months of the war he commanded a company of volunteers at the capture of Michilimackinac, was captured during Hull's advance and was freed when Detroit fell to Brock. He was again taken prisoner near Fort George in August 1813 but escaped a few days later. In 1814 he was made a lieutenant in the Indian Department and subsequently acted as a courier. He assisted in the defence of the *Nancy* at Nottawasaga and in the capture of the *Tigress* and *Scorpion* in September 1814.]

Foul weather prevented the American vessels from approaching the shore for several days, but on August 1st a party of soldiers was landed on Round Island where they had a skirmish with some Indians. After carefully reconnoitring the harbour and the vicinity of the forts, Croghan decided to adopt the advice of former residents of the island who accompanied him as guides and attempt a landing on its western coast where there was a break in the cliffs and his largest ships could anchor within three hundred yards of the shore. From this place, however, he would be compelled to advance for nearly two miles through dense woods before reaching an open space where a favorable position existed for assailing the works 'by gradual and slow approaches' under cover of his artillery which he knew to be superior in range and weight of metal. Nearly a thousand men, including a body of marines, were accordingly landed on the morning of August 4th and began their march across the island.

McDouall promptly advanced to meet them with one hundred and forty men of the Royal Newfoundland Regiment and Michigan Fencibles and about one hundred and fifty Indians, mostly of the Folles Avoines or Menomonee tribe from the Wisconsin River, whom he considered the bravest and best fighting men of any at his disposal. With this force he occupied an excellent position in which his men were hidden among thickets and underwood on the edge of a small clearing across which the enemy must pass in their advance, yet it could easily be turned as there were paths leading around either flank which he had not force enough to guard. When the enemy came in sight, he opened fire upon them from two field guns, without effect except to check their advance and cause them to attempt a movement around the clearing in the direction of his left flank. But the battalion of regular troops which undertook this flank march was suddenly assailed by a party of Menomonees from an ambush among the thickets. Their first fire killed Major Holmes and severely wounded Captain Desha, next in command. Two other officers, Captain Van Horne of the 19th and Lieutenant Jackson of the 24th Infantry, were mortally wounded and their men instantly fell into great confusion. A field piece was brought up, but the fire of their unseen foes was so effective and the disorder became so great that Croghan soon decided to retire to his shipping to avoid a worse disaster, leaving behind him two wounded men and the bodies of Major Holmes and others of the dead. . . .

Sinclair had learned from a prisoner taken in the *Mink* that reinforcements and supplies had arrived at Mackinac from the Nottawasaga River and that the *Nancy* had lately been despatched thither for more. By destroying her and blockading the river he hoped to retrieve his defeat and ultimately compel the garrison to surrender for want of provisions, and also prevent the Northwest Company from receiving any further supplies.

About the middle of July, Lieutenant Miller Worsley[7] of the Royal Navy, with a small detachment of seamen, had arrived at the mouth of the Nottawasaga, where he awaited the appearance of the *Nancy* for more than a week, suffering much discomfort from bad weather and swarms of mosquitoes. On her arrival, the schooner was loaded with three hundred barrels of provisions and a quantity of much-needed military stores, and on August 1st she again set sail for Mackinac. Before she entered the lake, Livingston met her with McDouall's instructions, and Worsley at once turned back. The *Nancy* was towed up the river about two miles to a place where she was hidden from view from the bay by intervening sandhills and the construction of a log blockhouse for her protection on a commanding position on the right bank was begun. Information of her perilous situation was sent to Lieutenant-General Drummond, who was then besieging Fort Erie, and he promptly gave orders for the assembly of a body of militia and Indians for her defence. But on the 13th of August, before these instructions could be fully carried into effect, part of the American squadron, consisting of the brig *Niagara* and the schooners *Scorpion* and *Tigress*, made their appearance in Nottawasaga Bay, having on board a detachment of artillery with several field guns and three companies of regular infantry under the command of Lieutenant-Colonel Croghan.

Lieutenant Livingston, who had returned that morning from York with despatches, was at once employed in assembling the neighboring Indians, but only succeeded in mustering twenty-three. Worsley had under his command Midshipman Dobson and twenty-one seamen of the Royal Navy and nine French Canadian boatmen. Three guns had been mounted in the blockhouse, two of which were twenty-four pounder carronades, taken from boats lying in the river, and the other was a six pounder field piece. With such inadequate means Worsley gallantly undertook to offer the stoutest resistance possible. Late in the afternoon, Croghan landed his troops on the narrow peninsula separating the lower reach of the river from the bay, and while exploring it for the purpose of selecting a suitable place for encamping, he discovered the *Nancy* lying on the opposite side of the stream close under the guns of the blockhouse. Next morning Sinclair anchored all his vessels near the shore within easy range and opened fire with little effect, as both vessels and blockhouse were screened from view by the sandhills, surmounted by a thin belt of trees and bushes. About noon, however, two howitzers were landed and placed in a favorable position within a few hundred yards. Their fire speedily became so damaging that Worsley determined to destroy the

[7] [Miller Worsley succeeded Lieutenant Newdigate Poyntz as British naval commander on Lake Huron. He was promoted to commander in July 1815 for his part in the capture of the two American vessels. He was a commander in the British Coast Guard in 1833.]

schooner and retire into the woods. The guns had accordingly been spiked and a train of powder laid to the *Nancy* when a well directed shell burst inside the blockhouse, setting fire to a quantity of combustible material near the magazine which soon blew up, communicating the flames to the schooner which was entirely destroyed with her valuable cargo still on board.[8] Worsley had defended himself 'very handsomely', as Sinclair said, but lost only one man killed and another severely wounded. The Indians continued to fire for some time from the edge of the woods and no pursuit was attempted. Eventually Sinclair sent a party of men across the Nottawasaga in boats who brought off the guns from the smouldering ruins of the blockhouse and took away a bateau which had escaped destruction, after which they endeavored to obstruct the river by felling trees across it.

On the following day Sinclair sailed for Lake Erie in the *Niagara*, leaving Lieutenant Turner in command of the *Scorpion* and *Tigress*, with instructions to maintain a rigid blockade until 'driven from the lake by the inclemency of the season, suffering not a boat or canoe to pass in or out of this river', but authorizing him at the same time to detach the *Tigress* to cruise for a week or two at a time in the vicinity of St. Joseph's to intercept fur canoes passing between Sault Ste. Marie and French River. Twenty-five picked men from the 17th United States Infantry were detailed to serve on these vessels as marines, and the *Scorpion* was provided with a boarding netting as a protection against a night attack by small boats.

'Against attacks of this kind, which he might be driven to by his desperate situation, as this blockade must starve him into a surrender, I must particularly caution you,' Sinclair said in his instruction. 'If we can keep their boats from passing until October, I think the bad weather will effectually cut off all communication by anything they have on float, and in the spring an early blockade will possess us of Mackinac.'

A brigade of boats from Montreal, by way of French River, under Captain J. M. Lamotte, laden with supplies for Mackinac, received timely warning of their presence before entering Lake Huron and turned back to a place of safety.

Upwards of a hundred barrels of provisions still remained in a store-house several miles up the Nottawasaga which the enemy had not discovered, and two bateaux and Livingston's large canoe had escaped destruction. In these circumstances Worsley determined to elude the blockading vessels. The obstructions were quietly removed from the river, seventy barrels of provisions were taken on board, and, on the night of the 18th, he entered the bay without being observed. Six days later, when within a few miles of St. Joseph's,

[8] For two round trips of the *Nancy* from Detroit River to Fort Erie, in 1812, the Northwest Company claimed and received £500. For her services in 1813-14, her owners were allowed £1,243 5s. 0d. and the further sum of £2,200 as compensation for the loss of the vessel.

after rowing three hundred and sixty miles along the north shore of the lake, he was greatly surprised to discover both the schooners which he had seen in Nottawasaga Bay a week before, cruising among the islands ahead. As it would be scarcely possible to pass them unobserved, with his heavily-loaded boats in the narrow channel known as the Detour which they were evidently watching, he turned back and concealed them in a secluded bay. His whole party of twenty-five persons then embarked in Livingston's canoe on the night of August 29th, and, after passing one of these vessels within a hundred yards in the darkness, arrived at Mackinac at sunset on September 1st.

Worsley lost no time after reaching the island in soliciting permission to lead an attack on the two schooners which were lying about fifteen miles apart when last seen by him. Next day four large rowboats were equipped for this enterprise. One of these, armed with a six-pounder, was manned by Midshipman Dobson, a gunner's mate and seventeen seamen of the Royal Navy, under Worsley himself. The other three were manned by a picked detachment of two sergeants, six corporals, and fifty privates of the Royal Newfoundland Regiment, commanded by Lieutenants Bulger,[9] Armstrong, and Radenhurst. Bulger's boat was armed with a three-pounder in charge of a bombardier and a gunner of the Royal Artillery. As it was reported that the blockading vessels were accompanied by a body of Indians, whom they had induced to co-operate with them, about two hundred warriors were also embarked in nineteen canoes, under the orders of Dickson and four officers of his department.

The expedition left Mackinac that evening, and at sunset on the 2nd of September arrived at the Detour, thirty-six miles distant, where they expected to find one of the schooners. The men were landed on the island and the boats concealed in a secluded bay. Early next morning Worsley and Livingston went out in a canoe to reconnoitre and soon discovered one of the schooners at anchor about six miles away. It was thought prudent to defer the attack until night when they could approach her unseen. At six o'clock the whole force was re-embarked and rowed as quietly as possible towards the enemy. When about three miles from the schooner the Indians were directed to remain behind and await further orders, but Dickson and three of their principal chiefs were taken on board the boats, making a total of ninety-two of all ranks. The night was very dark and still. About nine o'clock the outline of the schooner was described close ahead. It was then arranged that Worsley's and Armstrong's boats should board her upon the starboard side and

[9] [Andrew Bulger (1789-1858) was born in Newfoundland, joined the Royal Newfoundland Regiment in 1804, and reached the rank of captain in 1815. He saw action at Detroit, Fort George (December 1812), and Crysler's Farm, and commanded the military expedition for the relief of Michilimackinac in the summer of 1814. He served at Prairie du Chien (Fort Shelby) from November 1814 till May 1815 and in 1822-3 was governor of the Red River Colony.]

Bulger's and Radenhurst's on the larboard. Their approach was so noiseless that Worsley's boat was within ten yards of her and Bulger's not far behind when they were discovered and hailed. No answer being returned, a gun was fired without doing any injury and a hasty and ill-directed fire of musketry was opened upon them. In the face of this the boarders quickly gained the deck on both sides nearly at the same instant and within five minutes the commander of the schooner, Sailing Master Champlain, and all his officers were cut down with several of his men and the remainder driven below. From between-decks they kept up a desultory fire which killed one of Worsley's seamen. After all resistance had ceased it was ascertained that the prize was the *Tigress,* having a crew of thirty-one persons, of whom four were killed and four wounded. Worsley lost two seamen killed and one seaman wounded, but Lieutenant Bulger, Gunner McLaughlin, and six privates of the Royal Newfoundland Regiment were also wounded. The prisoners were sent away in boats under guard, and Livingston was despatched in a canoe to ascertain the position of the other schooner. In two hours he returned with information that she was apparently beating down toward the *Tigress* under sail.

As it seemed highly improbable that the firing could have been heard by her crew, Worsley determined not to alter the position of his prize and to keep the American colors flying. During the night of the 5th, the *Scorpion* anchored within two miles of the *Tigress* without making any effort to exchange signals or communicate with her in any way. At break of day next morning, Worsley slipped his cable and ran silently down towards her under the jib and foresail only with a dozen sailors in sight besides a few soldiers who were lying down covered with overcoats. Four or five of the *Scorpion*'s crew in charge of the gunner were scrubbing her deck, and although the approach of the *Tigress* was observed and duly reported it excited no suspicion in the minds of her officers. At the distance of a dozen yards the twenty-four-pounder on the *Tigress* was fired into the *Scorpion*'s hull as a signal for the remainder of the soldiers to rush on deck. Worsley then ran alongside and grappled with her. The boarders fired a single volley and sprang on her deck, meeting with scarcely any resistance from her bewildered crew, of whom two were killed and two wounded before they surrendered. Like the *Tigress,* the *Scorpion* mounted a single twenty-four-pounder but also had a twelve-pounder in her hold, the carriage of which had become unfit for use. She was commanded by Lieutenant Daniel Turner and had a crew of five officers and thirty-one soldiers, seamen, and soldiers.

It appeared that these vessels had been forced out of Nottawasaga Bay by a fierce gale which had nearly driven the *Niagara* on shore after parting from them and even compelled Sinclair to cut loose his launch and the captured boat which he was towing astern. For the last five days the *Scor-*

pion had been cruising between St. Joseph's and the French River in the hope of intercepting Lamotte's Brigade of boats from Montreal, of whose approach they had received some information. In her capture Worsley had but a single seaman wounded. He had regained entire control of Lake Huron and effectually relieved Mackinac from all danger of being forced to surrender from want of provisions. This expedition was admirably planned and executed and certainly richly deserved the success with which it was crowned. The prizes were fine vessels for lake service and were at once placed in commission under the names of the *Surprise* and the *Confiance*. They sailed at once for the Nottawasaga whence they returned in the beginning of October with a supply of provisions sufficient to maintain the garrison of Mackinac for six months.

FURTHER READING: W. C. H. Wood (ed.), *Selected British documents . . .*, volume 3, part 1, pages 250-82; A. R. Gilpin, *The War of 1812 in the old northwest* (Toronto, 1958); G. F. G. Stanley, 'British operations in the American north-west 1812-1815', *Journal of the Society for Army Historical Research*, volume 22 (1943), pages 91-106.

The character of the war changed appreciably in 1814. Operations were on a greater scale and involved larger bodies of trained soldiers, militia as well as regulars. The numerical superiority of the Americans was becoming felt increasingly in Upper Canada though victory in Europe at last permitted Britain to carry the war against the coasts of the United States. The summer brought a series of desperate engagements along the Niagara frontier, notably the battles of Chippawa and Lundy's Lane and the protracted siege of Fort Erie. That siege was prosecuted without success for more than two months at a cost of over 1,500 casualties to the besiegers. Then, after the siege had been abandoned, the fort was evacuated and blown up by the retreating Americans, an ironic final act of a war that had ground to a stalemate in Upper Canada. . . . The following extract from Mr. Cruikshank's study of the siege deals with the most harrowing single episode of the campaign, the costly effort to storm the fortress by a night attack. It is taken from 'The Siege of Fort Erie', published in 1905 by the Lundy's Lane Historical Society, and appears through the consent of Mrs. Cruikshank and of the Society.

Drummond's Night Assault upon Fort Erie August 15-16, 1814

BY ERNEST A. CRUIKSHANK

Drummond determined to make the assault in three columns with the intention of assailing simultaneously every accessible part of the fortifications. The first and strongest of these, commanded by Lieut.-Colonel J. Fischer of the Regiment de Watteville,[1] consisting of the remnant of the 1st Battalion of the 8th Regiment, the light companies of the 89th and 100th, as many volunteers from the Regiment de Watteville as could be obtained, and a dozen gunners of the Royal Artillery, was instructed to move from the camp

[1] [De Watteville's Regiment was a unit of Swiss soldiers raised by Abraham Louis Charles de Watteville and taken into British service in 1801. It fought in Malta, Egypt, Sicily, Italy, and Spain before reaching Canada in May 1813. Here de Watteville was appointed to the general staff with the rank of major-general, so the regiment was commanded in turn by lieutenant-colonels Victor Fischer and Rodolphe de May. The regiment played a leading part in the assault on Oswego in May 1814 before being added to the besiegers of Fort Erie. After the war, more than 150 of the men took up land in the Perth Settlement, Upper Canada.]

at four o'clock in the afternoon and march westward along the Concession or Garrison Road for about four miles, when turning to the left they would gain the lake shore at Baxter's farm. Until they reached this point their movements would be effectually screened by dense woods. Here they were to halt until eleven o'clock. No fires were to be lighted and no loud talking permitted, and every precaution was to be taken to prevent desertion. The rolls were to be called every hour and no officer allowed to leave his command. To further ensure silence and secrecy the flints were to be removed from the firelocks of all except a reserve of very steady men. It was anticipated that these precautions might enable this column to take the garrison in that part of the works by surprise and effect an entrance between Snake Hill and the water, where a space was reported as being sufficiently open to admit the passage of a small body of troops. If they succeeded in doing this they were to turn at once to the left and assail the occupants of the Snake Hill battery and adjacent line in flank or attack their reserves at the building known as the White House. It was hoped that the removal of their flints would 'effectually conceal the situation and number of our troops, and those of the enemy being exposed by his fire and his white trousers, which are very conspicuous marks to our view, it will enable them to use the bayonet with the effect which that valuable weapon has ever been found to possess in the hands of British soldiers'. If the storming party failed to penetrate into the camp at this point it was provided with hay-bags and short ladders to scale the works elsewhere. This attack was to commence at two o'clock in the morning. As nearly the whole of the Regiment de Watteville volunteered with alacrity, Fischer's command exceeded a thousand men, and as General Drummond had purposely avoided any previous demonstration on that flank he believed he had succeeded in drawing the attention of the garrison to their right. The Snake Hill battery was considered the key of their position, and if Fischer succeeded in carrying it there could be little doubt of his final success. . . .

The centre column, commanded by Lieut.-Colonel William Drummond of the 104th Regiment, a nephew of the General and a very gallant and distinguished officer, consisting of a small detachment of Royal Artillery under Lieut. Charleton, the flank companies of the 41st and 104th Regiments, fifty marines, and ninety seamen, about 360 officers and men in all, was designed to enter the fort itself by escalade when the attacks elsewhere were well developed. It was guided by Captain Barnes of the 89th Regiment, and Lieut-Colonel Drummond had personally selected Sergeant Richard Smith of his own regiment for the desperate service of leading the forlorn hope, encouraging him with the prospect of receiving a commission if successful.

The left column was composed entirely of the effectives of the 103rd Regiment, about 700 strong, under their colonel, Hercules Scott of Brotherton, an exceedingly brave and spirited but irascible officer, who had openly quarrelled with General Drummond and made no secret of his lack of confidence in him. He could, however, be trusted to lead his men into action at all times with the utmost gallantry and coolness. Before leaving his quarters that evening he had openly criticized the plan of attack, but at the last moment seemed in high spirits and shook hands with his surgeon, saying: 'We shall breakfast together in the fort in the morning.' Captain Eliot, Deputy Quartermaster General, was assigned as guide to this column, which was directed to attack the right of the American position between the fort and the river, and endeavor to penetrate through the opening next the salient angle of the bastion, using their ladders at the same to scale the intrenchment.

The remnants of the 1st Battalion of the Royal Scots, the Glengarry Light Infantry, Incorporated Militia, and the remainder of de Watteville's Regiment constituted the reserve under Lieut.-Colonel Tucker and was directed to occupy the ground where the picquets and covering parties had been posted during the day. The squadron of the 19th Light Dragoons was instructed to take post in rear of the battery nearest the fort, in readiness to escort prisoners to the rear. General Drummond also took his position at this battery to watch the assault. 'The Lieutenant-General *most strongly recommends the free use* of the bayonet,' his secret order added. If the assaulting columns met within the works they were to recognize each other by the watchword 'Prince Regent', answered by the countersign 'Twenty'. 'As proposals of surrender may possibly be made to you,' his instructions said, 'you are to attend to none which are not unconditional, not suffering yourself for a moment to be diverted from the prosecution of your attack. Clemency to prisoners it is unnecessary to recommend to you, but in removing them you must be careful not to detach too many men.'

As Lieut.-Colonel Fischer's column was as strong as the other two combined, it is evident that General Drummond based his chief hope of success upon its ability to carry the Snake Hill battery and take the remainder of the intrenchments in reverse. But, by thus dividing his force into two nearly equal bodies with an impassable forest between them, it is apparent that he exposed either wing to the danger of being overwhelmed by a sudden and vigorous counterattack. . . .

The signs of activity which he had observed in [the British] lines led General Gaines[2] to suspect that an assault might be attempted by them that

[2] [Edmund Pendleton Gaines (1777-1849) entered the army of the United States in 1797 and in 1807 arrested Aaron Burr and testified against him at his trial in Richmond, Virginia. For his defence of Fort Erie he was promoted to brigadier-general. After the war he served in the campaigns against the Creeks and Seminoles and in the Black Hawk War. He was in command of the Western Department at the outbreak of the Mexican War but was soon removed from his post on charges of exceeding his authority in the calling up of recruits.]

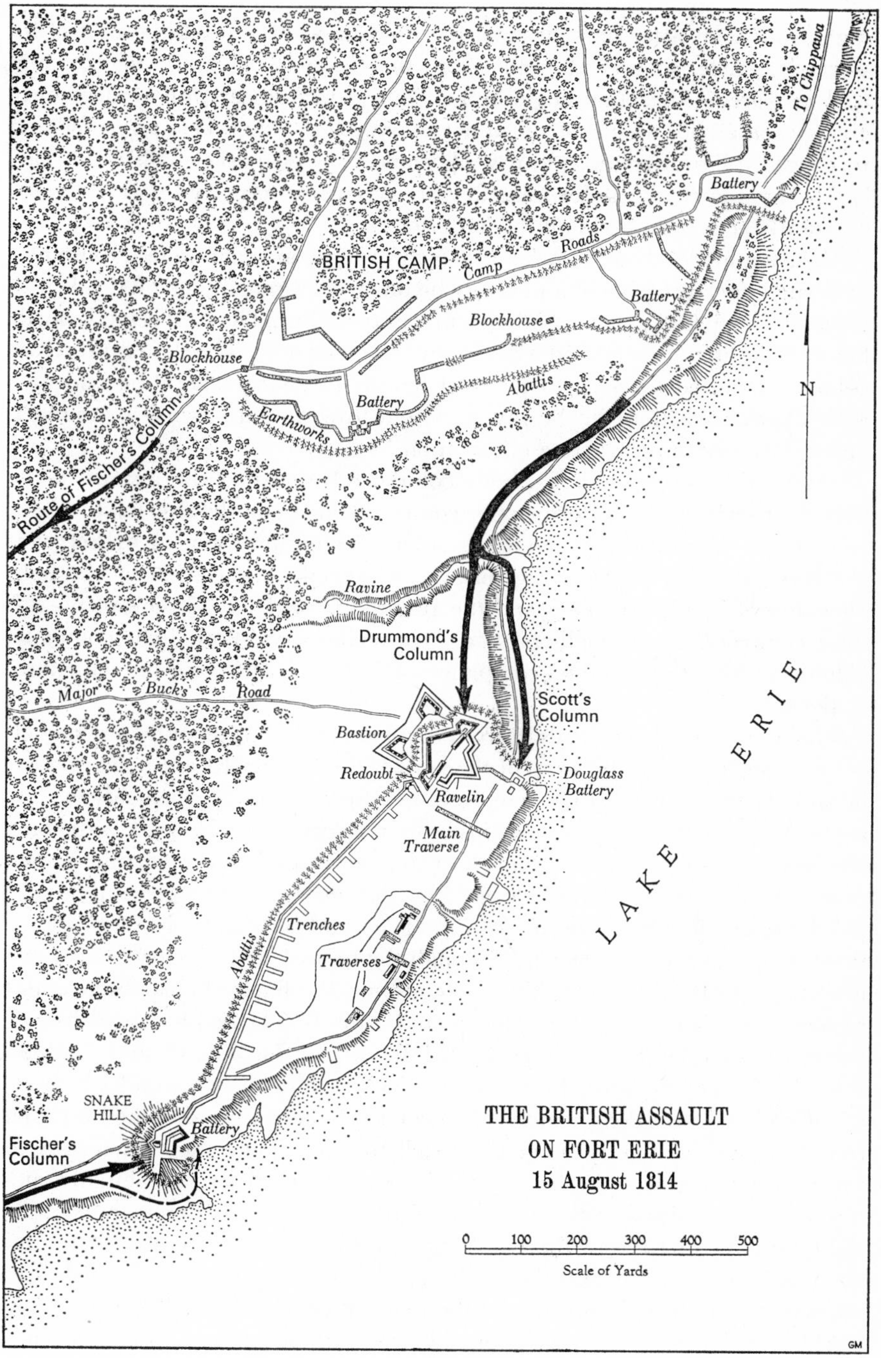

THE BRITISH ASSAULT
ON FORT ERIE
15 August 1814

night, and soon after dark he took the precaution of going the round of his works in person to urge the officers on duty to be particularly vigilant and well prepared. The chief engineer and other staff officers followed in turn, giving such advice as they deemed necessary. All the guns were unloaded and recharged, piles of round and case shot and bags of musket balls were piled beside them in readiness for immediate use. Dark lanterns and port fires were constantly kept burning in all the batteries.

Night set in cloudy and dark and a heavy rain soon began to fall, thoroughly drenching Fischer's column in its bivouac. The remainder of the British troops scarcely fared better as they had scanty shelter. The rain ceased shortly before midnight, but the darkness was little abated. The left and centre columns splashed forward to the trenches, and moving silently beyond took their allotted positions in the ravine within three hundred yards of the fort, apparently without attracting observation.

At the time appointed, Fischer's column advanced to the assault in the following order: the forlorn hope, composed of a sub-division of the light company of the 8th, commanded by Lieut. Young and guided by Sergeant Powell of the 19th Light Dragoons, . . . followed in succession by the light companies of de Watteville's and the 100th, a second sub-division of the 8th light company, the grenadiers of de Watteville's, the 89th light company, volunteers from the battalion companies of de Watteville's, and the remainder of the 8th.

About three hundred yards in front of Snake Hill a strong outlying picquet, commanded by Lieut. Belknap of the 23rd United States Infantry, was posted in an oak grove, which discovered and attempted to check their advance by a sharp fire of musketry. It was instantly charged and dislodged with some loss. Belknap himself received a severe bayonet wound in the pursuit. Young pressed swiftly onward until stopped by the *abattis*, when Sergeant Powell led the way without hesitation into the lake, and by wading in places up to their armpits, and even deeper, although the bottom was slippery and strewn with large rocks, they made their way around the flank of this obstacle and regained the shore behind it. They were promptly followed by about half of the de Watteville light company, led by Major DeVillatte and Captain Powell. The remainder of that company lost track of their comrades in front and wandered into deep water, where some of them were drowned and the rest had much difficulty in getting back to land. They then attempted to force their way through the *abattis*, in which some of them actually succeeded. But at this instant the guns of the battery and a tremendous discharge of musketry from the whole line struck the grenadiers of de Watteville's at once in front and flank with such appalling effect that all who remained unhurt turned and ran to the rear with such frantic haste that they literally swept the 89th light company before them for some distance, and communicated the panic to the men of their own regiment, who were behind it. So rapid and steady was the fire from the redoubt that it seemed to be wrapped in a constant sheet of flame. The light company of the 89th continued to keep their ranks with admirable firmness in the midst of this scene of confusion, and, strange to say, scarcely lost a man, but the whole of de Watteville's Regiment, with few exceptions, became utterly terror-stricken and ran over, beat down, or swept before them the weak fragment of the veteran 1st Battalion of the 8th, who gallantly attempted to stem the torrent of their shameful flight. Upon this confused and struggling mass the unaimed fire from the American works fell with deadly effect, and probably more men were hurt than if they had boldly advanced to the attack. Many disaffected men of de Watteville's Regiment seized this opportunity to desert their ranks and conceal themselves in the woods and thickets until they could give themselves up as prisoners of war to the enemy. This corps lost thirty-four killed, twenty-seven wounded, and no less than eighty-three missing.

Meanwhile Young and DeVillatte, with their followers, not exceeding in the whole fifty men, were attacked by three companies of the 21st United States Infantry, whom they charged and engaged in a hand-to-hand fight. But, the reserve of that regiment having come up, the British party was quickly overwhelmed, and all who were not killed or disabled were forced to make their escape by the route they had come in. Their loss was severe, particularly in the light company of de Watteville's, which behaved very gallantly. Lieut. Young was slightly wounded but succeeded in making his escape with all the other officers and sturdy Sergeant Powell, whose conduct was distinguished. In company with stragglers from other corps, by whom they were joined, they clung tenaciously to the front of the American works for half an hour, during which they made four or five resolute attempts to surmount them, forcing their way through the *abattis* and even raising their scaling ladders against the scarp of the redoubt, only to find them eight or nine feet too short to reach the crest of the parapet. Finally when this despairing effort failed they covered the retreat of the routed column. In this unequal conflict, the light company of the 8th lost Lieut. Noel, one sergeant, and fifteen privates killed, Lieut. Young and fourteen privates wounded, and one sergeant and fifteen privates missing, being fully two-thirds of its effective strength. Including wounded men and deserters, General Ripley reported the capture of one hundred and forty-seven prisoners on this flank. His own loss was trifling, not exceeding a dozen men, and even before the firing ceased he was able to detach four companies to the support of the right wing.

General Drummond did not hesitate to attribute the failure of this attack to the misconduct of de Watteville's Regiment, and it certainly seems probable that the intrenchments might have been carried had the forlorn hope been properly supported.

The other two assaulting columns lay quietly in the ravine until the boom of cannon and crash of musketry from Snake Hill told them that Fischer's advance had been discovered. They instantly rose from their cover and moved rapidly forward. Their approach was soon detected by an outlying picquet of the garrison posted near the river, who discharged their muskets at random and took to flight. Scott's column followed on their track along the beach, while Drummond, ascending the bank, directed his march straight upon the northeastern bastion. Both moved in close column of sub-divisions or half companies. The steady noise of battle and blaze of musketry and cannon on the other flank, which was reflected from a heavy bank of clouds overhead, indicated that a stubborn conflict was in progress there. The garrison of the works in front was already fully alert, but no attempt was made to check their approach until the measured tread of many men and the suppressed voices of their officers exclaiming: 'Close up! Steady men, steady! Steel! Steel! Captain Steel's company!' could be plainly heard. Then the storm burst. The guns of the fort and water battery, literally crammed to the muzzle with case-shot and bags of musket balls, and the muskets of a long line of infantry loaded with 'ball and buck' cartridges containing a bullet and three buckshot, opened upon them at short range with fatal effect. The 103rd Regiment, crowded together in the defile between the high bank and the water, suffered heavily both in officers and men. Their ranks were soon broken and they fell into much confusion, but by the strenuous efforts of Colonel Scott, Major (afterwards Lieut.-General) Smelt and other officers, they were rallied and the advance resumed. Officers and men fell fast, but, when the head of the column gained the point where the high bank recedes from the water, the leading sub-division swerved to the right and led the way towards the supposed opening between the *epaulement*[3] and the bastion, receiving the oblique fire of a body of infantry as they advanced. By this time the 9th United States Regiment, stationed on this line, had been reinforced by the 22nd, 25th, the greater part of the 11th, and several companies of Porter's volunteers, forming a body of fully one thousand men to occupy a front of about one hundred yards. Captain Eliot fell, desperately wounded, on the edge of the ditch, where he was afterwards taken prisoner. Colonel Scott was shot through the brain on the *glacis*,[4] but carried back to the trenches to die a few hours later. Major Smelt was severely wounded about the same time. For a quarter of an hour their efforts to struggle through the obstructions at this point were continued until many were shot down. Finding that it was impossible to effect an entrance here, some of the survivors made their way into the ditch and joined the centre column. Three captains, eleven subalterns, among whom was the adjutant, and 350 non-commissioned

[3] [An epaulement is an earthwork usually thrown up for flank protection.]

[4] [A glacis is the smooth grass slope leading up to the outer defences of a fortification, intended to give the defenders a good field of fire.]

officers and men of this regiment were numbered among the killed, wounded, and missing. The garrison along this line did not have a man hurt, and it is doubtful whether the 103rd fired a single shot in making the attack.

Although by far the weakest, Drummond's column came nearest being successful. Dashing boldly across the level open plain, as soon as it emerged from the shelter of the ravine, it gained the ditch with little loss. Here the men were pretty well covered from the fire of the fort, and hidden from view by the heavy cloud of smoke from its guns, which hung above their heads and rendered the darkness all but impenetrable. Raising their ladders against the scarp of the bastion, and led by Lieut.-Colonel Drummond and Captain Dobbs,[5] the stormers made their way through the embrasures with loud shouts of 'Give the Yankees no quarter!' The gunners abandoned their pieces in dismay, but were soon rallied by their officers, and a desperate hand-to-hand fight followed in which many fell. Captain Alexander John Williams and Lieut. Patrick McDonogh of the United States Artillery here died nobly. Observing that a blazing portfire in front of his men threw its light upon their position, Williams sprang forward and extinguished it with his sword, receiving a fatal wound in the act. While desperately defending himself with the rammer of a gun, McDonogh was shot dead by Drummond. The rest of their men then took refuge in or behind the stone barracks, from which they kept up an annoying fire of musketry at a distance of only a few paces. Lieut. Charleton, R. A., entering the bastion with a small party of Royal Artillery, soon turned one of the captured guns upon these buildings, from which he fired several rounds. Then the guns of the water battery and musketry from the adjacent line were directed upon the ditch and captured bastion. To check this, a British officer leaped upon the parapet and shouted: 'Cease firing! You are firing upon your own men!' For an instant the fire slackened, until a shrill countermand was heard, when it was renewed with increased vigour.

The end of the northeast barrack was built directly across the gorge of the bastion, leaving a passage of only seven feet leading to the parade, which was partly obstructed by masses of stone from its shattered walls. Through this the stormers made their way into the barrack square, expelling all they found there and endeavored to break open the doors of the barracks. A renewed burst of musketry from these buildings showed that they were strongly occupied. By this time the two new bastions had been wholly abandoned by the garrison, and all that side of the fort was in undisputed possession of the

[5] [Alexander T. Dobbs (1784?-1827) was born in Dublin, became a lieutenant in the Royal Navy in 1813 and a commander in 1814. He served with distinction on lakes Erie and Ontario, taking part in actions at French Creek (November 1813) and Oswego (May 1814), and capturing the American schooners *Somers* and *Ohio* on Lake Erie during the siege of Fort Erie (August 12-13, 1814).]

storming party. Captain John Barry Glew of the 41st Regiment, who had headed the final successful charge upon the American gun position at Lundy's Lane, was here disabled, and the command of the flank companies of that corps devolved upon Captain Richard Bullock, who led them again to the attack of the barracks. The door of one of these was soon forced and his party entered it, only to be driven out again after a stubborn struggle in which Bullock himself was badly wounded. Fischer's attack had already failed, and reinforcements were being hurried to the fort from the centre and left. The first to arrive was a party of artillerymen under Major Hindman, which united with a body of the 19th United States Infantry under Major Trimble in an attempt to regain the interior of the fort by the gateway between the barracks. They were easily repelled and driven back into the ravelin,[6] where they were soon joined by Captain Birdsall with his battalion of riflemen. Birdsall headed a second unsuccessful charge through the gate in which he fell severely wounded. Detachments from the 11th, 19th, and 22nd Infantry then came up and were formed in rear of Fanning's battery with orders to scale the southeastern bastion and attack the British in flank, while their attention was occupied in front by the force in the barracks and ravelin. This movement was so far successful that they regained possession of the bastion and threw a reinforcement from the 22nd Regiment into the nearest barracks. Several attempts made by them to charge through the gorge of the bastion were, however, summarily repulsed. Three companies of the 23rd and one of the 19th, detached by General Ripley from the left wing, then came up under Major Brooke and entered the ravelin with the intention of renewing the attack in front. By this time the assaulting column had been much reduced by the steady fire directed upon it. Lieut.-Colonel Drummond had fallen, mortally wounded, and several other officers had been disabled by wounds. The guns and musketry from the intrenchments on the right constantly swept the ditch, rendering it almost impossible for any reinforcement to join it. At the last moment General Drummond sent forward two companies of the Royal Scots from the reserve. They suffered heavily in their advance and few if any of them succeeded in entering the fort. Captain Torrens and thirty-two privates were killed and two sergeants and thirty-seven privates wounded during the short time they were under fire.

Having failed in two attempts to force their way into the barracks, the storming party was preparing for another, while the Americans were mustering in force in the ravelin to drive them out of the fort altogether, when an appalling explosion took place in the northeastern bastion. The gun-platform, with its guns and the men engaged in serving it, masses of earth, and fragments of stone were hurled into the air in the heart of a cloud of smoke and

[6] [A ravelin is a triangular outwork, usually in front of a curtain wall.]

flame. An expense magazine underneath the platform had become ignited, as the officers nearest it supposed, from a train of powder accidentally dropped in charging and firing a gun against the barracks. A story, however, became current in the British camp later on, that it had been exploded with a slow match by a corporal of the United States Artillery, who had disguised himself in the red coat of a British deserter and mingled with the men in the bastion until he was able to accomplish his design and slip away. If this was true, the brave fellow must have perished in the explosion, as it is not corroborated by any American account.

The American troops were almost entirely protected from the effects of this explosion by the barracks, but the stormers suffered terribly. Many were killed, some fairly blown in pieces, others crushed beneath falling masses of stone and timber. Those who remained unhurt were hurled violently from their feet and thoroughly dismayed and bewildered by his unexpected catastrophe. Scarcely an officer or non-commissioned officer remained unhurt, and the men could not be convinced that the explosion was accidental. They imagined that the whole fort was mined and would be blown up under them. Their natural impulse was to fly from that fatal spot, and when the enemy's fire was resumed they became panic-stricken and abandoned the works. Drummond's column had been practically annihilated. The little party of Royal Artillery lost eight men out of thirteen, Lieut. Charleton and others were blown into the ditch, scorched and bruised but otherwise unhurt. The detachment of seamen lost twenty-three, including Captain Dobbs, and three officers out of fifty, the Royal Marines thirty out of ninety. Every officer of the 41st flank companies was either wounded or missing, and only thirty-nine men out of one hundred and twenty escaped unhurt. Sergeant Hugh Clarke of the grenadiers and Private Robert Ball of the light company were particularly commended for their gallant conduct. Of the 104th flank companies, twenty-four non-commissioned officers were reported killed or missing, and Captain Leonard, Ensign McLaughlin, and twenty-nine non-commissioned officers and men were wounded. Sergeant Smith, the gallant leader of the forlorn hope, received no less than five wounds. Only twenty-six men of these companies returned unwounded.

When the fugitives began to stream into battery, at which General Drummond had taken post, he ordered forward the remaining companies of the Royal Scots to cover their retreat. Day was then breaking and the absolute discomfiture of both columns became fully apparent. The ditch of the fort in several places was choked with dead and wounded. The plain and river side was thickly strewed with bodies. Those who came back unhurt were thoroughly dispirited and exhausted. Drummond's effective force on that line was reduced to less than a thousand men, and a vigorous counterattack at that moment would probably have driven it from the siege batteries and camp before Colonel Fischer could have rejoined him. General Gaines, however, failed to take advantage of this favorable opportunity, and did not even attempt any organized pursuit beyond his own lines. Many wounded and a considerable number of unwounded men were taken here, and in all he reported the capture of 174 wounded, including seven officers, and 186 unwounded prisoners. Many of the wounded prisoners were fatally hurt. Two hundred and twenty-one dead, including fourteen officers, were found on the field. Drummond officially stated that he lost four officers and fifty-three non-commissioned officers and privates killed, twenty-four officers, twelve seamen, and 273 non-commissioned officers and privates wounded, nine officers, seven seamen, and 523 non-commissioned officers and privates missing, but added that the greater part of those returned as missing were supposed to have been killed by the explosion. Six of his battalions, the Royal Scots, 8th, 41st, 89th, 100th, and 103rd were now so much diminished by their losses in this and former actions as to be entirely unfit for field duty.

The loss of the garrison was comparatively insignificant, amounting only to two officers and fifteen men killed, six officers and forty-six non-commissioned officers and men wounded, and one officer and six men missing. . . .

FURTHER READING: E. A. Cruikshank (ed.), *Documentary history . . .*, part VII, pages 138-70, 434-5; W. C. H. Wood (ed.), *Selected British documents . . .*, volume 3, part 1, pages 178-94; F. H. Severance (ed.), 'Papers relating to the War of 1812 on the Niagara frontier', *Buffalo Historical Society*, volume 5 (1902), pages 63-98; J. D. P. Martin, 'The Regiment de Watteville: its settlement and service in Upper Canada', *Ontario History*, volume 52 (1960), pages 17-30.

This study outlines the naval situation during three campaigns on Lake Ontario. The emphasis upon more and larger ships has made 'A Shipbuilder's War' a not uncommon name for this aspect of the War of 1812. For a proper assessment of the conduct of Chauncey and Yeo, an understanding of the seemingly infinite permutations and combinations of sailing ships and guns is essential. This is rarely attempted in the literature of the war, so this article is all the more welcome in that it affords a new insight and perspective on the naval war upon Lake Ontario. It is interesting to note, too, how differences of nomenclature and measurement have increased the difficulties of reaching a true understanding of the relative strengths of the opposing fleets. . . . 'C. Winton-Clare' was the nom de plume of Dr. R. C. Anderson, Fordingbridge, Hampshire, England, author and editor of several volumes of naval history, trustee of the National Maritime Museum, and for fifty years associated with the Society for Nautical Research as founding member, editor, and president. 'A Shipbuilder's War' was first published in 'The Mariner's Mirror', volume 29 (1943), and appears through the kindness of Dr. Anderson and of the honorary editor of that journal.

A Shipbuilder's War

BY C. WINTON-CLARE

In a sense all naval wars are shipbuilder's wars, because the shipbuilder provides the tools which the sailor uses, but it is seldom that the tool-maker eclipses the workman to quite such an extent as was the case in the struggle for the command of the waters of Lake Ontario during the war of 1812-15. In that self-contained area of operations an increase of force could only be obtained by local effort; the enormous quantitative superiority of the British navy as a whole was of no avail, and the two sides were alike dependent on the skill, and above all the energy, of one or two designers and a handful of workmen.

Three factors combined to raise the shipbuilder's importance. In the first place, the two fleets were never of any great size, so that a single ship could represent a large fraction of one side's total strength. Secondly, both were at first made up of vessels belonging to classes which came well down the list of a normal sea-going navy, and yet both were produced and handled by men who were acquainted with ships of greater size and knew their advantages. To achieve superiority it was not actually necessary to build more vessels than the enemy of a particular standard type, for the same result could be attained by setting a small frigate against a sloop, a large frigate against a small one, or a ship-of-the-line against a frigate. Thirdly – and this was perhaps the determining factor – the chief commanders on the two sides were both inclined to look on their encounters in the spirit of chess players and to consider the game lost if the enemy achieved by any means a superiority of a single piece.

In one way the very fact that such emphasis was laid on material in these campaigns eases the historian's task. We are, at any rate, usually given the actual armament of the vessels concerned, and are saved the labour of disentangling it from the camouflage of a fictitious system of rating.

It is a well-known fact that in the early years of the nineteenth century the number of guns ascribed to a ship in her official rating had only a very slight relation to the number she actually carried. At one time a 32-gun frigate had been armed with 26 12-pounders, and 6 6-pounders, a 36-gun with 26 18-pounders and 10 9-pounders, and so on; then carronades were added, *but not counted*, the 32-gun having 6 24-pounders and the 36-gun having 8, so that their real total armaments were 38 and 44 respectively; after that, as the value of the carronade was recognized, most of the long guns on the quarterdeck and forecastle were replaced by carronades, *and these were counted*, because they were simply substitutes for the original long guns which had been included in the rating. In this way there arose the farcical situation that a 38-gun frigate had neither a total of 38 guns of all sorts, nor that number of long guns only, but in actual fact carried 30 long guns and 16 carronades, a total of 46 guns. She ought to have been called a 46; she might, with some vestige of reason, have been called a 30; as it was, she 'split the difference' and was called a 38. In the same way, a ship with 32 long guns and 22 carronades was neither a 54 nor a 32, but a 44. If she had carried carronades all along her spar-deck and had thus had a total of 62 or 64 guns, she would probably still have been called a 44, because the 8 or 10 additional carronades would have been extras, not replacements.

The English could, perhaps, advance some sort of excuse, far-fetched though it might be, for the inconsistencies of their rating, but I doubt if the Americans troubled about anything of the sort. They probably reasoned that a 32, a 38, or a 44 had so many main-deck ports, and that what other ports she had and what guns she actually carried made no difference to her rating. Something of this sort seems to be the only possible explanation of the fact that the *Essex* was called a 32, although she started life with 42 guns and ended with 46. Hers was, indeed, an extreme case; but, even so, it was no worse than that of the English *Cyane*, which at one time carried 32 guns (or 33 counting a boat-gun) and was still rated as a 22-gun ship.

The builders and organizers of the lake fleets were not altogether guiltless of this sort of obfuscation. The last three frigates laid down by the Americans appear in later lists as 44s, but there is no doubt that they carried, or were intended to carry, far more. The *Superior* actually had 62 guns (afterwards reduced to 58) and her two successors, which were never completed, were a good deal larger, but still called 44-gun frigates. The *New Orleans* too, the first American battleship on the lakes, was described as a 74, but is said to have been pierced for 102 guns. Still, these last three vessels were never completed; if they had actually taken the water, we should probably be well informed about their real armament.

There was, and still is, much dispute about the relative size of the ships on the two sides. Normally, the American method of measurement gave a slightly larger tonnage than the English; the *President*, for example, measured 1,576 tons by American measurement and 1,533 by English; but, unfortunately, besides the confusion caused by the occasional use of other formulae or other methods of taking the actual dimensions, there have been misstatements due either to genuine errors or to deliberate juggling with figures. . . .

When war broke out, the English appeared to have an overwhelming superiority. They had the ship-rigged *Royal George* of 330 tons and 22 guns, the much smaller ship *Prince Regent* of 141 tons and 16 guns, the brig *Earl of Moira* of 169 tons and 14 guns, the 10-gun brig *Gloucester*, and the two schooners *Seneca* and *Simcoe* of 8 guns each. On the American side there was at first only the brig *Oneida* of 243 tons and 16 guns; the addition of six purchased schooners gave them a bare numerical superiority, but neither these nor another four bought during the winter were of much value as men-of-war in spite of the few powerful guns which they carried.

The English fleet under a Canadian officer named Earl appeared off Sackett's Harbour on 19 July, just a month after the war began, with the object of taking or destroying the *Oneida*, but they were easily repulsed, and for the rest of the season the initiative – such as it was – remained with the Americans. In September, Commodore Isaac Chauncey was appointed to command all American forces on the Great Lakes, while at the same time shipwrights were sent to begin the construction of new vessels. The first of these, the ship *Madison*, was launched on 26 November, having been little more than two months in building. She was slightly more powerful and very much larger than the *Royal George*, since she carried 24 guns and measured 593 tons; her launch came, however, too late to affect matters before the winter. In the meantime, on 8 November, Chauncey had left port with the *Oneida* and six schooners and had met the *Royal George* and chased her into Kingston. Next day he closed in and opened fire on both ship and fortifications. The *Royal George* was forced to run right inshore for safety; but that was all; a gun-burst in the schooner *Pert*, and the Americans withdrew without accomplishing much more than the English had done at Sackett's Harbour in July.

As a reply to the *Madison* the English now laid down two 24-gun ships, one at Kingston and one at York, while the Americans, to keep their advantage, prepared to build a second ship, larger than the *Madison* and better armed. Without waiting for this reinforcement, Chauncey began operations in 1813 by an attack on York. He arrived there on 27 April with the *Madison*, *Oneida*, ten schooners, and a transport, landed his troops under cover of a bombardment, and had little difficulty in taking the place. The new ship was burnt and the *Gloucester*, which was in the port, was captured. A month later an attack was made on Fort George, the English position at the mouth of the Niagara River. Again the schooners covered the landing and again the attack succeeded. What was more, the remaining English forces were compelled to withdraw from the upper river and thus left the way open for American vessels from Buffalo to reach Lake Erie.

Meanwhile, the *Wolfe* had been launched at Kingston on 6 May, and on the same day a new officer, Commodore Sir James Yeo, had arrived at Quebec to take command of the English forces on Lake Ontario. His new ship, the *Wolfe*, was of 426 tons and carried 23 guns, four of them 68-pounder carronades. She was about equal in force to the *Madison*, and for the moment the strength of the English squadron was distinctly greater than that of the enemy. With the completion of the new American ship the position would be reversed, and accordingly, on 27 May, when Chauncey was landing at Fort George, Yeo sailed for Sackett's Harbour in the hope of destroying her on the stocks. The attack took place on the 29th and was unsuccessful, though the alarm led to the burning of the recently captured *Gloucester*. The new ship, the *General Pike*, was also fired by the defenders, but was saved on the retreat of the English.

Yeo went back to Kingston, and a few days later Chauncey returned to Sackett's Harbour. Yeo used his temporary command of the lake by taking his force of two ships, two brigs, and two schooners, and effecting landings at several points to the westward to destroy stores intended for the American army; he was away from his base from 3 to 29 June, and while he was thus employed the *General Pike* was launched.

According to James, that ship 'alone was nearly a match for the whole of Sir James Yeo's squadron'. That, like most of James's statements with regard to the strength of American ships, was a gross exaggeration, but she was certainly the most powerful vessel that the lakes had seen up to that time. She was of 875 tons and carried a battery of 28 long 24-pounders. Roosevelt reckons that she was about equal to the *Wolfe* and the largest English brig together; the English ships had heavier guns, but the majority of them were carronades, so that the advantage at long range would be with the American. . . .

Chauncey left Sackett's Harbour on 21 July with two ships, one brig and ten schooners; he reached Niagara on the 27th, embarked some troops with which he made a second successful attack on York on the 30th, and returned to Niagara on 3 August. Yeo with his six vessels left Kingston on 2 August and found the Americans at anchor off Niagara on the 7th. Both sides claim to have been anxious to engage, but all that happened was that two of the American schooners, the *Hamilton* and *Scourge*, capsized and sank in a squall during the following night. On the 10th there was a little firing and some manoeuvring which led to the capture of two other schooners, the *Growler* and *Julia*; next day, neither commander seemed eager to fight, and on the 13th the Americans were back at Sackett's Harbour for provisions. For the next month Yeo and Chauncey, according to their own accounts, pursued one another round the lake; but, as one was only prepared to fight in calm weather at long range and the other in heavy weather at close quarters, it was not strange that no action took place.

On 11 September there was some long-range fighting off the Genesee River (near the present Rochester); the English had the worst of it and retired towards Kingston. At length on 28 September something more like a real fight took place at the western end of the lake. Yeo had his usual six vessels, while Chauncey had the *Pike*, *Madison*, and *Oneida*, the new schooner *Sylph* of 300 tons and 16 guns, and seven smaller schooners. The *Wolfe* lost her main and mizen-topmasts and at once ran for Burlington Bay with the *Royal George* covering her retreat. Chauncey followed till the English were out of reach, then went to Niagara to refit, and finally reached Sackett's Harbour on 6 October, having taken a few English transports on the previous day, among them the former American schooners *Growler* and *Julia*, now called *Confiance* and *Hamilton*.

A day later the English returned to Kingston, and there they were more or less blockaded for the next few weeks, till winter put an end to operations. After this the two fleets never met. Command of the lake became simply a matter of shipbuilding, and whichever fleet was temporarily inferior stayed in port until it was reinforced.

During the winter and spring the English built two large frigates and made preparations for building a battleship; at the same time they renamed their former six vessels and converted the two schooners to brigs. The *Wolfe* became the *Montreal*, *Royal George* – *Niagara*, *Moira* – *Charwell*, *Melville* – *Star*; while the schooner *Beresford* (once the ship *Prince Regent*) was transformed into the 14-gun brig *Netley* and the schooner *Sidney Smith* became the brig *Magnet*. The two new ships, both launched on 15 April, were the *Prince Regent* of 1,294 tons and 58 guns and the *Princess Charlotte* of

756 tons and 42 guns. The American additions were the brigs *Jefferson* and *Jones* of 500 tons and 22 guns, the frigate *Superior* of 1,580 tons and 62 guns, and later the *Mohawk* of 1,350 tons and 42 guns. The two brigs were launched on 7 and 10 April, the *Superior* on 1 May, the *Mohawk* on 11 June. This last vessel is said to have been built in 34 days. The *Sylph* was rerigged as a brig and rearmed, but the rest of the schooners were relegated to service as transports or gunboats.

By including the schooners, by adding 8 to the 42 guns that the *Mohawk* carried,[1] and by counting her 32-pounder carronades as 42s, James managed to prove to his own satisfaction that the English fleet was only just superior to the American at the beginning of the season, distinctly inferior when the first new American frigate appeared, and inferior in the proportion of about 3 to 5 when the *Mohawk* joined her. Roosevelt, on the other hand, though fair enough as regards guns, makes the tonnage of the English fleet at least 2,000 tons too great. Even when we allow for the slight excess due to American measurement, he makes the *Prince Regent* at least 100 tons too large and the *Princess Charlotte* about 400. In the case of these two ships James appears, for once, to have overestimated English tonnages. He gives them as 1,310 and 815 tons, later official lists give 1,294 and 756, Roosevelt gives 1,450 and 1,215. As far as I can judge, the two fleets were about equal in strength at the beginning of June, when the *Superior* was in service but not the *Mohawk*. Before that the English had a distinct advantage; afterwards the advantage was with the Americans, but not to quite the same extent.

The *Superior* was rated as a 44 and was roughly the same size as the sea-going vessels of that class. Chauncey himself described her as 'something larger than the *President*', and her tonnage of 1,580 confirms this estimate. The *Prince Regent* was of a size intermediate between a 44 and a 38; she was 3 ft. shorter than the *Congress* or *Constellation* but about 2½ ft. wider. The *Mohawk* with her 1,350 tons (American) was of almost exactly the same size, but the *Princess Charlotte* was hardly as big as the *Pike*, though she carried a much heavier armament.

The new ships were armed as follows: The *Superior* had 30 long 32-pounders, 2 long 24-pounders, and 30 42-pounder carronades. Four of these last were soon taken out, ostensibly to make her equal on paper to the *Prince Regent*, but more probably because she was found to be over-gunned. The *Prince Regent* carried 32 long 24-pounders, 4 68-pounder carronades (taken from the *Wolfe*) and 22 32-pounder carronades.[2] The *Mohawk* had 26 long 24-pounders, 2 long 18-pounders, and 14 32-pounder carronades.

[1] She was rated as a 32.

[2] A contemporary engraving of the attack on Oswego shows her as a double-banked frigate with 30 ports on each deck.

The *Princess Charlotte*, though a much smaller ship, carried the same with the addition of 2 68-pounder carronades from the *Royal George*.

Whatever the real facts of the case may have been, there was little doubt as to what the two commanders thought about their relative strength. Until the *Superior* was ready, Chauncey stayed in port and Yeo did as he liked on the lake. After that, until Yeo's new battleship, the *St. Lawrence*, appeared, the positions were reversed; then it was Chauncey's turn to retire to Sackett's Harbour for the last few weeks of the season of 1814.

The operations of 1814 can be described quite briefly. Yeo left Kingston on 3 May and effected a landing at Oswego on the 6th, just as Chauncey had done at York in the previous year. He took the place, captured the *Growler* for the second time, and returned to Kingston. On 19 May he appeared off Sackett's Harbour, where the *Superior* was awaiting her guns and gear, which had to be brought by water from Oswego. A number of boats employed on this duty left Oswego on 28 May and had to take refuge on the following morning in a creek some 8 miles short of their goal. Yeo at once sent two gunboats and some ship's boats to attack them, but the party were ambushed and captured after suffering heavy losses.

The blockade was raised early in June, but the Americans were not ready to sail till the end of July; the only incidents of note were the capture of an English gunboat by American boats and the destruction of a new English 14-gun schooner at Presqu'isle. During August and September it was Chauncey's turn to control the lake. Leaving Sackett's Harbour on 31 July, he caught the brig *Magnet* at the top of the lake and forced her crew to run her ashore and burn her. He then detached his smaller vessels and blockaded Kingston with the four largest. Yeo declined an engagement and Chauncey refused to undertake any form of co-operation with the army that would hinder what he considered his primary object, the destruction of the English fleet. His only activity in this way was the transport of some 3,000 men as far as the Genesee River on 21 September.

That same day the English battleship *St. Lawrence* was launched at Kingston, and with that the days of American superiority were ended. Chauncey soon withdrew to Sackett's Harbour, and on 15 October Yeo at last ventured out. His new ship was 191 ft. 2 in. long and 52 ft. 7 in. wide; her tonnage was 2,305 and she carried 112 guns, for the most part 32-pounders. Roughly speaking, her broadside was equal to those of the two largest American ships together, and since the rest of the English fleet would be in a superiority of 7 to 6 with an advantage in guns of nearly 2 to 1, Chauncey can hardly be blamed for considering himself helpless.

Again he called on his shipbuilders and again they responded to the call. If the English could build a battleship, they could build a bigger one, and accordingly they began work on a ship intended to bear much the same relation to the *St. Lawrence* as the *Superior* bore to the *Prince Regent,* at least in size. This ship, the *New Orleans,* was called a 74, but was probably intended to carry at least 100 guns, and some of these would probably have been 42-pounders.[3] Her dimensions are said to have been 214 ft. by 56 ft. as against 191 ft. 2 in. by 52 ft. 7 in. for the *St. Lawrence*; their actual keels measured 183 ft. 7½ in. and 171 ft. 6 in. respectively; in tonnage they were 2,805 to 2,305. Work was also begun on two other ships, the *Chippewa* and *Plattsburg.* Accounts vary as to whether the former was to have been a large frigate (a so-called 44) or another battleship, but the *Plattsburg* was certainly an enlarged *Superior* of 1,748 tons, also classed as a 44, but no doubt designed for at least 64 guns.

On the English side it was no longer a matter of trying to catch up with the enemy, but one of keeping an advantage already obtained. To make sure of this they began two more battleships and a small but heavily armed frigate. Apparently they considered that the *St. Lawrence* had already passed the limit of useful size, for the two new battleships were smaller. The *Wolfe* and *Canada,* as they were to have been called, were to be 191 ft. 3 in. on the gun deck and 50 ft. 8 in. wide, the same length as the *St. Lawrence* and 2 ft. narrower; their tonnage was to be 2,152. They were, however, to carry a more powerful armament and one consisting almost entirely of long guns. It is interesting to notice that, even at a later date, when the *St. Lawrence* was rated by her actual number of guns, although a large number of them were carronades, the two later ships were also called 112s in spite of their carrying 6 carronades in addition to that number of long guns. The explanation is that the order of 1817, by which the fictitious system of rating was supposed to be abolished, omitted to mention guns on the poop, and this is where the carronades were carried. James mentions this remarkable state of affairs in the last volume of his *Naval History* (p. 293), and goes on to discuss the American sea-going 74s built shortly after the war. . . .

The last English frigate to be built on the lake also showed a tendency towards moderate dimensions. It is true that she was very slightly larger than the *Princess Charlotte,* but she was much smaller than the *Prince Regent,* though very heavily armed for her size. On a tonnage of 769 she had 28 24-pounder long guns and 28 32-pounders.

This frigate, the *Psyche,* was the only one of these final efforts of the war to be actually launched. When news of the Peace of Ghent, signed on 24 December 1814, reached Lake Ontario, the *New Orleans* was nearly ready for launching, but work was at once suspended. A house was built over her on the stocks and she remained thus protected for many years, but most of

[3] A photograph of her before she was broken up shows 17 ports a side on the lower deck and 18 on the upper. It also shows the top-timbers extending the whole length for another complete deck.

the other American ships were sold or broken up soon after 1821. Their English counterparts remained on the lists a little longer, but they too were sold between 1832 and 1837.

FURTHER READING: E. A. Cruikshank, 'The contest for the command of Lake Ontario in 1812 and 1813', *Royal Society of Canada*, third series, section 2, volume 10 (1916), pages 161-223; E. A. Cruikshank, 'The contest for the command of Lake Ontario in 1814', *Ontario Historical Society*, volume 21 (1924), pages 99-159; C. P. Stacey, 'The ships of the British squadron on Lake Ontario, 1812-14', *Canadian Historical Review*, volume 34 (1953), pages 311-23; F. B. Cumberland, 'The navies on Lake Ontario in the War of 1812 . . .', *Ontario Historical Society*, volume 8 (1907), pages 124-42; A. T. Mahan, *Sea power in its relations to the war of 1812* (London, 1905).

The important part in the War of 1812 played by the Indians, particularly in the sparsely settled western portion of Upper Canada, has never received the attention it merits. As they figured in many actions of the war, various of their activities have already been encountered. Here for the first time, however, the Indian is presented as the central subject and not merely as incidental to some action or other. This study places the war in a different frame of reference, lays the ground for further reading and investigation, and serves as a reminder of Canada's debt to the Indian during the War of 1812. . . . GEORGE STANLEY *has published many articles and several volumes on Canadian military history and on the history of western Canada. He is Professor of History and Chairman of the Arts Division, Royal Military College of Canada, Kingston, and a member of the Archaeological and Historic Sites Board of Ontario. The following study appeared in the 'Canadian Historical Review', volume 31 (June 1950), and appears with Dr. Stanley's and the editor's permission.*

The Indians in the War of 1812

BY GEORGE F. G. STANLEY

The use of primitive peoples to fight the battles of civilized nations has, from time to time, been condemned by moralists. And yet, despite such condemnation, the practice has been frequent in our history. Certainly today few nations would cavil at the employment of Senegalese by France or Ghurkas by Great Britain – except, perhaps, such nations as do not possess colonies providing coloured manpower. In the past, in North America, all nations have been prepared to employ the native Indian peoples as military auxiliaries. Each country, be it France, England, or the United States, while admitting the difficulties of keeping their aboriginal allies within the recognized bounds of civilized warfare, has been prepared, not only to use, but to employ every device to solicit the assistance of the Indians. In the seventeenth and eighteenth centuries the French relied to a great extent upon the Indians for the defence of Canada. The British sedulously cultivated the friendship of the League of the Iroquois, and in particular that of the Mohawk nation. During the American Revolution the United States succeeded in detaching many Oneida from the League through the efforts of the Reverend Samuel

Kirkland. Thus in 1812 when President Madison declared war upon Great Britain and Henry Clay boasted that the Kentucky militia alone could take Canada, it is not surprising to find both contestants seeking the aid of such Indian warriors as were prepared to take up the tomahawk on their behalf.

As far as the Indians were concerned, Great Britain enjoyed certain marked advantages. The British Indian Department had behind it a long tradition of successful dealing with the Indians ever since the day when William Johnson had been appointed superintendent of the Six Nations in 1755. The department had extended its activities to Canada after the Seven Years' War, and after the American Revolution removed its main office to Montreal. In 1774 Colonel Guy Johnson was appointed to succeed Sir William, and in 1782 Sir John Johnson, Sir William's son, was appointed superintendent-general of Indian affairs. The expanding needs of the service necessitated a division of responsibility and at the end of the eighteenth century the department was divided, with the superintendent-general remaining at Montreal and a new office, that of the deputy superintendent-general, being opened at Fort George. . . .

One of the most significant features of the Indian Department in its early days was the strong personal hold which the officers of the department acquired over the Indians. For many years, the men who ran the department were men who had been schooled in the tradition of Sir William Johnson; when they passed on, their sons succeeded to their appointments and to their influence. Many of the officers of the department were related to one another, and, in some instances, to the very Indians whose affairs they administered. Names like Johnson, McKee, Claus, Elliott, Caldwell, Chew, and others were names familiar to more than one generation of Indians; and they were still names to conjure with in 1812. This fact gave the Indian Department a strong sense of independence, one which brought it into conflict with the military authorities after the war broke out.

To swing the Indians to the British side was not a difficult task. The western tribes, in particular, had never ceased to hate the Americans. They had refused to lay down their arms when the white men had stopped fighting in 1783, preferring to carry on an unequal struggle to preserve the Ohio as the boundary of the Indian territory until they were finally defeated at the hands of 'Mad Anthony' Wayne and compelled to accept the peace of Greenville in 1795. Although the United States claimed territorial sovereignty over their lands, the western Indians continued to look to Great Britain for assistance and advice. And these Great Britain was prepared to give. To have refused would have been to impose unnecessary hardship and undue distress upon the Indians who were completely dependent for their very subsistence upon periodical handouts of ammunition. There is no evidence to show that the British ever used their influence with the western Indians deliberately to stir them up against the United States – and much to the contrary – but there is truth in the charge that the Indians were encouraged by Great Britain never to let the ancient covenant chain of friendship grow brown with rust. Political and military factors made it essential for the British to retain the confidence of the Indians. Against the western Indians the colony of Upper Canada had no defence whatever; against the Americans, unfriendly and threatening, Canada's greatest assurance of protection seemed to lie in the support of the red men. The fur trade too, still one of the principal economic activities of Canada, required the friendship of the western Indians. That is why the Indians continued to receive presents in large numbers from the British government through the agency of the British Indian Department. Undoubtedly these presents, the official expressions of sympathy, the retention of the western posts until 1796, the presence of British agents at Indian councils, must have worked strongly upon the minds of the Indians to convince them that Great Britain was still their ally and that in a final test of strength with the United States, Great Britain would defend them; even when no official encouragement was actually given them so to believe. . . .

THE WESTERN THEATRE OF OPERATIONS 1812-13

. . . That the Indians must constitute an important component of the defence forces of Canada was always appreciated by Major General Brock. He was aware of the temper of the Shawnees and knew of Tecumseh's efforts to form a western Indian confederacy, and although he took care to direct the officers of the Indian Department at Amherstburg to exert their whole influence to dissuade the Indians from attacking the Americans in 1811, he took equal care to secure that, should war break out between Great Britain and the United States, the Indians would be found on the British side. He realized that the best way to engage their active support would be a quick, decisive action against Detroit and Michilimackinac; only in this way would it be possible to convince those Indians who felt that they had been deserted by the British when Major Campbell refused to help them against Wayne in 1794 and when the red coats marched out of the western posts in 1796 'that we are earnestly engaged in the War'.

It was in accordance with this policy that Brock wrote in February 1812, four months before the actual declaration of war, to Robert Dickson, a British fur trader then in Wisconsin, asking him 'to ascertain the degree of cooperation that you and *your friends* might be able to furnish, in case of . . . an Emergency taking place'. Dickson received this communication in June and hastened to assure Brock of the services of 250 to 300 Indians, 79 of whom he sent at once to Amherstburg while hurrying himself with the remainder directly to St. Joseph's.

Meanwhile, General Hull at Detroit was engaged in similar efforts to gain Indian support, or at least to ensure Indian neutrality. He had been instructed to 'adopt such measures with the chiefs of the several tribes of Indians as may . . . appear to be the best calculated to secure the peace of the country'. He therefore despatched Huron agents to the Grand River with a promise that the Six Nations would be undisturbed in the occupation of their lands and invited all the Indians in the vicinity of Detroit, including those under Tecumseh and Roundhead who had already joined the British at Amherstburg, to attend an Indian council at the Wyandot village at Brownstown. Both chiefs, however, remained firm in their refusal to have anything to do with the Americans and Colonel Matthew Elliott wrote to [William] Claus[1] that Tecumseh 'has shewn himself to be a determined character and a great friend to our Government'. This was good news to Brock's ears, for he had always been apprehensive lest the scale of American preparations at Detroit should so impress the Indians with the strength and determination of the United States that they would be reluctant to support a side which might appear to have little chance of victory.

The first success of the war went to the British, not to the Americans. The small British force at St. Joseph's, taking advantage of a prior knowledge of the official declaration of war, immediately seized Michilimackinac, a fort long known to the Indian trade. The effect of this victory was all that Brock had hoped for; to quote General Hull:

> . . . after the surrender of Michilimackinac, almost every tribe and nation of Indians, excepting a part of the Miamis and Delawares, north from beyond Lake Superior, west from beyond the Mississippi, south from the Ohio and Wabash, and east from every part of Upper Canada and from all the intermediate country, joined in open hostility, under the British standard against the Army I commanded. . . . The surrender of Michilimackinac opened the northern hive of Indians, and they were swarming down in every direction.

One must make allowances for the fact that Hull, when he penned this report, was seeking to find excuses for his own supine conduct at Detroit in August; but there is no doubt that the initial British success at Michilimackinac made an impact upon the Indians far out of proportion to its broader military significance.

On the Detroit front Hull made the first move by crossing the river and penetrating into Upper Canada. He issued a belligerent manifesto threatening reprisals against those taken in arms with the Indians but made no hostile

[1] [William Claus (1763?-1826) was the son of Colonel Daniel Claus and grandson of Sir William Johnson. He succeeded Alexander McKee as deputy superintendent of Indian affairs in 1799 and held this position to his death. He was lieutenant-colonel of the 1st Lincoln militia regiment during the war. He became a member of the legislative council of Upper Canada in 1812 and of the executive council in 1818.]

move against the British position at Amherstburg. Then came the news of the British success at Michilimackinac, quickly followed by rumours that the British forces on his flank included 5,000 Indians![2] The report was false, but Hull was gullible enough to believe it, and, finding his line of communications cut by Tecumseh, he succumbed to the war of nerves and surrendered his entire command to General Brock on August 16 without striking a blow. The American frontier was thus thrust a long way back towards the Ohio, the line the Indians sought to establish as their boundary. Brock reaped great credit for his spectacular victory, but without the aid of Tecumseh and the Indians it could never have been so easily achieved, a fact which Brock willingly admitted. From the day the two men met face to face at Amherstburg each respected the other, and Brock wrote of his ally, 'a more sagacious or a more gallant Warrior does not I believe exist'.

During the autumn and winter Robert Dickson continued to hand out presents and to send Indians to Amherstburg. Behind him was the full support of the fur barons of Montreal. James McGill wrote to Sir George Prevost on Dickson's behalf, pointing out: 'The Indians are the only Allies who can aught avail in the defence of the Canadas. They have the same interest as us, and alike are objects of American subjugation, if not extermination.' He urged that Dickson's requests for further supplies be given favourable consideration. Sir George was more than favourably disposed towards Dickson. Not only was he prepared to compensate him for the sums which had been spent upon Indian presents[3] but commissioned him as a special agent for the Indians west of Lake Huron with a staff of five officers and fifteen interpreters and authority to 'make such requisitions as may be necessary upon H.M. Indian storekeepers and other proper officers for such goods and provisions as from time to time shall be considered needful'; all this 'in the expectation that upwards of 1,000 picked warriors will be collected'.

The Indians, however useful their services may have been at Michilimackinac, Brownstown, and Detroit, were at best unsatisfactory soldiers. They were devoid of discipline. They lacked tenacity and were easily discouraged by failure. They were restless, dissatisfied during periods of enforced inactivity, and yet inclined to fight for only brief periods at a time.

[2] Owing to the capture of Hull's orders and despatches at Brownstown as a result of an Indian ambush, the British were fully informed of Hull's weakness and his fear of the Indians. It was thus possible to play upon his fears by planting a letter purporting to be from Procter to the commanding officer at Michilimackinac asking that no more Indians be sent to Amherstburg as there were already more than 5,000 there!

[3] A board of commissioners including General de Rottenburg, McGill and his associates, John Richardson and Wm. McGillivray, and officers of the Indian Department, awarded Dickson the sum of £1,875 to cover the cost of the goods which he distributed among the Indians during the summer and autumn of 1812.

Tactically they offered great advantages in ambuscades and forest warfare, but, when it came to besieging a fort protected by walls and cannon, they were invariably useless.

This weakness on the part of the Indians as a fighting force became painfully apparent during the campaign of 1813. In January Colonel Procter administered a check to General Winchester at Au Raisin River where the issue was decided by the Indians outflanking the Americans on either side and gaining their rear; at Fort Meigs, however, the Indians drifted away after several days' siege leaving Procter, according to his own report, with 'less than twenty Chiefs and Warriors'. Well might Procter add that 'under present Circumstances, at least, our Indian Force is not a disposable one, or permanent, tho' occasionally a most powerful Aid'. Throughout the spring and summer western Indians flocked to Amherstburg adding both to Procter's strength and to his embarrassment. They consumed vast quantities of food and Procter's supplies were never abundant. It was, therefore, as much with the object of finding employment for his Indians as in the hope of administering a defeat to the Americans that he led his force against Fort Stephenson late in July. But a cannon, a stockade, and a determined Irishman stopped the Indian assault and the British force returned to Amherstburg with both Procter and the Indians indulging in mutual recriminations.

During the autumn it became clear that the reverses suffered at Fort Meigs and Fort Stephenson had not been without their effect upon Indian morale. Procter was aware of what was happening and begged that reinforcements of regulars be sent him in order 'that our Dependence on the Indian Force may not appear to so great a Degree as it has hitherto done', also 'to prevent Defection among the Indian Tribes, which ought strenuously to be guarded against, from the Propensity of Indians to follow each other, on the most unaccountable Impulse at Times'.

If the Indians needed a stimulant for their morale, so too did Procter. He was not a man of great courage nor did he ever enjoy the respect of his redskin allies. He seems to have been very much alarmed at the extent of the American preparations for a counter attack and was inclined to pull out of his exposed position. He feared, however, that such a course might lead to trouble with the Indians and endeavoured to cloak his intentions from his allies. Finally, after Barclay's defeat at Put-in-Bay and the loss of Lake Erie to the Americans, he felt that he had no choice but withdrawal, even though Tecumseh, anxious to fight it out where he stood, likened the British commander to a whipped dog crawling away with its tail between its legs. And there was some aptness to the metaphor. For when Procter was finally shamed into making a stand at Moraviantown on October 5, 1813, it was Tecumseh and the Indians who did the fighting, not Procter's red coats. Tecumseh gave his life; Procter saved his by flight.

The effect upon the Indians of the defeat at Moraviantown was as decisive as that of the victories at Detroit and Michilimackinac. With military defeat and the death of the soul and inspiration of the Indian resistance, organized Indian opposition in the Michigan and Lake Erie region came to an end. Small bands of Indians might harass the American army on its withdrawal from Moraviantown, but no large forces of Indians were again mustered on the Detroit front. Only in the upper reaches of Lake Huron and in Wisconsin, where Robert Dickson continued to hand out large numbers of presents and larger numbers of promises while arranging with Sir George Prevost for still larger supplies of both, did the British influence over the Indians remain unimpaired.

THE NIAGARA FRONTIER 1812-13

The response of the western Indians to the British appeals for assistance was by no means equalled in alacrity or ardour by that of the Six Nations. The Iroquois tribes had, after the American Revolutionary War, accepted land reserves not only in Canada but in the United States as well and they had little stomach, at this time, to engage in fratricidal war. Hoping to take advantage of this disinclination on the part of the Six Nations to join in the hostilities, the United States prevailed upon the old Seneca chief, Cornplanter, to send a deputation of American Iroquois to Canada to talk in terms of Indian neutrality with their kindred at Grand River. There is no doubt that the Canadian Six Nations were disposed to toy with the idea of neutrality, but to the American deputation they returned the answer: 'It is the President of the United States makes war upon us. We know not your disputes. . . . The British say the Americans want to take our lands. We do not want to fight, nor do we intend to disturb you; but if you come to take our land, we are determined to defend ourselves.'

Brock was just as anxious to bring the Six Nations into the war as the Americans were to keep them out. On July 3, 1812, he wrote: 'About 100 Indians from the Grand River have attended to my summons, the remainder promise to come also, but I have too much reason to conclude that the Americans have been too successful in their endeavours to sow dissension and disaffection among them.' Three weeks later he learned to his disgust that only fifty Grand River Indians were willing to go to Detroit; the remainder had determined to follow a cautious policy of wait and see.[4] This was a great source of apprehension to the commanding general, for as long as the Indians remained undecided as to their course of action, the civilian population living in the Niagara peninsula would be reluctant to leave their homes and

[4] Brock attributed this change of sentiment to the agents whom Hull had sent to Grand River with his letter to the Six Nations.

join the militia at Amherstburg or Fort George.[5] Brock therefore hastened to answer Hull's letter to the Indians by drawing attention to Hull's inconsistency in making threats in his proclamation while making promises in his letter, and by sending Joseph Willcocks to Grand River to counter the American propaganda.[6]

However cool the Six Nations Indians may have been at the beginning of hostilities, they warmed to enthusiasm after the British victories at Michilimackinac and Detroit. On September 7 Brock reported to Prevost that he had now three hundred Indians assembled at Fort George with 'two hundred more . . . expected tomorrow'. 'They appear ashamed of themselves,' he wrote, 'and promise to whipe away the disgrace into which they have fallen by their late conduct.' Even so he was not inclined to place too much reliance on their loyalty. He felt that so long as he was able to maintain his position at Niagara and keep open the line of communications with Montreal the Indians would remain firm in their attachment to the Crown, but 'the moment they are convinced that we either want the means to prosecute the War with spirit, or are negotiating a separate peace, they will begin to study in what manner they can most effectually deceive us.'

When put to the test, the Six Nations Indians fought well. At Queenston Heights they played an important role under the command of John Brant, a son of the immortal Joseph, Captain Jacobs, and Captain Norton, and suffered the loss of two Cayuga chiefs, one Onondaga and two Oneida warriors, and several wounded. Following the traditional Council of Condolence at Fort George on November 6, the bulk of the Indians, under the command of Major Givins[7] of the Indian Department and captains Norton and Kerr, proceeded up the Niagara River towards Fort Erie where they assisted in repelling the second attempt made by the Americans to cross the river. Subsequently they returned to Fort George whence Lieutenant Thomas Ridout wrote to his cousin on January 5, they 'are encamped on the skirts of

[5] Brock wrote: 'I meditated, the moment I could collect a sufficient number of Militia, a diversion to the westward, in the hope of compelling General Hull to retreat across the river, but this unexpected intelligence has ruined the whole of my plans. The Militia, which I destined for this service, will now be alarmed, and unwilling to leave their families to the mercy of 400 Indians, whose conduct affords such wide room for suspicion – and really to expect that this fickle race would remain in the midst of war in a state of neutrality is truly absurd.'

[6] This appears to be the same Willcocks who later went over to the Americans and led a force of renegades calling themselves the 'Canadian Volunteers' who ravaged the Canadian frontier during 1813 and 1814. . . . An odd selection, to say the least, for the purpose of inducing the Indians to fight on behalf of Great Britain.

[7] [James Givins (1759?-1846) was a clerk in the North West Company and became a lieutenant in the Queen's Rangers in 1791. He was appointed Indian agent at York in 1798 and superintendent in 1816, becoming chief superintendent of Indian affairs for Upper Canada in 1830. He was appointed aide-de-camp to General Brock with the rank of major and was present at the capture of Detroit and at the defence of York in April 1813.]

the woods back of the town' keeping the troops 'alive with their war dances' and making 'the dark cedar woods echo with savage yells'.

Indian morale suffered something of a slump after the British reverses at Fort York and Fort George, nevertheless a number of Indians remained with the British troops and accompanied them on the retreat towards Burlington. They were therefore on hand to participate in the pursuit of the Americans after the night attack at Stoney Creek. On this occasion they appear to have acquired considerable booty: on June 11 Harvey wrote from Forty Mile Creek that 'the greatest part' of the enemy baggage and equipment 'are in the hands of the *Indians* or scattered throughout the Country'.

Following the setback at Stoney Creek the Americans withdrew to Fort George closely followed by the troops and the Indians. The latter had, incidentally, received a strong reinforcement from Lower Canada. On May 26 Sir John Johnson had informed Claus that he had succeeded in raising a substantial force in Lower Canada and would send about 300 Indians to Sir George Prevost 'either to attack or defend'.[8] These Indians were led by Captain Dominique Ducharme. At Forty Mile they were joined by John Brant and William Kerr with about 100 Mohawk. On June 20 the combined force of Indians encamped at Twenty Mile Creek, near a spot known as Beaver Dam. Learning from scouts that the Americans were preparing a reconnaissance in force, Ducharme notified Major de Haren and then, placing himself in the centre, Kerr on the left, and J. B. de Lorimier and Isaac Leclair on the right, he set the stage for an ambush. After two hours' fighting the Americans under Colonel Boerstler[9] surrendered. The actual capitulation was received by Lieutenant Fitzgibbon and completed by de Haren both of whom, however, arrived on the scene with regular reinforcements after the day had been won; it is clear from all contemporary accounts that Beaver Dam was an Indian victory. Indeed, there seems to be more than one grain of truth to Norton's jibe that 'The Cognauaga Indians fought the battle, the Mohawks got the plunder, and Fitzgibbon got the credit'.[10] In the fighting the Indians suffered five principal chiefs and warriors killed and 20 wounded.

[8] According to a letter written by Ducharme on June 5, 1826, he commanded 340 Indians comprising 160 from Caughnawaga, 120 from Lake of Two Mountains, and 60 from St. Regis.

[9] [Charles A. Boerstler of the 14th Infantry Regiment, United States army, was a native of Maryland and had been commissioned a lieutenant-colonel in March 1812. He participated in the attack at Frenchman's Creek in November 1812 and had been promoted to colonel only three days before the ill-fated expedition against Beaver Dam.]

[10] In 1818 FitzGibbon wrote to Captain Kerr of the Indian Department: 'With respect to the affair with Captain Boerstler, not a shot was fired on our side by any but the Indians. They beat the American detachment into a state of terror, and the only share I claim is taking advantage of a favorable moment to offer them protection from the tomahawk and scalping knife. The Indian Department did all the rest.' According to Ducharme the only reason that

Beaver Dam was an important victory for the British. The old fear of the Indians took possession of the American troops at Fort George and following Colonel Boerstler's disaster they did not venture to send a patrol more than a mile from the fort. Perhaps there was justification for such caution, for, despite the return home of the Lower Canada contingent,[11] the Indian forces in the Niagara peninsula had received a new reinforcement with the arrival, on July 5, of a number of Ottawa Indians under Captain Matthew Elliott and their chief, Blackbird. It was the new arrivals from the west, along with some of Norton's Mohawk, who fought a sharp engagement with Americans on July 8 at Ball's Farm in an effort to recover a quantity of medicines and surgical instruments which had been buried when the British had abandoned Fort George earlier in the year. Unlike the engagement at Beaver Dam the proceedings at Ball's were marred by scalping, notwithstanding all that could be done by the officers of the Indian Department to prevent it.

The net around Fort George tightened as the weeks passed. Each day the Indians were employed harassing and teasing the enemy outposts. On July 27 the American General Peter B. Porter wrote disgustedly:

> The truth is . . . that we have had an army at Fort George for two months past, which at any moment of this period might by a vigorous and well-directed exertion of three or four days have prostrated the whole of the enemy's force in this division of the country, and yet this army lies panic-struck, shut up and whipped in by a few hundred miserable savages, leaving the whole of this frontier, except the mile in extent which they occupy, exposed to the inroads and depredations of the enemy.

No more eloquent tribute could have been paid to the services of the Indians to the British cause in the Niagara peninsula in 1813 than this.

Meanwhile, the Americans were using every effort to scrape up a few native warriors for themselves. The failure of Cornplanter's mission to the Grand River in 1812 had not, perhaps, been wholly unexpected; but the chilly reply of the Seneca to the American request that they take up the hatchet and the letter sent by a number of Oneida, Onondaga, Stockbridge, and Tuscarora Indians to the president of the United States on September 28 expressing their desire to remain neutral and their regret that they should ever have been asked to take up arms in a white man's war, must have been a great disappointment.

he did not demand the surrender and receive the capitulation was because he did not speak English.

[11] Following the victory at Beaver Dam the Lower Canada Indians became restless. They were dissatisfied with the rewards which they had received and the long standing jealousy between the Iroquois of Caughnawaga and the Iroquois of Grand River flared up. Many of them returned home and the others followed a few weeks later owing to the necessity of looking after their crops.

Early in 1813 a determined drive was made to enlist Indian support. The United States Indian Department might point out that the president had never authorized the employment of the Indians, but the army needed them, and General Dearborn, the commander-in-chief at Niagara, made it clear that he wanted 150 'young warriors of the Six Nations' to meet him at Fort George. The Indians replied by holding council at Buffalo and on July 25 Red Jacket told the American Indian agent, Erastus Granger, that 'the part we take in this war is not voluntary on our part; you have persuaded us into it. . . . Your voice was for us to sit still, when the war began, but you have beat us – you have got us into the war.' The reluctance on the part of Red Jacket and some of the other Indians to take up the tomahawk was probably promoted less by their distaste for war than the fact that, by this time, they had been fully informed of the American reverses at Stoney Creek and Beaver Dam. Under the circumstances neutrality was perhaps the safest course. This, at least, was Granger's explanation of the Indian attitude. Farmer's Brother and Henry O'Bail of the Seneca were, however, less inclined to argue than was Red Jacket, and the American military authorities succeeded in enlisting a number of Indian warriors who took part in the defence of Black Rock and Buffalo in July 1813. A few Seneca and other Six Nations Indians joined the American forces at Fort George but, with the exception of one slight skirmish, their services did not merit much comment. . . .

THE CAMPAIGN OF 1814

The decisive year was 1814. With the entrance of the Allies into Paris and the fall of the French Empire it was obvious that if the Americans were to achieve victory in Canada they would have to do so before the arrival of the reinforcements from Wellington's armies which events in Europe would now set free.

The American advance began with the crossing of the Niagara and the surrender of Fort Erie. Moving northwards along the Niagara River the American troops encountered General Riall near the Chippewa River. With Riall were 300 Indians, including 100 western Indians and 200 Six Nations under Norton. These Indians very nearly succeeded in capturing Winfield Scott, one of the American brigadiers, while he was taking his morning coffee in a Canadian farmhouse, but Scott and his aides proved to be fleet of foot and succeeded in effecting an escape. In the battle which ensued the Indians penetrated too far into the woods on the British right to afford Riall the assistance he required of them and when the retreat began they melted into the surrounding country in a fashion which drew forth his indignation: 'The Indians . . . have behaved most shamefully; literally speaking, not one remaining, of the hundreds that were with him, prior to the retreat.'

This marks the virtual end of the Indian participation in the war in the Niagara area. Only a small number of them took part in the battle of Lundy's Lane and these, together with the light troops, were sent to follow the Americans and harass them during their withdrawal. There were also a few Indians at the siege of Fort Erie but they played no significant role.[12]

Nor did the American Indians play much part in 1814. General Porter had enlisted the aid of Red Jacket and Erastus Granger to raise a force of Indians for his command, and 600 Indians appear on the United States payroll. It is hardly likely, however, that anything like this number actually crossed the Niagara River or participated in the battle at Chippawa. When, after the battle, the Indians appeared before Porter and demanded payment for their scalps, Porter indignantly refused, and his Indians promptly returned home. There were no American Indians present at Lundy's Lane.

The problem of handling the Indians during the war was not simply a matter of preventing them from indulging in the barbaric practices usually associated with Indian warfare; it was also a matter of preserving good relations between the army and the Indian Department. And these, unfortunately, were never very satisfactory during 1812-14. Even prior to the outbreak of hostilities Captain Norton, an Indianized Scotsman[13] who sought to step into the shoes of Joseph Brant as the principal leader of the Six Nations, had come into conflict with the officers of the Indian Department, and in particular with William Claus, the deputy superintendent-general. Brock was not unaware of this personal antagonism and the effect which it had upon the tribes on the Grand River. As early as May 1812 he had noted that while the Six Nations seemed 'well disposed' they were, unfortunately, divided 'on points which some white people find an interest in keeping alive'.

The issue raised by the quarrel between Norton and Claus was a fundamental one. Norton had proved himself to be a good fighting man, and for that reason he received the support of officers like Prevost, de Rottenburg, Harvey, and others who felt that the first consideration should be that of winning the war. The political implications of Norton's activities were of no

[12] Following the battle of Chippawa, two American Indians bringing with them a Cayuga Chief taken prisoner at Chippawa attended a council of the Six Nations at Burlington where they endeavoured to persuade the Canadian Indians to withdraw from the war promising the American Indians would do likewise. 'Whatever those fellows have said', wrote Riall, 'has caused much dissatisfaction among the Indians, and the western people have reason to suspect the Six Nations of treachery.' In any event very few Cayuga or Onondaga came forward with the other Indians.

[13] Norton was a Scotsman by birth who came to Canada as a private in the 65th Regiment. He was discharged in 1788 and after a brief stay in Kingston went to the villages of the Six Nations where he learned the Mohawk tongue. After a period as a trader he made the acquaintance of Joseph Brant and at Brant's instigation was appointed interpreter to the Mohawk. He resigned this appointment in 1800 and assumed the habits and manners of an Indian.

concern to them. On the other hand, the Indian Department and the civil authorities had to look to the future. They were obliged to consider what problems might arise were Norton to achieve his object of becoming the leader of the Six Nations; better by far that the Indians should remain peaceful and submissive than stirred up to make embarrassing demands. For that reason Claus not only attempted to play down Norton's ability as a leader of the fighting Indians, but also endeavoured to undermine Norton's authority with the tribes at Grand River and obstinately opposed all proposals that he be given a free hand in the distribution of presents to the Indians.

It was thus a matter of concern to Claus that Prevost, who was always suspicious of the Indian Department as a jealous clique, agreed in 1813 to give Norton a discretionary power to distribute presents and rewards to Six Nations warriors who fought in the British interest. And events soon proved that Claus had some justification for his alarm. It was not long before Norton, not content with controlling the Six Nations Indians, endeavoured to extend his influence over the western Indians as well by bribing them with liquor and supplies. When Colonel Caldwell, the superintendent of the western Nations, addressed his Indians on June 14, one of their chiefs replied: 'As to the Snipe [Captain Norton] having got some of our young men to join him, I only say, He speaks loud, and has Strong Milk and Big Breasts, which yield plentifully. You know Father, your Children are fond of Milk, and he gives when they go to him, and promises them Provisions as they want and Goods at discretion. If you will do so Father they will not go to him, but we cannot keep our young men in our hands.'[14]

THE MISSISSIPPI VALLEY

Despite the events on the Thames River in 1813 which had led to the virtual extinction of Indian resistance on the Detroit front, the British still hoped to revive the fighting spirit of the western Indians. Tecumseh's sister was heaped with presents of condolence, his son was given a commission in the British Army, and his brother, the Prophet, was given a pension and installed as principal chief of the western Indians. But these investments yielded no dividends, for the Indians were not prepared to take up arms in any large numbers until the British themselves were in a position to send regular troops to reoccupy the abandoned territory. General Drummond was confident that the Indians around Detroit were still loyal to Great Britain and that, could he but spare the men, he could, without difficulty, recover everything that had been lost. But there were no troops available for this task, and the Indians would not fight alone.

Beyond Lake Michigan the British position was still reasonably secure.

[14] Extract of a Speech delivered to the Western Warriors, June 14, 1814, and the answer of Neywash.

Michilimackinac was well defended; an Indian store depot had been established at Green Bay, and Dickson's agents, Rolette and Brisbois, with the assistance of the loyal Winnebago, maintained British influence throughout the upper reaches of the Mississippi River between Michilimackinac and Prairie du Chien. Against these two positions the Americans directed their western operations during 1814 without success. The little post at Prairie du Chien was taken but quickly recovered and the attempt against Michilimackinac ended in failure. A later effort by Zachary Taylor[15] to dislodge the British from the Mississippi met with failure at the hands of the Winnebago, Sioux, and Sauk Indians. The British thus retained their hold on Prairie du Chien and even began to plan offensive operations for the Wisconsin Indians against St. Louis for the spring of 1815.

THE TREATY OF GHENT

One of the great blunders committed by the British delegates to Versailles in 1783 had been failure to secure some guarantees for the Indian allies of the Crown, in the final treaty of peace. The problem of obtaining Indian assistance during the War of 1812 had kept this lesson before the minds of the British authorities and when their representatives left London for Ghent in 1814 they were bound by instructions to make some effort to arrive at an understanding with the United States over the Indian boundary line. It was to the credit of the British that they would not consent to any arrangement which excluded the Indians, and righteously asserted of Great Britain that 'it is utterly inconsistent with her practice and her principles ever to abandon in her negotiations for peace those who have co-operated with her in war' – an assertion which would have stuck in any Indian throat at that date.

The original British proposal called for the establishment of a clearly defined Indian territory in which the Indians might live their own independent existence, the boundaries to follow those fixed at Greenville in 1795. This was, at least in principle, what the Indians had been fighting for. But the defeat at Moraviantown and the loss of that territory beyond Lake Erie which the capture of Detroit by Brock and Tecumseh had given them, made it difficult for the British to press their point in the face of the adamant refusal of the American delegates to agree to the setting up of an Indian buffer state. The final compromise was one by which the United States agreed to restore to the Indian nations who had been at war 'all the Possessions, Rights,

[15] [Zachary Taylor (1784-1850) was commissioned in the United States army in 1808, and during the war distinguished himself by his defence of Fort Harrison, Indiana Territory, against a large force of Indians led by Tecumseh. After the war he held a series of garrison commands and administrative positions and fought in various campaigns against the Indians. In 1846-7 he led the victorious assault on Mexico from the north, was promoted to major-general, and was nominated for the presidency by the Whig party. He won the election of 1848 but died after sixteen months in office.]

and Privileges' which they had enjoyed or been entitled to enjoy before the commencement of hostilities. It was not what the Indians wanted nor what the British would like to have gained for them; but, while conceding the United States claim to territorial sovereignty over the area which the western Indians had striven to maintain for themselves ever since the days of Pontiac, the Treaty of Ghent did place the United States under a moral obligation to restore the Indians to the *status quo ante bellum.* If the Indians did not gain anything from supporting the British in 1812-14, at least they did not lose anything.

FURTHER READING: W. C. H. Wood (ed.), *Selected British documents . . .*, volume 3, part II, pages 714-34; W. Claus, 'An account of the operations of the Indian contingent with our forces on the Niagara frontier in 1812-13', *Niagara Historical Society*, no. 9 (1902), pages 23-46; E. A. Cruikshank, 'The employment of Indians in the War of 1812', *American Historical Association*, 1895 report, pages 319-35; R. Horsman, 'The role of the Indian in the war', in *After Tippecanoe*, P. P. Mason (ed.), pages 60-77; J. M. Oskison, *Tecumseh and his times: the story of a great Indian* (New York, 1938).

PART TWO

The People and the War

The modern reader with his experience of total war may find it hard to grasp the fact that in most of Upper Canada everyday life continued much as usual despite the war. Only the Niagara frontier was a more or less permanent battleground. Elsewhere, the inhabitants expected to carry on as usual and did not take kindly to restrictions upon their customary liberties. Furthermore, the large numbers of recent arrivals from the United States made it inexpedient to exercise undue severity lest it kindle resentments and win allies for the American cause. Consequently the commanders and administrators struggled to obtain funds and authority from a recalcitrant legislature and only resorted to martial law in great emergencies. The failure of the Americans to secure widespread support in Upper Canada indicates the wisdom of the policy of limited interference with civil jurisdiction followed by commanders in Upper Canada and Governor-General Sir George Prevost. . . . WILLIAM M. WEEKES *is a graduate of Carleton University, the University of Western Ontario, and Osgoode Hall. He lives and practises law in Ottawa. This article appeared in the autumn 1956 issue (volume 48) of 'Ontario History' and is presented with the permission of the author and of the Ontario Historical Society.*

The War of 1812: Civil Authority and Martial Law in Upper Canada

BY WILLIAM M. WEEKES

MAJOR-GENERAL SIR ISAAC BROCK
October 1811 – October 1812

On 9 October, 1811, Brigadier-General Isaac Brock, Commander of the Troops in Upper Canada, issued a proclamation at York declaring himself President of the Council and Administrator of the Province, *vice* Lieutenant-Governor Sir Francis Gore, who had been granted twelve months' leave of absence to return to England to attend to personal affairs.[1] This appointment had been sanctioned by the home government. A proclamation vesting him

[1] During the War of 1812, the British government ordered that in 'the event of the absence of the civil governor from the Province the Senior Military officer assumes the Presidency of the civil Council'.

as administrator in the absence of the governor or lieutenant-governor was issued on 9 April, 1812.[2] With this assumption of power Brock became Major-General on the Staff in Upper Canada.

The character and ability of Major-General Brock are too well known to necessitate reiteration here. Some brief description, however, of the military relationship between this man and his superior officer, Sir George Prevost, might assist in understanding subsequent events.

Lieutenant-General Sir George Prevost was Governor-in-Chief and nominally Commander-in-Chief of the British forces in North America, but he left most of the conduct of the War of 1812 to others. On the two occasions when he appeared personally in the field – Sackett's Harbour and Plattsburg – British arms suffered reverses. An able civil governor, he failed to comprehend the effective decisions necessary to bring the war to a successful conclusion. It is true that during the first months of the war he was under the express injunction of the home government not to do anything which would antagonize the Americans, but his vacillations during later months are entirely inexplicable.

Though disagreements arose between Brock and Prevost over the conduct of military operations, the former's chief difficulties during his wartime command developed in the hazy, undefined area between civil and military government. For war meant the usurpation of many civil rights and as Brock was civil administrator as well as military commander obstacles were inevitable. The military question, of course, had to dominate the whole, but that ascendency was achieved as diplomatically and as painlessly as possible. Brock's problems here were very real. Militiamen were half soldiers, half civilians (usually farmers). As far as they were soldiers, Brock had to obey the directions of Prevost; yet as President of the province he was responsible for the well-being of the militia. This dualism had many implications on the problems of supplies, finances, recruiting, martial law, habeas corpus, etc. The two functions were inevitably, inextricably, intertwined and when the line between the two was drawn the civil side invariably suffered.

In preparation for the approaching crisis with the United States Brock drew up a Militia Act which provided for militia flank companies. 'No exertions [he wrote] . . . shall be wanting in my civil capacity to place that body upon a responsible footing'. But even though this bill had no real teeth in it it failed to pass the spring session of the legislature in 1812. The members refused to institute the oath of abjuration into the bill; the bill for the suspension of habeas corpus also failed to pass. Both Prevost and Brock deplored the limitation – until the end of the ensuing session – in the operation

[2] Under colonial regulations of the period, the lieutenant-governor of each province, except on those occasions when the governor-general was present within the province, was responsible on civil matters directly to the home government.

of the Militia Act, but they believed that the bill would continue in force throughout the winter. For if war came and the legislature was not convened, the act would continue in force during the war – unless Brock made efforts to change it.

Towards the end of April and the beginning of May Brock became optimistic. The militia bill had been put into operation and was showing success; the flank companies throughout were filled with volunteers. There was a clause in the new Militia Act for training flank companies six times a month (non-harvest and non-winter months) for which there were rations but no pay. 'I shall proceed to extend this system now that I have ascertained the people are so well disposed – but my means are very limited.'

Unfortunately, however, Brock's optimism was not well founded. By mid-July the state of the militia was rather a sorry one. The new militia law made provision for a fine of five pounds or three months in gaol for those who refused to march, while those who left the force without permission to harvest their crops were fined twenty pounds. The Long Point militia, concerned about the safety of their families, refused to move as long as the Grand River Indians remained neutral, and the Long Point magistrates refused to act upon their disobedience. Although he wished to have the militia acquire some degree of discipline without interruption, Brock was unable to engage in any operations on the Niagara front. Some of the militia had been permitted to return to their homes but these had to be recalled. Some left their units in spite of the fine. There was much discontent. The militia was clamouring for its pay, taking all the available specie, and Brock had to request government paper money to enable him to carry on.

The advance to Detroit of the American Brigadier-General William Hull threw the province into a panic.

> Legislators, magistrates, militia officers, all have imbibed the idea [that the province must fall], and are so sluggish and indifferent in their respective offices that the artful and active scoundrel is allowed to parade the country without interruption and commit all imaginable mischief. They are so alarmed of offending that they rather encourage than repress disorders and other improper acts.

Brock had to have more power.

A session of the Legislature of Upper Canada was called on 27 July, 1812, and was prorogued on 3 August, when it became apparent that Brock was not to be granted his wishes. The Assembly refused to strengthen the Militia Act, to suspend partially habeas corpus, to authorize 'a partial exercise of Martial Law concurrently with the ordinary course of Justice', or to give Brock monies not used from past appropriations. To Prevost he wrote that, though this was the best House yet called, he would get no good from them;

they, like the magistrates, would remain passive. 'The repeal of the *Habeas Corpus* will not pass and if I have recourse to the Law Martial I am told the whole armed force will disperse. . . . The Militia cannot possibly be governed by the present Law. All admit the fact, yet the fear of giving offence, will prevent anything effectual being effected.'

On prorogation, the Executive Council advised Brock that it was expedient to proclaim and exercise martial law according to the powers of His Majesty's Commission to the Governor-General. In endeavouring to resolve his dilemma, Brock wrote to the Commander of the Forces:

> My present Civil Office not only authorizes me to Convene General Courts Martial for the trial of offenders belonging to the Militia but likewise the infliction of the Sentence of death. Whilst in regard to the Military my power is limited to the mere assembling of the Court I beg leave to submit to the consideration of Your Excellency whether in times like the present I ought not to be invested with equal authority over each Service.

On 20 August, Prevost signed a warrant giving Brock more extensive power over the sentence of such general courts martial as Brock might be called upon to assemble.

Faced with the prospect of having to declare martial law, further doubts arose in Brock's mind; these he submitted to Prevost for the latter's opinion:

> 1st In the event of declaring Martial Law can I without the Sign Manual Approve and Carry into effect the Sentence of a General Court Martial.
> 2d Can I put upon a General Court Martial, after Martial Law is proclaimed, any person not a Commissioned Officer in His Majesty's regular forces. In other words, can Militia Officers sit in conjunction with those of the line?
>
> Your Excellency, I feel confident, will readily excuse the direct manner with which I presume to put my queries. Should Militia Officers be disbarred sitting, the proclamations of Martial Law will be a perfect nullity. There is now a want of a sufficient number of officers at any one place in this widely extended Province to compose a Court Martial and unless Militia officers be admitted as members, the Law cannot operate.

Several of Prevost's letters dealt with these requests for advice:

> I believe you are authorized by the commission under which you administer the government of Upper Canada, to declare martial law in the event of invasion or insurrection; it is, therefore, for you to consider whether you can obtain any thing equivalent to that power from your Legislature. I have not succeeded in obtaining a modification of it in Lower Canada, and must therefore, upon the occurrence of either of those calamities, declare the law martial unqualified, and of course shut the doors of the courts of civil law.

In a further communication Prevost added:

> . . . it has not fallen within my Experience to see Martial Law Proclaimed

> except in those places where it has been declared under the authority of a Provincial Legislature which of course regulated the model in which it was to be executed.
>
> As the Martial Law which you propose declaring is founded upon the King's Commission and upon the extreme case of an Invasion alluded to in it, I am inclined to think that whatever power is necessary for carrying the measure into effect must have been intended to be given you by the commission and consequently that the power of Assembling Courts Martial and of carrying the Sentence into execution is included in the authority for declaring Martial Law.
>
> The Officers of the Militia being themselves subject to Martial Law when it is declared I conceive they may sit upon Courts Martial with Officers of His Majesty's Regular Forces. But upon both these points I desire not to be understood as speaking decisively – extreme cases must be met by measures which in ordinary occasions would not perhaps be justified.

This policy Brock adopted, apparently, but these were not to be the final words on the subject during the war.

Until the battle at Queenston Heights there was a chance that a prolonged war could be averted and that a definite armistice might be arranged. Thus Brock was urged to rigid economy. Even so, specie – always in short supply in Upper Canada – soon disappeared. In December 1811, £3,000 had been sent to the Administrator of the upper province for use in the civil government, to be followed by £2,000 more as soon as the military chest was replenished. These funds were to be devoted partly to authorized construction of roads and other public services at York.

It became necessary immediately after war broke out to institute paper currency. The issue of army bills was sanctioned by the legislature of Lower Canada – which saved the day, for the assembly of Upper Canada refused to make the innovation. Money became so scarce in Upper Canada that it was unobtainable at any discount of government bills of exchange.

All money, whether in the form of specie or of paper currency, came from Lower Canada, that is, the military chest. Sir Roger Sheaffe, Brock's successor, was forced, however, to sanction the Deputy-Commissary-General to issue notes to supplement the military chest of Upper Canada. There appears to be no instance in which a money requisition from Upper Canada went unhonoured by the Commander of the Forces; usually, these would be in amounts of £5,000 – totalling, for some of these war years, over £200,000.

MAJOR-GENERAL SIR ROGER SHEAFFE
October 1812 – June 1813

Major-General Sir Roger Sheaffe had been Brock's second-in-command in Upper Canada. He was by no means so popular as his senior and shortly after he assumed the command he aroused a cabal of ranking officers against him. Though Prevost supported him in this quarrel, it, together with subsequent events, did not enhance his reputation.

While Brock was killed at Queenston, 13 October, 1812, it was not until 20 October that Sheaffe was able to reach York and be sworn in as President and Administrator of the province. Very soon he had to devote his attention to a matter which was to be of some concern to him and his successors: the question of aliens in the province.

The alien faction in Upper Canada, particularly along the north shores of lakes Ontario and Erie, was considerable. As recent American immigrants, they assisted in instigating disaffection and were a continual nuisance and source of anxiety to the administration. Sheaffe posed the question of their control to his council, and it was decided to permit the aliens to reside where they wished during good behaviour. It was deemed impolitic to let them go to the United States.

It was during Sheaffe's régime that the real effects of the war, in the form of shortages, scarcity of supplies and men, disgruntled populations, and so on, began to come to the fore. In this situation the aliens naturally played an exaggerated role. Yet the home government advised against antagonizing any element of the population '. . . not to interfere with the ordinary occupations of the inhabitants beyond what may be necessary for the defence of the Province, and by demanding no sacrifice beyond what are absolutely required to ensure their being easily and cheerfully borne.'

In his speech to the legislature on 8 March, 1813, Sheaffe sought more money for defence purposes; authorization to grant a sum for clothing to each militia volunteer since a shortage existed; and a revised and more efficient militia law. He also requested authority to pay in advance half-yearly annuities to widows, children, and disabled; and because the crops were so poor, control of the export and distillation of grain. In all these requests he was eventually successful. In the matter of the grant to the militia volunteers Sheaffe had to consult the Governor-in-Chief. Prevost, however, had already encouraged him in this for, in January, the governor had asked Sheaffe to raise three battalions, assisted by a promise of land. These corps were to be officered, not by militia, but by captains of the line. He left the handling of the question to Sheaffe's judgment.

The militia bill was amended as desired. An incorporated militia was to be formed with a bounty of eight dollars being granted to each volunteer for his clothing; the assembly could raise no money to pay more, but all unappropriated funds were given to Sheaffe. He sought Prevost's aid and authority to increase the bounty, which he considered too small, by ten or twelve dollars. Before receiving Prevost's approval, he increased the bounty to eighteen dollars on his own initiative. However, Prevost gave his unqualified approbation to this increase. As an added inducement, Sheaffe decided to offer grants of land. All this was done to raise a more permanent militia, for Prevost had intimated that there was little hope of reinforcement from Europe (an opinion which was correct at the time but soon proved erroneous).

The same session of the legislature passed a bill which gave currency to army bills issued by the authority of the legislature of Lower Canada, though, in the previous December, Sheaffe had authorized the Deputy-Commissary-General to issue notes because of the exhausted state of the military chest. Money continued to flow from Lower Canada in lots of £5,000 and £10,000 for the civil government.

The question of martial law arose only twice during the time that Sheaffe was President of the Council. Brigadier-General Henry Procter, in command of operations in the western areas with headquarters at Amherstburg, had been empowered by Prevost (through Sheaffe) to invoke martial law in the Western District if he deemed it necessary.[3] Because of a shortage of supplies and a reluctance on the part of the local inhabitants to bring forth their produce for sale,[4] Procter had been forced to institute a partial operation of martial law. Prevost conceived that Procter had 'acted with proper precaution, to preserve Order in the newly acquired Territory, & that the Circumstance which led to it fully justified such a measure'.

When Sheaffe retreated from York, Prevost had authorized him to institute martial law within the district for troop subsistence and the protection of Upper Canada from disaffection. Sheaffe declined to do so as President, claiming that he had no constitutional authority to exercise martial law partially, and he manifested that conviction by soliciting his legislature to empower him to do so. Thereupon Prevost gave him an absolute military command to authorize Brigadier-General Vincent, at the latter's discretion on the ground of necessity, to exercise martial law as limited.

Sickness, desertion, lack of clothing, lack of supplies, disaffection and distress in the militia – all of these began to plague Sheaffe. The Barrack Department and the Commissariat Department were quite inefficient, and while this was not the fault of Sheaffe he had to accept the responsibility.[5] He sought from Prevost advice as to whether he had the right to demand military service against the United States from the inhabitants of the Michigan Territory. But this right was not granted.

Sheaffe, however, had only a little longer to worry about such matters. Routed from York in the first week of May by the Americans, he retreated

[3] Brigadier-General John Vincent, in command of the forces in the Niagara peninsula at the time, with headquarters at Burlington, was likewise empowered.

[4] Supplies in this region became very scarce for the remainder of the war, mainly because the commissariat failed to pay the farmers' receipts for their produce.

[5] Brigade-Major T. Evans blamed Brock's refusal to attend to details as the reason for the state of these two departments.

hastily to Kingston and never returned westward. On 19 June, 1813, he was succeeded as Commander and Administrator by Major-General Sir Francis de Rottenburg.

MAJOR-GENERAL SIR FRANCIS DE ROTTENBURG
June-December, 1813

Baron de Rottenburg seems to have been a considerably stronger character than Sheaffe but he suffered from the fact that during the few months that he held the command the tides of war tended to go against the British. The Battle of Lake Erie, in which Captain O. H. Perry overwhelmed the smaller forces of Captain R. H. Barclay, gave the Americans the command of Lake Erie for the balance of the war. Control of Lake Ontario had been lost for all practical purposes to the enemy. The war entered a rather desultory phase with most of the successes falling to the Americans.

Along with this military situation, de Rottenburg had to contend with growing unrest and dissatisfaction within the province. There were complaints over the lack of money to pay the troops and civilians and to buy supplies. Civilian artificers were leaving their employment because they were not being paid. Army foragers were forced to buy by receipt though army credit was very bad, and the shortage of money meant high prices.[6] Such conditions raised again the alien question and the problem of martial law.

The new commander's first act was to prohibit the distillation of rye. He took over the grain and the stock of farmers who joined the enemy.[7] He ordered the militia to prepare Dundas Street for the transport of troops, stores, and ordnance, and planned to erect at Burlington Heights barracks to accommodate 1,000 men. As a precautionary measure he arranged for forty canoes of the Northwest Company to bring Procter's army to Montreal should such a move prove necessary. Yet not long after he had undertaken these measures he was ordered by Prevost not to incur any expense whatever out of the ordinary course unless previously sanctioned by the latter. Contrasted to this was the attitude of de Rottenburg [as described by Justice W. D. Powell[8] in a letter of June 28, 1813 to Prevost]:

> The greater or less energy of public functionaries will ever take its tone from the head. In the absence of General de Rottenburg we should not expect any-

[6] Some idea of the supply problems in Upper Canada during the latter half of the war may be gained from the fact that over eighty per cent of the army's fresh beef was supplied by drovers of Vermont and New Hampshire.

[7] Funds so provided were to be applied to the relief of war victims.

[8] [William Dummer Powell (1755-1834) came to Canada in 1779, practised law in Montreal for a time, was appointed justice of the Court of Common Pleas at Detroit in 1789, puisne judge in the Court of King's Bench in 1794, and Chief Justice of Upper Canada and speaker of the legislative council in 1816. He was one of the trial judges at Ancaster in 1814. See pages 241-50.]

thing decisive in the civil administration if the measures depended on every individual, but the President has authorized the Council to deliberate any propositions supposed to be important without waiting for a special reference, so that little delay need interpose between the necessity for any vigorous proceeding and its sanction. I think I may assure Your Excellency that under this arrangement there will be no display of weakness.[9]

Inefficient subordinates handicapped de Rottenburg. 'With the exception of Lieut.-Colonel Harvey . . . the heads of the departments here are deficient in activity and cleverness, and the militia staff is most miserable.' The chief justice felt that 'the Commissary is laborious and well acquainted with the resources of the country, but the habits of his department restrain in some degree of the energy of personal character by its rigid regulations to ensure economy'.

Both Prevost and de Rottenburg were anxious about the disaffected and alien population. The Commander of the Forces called the major-general's attention to 'the traitorous characters who are in league with and giving information to the Enemy to suggest to you the necessity of immediately Submitting . . . to the consideration of your Executive Council for their advice upon the best means of Suppressing the growing evil'.

In July de Rottenburg received a warrant from Prevost empowering him to convene general courts martial in Upper Canada, and authorizing him in cases where de Rottenburg felt it necessary that an immediate example should be made to approve and carry sentences into effect.[10] Increasing disaffection and arrests for treason in the Niagara district raised a problem for de Rottenburg which he carried to Prevost for solution.

Persons charged with treasonable practices being frequently arrested in this District, for the trial of whom a Summary method of proceeding would be desirable, as well to prevent an accumulation of prisoners of that description, which, from the Ordinary course of the law must be the consequence, as to awe the disaffected, whose cautious demeanor does not expose them to arrest – and not knowing myself how to act, under circumstances which, while Martial law exists in the District of Niagara, the functions of the civil officer remain unimpaired, I am induced to request you will favor me with Your Opinion and advice on the Subject – and Should it appear that those persons can be

[9] It appears that Powell was the most important of several confidential informants that Prevost had in the upper province. That de Rottenburg suspected this is evident. 'The President had not invited me to similar confidence as Sir G.P. [Prevost] had, and on the few occasions when my zeal prompted suggestions they were read with silent neglect by Maj.-Genl. De R. [Rottenburg].' From a note in Powell's handwriting, 18 November, 1813.

[10] De Rottenburg also wanted a warrant to appoint acting judge advocates. In 1764, the Judge Advocate's office in London challenged the right of the military courts to exercise jurisdiction over civilians. In 1777, the Chief Justice of Quebec, Peter Livius, complained of the use of military authority to tie the hands of the civil courts.

arraigned before a Military Tribunal, You will be pleased to furnish me with an authority from His Excellency the Commander of the Forces, for the assembling of such a Tribunal, if necessary.

To which request Prevost replied:

> . . . if Martial Law has in fact been regularly proclaimed in the Niagara District I conceive that little difficulty will exist upon this Subject, as in that case under the 15th. & 16th. Articles of the 14th. Section of the Articles of War persons accused of the crimes you mention may be brought before a Genl. Court Martial which you are already authorized to convene and may be tried and published by it, but I have some doubts whether Martial Law does at present exist in the Niagara district, to the extent that would Warrant a Court Martial to take Cognizance of such Offences if committed by those persons.

Prevost went on to refer to the authority given to Vincent by Sheaffe and concluded with the belief that if, in de Rottenburg's opinion, the situation in the Niagara district became sufficiently serious, the latter as president of the province should suspend the ordinary courts of law by the imposition of martial law and try accused persons before general courts martial.

By August the food and forage position for the large garrison stationed at Kingston had become so critical and disaffection so prevalent that de Rottenburg advocated martial law. In September, at Sandwich, Procter proclaimed martial law to supply the wants of his troops and to handle traitors and the disaffected. Prevost, who had come up to Kingston from Montreal (thus assuming direct civil control in Upper Canada as Governor-in-Chief) proclaimed that he would deal with anyone who sought American parole in order to avoid his obligation to the province. On 22 November, 1813, de Rottenburg proclaimed a partial existence of martial law in the Johnstown and Eastern districts. This act, the House of Assembly declared, was 'arbitrary and unconstitutional and contrary to and subversive of the established laws of the land'. It was also claimed by the assembly that Bathurst erroneously supposed de Rottenburg to have acted in his civil capacity, when he supported the latter's act.

LIEUTENANT-GENERAL SIR GORDON DRUMMOND
December 1813 – April 1815

Lieutenant-General Sir Gordon Drummond had been appointed second-in-command to Sir George Prevost on 4 June, 1811. On 13 December, 1813, he replaced de Rottenburg as Commander of the Troops in Upper Canada and as President and Administrator of the province. A firm, able military figure, he stood up to Prevost considerably more than had his predecessors, including Brock. As the war continued, his problems, particularly of supplies and maintenance of order, became increasingly acute.

Availability of supplies in the province varied as to district and circumstance; where the army was grouped in large numbers, the supply situation could and did become progressively severe. After Drummond took over the command, his second-in-command, Major-General Phineas Riall, set about determining the resources of the country. At that time he found the province in a fair state save for a lack of meat, which would have to come from the commissary in Lower Canada. Riall suggested setting up a corps of waggoners which would be attached to the commissariat, thus permitting farmers to remain at their homes to attend to agriculture, thereby increasing the amount of supplies available. Then when the need to call on the farmers did arise they would be much more willing to give their services and equipment. Prevost approved of this suggestion, and also of Drummond's plan that Riall investigate all claims of individuals for supplies furnished to government, and that those that were equitable be settled without delay.

Drummond suggested to Prevost that the critical situation at Kingston be eased by the dispatch of supplies from the lower province, and as a means of relieving the general distress he advocated sending some of the Indians at the head of the lake to Lower Canada. These people were very troublesome and a number of farmers had left their farms in fear of them, while the Indians were consuming about sixteen head of cattle and twenty-five barrels of flour daily. But Prevost refused to accept any Indians into Lower Canada, giving as his reason that they would be too troublesome to the Canadiens and the American borderers.

Supply conditions at Burlington and in the Western District if anything were worse than those at Kingston. Drummond needed £30,000 to discharge debts at Burlington alone. There were some claims in the Thames valley area dating from Brock's march which had not been paid. Though a board had been directed to investigate such claims, there were

> . . . many people, who, either living at a great distance, or not having heard of the establishment of the Board, or from many other causes, never preferred their claims to it; and are, in consequence, now refused the payment due to them. Yet in this, in one respect, they do not appear to be much worse placed, than those who did receive payment; many of the latter still being [?] out of their money; from two causes; first, as the Commissary reports, that he seldom has money in sufficient quantity to pay them; and, secondly, from the kind of money in his possession, he has it not in his power to discharge small sums: for, if a person has due to him a lesser sum than 25 dollars, he cannot be paid at all; and, if more than 25 dollars and less than 50, he gets but the 25, unless he can bring the difference in change between the other 25 and the fifty.

The soldiers also were not being paid and when they were the inhabitants would not give value for soldiers' bills.

Drummond's need for money grew more pressing. To uphold his credit he had to have money for York and Burlington. What was received only paid old debts. On one occasion he took matters into his own hands and authorized the Receiver-General of Upper Canada to draw upon the Commissary-General for £8,000 payable at Montreal.

On 25 January, 1814, Drummond repealed de Rottenburg's proclamation regarding martial law at Kingston. Within two weeks he was to regret this action[11] for the commissary at Kingston found that the local farmers continued to withhold supplies. He decided that the measure would have to be re-introduced, and he transmitted to Major-General [Richard] Stovin[12] at Kingston a proclamation 'to issue in the Midland and Newcastle Districts, declaring martial law to be in force as far as relates to provisions and forage for the use of His Majesty's troops in that vicinity'. However, as this proclamation was for Stovin's discretionary use, that officer felt that it was not necessary, since the inhabitants had brought their produce to the commissariat. But Stovin decided to retain the proclamation until such time as circumstances called for its distribution.

Drummond's repeal and reimposition of martial law at Kingston caused a sharp exchange between him and Prevost. Particularly did the latter object to Drummond's issuance of the proclamation in his role of Commander of the Troops in Upper Canada. Prevost stated:

> Whilst I was in Upper Canada, I gave authority to the General Officers in Command at Detroit & Niagara to do so in their respective districts, whenever the emergencies of the service should render it an indispensible act for the preservation of their Command or the subsistence of the Troops but when I withdrew to the Lower Province I considered my power to have ceased, therefore when M. Genl. de Rottenburg took the command and was under the necessity of declaring Martial Law, he modified its operation, but he did it as administrator of the Government & in that capacity alone during the existence of a Civil Government do I apprehend it ought to be done.

Drummond, however, persisted in his course and by midsummer of 1814 martial law prevailed throughout the province.[13] But he maintained strict control over its operation, was liberal and just, and insisted upon fair prices.

Following Drummond's complaint of a lack of small notes, Prevost advised doing as Lower Canada had done – have the assembly issue them (not redeemable in cash). However, he also forwarded such specie and small notes as he had available, for Prevost himself was running low on funds and was

[11] At one time the commissariat at Kingston, responsible for supplying 5,000 rations daily, had in stock sixteen barrels of flour.

[12] [Richard Stovin (d.1826 or 1827) became an ensign in the British army in 1780, a captain in 1788, a lieutenant-colonel in 1798, and a major-general in 1811. He commanded the Montreal District during the war.]

[13] Drummond's proclamation declaring partial martial law throughout the province, for provisions and forage, was issued at Kingston, 12 April, 1814.

demanding money, especially specie, from the home government. He reasserted the absolute necessity of employing every expedient to remove those difficulties in Upper Canada and stated that he would support Drummond in any move towards that end. The monetary problem became further complicated in the autumn of 1814 when forged notes began to appear at Quebec, Brockville being the suspected place of entry. To keep this practice to a minimum, Prevost asked Drummond to restrict intercourse at that place.[14]

By and with the advice of his Executive Council, Drummond prohibited the use of grains for the making of alcoholic beverages from 16 January to 1 March, 1814; and at the following session of the provincial parliament he obtained authorization to extend this prohibition, excepting His Majesty's military service. As President he later banned exports of most produce, including beef, pork, wheat, corn, grain, and meal flour. In his address on the opening of the third session of the sixth provincial parliament at York on 15 February, 1814, he sought new and more efficient ways of incorporating battalions of militia for permanent service; one great military road through the province; and an increase in the fine paid by conscientious objectors. In seeking a modification of habeas corpus he pointed out that two of the legislators were fighting for the enemy. He also sought acts of attainder, the returns from which were to be applied to war relief. The Assembly authorized acts to suspend habeas corpus; to provide for the more effective trial and punishment of treason and treasonable practices; and to declare certain persons aliens and to confiscate their estates. There was also a fair appropriation for the improvement of roads for military service, but 'It is a matter of much regret to me that the House of Assembly would not consent to strengthen the executive in this Province by authorizing the person administering the government to proclaim martial law in special districts only where so violent a measure became indispensable. The question was negatived by a decided majority.'

The Colonial Secretary also queried the legality of Drummond's martial law provisions. Lawsuits were brought against the officers and agents of the commissariat because of the seizures under these proclamations; these officials were defended by crown officers of the province. Bathurst informed Drummond that when decisions were rendered

> . . . unfavourable to the Individuals against whom the Suits may be brought; in all cases where the Verdict shall be found in any degree proportionate to the loss or damage sustained, His Majesty's Government are fully disposed to make good the same, according to the just and liberal principle which you have so properly laid down in the directions you have given to the Magistrates in each

[14] A year later Gore requested the assistance of the commanding officer of the Glengarry Light Infantry Fencibles in apprehending American counterfeiters, operating in the District of Newcastle, 'by ordering a sufficient party to proceed in aid of the Civil power'.

> District, to fix a fair price to be paid upon all articles discovered. In any case however where the warmth of popular feeling may lead to a Verdict to such an extent as will admit of Appeal, it will be proper to refer it to the decision of a higher tribunal.

Later, Gore wrote that these '. . . attempts to create dissatisfaction, by multiplying Suits at Law . . . have been check'd by the prudence of the Judge and all irritation on that account, will I trust subside, in a fair liquidation of just demands, by the Commissioner appointed for that purpose, by the Officer Commanding His Majesty's Forces'.

Drummond, too, had his problems in securing sufficient numbers of militia volunteers. The session of the Legislature, February-March 1814, however, assisted him considerably in obtaining what he wanted. The existing militia law was amended so that battalions of incorporated militia, numbering about six hundred men each, could be called out; and once called out, the executive government would have the power to continue their service for a period of one year. These troops were to be like troops of the line, even to scarlet clothing. However, Drummond bemoaned the fact that in this way men were being taken from their farms, and he hinted to Bathurst that he needed more regulars. His fears became realized later, at harvest time, when it proved essential that the sedentary militia be permitted to return home 'to save their produce from being totally lost to the country'. By January 1815 the bounty to the incorporated militia had been increased to ten pounds, partly to induce them to settle on the land. For Drummond's plan envisaged discharging any soldier who so desired on the spot, thus providing settlers. To this scheme Prevost was quite receptive.

The foregoing, perhaps, will present some picture of the relations between civil and military administration in Upper Canada during the War of 1812. . . . The examples given will point up at least the highlights of the association, and in some way reveal the personalities and characters which were involved. During this period the area in which administrative or non-military functional conflict could arise was in reality quite limited. The old concept of colonial governorship still prevailed, and during a time of war both the civil and military administration became dominated by the army. The border between the two administrations was rarely a clear one and, as has been shown, almost invariably the wishes of the Commander of the Forces prevailed.

FURTHER READING: W. C. H. Wood (ed.), *Selected British documents . . .*, volume 1, pages 164-86; C. F. Hamilton, 'The Canadian militia; universal service', *Canadian Defence Quarterly*, volume 5 (1927-8), pages 288-300; W. R. Riddell, 'The first Canadian war-time prohibition measure', *Canadian Historical Review,* volume 1 (1920), pages 187-90.

Given the background of extensive recent immigration from the United States, it would indeed have been surprising if the American cause had not elicited some support from among the inhabitants. The administrators of the province, knowing the delicacy of the situation, took steps to assure themselves of the loyalty of the militia, expelled aliens from the colony, frightened waverers from lending overt assistance to the invader, and proceeded with the fullest severity of the law only against those American partisans who crossed the thin line into treason. They were powerfully assisted by committees of loyalists, chiefly of the office-holding class and members of the governing 'establishment'. How much danger was there from these disaffected elements? This article is more useful for marshalling numerous instances of disloyal or suspicious activities than for attempting conclusions as to their total effect and their significance for the outcome of the war. It appeared in the 'Transactions' of the Royal Society of Canada, series three, section 2 (1912), and is reprinted with the permission of Mrs. Cruikshank and of the Society.

A Study of Disaffection in Upper Canada in 1812-15

BY ERNEST A. CRUIKSHANK

Travellers from the United States who visited Upper Canada during the first decade of the nineteenth century generally agreed in reporting that they had observed among the inhabitants 'a determined partiality to the United States and a decided and almost avowed hostility to the British Government'. One of these, Christian Schultz, related that while he was in a tavern at Niagara in 1807 he heard a man say in the presence of ten or twelve others who gave no sign of disapproval that 'if Congress will only send us a flag and a proclamation declaring that whoever is found in arms against the United States shall forfeit his lands, we will fight ourselves free without any expense to them'.

War was then believed to be almost inevitable in consequence of the collision between the frigates *Leopard* and *Chesapeake.*

Indeed, Lieutenant Governor Gore wrote officially to Sir James Craig about the same time:

> I think I may venture to state that the generality of the inhabitants from Kingston to the borders of the lower province may be depended upon, but I cannot venture to assert from the industry that has been used by certain characters now and lately in the province that the inhabitants about the seat of this government, Niagara and Long Point are equally to be relied on. I have also to observe that excepting the inhabitants of Glengarry and those persons who served in the American War and their descendants, which form a considerable body of men, the residue of the inhabitants of this colony consist chiefly of persons who have emigrated from the States of America, and of consequence retain those ideas of equality and insubordination much to the prejudice of this government so prevalent in that country. . . .

[In 1808], soon after his arrival at Halifax as Lieutenant Governor of Nova Scotia, Prevost had despatched John Howe to Boston as a confidential agent with instructions

> . . . to ascertain what ideas are entertained as to the feasibility and mode of attacking Canada, New Brunswick, and Nova Scotia, and whether by sea or land, whether the inhabitants of those provinces, or any or what part of them are considered as having any partiality or attachment to the United States, whether it is supposed that there is any disposition to favor or assist the United States in case of War with Great Britain or to Separate from Great Britain and enter into the confederacy of the United States.

Howe had reported after careful enquiry among men of all parties both at Boston and Washington:

> The Conquest of Canada, they contemplate as a matter perfectly easy; and whenever they speak of it they build much on the disposition of the Canadians as friendly to them. They reckon also, on a ready welcome from a number of Americans who have of late years become Settlers in Upper Canada. And this last circumstance at least, may well lead His Majesty's Government to consider whether it is politic to admit as settlers near the Frontiers, men of this description.

Since that time the number of American settlers in Upper Canada had steadily increased, and, writing in 1810, the traveller John Melish had affirmed his belief 'that if 5,000 men were sent into Upper Canada with a proclamation of independence the great mass of the population would join the American Government.'. . .

In March 1811, an address was presented to Lieutenant Governor Gore from 'the magistrates, clergy and principal inhabitants of the Eastern District' wherein they said:

> Your petitioners . . . cannot conceal from Your Excellency that the sudden and indiscriminate influx of foreigners, sometimes openly, and at other times secretly hostile to the British Government, gives them great uneasiness and begins to render their situation much less comfortable than it might have

otherwise been, and when they look at their children, they are filled with serious apprehensions lest they should imbibe principles very different from those which induced their parents to fight for their King and country and which still induce them to cling with delight to that happy Island, the birthplace of true liberty, and now her last hope in the general wreck of nations.

Far the larger number of the inhabitants, they affirmed, were still unquestionably loyal but this majority was rapidly decreasing and they strongly urged the 'necessity of introducing some check to the admission of strangers from the neighboring States in proper time before their numbers become formidable and the evil incurable.' . . .

[On February 24, 1812] Major General Brock, on whom the civil administration of Upper Canada had devolved in the absence of Gore, published a proclamation announcing that 'divers persons had recently come into the province with a seditious intent and to endeavor to alienate the minds of His Majesty's subjects' and instructing the commissioners lately appointed to enforce the act of the Legislature for the better security of the province to be vigilant in the discharge of their duty.

On the following day he was obliged to report his bitter disappointment at the defeat of an important amendment to the Militia Act which had been proposed at his request.

The many doubtful characters in the militia [he wrote] made me anxious to introduce the oath of abjuration into the bill. There were twenty members present when this highly important measure was lost by the casting vote of the chairman. The great influence which the fear and number of settlers from the United States possess over the decisions of the Lower House is truly alarming and ought by every practical means to be diminished.

In a letter to Lord Liverpool, dated March 23, 1812, referring to the recent session of the Legislature, Brock wrote:

My observations convinced me of the expediency of every militiaman taking an oath abjuring every foreign power. The many settlers from the United States who openly profess a determination of not acting against their countrymen, made some test highly necessary. The number of aliens emigrating from the United States, who have acquired property and consequently votes for the Assembly, alarmed at the novelty of an oath of abjuration, exerted their utmost efforts and ultimately succeeded (so extensive is the influence of these people that it even masters the Legislature), in preventing by the casting vote of the chairman, the adoption of this. A bill for the suspension of the Habeas Corpus was also defeated by their influence. Liable to the constant inroads of the most abandoned characters who seek impunity in this province from crimes of high enormity committed in the States and surrounded by a population, a great part of which profess strong American feelings and attachments, it will not, I hope, be deemed unreasonable at a time like the present, if I should be desirous to be clothed, in conjunction with His Majesty's Executive Council, with the means so well calculated to maintain public tranquility.

. . . In his well known proclamation, dated the day after entering the Western District at Sandwich, General Hull made a direct appeal to the recent immigrants in the most significant terms.

> Raise not your hands against your brethren. Many of your forefathers fought for the freedom and *Independence* we now enjoy; being children therefore of the same family with us and heirs to the same heritage, the arrival of an army of friends must be hailed by you with a cordial welcome. You will be emancipated from tyranny and oppression and restored to the dignified position of freemen. Had I any doubt of eventual success, I might ask your assistance, but I come prepared for every contingency. I have a force which will look down all opposition, and that force is but the vanguard of a much greater. . . . If you tender your services voluntarily they will be accepted readily.[1]

Two hundred copies of this proclamation were printed in English or French and distributed as rapidly and widely as possible, with such effect that half of the militia assembled at Amherstburg promptly deserted. Sixty of these men reported at Hull's headquarters within twenty-four hours to claim the protection promised by him and some of them enlisted under his command. A scouting party which advanced up the Thames as far as Allen's Mills in the township of Delaware was immediately joined by Simon Zelotes Watson, Ebenezer Allen, and Andrew Westbrook, who had quarrelled fiercely with Colonel Talbot over the location of lands. Watson was a land surveyor and speculator who had formerly held the office of justice of the peace in the Montreal District. Allen had served as a volunteer in the British Indian department during the Revolution but bore a very doubtful character. Westbrook was a blacksmith lately from the United States who had acquired a considerable quantity of land and desired more. These three men accompanied the invaders to Sandwich and possibly gave Hull an exaggerated account of the disaffection and apathy of the inhabitants. . . .

On July 20 a copy of Hull's proclamation was obtained by General Brock and he was informed at the same time that 'it had been productive of considerable effect on the minds of the inhabitants'. Further intelligence of an alarming nature induced him to direct the march of a small force of regulars and militia to Delaware to overawe or arrest the malcontents.

> Numbers have already joined the invading army [he wrote], commotions are excited and late occurrences have spread a general gloom. . . . The enemy's cavalry amounts to about 50. They are led by one Watson, a surveyor from Montreal, a desperate character. This fellow has been allowed to parade with about 20 men of the same description as far as Westminster vowing as they

[1] Proclamation to the inhabitants of Upper Canada, July 13, 1812.

went along the most bitter vengeance against the first characters in the province. Nothing can show more strongly the state of apathy in that part of the country. I am perhaps liberal in attributing the conduct of the inhabitants to that cause.

In a few days, however, a party of militia led by two enterprising young officers succeeded in arresting both Allen and Westbrook and learned that Watson had returned to Sandwich. The apprehension of these two men had a marked effect upon the disaffected. . . .

In his speech to the Legislature delivered on July 28, Brock again strongly advocated the suspension of the Habeas Corpus Act, saying:

> A few traitors have already joined the enemy, have been suffered to come into the country with impunity and have been harbored and concealed in the interior, yet the general spirit of loyalty which appears to pervade the inhabitants of this Province is such as to authorize a just expectation that their efforts to mislead and deceive will be unavailing. The disaffected, I am convinced, are few. To protect and defend the loyal inhabitants from their machinations is an object worthy of your most zealous deliberations.

Next day after learning that the Norfolk militia as a body had refused to march to Oxford he became deeply depressed and wrote:

> The population, although I had no great confidence in the majority, is worse that I expected to find it and the magistrates, &c. &c., appear quite confounded and decline acting – the consequence is the most improper conduct is tolerated. The officers of militia exert no authority. Everything shows as if a certainty existed of a change taking place soon. But I still hope the arrival of reinforcements may yet avert such a dire calamity. Many in that case would become active in our cause who are now dormant.

. . . Finally on August 3 the Executive Council was convened and Brock informed the members that all his expectations of support from the Legislative Assembly had been disappointed as that body had consumed eight days in debating a single partisan measure, the repeal of the School Bill, and in passing an act for the disclosure of treasonable practices before a magistrate should have power to commit without bail, and requested their advice whether it would be expedient for him to prorogue the Legislature at once and proclaim martial law. . . .

The Council adjourned overnight for deliberation and informed him next day that it was their unanimous opinion that it was expedient to prorogue the Legislature immediately and proclaim martial law.

In a letter to Colonel Baynes[2] Brock stated that the Legislature had declined to do anything that they were asked.

[2] [Edward Baynes (d.1829) became a lieutenant in the British army in 1776 and achieved the rank of major-general in 1814. After serving in South Africa and India he came to Canada in 1807 to take up the position of adjutant-general to the forces in North America. He was

> Everybody considers the fate of the country as settled and is afraid to appear in the least conspicuous to retard it. A petition has already been carried to General Hull signed by many inhabitants about Westminster inviting him to advance with a promise to join him. The ungrateful and infamous conduct of the Indians on the Grand River is still more mortifying. . . .

A hasty examination of a number of contemporary newspapers furnishes evidence that a considerable number of persons were either being deported or were voluntarily leaving the province by stealth. For instance, a letter from Buffalo, dated July 14, records the arrival of four citizens of the United States who had made their escape from Long Point in a skiff. The *Buffalo Gazette* of July 21 reports that three others had been arrested but released and sent across the river, and a week later the same paper relates that another had been deported in the same way. On August 11, the arrival of eleven fugitives is recorded. A correspondent of the *New York Statesman*, writing from Lewiston, New York, on August 17, sarcastically remarks:

> Canadians arrive daily. The Niagara river which in peaceable times can only be crossed in safety in boats, flats, &c., can now be passed in apparent safety on logs, rails, slabs, and even by many without any buoy whatever. Lakes Ontario and Erie, formerly considered extremely dangerous to cross with open boats, no longer present any obstacle to those who are so fortunate as to get possession of a boat – the perils of the sea are absorbed by the fear of being taken by their friends.

Three young men, who had lately arrived at that place from York, having crossed Lake Ontario in a rowboat, stated that

> . . . a Mr. Wilmot, [Watson?] Surveyor General of Upper Canada, who lived near York for many years, has collected a respectable number of men, (about 60 in number), attached to the American cause and proceeded on his march through the wilderness to join General Hull. Wilmot, they say, is much exasperated against the Government of Canada and his followers not unlike their leader. Other reports of this nature there are in circulation, the truth of which cannot be ascertained.

. . . On October 29 Major-General Sheaffe, having become administrator of the civil affairs of the province in consequence of Brock's death, informed the Executive Council that there were a number of persons in the province, some of whom were actually under arrest, who had refused to take the oath of allegiance as required by the 45th clause of the Act passed on the 5th of August, 1812, pleading in justification that they were citizens of and owed allegiance to the United States, who had desired permission to return to their own country. The advice of the council was required whether it was ad-

military secretary to Prevost during the war and commanded the troops in the attack on Sackets Harbor in 1813.]

visable to deport these persons as alien enemies. It was recommended that ten of them who were natives of the United States should be permitted to leave the province, but that two British subjects who had emigrated from Ireland less than two years before and had actually been residents of Upper Canada for more than twelve months should be prosecuted under the 14th clause of the Act. . . .

Early in November, boards were appointed to assemble at Niagara, York, and Kingston for the purpose of examining all persons reporting themselves as subjects of the United States and as such claiming exemption from military service and thereby becoming liable to be sent out of the province. When satisfied of the truth of their statements, these boards were empowered to issue passports to enable them to cross the frontier at such places and in such manner as seemed most expedient. If it became apparent that very serious injury might accrue to 'such persons being settled and having families in the country who have not received lands from the Crown or taken the oath of allegiance', they were directed to report the facts with their opinion as to 'the terms of a modified allegiance or security for good conduct on which they may be permitted to reside'.

A proclamation was published at the same time announcing that 'every citizen of the United States who did not report himself to one of these boards before the first day of January, 1813, should be considered as an alien enemy and become liable to be treated as a prisoner of war or a spy as circumstances might dictate.'

One of those who appeared before the board sitting at Kingston was Michael Smith,[3] the Anabaptist preacher and author of the *Geographical View of Upper Canada*. He relates in his book that

> . . . twelve days after the battle of Queenston, Colonel Graham on Yonge Street ordered his battalion to assemble that a number might be drafted to go to Fort George. Forty of them did not come but went out to Whitchurch township which was nearly a wilderness and joined thirty more fugitives that were already there. Some men who were home for a few days volunteered to go and bring them in but since they were not permitted to take arms, they failed and the number of fugitives increased by the first of December to 300. When on my way to Kingston to obtain a passport I saw about fifty of these people near Smith's Creek in the Newcastle District on the main road with fife and drum beating for recruits and huzzaing for Madison. Some of these men remained in the woods all winter and Indians went out in the spring of

[3] [Michael Smith, a Baptist preacher who came to Upper Canada in 1808, purchased a farm and began collecting material for a book on Upper Canada. By 1812 he was living in Niagara and had completed arrangements for the publication of his book in Buffalo. When the war broke out he was deported to the United States. His book, a most valuable survey of the colony, went through four editions in 1813, a fifth in 1814, and a sixth in 1816. The titles and the contents differ slightly from edition to edition.]

> 1813 and drove them into their caves where they were taken. None of the militia in the Newcastle District bore arms except twelve at Presqu'Isle harbour. They were universally in favor of the United States.

About the end of December a number of aliens were sent under escort from York to Niagara to be put across the frontier but it was finally decided that it would be imprudent to allow them to enter the United States at that time and General Sheaffe directed their passports to be suspended and granted them permission to reside without molestation at their former homes, when these were situated at a safe distance from the frontier, until further notice. Many aliens appeared before the board at Niagara of whom a considerable number were permitted to cross the river. . . .

Fugitives continued to make their way to Buffalo and other American posts on the frontier during the winter, generally crossing Lake Erie on the ice. They agreed in reporting that the province was ravaged by disease and that 'the most rigid iron despotism reigns. No person can speak his sentiments with freedom in relation to the Government.' . . .

The temporary occupation of the provincial seat of government by the enemy at the end of April [1813] was accompanied by some remarkable demonstrations of disaffection. Several persons confined in the jail for seditious conduct or disobedience to orders were at once liberated and the invaders 'were joined by a number of vagabonds who gave them every information' and seized the opportunity to plunder the public stores and private dwellings.

After the enemy's departure the situation became so alarming that a special meeting of the magistrates was convened which was attended by the judges and by the Reverend John Strachan.[4] It was unanimously resolved that energetic measures 'should be instantly adopted to preserve order and prevent anarchy, to support and encourage the loyal and to inspire the wavering'. They affirmed their opinion that 'it is equally now as before this invasion high treason to aid, assist, counsel or comfort the enemy' and called upon all persons 'desirous to testify their abhorrence of anarchy which must prevail if principles adverse to the above declaration gain ground to associate in support of and afford their aid to the civil authorities and their officers'. The High Sheriff was instructed to promulgate and enforce this declaration. . . .

[4] [John Strachan (1778-1867) came to Upper Canada from Scotland in 1799, was ordained a priest in the Church of England in 1803, and operated schools at Kingston and Cornwall. In 1812 he became rector of York, where he distinguished himself as a patriotic spokesman during the war. He was a member of the executive council of Upper Canada from 1818 to 1836 and of the legislative council from 1820 to 1841 and exercised so great an influence upon the government that he is regarded as the central figure of the Family Compact. He was appointed archdeacon of York in 1825 and first bishop of Toronto in 1839.]

[On June 3, 1813], a week after he took possession of Niagara, General Dearborn reported that numbers of the inhabitants of the surrounding country had come voluntarily into his camp to give their paroles. 'A large majority are friendly to the United States,' he asserted, 'and fixed in their hatred to the Government of Great Britain.'

A contemporary Buffalo newspaper stated that many residents of Canada opposite that place had come into the American garrison established at Fort Erie to be paroled and seemed 'well suited by the recent change'. A list containing the names of more than five hundred persons thus placed under parole was actually forwarded to Washington. . . .

Late in June, Justice William Dummer Powell stated that the march of troops on their way to Niagara 'through the country has occasioned an obvious change in the manners and language of the people' and that the establishment of a garrison of regular soldiers at York would 'have an excellent effect in confirming the loyal and overawing the disaffected, especially if a party of dragoons could occasionally make excursions through the country' but affirmed his opinion that in the event of a serious reverse 'little reliance is to be had in the power of the well disposed to repress and keep down the turbulence of the disaffected who are very numerous.'. . .

. . . The second occupation of York by the enemy [on July 31 and August 1, 1813], although of very brief duration, was attended by another convincing demonstration of disaffection.

> There was several of the inhabitants constantly wt them [Major Allan[5] wrote] who are known to be as great enemys as are in the country, to wit, a Mr. John Young, mercht, Mr. Stebbins, a tavern keeper, Mr. Gilbert, blacksmith, Mr. Peters, a lawyer, who receives *half pay & a pension besides,* a notorious man, and a great many in the country well known. In short Commodore Chauncey owned to the Revd. Dr. Strachan that he never heard of any place that contained half the number of persons publicly known and avowedly to be enemys to the government & country to be allowed to remain at rest in these parts and for our peril. I can positively assert that if immediate steps (more ready than by civil process) is not taken to apprehend & send away those people from the country the consequence will be serious. . . . I most fervently pray as does several good & faithful subjects that some establishment may be kept at York and that something may be done about taking up those characters, otherwise neither our life or property is safe when so many surround us as long as we are liable to be visited by the enemy's vessels and boats.

[5] [William Allan (1770-1853) came to Canada in 1787 and opened a general store at York in 1796. He held a variety of minor civic appointments before 1812 and was active during the war as major, then colonel, of the 3rd York militia. Afterwards he became the leading businessman of York and one of the wealthiest men in the Canadas, prominent in banking, insurance, real estate, and transportation enterprises. He was a member of the legislative council after 1825 and of the executive council after 1836 and a central figure in the Family Compact.]

. . . Major Allan appeared before the committee of the Executive Council to whom his letter had been referred for investigation but he was unable to instance any specific acts of treasonable conduct on the part of any of the persons named by him. The committee, however, took this opportunity of making a special report in which they remarked:

> Since the first organization in 1792 the adventitious increase of population has, with very few exceptions, proceeded from the United States, whose subjects, enticed by the facility of obtaining grants of land, have settled amongst us without any predilection for His Majesty's Government. This District, it is but reasonable to suppose, from the period of its establishment, contains a very large proportion of such characters. To guard against the probable consequence of such a population in the event of hostilities with the United States, the Executive Government has made frequent but fruitless efforts to obtain from the Legislature suitable provision for the security of the Province. An occasional suspension of the Habeas Corpus could only be obtained with such clauses as would defeat the intention of Government. A power to exercise martial law concurrent with the law of the land in cases of invasion and other emergency was also solicited but refused. So circumstanced it is not surprising that the enemy should receive intelligence fatal to the interests of the service. During the several visits of his fleet to this seat of Government, it is obvious to general apprehension that it has received aid, comfort and assistance from many and the general sentiment points out amongst others to the persons named in Mr. Allan's letter, but it must not be concealed that the police is too weak to act with effect in securing and detaining all the persons, even if any probability existed that prosecution would issue in conviction. Such has been the complexion of civil juries in this District that such a result is quite hopeless. The enemy has profited by the large supply of stores and provisions found unprotected in this post to bribe the good will and complacency of many who were not before addicted to their cause. Exertion was made by the magistrate after the first invasion to repress this evil by taking from its possessors the insidious gift of the enemy but abandoned and exposed a second time to the threatened vengeance of an exasperated banditti, the gaoler refused to take charge a second time of such as the vigilance and exertion of the magistrate had apprehended.
>
> Your Committee has judged it expedient to offer to Your Honor this view of the subject as a justification of the advice in which they unanimously concur.
>
> It is recommended to Your Honor that until a suitable force can be afforded for the protection of this place from the enemy, a detachment of infantry and cavalry should be stationed here under a prudent officer, whose duty it should be to cause to be arrested such persons as may be pointed out to him in writing by some confidential person in the Commission of the peace as justly suspected of any treasonable practice in respect of the enemy or dangerous design against the persons of His Majesty's subjects or the peace of the Government. That such persons when apprehended should as soon as may be with the concurrence of the Commander of the Forces, be transferred to Lower

> Canada and there detained during hostilities or until His Honor; the President of the Province should recommend his release. . . .

In consequence of the representations contained in the report of the Committee of the Executive Council a small detachment of regular troops was stationed at York and the construction of blockhouses for the protection of the place was commenced. The officer commanding this force was directed to consult the acting attorney general [J. B. Robinson[6]] before making any arrests of suspected persons, but that acute lawyer felt constrained to inform him that he could afford no official assistance 'as the measures contemplated were not of a nature to admit of legal interference', but he would gladly furnish any information in his possession and put him in the way to obtain more.

At the same time he took care to inform General de Rottenburg that

> . . . by a participation with other members of the community in a measure which self-preservation demands, I am not giving any official direction to a step which considered in the abstract is illegal and nothing but the extreme necessity of the case could warrant. If called upon on the contrary, I am obliged to acknowledge its illegality and to say as I do now that measures of the nature contemplated must rest entirely upon the responsibility of Your Honor's military command. I can neither officially advise nor share in anything repugnant to the strictest letter of the law.
>
> Still, however, in a private communication which I wish this to be considered, I have no objections (if Your Honor will allow me the liberty), to give my opinion merely as a member of society as to what under present circumstances is expedient. The country must not be lost by a too scrupulous attention to forms, and when the civil administration of justice is found inadequate to our protection in times perilous and unusual as the present, recourse must be had to measures more efficacious and the necessity must and will justify their adoption. These measures Your Honor seems resolved to take and in another part of the Province where certainly the reasons are not more urgent, they have been acted upon and the public have felt the beneficial result. I would suggest that Your Honor should by private letters of instruction, something in the form of that which I presume to enclose, beg several of the most respectable gentlemen of the place to report to you what characters they deem suspicious and transmit as regular and full information as they can obtain of any act committed by those persons in opposition to the Government and our common cause. . . .

[6] [John Beverley Robinson (1791-1863) was educated at the Reverend John Strachan's school, studied law, and was appointed acting attorney-general in 1813. In 1815 he became solicitor-general, in 1818 attorney-general, and in 1829 chief justice. He represented York in the provincial assembly from 1821 to 1829 when he entered the legislative and executive councils. During the war he served in the York militia and was present at Detroit and Queenston Heights.]

In a letter from Downing Street under date of August 11, the Secretary of State for the Colonies directed the Governor General to instruct the officer acting as Lieutenant Governor of Upper Canada to take the most effectual measure to induce the Legislature to pass an act for the banishment of all persons who had aided the enemy and confiscating their property to form a fund in the first instance to be applied to the indemnification of all persons who had suffered loss by the war within the limits of the province. It was recommended that all persons who had voluntarily withdrawn from the province into the United States since the declaration of war, and who failed to return after receiving a reasonable notice to reclaim their property, should be included in the act.

In a proclamation dated September 4, after stating his belief that in several instances, paroles from the enemy had been sought and obtained by inhabitants of the province as a means of evading the performance of militia duty and anticipating that others might be animated by similar or worse motives to withhold their services when required for the construction of public works for the defence of the country, Sir George Prevost announced his intention of sending 'all such useless and disaffected characters out of the country to the enemy to whom they consider themselves as belonging as prisoners of war, there to remain as such until regularly exchanged'. . . .

The situation with respect to internal disaffection had become so very acute and serious that in his speech on opening the session of the Legislature (February 17, 1814), Sir Gordon Drummond used the following language:

> It has been more a subject of regret than surprise to have found two members of the legislative body in the ranks of the enemy. This disgrace could not have been had their malignant influence in the last session failed to reject the call of the Executive Governmnt for a suitable modification of the Habeas Corpus Act. I rely upon the good sense of the two houses so to strengthen the hands of Government as to obviate all apprehensions of a recurrence of a similar reproach.
>
> A due regard to the interests of the loyal subjects requires that means should be adopted to punish such traitors as adhere to the enemy by the confiscation of their estates. It may often happen, as in the instance of the two representatives of the people, that they may withdraw from the process necessary for legal conviction. To obviate this an Act of Attainder by the legislature may subvene to the usual process of outlawry.
>
> In submitting such a measure it is my duty to apprise you of the gracious desire of His Royal Highness, the Prince Regent, that all such forfeitures shall be applied to the relief of the sufferers by the war in this province.

Of the two members of the Legislative Assembly referred to as having deserted to the enemy, one was Joseph Willcocks,[7] representing the first riding

[7] [Joseph Willcocks (d.1814) came to Upper Canada from Ireland and settled at York in 1800.

of the County of Lincoln, and the other was Abraham Markle,[8] the member for the west riding of York and the townships of Ancaster and Saltfleet. Benajah Mallory,[9] who had represented Norfolk, Oxford, and Middlesex from 1804 to 1808, and Oxford and Middlesex from 1808 until 1812, and owned a considerable tract of land in the township of Burford, had also joined the enemy, and was rewarded by a commission as major in the corps of Canadian Volunteers commanded by Willcocks, in which Markle became a captain.

Resolutions for the expulsion of Willcocks and Markle were passed without debate or opposition.

The Legislature no longer hesitated to take prompt and energetic measures. Acts were passed to enable the government to arrest and detain for a limited time all persons suspected of a treasonable adherence to the enemy and for the more impartial and effectual trial and punishment of high treason, misprision of high treason, and treasonable practices. By a third act all persons who had become seized of lands in the province, by inheritance or otherwise, and had voluntarily withdrawn to the United States since the first day of July 1812, or who might thereafter withdraw without licence, were declared aliens and incapable of holding lands, and the confiscation of their estates was authorized upon due inquiry. . . .

Indictments for treason or treasonable practices were prepared by the acting attorney general against some fifty persons, most of whom, however, including the most notorious offenders, had already sought refuge in the enemy's lines, and consequently were beyond reach of punishment, except by the confiscation of their estates. Three of those held in custody, according to the ordinary rules of procedure, were subject to trial in the Niagara district, and the remainder in the district of London. On mature deliberation it was

Appointed sheriff of the Home District in 1803, he was dismissed in 1807 for joining the opposition against the lieutenant-governor. He founded a party newspaper and was a member of the legislative assembly between 1808 and 1812. At the outset of the war he was appointed to deal with the Mohawks of the Grand River but in 1813 went over to the Americans. On October 4, 1814, he was killed during the siege of Fort Erie while commanding a unit of Canadian Volunteers.]

8 [Abraham Markle (also written as 'Marcle' and 'Maracle'), an innkeeper and partner in the Union Mills at Ancaster, was elected to the legislative assembly of Upper Canada in 1812. In 1813 he was detained briefly in Kingston on suspicion of disloyalty but was permitted to return to his farm. Later he became implicated in the activities of American partisans in Norfolk County, joined the Canadian Volunteers, and participated in raids upon Port Dover and Point Abino. He was expelled from the legislature in 1814 and was attainted of treason in 1817. Markle eventually settled in the United States.]

9 [Benajah Mallory fought on the side of the Americans in the Revolutionary War but afterwards settled in Upper Canada where he received a militia commission in 1798 and was granted 1,400 acres of land in Oxford County. He went over to the Americans in 1812 and after the war settled at Lockport, New York, where he was living as late as 1852.]

decided to issue a special commission for the trial of the whole at Burlington, which was understood to be a place within the limits of the former district. Mr. Robinson at first dissented on grounds of expediency:

> Executions of traitors by military power [he remarked] would have comparatively little influence. The people would consider them arbitrary acts of punishment but would not acknowledge them as the natural effects of justice. Now to give the condemnation of traitors by the law of the land and by a jury the full effect, the common course of justice should, as much as possible, be observed. If these offenders are tried out of their proper district by virtue of this statute, it will be said, and perhaps with some appearance of reason, that the law was passed with a view to try them out of the ordinary course, and in so far in its intention, ex post facto. The reason of the law requiring trials to be had only in the district where the offence was committed is just and obvious, and whether the jury's local knowledge of the characters of the accused and the witnesses be to the advantage of the prisoners or against him, it is in favor of public justice they should have it.
>
> But it appears to me and this I take the liberty of urging as a very powerful reason for wishing these trials to be had if possible in their proper districts, that the local acquaintance of the jurors if taken from the District of London, will be much in favor of the success of the prosecutions. Here (York) as in the District of Niagara, and indeed in most other districts, more especially in those inhabited by emigrants from the United States, the jurors, I fear, are very indifferent to the interests of Government; indeed, if they are not wholly indifferent, their bias is the other way. The inhabitants of the District of London, however, know perfectly well the designs and intentions of the rebellious party. They felt that their persons and property were in danger from their violence, so much so that they voluntarily resorted to arms, to subdue them, and it is fair to suppose that men who risked their lives in the apprehension of these traitors will be well satisfied to have them punished as they deserve. Add to this that our witnesses, not a few, live in this District and may not easily be obtained out of it, besides that being in the District gives the prosecutor the opportunity of making continual inquiry and discovering testimony that might not otherwise be had.

Drummond, on the contrary, held with good reason that the district of London was insecure, and so liable to be disturbed by incursions of the enemy that courts could not sit with reasonable safety, nor juries be summoned, and the judges themselves very strongly favoured holding the court at Burlington. Oddly enough it was then discovered that although the 'little lake' had received the name of Burlington Bay . . . yet there was neither town nor township of that name in the province and the place of sitting was altered to the township of Ancaster.

The court was opened on May 23 and sat until June 21 when it was adjourned until August 10. It was composed of three judges of the King's

Bench who took turns in presiding, three being always present. Nineteen prisoners were brought to trial, but indictments were laid against more than seventy former residents of the London, Niagara and Western districts, most of whom had fled the country. Cornelius Hovey, who was so ill that his recovery seemed doubtful, pleaded guilty. Fourteen others were convicted by the jury.[10] All of these men were sentenced to be hanged on July 20, but seven of the least guilty were recommended for mercy by Chief Justice Scott[11] and reprieved by Sir Gordon Drummond until the pleasure of the Prince Regent could be ascertained. Four others were tried at a subsequent session, of whom two were convicted. . . .

By the end of August 1813, Joseph Willcocks had succeeded in enlisting about 120 refugees in the corps known as the Canadian Volunteers, which during the next two months formed part of the American garrison of Fort George and was engaged in several affairs between the outposts.

On leaving that post in November, General W. H. Harrison advised his successor, Brigadier-General McClure of the New York militia, 'to make use of the zeal and activity which Colonel Willcocks certainly possesses to counteract the machinations of the enemy and ensure the confidence of our friends among the inhabitants'.

About the same time, his command was considerably augmented by the arrival of a party from the Grand River under Mallory who was appointed second in command, with the rank of major. Some days later Willcocks led a reconnaissance of mounted men within sight of the British piquet line at Stoney Creek. A week after, he again advanced as far as Grimsby, but was discovered and pursued so vigorously that his force was obliged to disperse to effect its escape. In the course of these raids he arrested several militia officers and other loyalists at their homes and carried them away as prisoners of war. On December 10 a scouting party belonging to his corps was routed at the Ten Mile Creek, losing one man killed and four captured. Of the latter it was reported that one was tortured and killed by the Indians.

It is not unlikely that exasperation over this check caused Willcocks and his followers to take a remarkably active hand in setting fire to the town of Niagara that night. Lieut.-Colonel Chapin of the New York militia, who from a warm friend had become a bitter enemy, afterwards stated in a printed address to the public:

> In the destruction of this town he (General McClure) was aided by the most active exertions of Joseph Wilcox, who had for a number of years resided in

[10] [Four other prisoners were acquitted. For the trials at Ancaster see pages 241-50.]

[11] [Thomas Scott (1746-1824) was attorney-general of Upper Canada from 1801 to 1806 and chief justice from 1806 to 1816 with a seat on the legislative and executive councils of the province.]

> this pleasant village and had been patronised far beyond his merits; and at that time when it became his duty, as a man of justice and as a subject of His Majesty whom he had sworn to protect and defend, he like a cowardly sycophant deserted the cause of his country and actually led a banditti through the town, setting fire to his neighbors' dwellings and cursing every American – applying the epithet of tory to every one who disapproved of that act of barbarity.

Two of Willcocks's men were killed and several captured on the evacuation of Fort George and as his corps had become reduced by casualties to about sixty of all ranks, it was ordered to retire to Buffalo to recruit. 'He (Willcocks) was among the last to leave the place,' McClure wrote to the Secretary of War, 'and from his vigilance and attention to our cause, I think he deserves your notice.'. . .

During the following spring a considerable number of recruits were enrolled and a reorganization effected. Abraham Markle was commissioned as captain of a company and sent to Erie accompanied by Oliver Grace, another refugee, to conduct an expedition against Port Dover, where he had the satisfaction of witnessing the destruction by fire of the mills and dwellings of several militia officers and other active loyalists.[12] Robert Nichol who had moved that Markle should be expelled from the legislature suffered a loss of property on this occasion valued at £5,000. In his report of this raid, Captain Sinclair of the United States navy remarked:

> . . . I think it proper to inform you that Genl. Scott sent with a letter of introduction to me about two weeks since, a Captain Markle, who it appears is a Canadian of respectable standing, and one who has taken a decided and active part in our cause during the present war. He brought with him a confidential and enterprising man selected by the Genl. as a spy. Through this man, who I have landed several times in the enemy's country, Capt. Marcle has been enabled to correspond with his friends who are favorable to our cause, and has gained considerable information as to the numbers, situation and movements of the enemy in the upper province. . . . Marcle appears to be a man who can be relied on and places implicit confidence in those friends who gave the information.

The battalion of Canadian Volunteers formed part of the invading force under General Brown which entered Upper Canada at Fort Erie on July 3, 1814. It was not engaged in the action at Chippawa, but both Willcocks and Mallory were particularly active in reconnoitring and foraging during the two weeks following, and are mentioned several times in the official correspondence on both sides. In his report of the operations of his brigade in the battle of Lundy's Lane, General Porter stated that 'Lieut. Colonel Willcox of the Canadian Volunteers (a corps which though small is surpassed

[12] [For the raid on Port Dover see pages 233-5.]

by none in enterprise and bravery) was most actively and usefully engaged during the whole action and had his horse killed.'

Two men of that corps were killed, two others wounded, and eight reported missing on that occasion.

After the American army had retired into an entrenched camp at Fort Erie, the command of the brigade of volunteers devolved temporarily on Willcocks during Porter's absence for three weeks on recruiting service. He soon incurred the pronounced ill-will of the regiment from the State of New York, which became so marked that, being directed to reinforce the piquet line with that corps on the afternoon of September 4, he declined to take command although he accompanied it into action. While thus engaged he received a mortal wound in the breast from a rifle bullet. The official report stated that 'he behaved worthy of a hero and a patriot. Calm and unruffled he rushed on in defence of our country's rights until he fell entwined with the laurels of glory.' . . .

Markle, who had been promoted to the rank of major, succeeded Willcocks in command of the corps and was mentioned in despatches for gallant conduct in the sortie on September 17. . . .

Markle is named as the leader of a foraging party which was surprised in the vicinity of Point Abino on October 1 and sustained some loss. After the conclusion of peace he boasted to a former acquaintance that the government of the United States had rewarded his services by a grant of 3,000 acres of land and had promised compensation for all his losses. . . .

The refugees from the Western and London districts who had fled to the American garrisons at Amherstburg and Detroit were less numerous but scarcely less active in their hostility, although not organized as a separate military force, being chiefly employed as scouts and guides for raiding expeditions. The most enterprising of these partisans were Andrew Westbrook, Daniel Norton, Samuel Doyle, and James Pelton. The first-named of these, a man of great strength and stature and animated by an insatiable desire for revenge, was the most formidable and merciless. The policy of destroying the dwellings and property of the loyal residents, and disorganizing the militia by carrying off the local officers, was relentlessly carried out by him. On the last night of January 1814, a party under his guidance captured a guard composed of Captain Daniel Springer and twelve men of the Middlesex militia, posted at Westbrook's own house in the township of Delaware. The house and other buildings containing several hundred bushels of grain were set on fire with his own hand and consumed. Lieut.-Colonel Francis Baby, captains Brigham, Dolsen, and Springer were carried off by the raiders on horseback, bound hand and foot to prevent their escape.

On February 24, he led a party across from the Thames by a little known path to the new settlement at Point aux Pins where several houses were burned and a number of the inhabitants compelled by threats to take an oath of neutrality. About the middle of April he made a descent on the village of Oxford and carried off Major Sykes Touseley. On May 20 he appeared at Port Talbot after midnight at the head of thirty riflemen. Captain Patterson and Wilson were taken prisoners at their homes, but the man in charge of Colonel Talbot's mill escaped and gave the alarm. By daybreak Lieut.-Colonel Burwell[13] had assembled a considerable force of militiamen, but it was then ascertained that the raiders had stolen off under cover of darkness without doing much damage, evidently fearing that their retreat might be cut off. This settlement was again over-run in the middle of July by a body of some 300 men of whom eighty were mounted. Many houses were plundered and much of the growing crops destroyed. On August 16 a party headed by Westbrook succeeded in taking Burwell in his own house, while Talbot narrowly escaped by jumping out of a window. The horses, cattle, and other valuable property of the latter, who was a particular object of their animosity, were killed or carried off. Two weeks later Westbrook ascended the Thames as far as Oxford, paroled many of the inhabitants, and carried off three captains and a sergeant of the militia. On September 1 this party was ambuscaded and dispersed with the loss of their leader and several others by a party of militia hastily assembled under the command of Lieut. Daniel Rapalje of the Middlesex regiment. The remainder made their escape by a path through woods under the guidance of Westbrook, who had marched with the rear-guard, but they were compelled to abandon the horses and cattle they had taken. Four days later this indefatigable marauder revenged this reverse by another raid on Port Talbot, where he burned the mills and a number of houses and ravaged the settlement along the Talbot Road for fifteen miles.

The situation of many of the inhabitants of the western district had then become so miserable and hopeless that a considerable number of the leading men united in a petition to Brigadier General McArthur[14] who had lately taken over the command of the American troops at Detroit and Amherstburg, particularly directing his attention to a proclamation issued in September

[13] [Mahlon Burwell (1783-1846) trained as a surveyor and surveyed a large portion of western Upper Canada between 1809 and 1840. He represented Middlesex in the legislative assembly between 1812 and 1824 and from 1830 to 1834 and London after 1836. He served in the 1st Middlesex militia regiment.]

[14] [Duncan McArthur (1772-1839) served in the Indian wars of the early 1790s, became a surveyor and land speculator in Ohio, was elected to the state legislature in 1805, and became major-general of the state militia in 1808. During the war he was commissioned a brigadier-general in the United States army and eventually he succeeded General W. H. Harrison in command of the army of the west. He afterwards resumed his political career, becoming governor of Ohio in 1830.]

1813 by General Harrison and Commodore Perry, promising protection to their lives and property which they complained had been persistently violated and alleging that most flagrant wrongs had been committed in the impressment of horses and carriages....

More than a year after the ratification of the treaty of peace in consequence of a complaint to Sir George Murray, then administering the civil government of Upper Canada, that certain persons who had withdrawn to the United States during the war without a licence were returning, he deemed it expedient to issue a proclamation calling on the judges and commissioners appointed to carry out the provisions of the Sedition Act of 1805, to be vigilant in the discharge of their duties.

An official list of such persons possessing lands in the province contains three hundred and thirty-six names and it is probable that the number of landless men of whom no record has been kept was considerably greater.

An act was passed by the Congress of the United States indemnifying for their losses all refugees from Canada who had performed military service in its behalf during the contest and authorizing free grants of public land in the territories to be made to them in proportion to their rank. Westbrook's exploits in particular had given him a certain celebrity and a traveller relates that in 1817 he found him residing on lands granted to him near Fort Gratiot in Michigan.

[The article concludes with a number of lists: of persons who fled during the war, the commissioners appointed to inquire into forfeited estates and under the Alien Act of 1804, names and details of disaffected persons in the London and Western Districts, etc.]

FURTHER READING: W. R. Riddell, 'Joseph Willcocks', *Ontario Historical Society*, volume 24 (1927), pages 475-99; W. R. Riddell, 'Benajah Mallory, traitor', *Ontario Historical Society*, volume 26 (1930), pages 573-8.

Norfolk County, a pocket of settlement along the coast of Lake Erie, was much exposed to enemy attacks from the lake, by raiding parties overland from Michigan, and the activities of American partisans among the settlers of the district. Valuable though Norfolk was as a source of provisions for military forces in the western district and as a potential naval base for the reconquest of Lake Erie, regular forces could not be spared to guard the county. Its defence, therefore, fell to its own militia, who did their best to fight off attacks from outside, occasionally contributed men to campaigns on the Detroit and Niagara frontiers, and held dissident elements in check. Norfolk undoubtedly suffered worse ravages than did most sections of Upper Canada and was left with a legacy of anti-Americanism and suspicion concerning the loyalty of certain sections of the population. . . . This study, published in the 'Papers and Records' of the Ontario Historical Society, volume 20 (1923), is reprinted by permission of the Society and of Mrs. Cruikshank.

The County of Norfolk in the War of 1812

BY ERNEST A. CRUIKSHANK

[The article begins by reviewing Lieutenant Governor Simcoe's efforts to establish a settlement at Long Point as being 'the best adapted situation for the Naval Arsenal of Lake Erie'. From this arose the first settlement of United Empire Loyalists in the county of Norfolk. By 1812, Norfolk's twelve townships contained probably 3,000 inhabitants. Descriptions of the various settlements, drawn from Michael Smith's 'A Geographical View of the Province of Upper Canada and Promiscuous Remarks upon the Government' (1813), are presented.]

. . . It will thus be seen that the inhabitants of the county formed a self-dependent and largely self-sustained community, well provided with the means of supplying their most essential wants. It was in a sense isolated, being cut off from the nearest settlements in the Niagara district by the intervening lands of the Six Nations and from those in the Western district by a long stretch of thinly peopled woodland. The principal merchant and mill-owner was Robert Nichol of Dover, and the only lawyer was Henry Bostwick of the same place. The Sovereigns had large mills near the site of the present town of Waterford. It is probably significant of the sentiments of many of the more recent immigrants from the United States that Benajah Mallory, a particularly turbulent and disloyal man, who had served in the Continental army during the Revolution, represented the counties of Norfolk, Oxford, and Middlesex in the Legislative Assembly from 1804 until 1808, and the counties of Oxford and Middlesex from 1808 until 1812, when he was displaced by Mahlon Burwell. Philip Sovereign sat for Norfolk from 1808 until 1812, when he was displaced by Robert Nichol. It must have been particularly galling to the loyalists of Norfolk to be represented by Mallory, who was beyond doubt a most disreputable person.

The most notable events that occurred within the county during the war were the concentration and departure of General Brock's expedition for the relief of Amherstburg; the occupation of the bay near Long Point as a harbour of refuge and a temporary base of supplies by the British squadron on the lake; the defeat of a band of marauders by volunteers at Nanticoke; the destruction of the village of Dover by an invading force; the raid of General McArthur through the northern part of the county; and the fortification of Turkey Point as a naval station just before the close of hostilities.

The reorganization of the local militia into two regiments was accomplished early in the spring of 1812. Robert Nichol was appointed to command the second regiment and Joseph Ryerson was continued in command of the first. Each of these regiments was called upon to form two flank companies for active service in any part of the province, consisting of three officers and thirty-seven other ranks. Nichol was soon after elected as a member of the Assembly and held the seat until his accidental death twelve years later.

The annual muster of the militia took place as usual on June 4, the King's birthday. In a letter to the Adjutant-General of Militia, dated June 12, Lieut.-Colonel Ryerson reported the strength of the 1st Regiment at twenty-two officers and two hundred and forty other ranks. This, of course, included all men of military age within the regimental area. He added:

> Presuming that the men subject to militia duty would be equally divided, I had with the President's leave authorized Capt. Danl. McCall to raise a company of riflemen, which I thought, and still think, would be very useful in case of hostilities. The company was filled up immediately by active young men, who volunteered for the express purpose. It might occasion discontent to consider them as a flank company and I have thought it would weaken my battalion too much to organize more than one flank company at present, unless the President after seeing the annual return should think it would admit of two.

The officers of the flank company of the 1st Norfolk were Captain John Bostwick, Lieutenant George Ryerson, and Ensign George Rolph. The officers of the rifle company of that regiment were Captain Daniel McCall, Lieutenant Samuel Ryerson, and Ensign James McCall. The officers of the two flank companies of the 2nd Norfolk were captains Nathaniel White, Abraham Rapelje, and William McCracken, lieutenants William Gordon, Jonathan Austin, and Titus A. Williams, ensigns Isaac Gilbert and Philip Beemer. . . .

Lieut.-Colonel Nichol of the 2nd Norfolk Militia was immediately appointed Quartermaster-General of Militia, in which station he performed most efficient service, and the command of that regiment devolved upon Major George C. Salmon. As senior officer, resident in the district of London, Colonel Thomas Talbot was put in command of the flank companies and all embodied militia within its limits. He took up his headquarters at Charlotteville about the middle of July. On July 22, two days after he had received official information of the landing of the enemy at Sandwich, General Brock issued an order to Talbot to make a detachment of two hundred men from the militia of the London district with a due proportion of officers, under command of Major Salmon, who were to march at once to join a small force of regular troops under Major Chambers at the Moravian village on the Thames.

This order probably reached Talbot on July 24, and he made an effort to execute it, with highly unsatisfactory results. On July 27, he wrote to Brock from Oxford:

> I arrived at this place from Long Point where I had been two days, one spent in endeavouring to procure 100 Volunteers from the Norfolk Militia, and I am sorry to inform you that notwithstanding the apparent readiness manifested by the Flank Companies of these Battns on former occasions, when it was understood that the men required were absolutely to proceed to the River Thames, very few turned out for that service, after much explanation of the expectations of the Government and the disgrace that would attend their Regts, I made out about 60 men, I then ballotted 40 more and ordered the detachment to march to join Major Chambers as yesterday morning, when I reached the ground from whence the detachment was to march, I found a large assembly of Farmers with their Women, who upon my approach addressed me by declaring that their men should not March; upon this I enquired if there were any Magistrates present; the answer was, several. I required one to come forward, on which Mr. Bemer appeared. I asked him how he as a Magistrate could permit such proceedings; he offered no excuse, but said that he conceived the measure of withdrawing any of the Militia from Long Point was highly improper. I then ordered the party to March, when about half obey'd and after proceeding a short distance the men fell out, all but about 20, who continued their march, and even these few seemed unwilling. I therefore thought it most prudent to allow these few to return as I could not flatter myself with any material benefit that could result from their weak and uncertain assistance. Major Salmon who was present I directed to proceed to Head Quarters and state the circumstances as they occurred to you.

The reluctance of the militia to volunteer for service at a distance from their homes at this time seems to have been largely due to their distrust of the Indians on the Grand River, who had already received a message from General Hull inviting their assistance, but partly also to the personal unpopularity of Colonel Talbot himself. Michael Smith relates that John Beemer, a justice of the peace, Timothy Collver, an officer in the militia, and a third man, whose name is not given, rode about for three days from house to house, advising the militia to disobey Talbot's orders. This statement is to some extent corroborated by the subsequent arrest of Beemer, against whom a true bill on a charge of sedition was found by the Grand Jury at the sessions of the Court of Oyer and Terminer, held at Charlotteville on September 4 following.

Next day, however, Talbot wrote in better spirits from Oxford to Lieut.-Colonel Ryerson that finding 'a general disposition of zeal and Loyalty prevailed' in the flank companies of that county, he thought if a body of the Norfolk militia was again assembled and the situation properly explained to them, a considerable number of volunteers could be obtained. Major Chambers soon afterwards decided to march to Dover, and his arrival there with 150 regulars and volunteers caused an immediate change of feeling. Colonel Talbot disappeared from the scene and seems to have retired to Port Talbot in ill humour. . . .

Brock sailed from York on [August 5] in a small boat for Burlington on his way to Dover, where he had directed the flank companies of the Lincoln and York militia to assemble. Writing that night to Colonel Baynes, his aide-de-camp, Captain Glegg, made the following accurate prediction:

> I cannot refrain from intruding an assurance that the General's presence at Long Point and elsewhere at the Head of the army will have the very best effect, and such is his popularity, amongst the best *classes* of our population, that I feel confident in saying that provided Genl. Hull has not overwhelmed our small but gallant force at Amherstburg before the arrival of this Reinforcement, our united troops will give a good account of his army.

Brock reached the Indian council house at the Grand River next day, where he met the principal chiefs and warriors and quickly obtained a satisfactory assurance of their support. Then without the least delay he continued his journey. Mr. Owen states,[1] probably from local tradition, that the militia of the neighbourhood assembled at the tavern of William Culver, in the gore of the township of Woodhouse, near St. John's church, south of this town, where, after a short speech from Brock, 173 men volunteered to accompany him. On the evening of August 7, he arrived at Dover and made Nichol's house his headquarters. Chambers had already been joined by the volunteers from Lincoln and York. Altogether more than five hundred men were as-

[1] [See E. A. Owen, *Pioneer sketches of Long Point Settlement* . . . (Toronto, 1898), page 561.]

sembled, nearly three-fifths of whom were volunteers from the militia of the counties of Norfolk and Oxford. Nichol had sent one of his assistants, James Cummings of Chippawa, to collect boats and supplies. Brock possessed the art of winning the confidence and affection of the average man, and when he addressed the militia next morning, they declared that they were willing to follow him anywhere. Only four hundred men could be transported in the boats that had been procured. Seven officers and seventy-five other ranks were selected from the Norfolk and Oxford volunteers to proceed by water, with the companies from Lincoln and York and the soldiers of the 41st, while one hundred more were ordered to join Lieut.-Colonel Bostwick at Oxford and march to Amherstburg by land. Major Salmon was put in command of the detachment that embarked from Port Dover on August 8, 1812, in the little schooner *Chippawa.* Under him served captains John Bostwick and William McCracken, lieutenants George Ryerson, George Rolph, and Titus Williams, three sergeants, and fifty-nine privates of the 1st and 2nd Norfolk, and Captain John Eakins, two sergeants, and eleven privates of the Oxford regiment. Major William D. Bowen, a competent drill instructor, was left in charge of those who remained at Dover. . . .

Three days after the battle of Queenston, a district general order was issued for two-thirds of the whole establishment of the four militia regiments in the London district to march to the Niagara, the 1st and 2nd Norfolk being directed 'to repair with the greatest possible dispatch' to Chippawa and the other two regiments to Queenston. Each man was required to bring a blanket and the arms and ammunition in his possession. Three days later, a second armistice having been concluded,[2] Captain Glegg informed Talbot that as this cessation of hostilities extended 'only between the Lakes Erie and Ontario, or in other words the extremities of our mutual Posts on this communication, it was considered not improbable that the enemy might make some attempt to land above Fort Erie'. He was accordingly instructed to distribute the militia under his command between Long Point and Fort Erie, placing strong detachments at or near Long Point, Dover Mills, Grand River, and the Sugar Loaf, and a small party between the latter place and Fort Erie. Sixty-four non-commissioned officers and men of the 1st Norfolk and sixty of the 2nd Norfolk were detailed for this duty. A chain of posts of mounted men was established connecting the headquarters at Niagara with Long Point for the rapid conveyance of messages. Until the middle of November, a flank company of the 1st Norfolk, commanded by Captain John

[2] [After the battle of Queenston Heights Major-General Sheaffe agreed to a three-days' armistice along the whole of the Niagara frontier. This armistice was afterwards extended indefinitely, subject to thirty hours' notice by either party. The notice was given on November 19 by the American commander, Brigadier-General Smyth, and hostilities recommenced on November 21 after an elapsed interval of some 39 days.]

Bostwick and one of the 2nd Norfolk commanded by Captain A. A. Rapelje, and the Oxford rifle company commanded by Captain B. B. Brigham, in all 114 of all ranks, were stationed at the Sugar Loaf, when the two first named companies were moved to Fort Erie and placed in support of the batteries at Frenchman's Creek. Here, before dawn on the morning of November 28, they were attacked by a strong body of seamen of the United States navy and regular infantry. A fierce struggle in the dark took place, until the assailants retired or were driven off, leaving several dead and upward of thirty prisoners behind. In this conflict the two Norfolk companies suffered severe loss. . . . In his official letter, Lieut.-Colonel Bisshopp[3] stated that 'The Norfolk Militia under Captain Bostwick gave a strong proof of the valour which has uniformly distinguished the militia of this country when called into action.'

During these operations, sergeants Richard Drake and Henry Medcalf and eight privates volunteered to assist a few men of the Royal Artillery in working the guns of their batteries.

The remnant of these two companies were next stationed for several weeks during the winter at Carter's Point on Lake Erie to resist any attempt at an invasion by crossing on the ice. Each of the companies was allowed a furlough of three weeks to visit their homes.

The internal peace of the county had not been disturbed, but the absence of so large a proportion of the young men must have seriously affected agriculture and other industries. This was probably compensated to some extent by the increased demand for all kinds of supplies and higher prices caused by the war. The assemblage of large bodies of troops and Indians at Amherstburg and Detroit soon exhausted the resources of the neighbourhood and the farms and mills in Norfolk were called upon to supply their wants.

In the spring of 1812, a government schooner was built at Turkey Point as an addition to the small squadron on Lake Erie, which was named the *Lady Prevost* and duly commissioned in July. Dover became a regular port of call for vessels of the squadron in their frequent voyages between Fort Erie and Amherstburg, and considerable cargoes of flour, grain, and lumber were shipped in them.

By an order of April 7, 1813, in anticipation of another invasion, an additional militia force was called into service, consisting of three officers and fifty-two other ranks from each of the Norfolk regiments and smaller detachments from Oxford and Middlesex. Major William D. Bowen of the 1st Norfolk was placed in command and instructed to station one field officer,

[3] [Cecil Bisshopp (1783-1813) entered the British army in 1799 and served in Flanders, Portugal, and Spain before coming to Canada in 1812. He took part in the campaigns in the Niagara peninsula, winning an engagement at Frenchman's Creek near Fort Erie on November 28, 1812. He was mortally wounded in a raid on Black Rock, July 11, 1813.]

five other officers, and eighty-four other ranks at Turkey Point as his headquarters; three officers and fifty-three other ranks at Dover Mills, and one officer and twenty-three other ranks at Port Talbot.

The occupation of the whole line of the Niagara River by the enemy at the end of May cut off all communication between lakes Ontario and Erie by that route and forced the officers of the supply service to seek an alternative by using the road from Burlington to the Grand River and thence by boat or road to Dover, which then became the base of supply for Amherstburg and Lake Erie. Several small armed vessels of the United States navy that had been blockaded at Black Rock were also liberated to join others under construction at Erie. Symptoms of disaffection among the recent settlers in the county became more pronounced and many went voluntarily to meet the invaders and secure a parole as prisoners of war and thus evade military service. A list of persons who joined the enemy from the limits of the 2nd Regiment of Norfolk from the month of June 1812 until June 1814 certified by Major Salmon, contains forty-eight names. . . .

On August 28 [1813] Lieut.-Colonel Hamilton with two companies of the 100th Regiment was despatched from Burlington with instructions to occupy a position near Long Point, organize the militia, and protect inhabitants from depredations.

The total defeat and capture of Barclay's squadron on September 10 threw the command of Lake Erie into the hands of the enemy, and General Procter, in view of an immediate retreat, advised the occupation of Turkey Point 'by blockhouses connected by picketing that may be defended by from three to five hundred men'. On September 17, Colonel Harvey replied from Kingston that an engineer officer would be sent on at once to construct the fortifications, and that Colonel John Murray would take command of the troops and call out the militia. After Procter's defeat, it was over-hastily decided to withdraw the regular troops to Kingston, disband the militia, and abandon the whole of the province west of that place. The detachment at Long Point accordingly retired to Burlington. Within a few days two bands of refugees and others, organized at Buffalo, made their appearance. One of these, led by William Sutherland and Frederick Onstone, advanced along the lake shore towards Long Point. The other, commanded by Benajah Mallory, the former member of the Assembly, moved up the Grand River. Their avowed object was to recover property they had abandoned and make prisoners of the most active officers of the militia, but they soon proved by their conduct that they were marauders of the worst type. Sutherland's party captured several militia officers, whom they sent off as prisoners of war, among them being Captain William Francis of the 2nd Norfolk. They then approached Dover, stealing horses and cattle, and plundering houses. The inhabitants were greatly alarmed and upon two hours' notice thirty-six persons met for consultation at the house of Captain William Drake. Among them were not less than twenty-one militia officers, including lieutenant-colonels Bostwick and Burwell, and captains John Bostwick, William Drake, Daniel McCall, William McCracken, William Parks, Samuel Ryerse, and Jonathan Williams. Thomas Bowlby, J.P., was elected chairman and John Ten Broeck, secretary of the meeting. . . .

The following resolutions were then adopted.

> Resolved, that it is the opinion of this meeting that some effectual means should be immediately adopted for the purpose of defending the District against any attempt that may be made against the persons or property of the inhabitants until some more effectual means can be devised for its defence.
>
> Resolved, that it is the desire and determination of every person in this meeting to defend not only this District but any and every part of this Province to the utmost of his power, and at the risk of his life and property, against any attack that may be made against it.
>
> Resolved, that every person in this meeting do volunteer his services to go from this place for the purpose of attacking and driving from their position any maurauders that may be found, and also that it is highly expedient that every person in this meeting do use his endeavors to procure volunteers for that purpose and to be in readiness to march on the 13th inst., at 6 o'clock a.m. . . .

Lieut.-Colonel Bostwick was chosen to command the volunteers. His report to Major Glegg, dated at Woodhouse, on November 14, relates the result of the expedition in a modest and straightforward manner.

> On the night of the 12th instant we received information that the party of brigands mentioned in my last letter was in this neighborhood; the few militia that were here immediately proceeded in search of them. They, however, suspecting our intentions hastily returned down the lake.
>
> Yesterday, as early in the morning as possible, the number of volunteers proposed commenced their march down the lake in pursuit of them. After a tedious and circuitous route through the woods we surprised them at the house of John Dunham, which had for some time been one of their principal places of rendezvous. After having ascertained that they were there, a small party under the command of Captain Daniel McCall was detached across a point of woods in order to intercept them should they attempt to escape that way. Captain Jno. Bostwick with another small party proceeded towards the house near the lake shore, while the remainder, being the greatest number, with myself, took a circuitous direction through the woods in order to come in rear of the house and surround it. Capt. Bostwick in coming near the place, not observing any person about there, immediately entered the house with Lieut. Austin and was not a little surprised to find it crowded with the band we were in pursuit of. They instantly flew to their arms but he desired them to surrender themselves, telling them they were surrounded. Most of them consented and gave up their arms. Captain Bostwick, however, not being supported

as soon as he wished, they resumed possession of their arms, discharged two muskets at him and he in turn became a prisoner. On hearing the report of the guns, the whole of the party with me hastened with as much expedition as possible towards the place, and on their discovering us they commenced a fire from the house upon us, which was immediately returned, we not knowing that Capt. Bostwick was there. After a warm fire on both sides, some of them escaped from the house and fell in with Capt. McCall's party, who attacked them with spirit, when a few took to the woods, the remainder being either killed or wounded, and those in or near the house surrendered. . . .

Eighteen prisoners were taken of whom four, Adam Crysler, John Dunham, Dayton Lindsay, and George Peacock, were convicted of treason and sentenced to be hanged at Ancaster on July 20, 1814. One of the men killed was identified as John Schofield, a refugee. Mallory immediately retreated and made his escape. It was afterwards stated by Colonel Nichol that upwards of seven thousand barrels of provisions were saved by this action for the use of the army, thereby enabling General Vincent to hold his position at Burlington, and recover within a month possession of the entire Niagara district.

General de Rottenburg made it the subject of a general order, in which he said:

The Major-General commanding and President, having received from Major-General Vincent a report of the very gallant and patriotic conduct of Lieutenant-Colonel Bostwick and an association of 45 officers and men of the militia of the County of Norfolk in capturing and destroying a band of traitors who in violation of their allegiance and of every principle of honour and honesty had leagued themselves with the enemies of their country to plunder and make prisoners the peaceable and well disposed inhabitants of the Province, Major-General de Rottenburg requests that Colonel Bostwick and every individual of the Association will accept his best thanks for their zeal and loyalty in planning and gallantry in carrying into execution this most useful and public-spirited enterprise.

. . . As soon as navigation on Lake Erie again became practicable, two of the enemy's ships of war were constantly kept cruising between Erie and Long Point and spies were landed to obtain intelligence. On May 13, Captain Sinclair, the new naval commander, wrote from Erie to the Secretary of the Navy:

The troops from this place, both Regulars and Militia, are ordered to Buffalo. I do not, however, apprehend any danger from their departure, as I have acquired the best information, within a few days past, from the opposite shore, by which I learn they are building nothing on any part of the lake, which can give transportation to troops. I learn that near Long Point they have a considerable quantity of flour deposited in five or six large manufacturing mills,

> standing within the compass of as many miles, and guarded only by a company, and distant forty or fifty miles from any military post. These mills supply all the upper part of the Province with breadstuff. I have proposed to the Commander of the Military, (Col. Campbell[4] of the 19th Regiment, an intelligent and apparently enterprising officer), that I will transport as many of the troops from this to Buffalo, as can be embarked on board the small vessels, say 750, which will not interfere very materially with my outfits, and that we shall wait a favourable opportunity, touch on the shore, land before daylight, and by a rapid move destroy those mills, embark the same day and proceed down. He seems full of the enterprise, and if the weather favours, I am in hopes that it may be accomplished.

. . . This squadron cast anchor in the bay off the mouth of Patterson's Creek, late in the afternoon of May 14. Several hundred men were at once landed, without opposition from a look-out party of the 19th Dragoons, which retired by the road to Sovereign's Mills, leaving a few men behind at a storehouse to remove its contents. Nearly all the flour at the mills had already been taken away in anticipation of such a descent.

The invaders were accompanied as guides by Abraham Markle, lately a member of the Legislative Assembly for the Fifth Riding of Lincoln, who had been expelled at the recent session for having joined the enemy, on a motion by Colonel Nichol, and by Oliver Grace, Samuel Green, and John Dixon, three refugees from the county. Markle had kept a tavern near Ancaster and was well known. He was sent forward with a white flag, but at the same time the American militia opened fire at the men at the storehouse, who beat a hasty retreat. No further advance was made by the body that had landed, who encamped near the shore and built huge fires. In the early morning some men sent forward to burn the storehouse were fired upon from the neighbouring woods. The whole force was then put under arms and marched to the village of Dover about three miles away.

Alexander McMullen, a private in Fenton's regiment, wrote an account of what he observed on this occasion, of which one of his descendants favoured me with a copy some years ago. From this I will now quote as the evidence of a friendly witness.

> The situation of this village was pleasant, the houses generally frame, near a beautiful creek with a fine, large fulling-mill, grist-mill, and saw-mill. The inhabitants had principally left town at our approach. We were then placed in line of battle, the artillery in the centre, the regulars on the right, a reserve in the rear, and a company, I suppose of observation, some distance off. An

[4] [John B. Campbell (d.1814), a native of Virginia and lieutenant-colonel of the 19th Regiment of Infantry, led an attack upon the Indian allies of Britain in the Wabash River country at the end of 1812. Following the raid of May 14-16, 1814, upon the county of Norfolk, Campbell was employed on the Niagara front. He was severely wounded at the battle of Chippawa and died of his wounds on August 28, 1814.]

order from Campbell to set fire to the houses was now executed by men detailed from all the companies. A scene of destruction and plunder now ensued, which beggars all description. In a short time the houses, mills and barns were all consumed, and a beautiful village, which the sun shone on in splendour that morning, was before two o'clock a heap of smoking ruins. The women and children had remained in the village and were permitted to carry out the valuable part of their moveable property. A party of sailors appointed to man the artillery killed the hogs in the streets, and severing them in the middle carried off the hind parts, while the head and shoulders were left in the street. . . .

The sun was setting as the troops re-embarked, and shortly after dark we set sail, expecting to wake in the harbor of Erie, but judge of our surprise in the morning to find that we were not more than a mile from the Canadian shore and four miles from where we started the evening before. The sails were lowered, the fleet stopped, and boats manned for shore. A troop of horse, formed on the shore, seemed determined to oppose our landing, but the turning of a long 32-pounder on board the *Porcupine* gun-boat to bear on them, made them gallop off without firing a gun. There was a grist-mill and saw-mill, to which our troops set fire. Orders were then given to re-embark, and the fleet set sail for Erie, where we arrived next evening at dark, generally disgusted with the conduct of Campbell.

Mathias Steele, who was agent for Colonel Nichol, made an affidavit in which he stated that altogether twenty dwelling houses, three flour-mills, three saw-mills, three distilleries, twelve barns, and other buildings were destroyed by the invaders, and that they shot all the cows and hogs they could find, leaving their bodies to rot on the ground. 'On Colonel Campbell being asked the reason of this wanton and barbarous conduct, where he had met with no opposition,' Steele added, 'he answered that it was done in retaliation for the burning of Havre de Grace, Buffalo and Lewiston.' The Loyal and Patriotic Society of Upper Canada assessed the loss of twenty-five persons at the considerable sum of £12,125. The principal sufferer at Dover was Colonel Nichol, whose property was valued at £5,000. . . . At Ryerse's Mills, the chief losers were Sarah Ryerse £2,500, and Henry Medcalf, £300. At Finch's Mills the loss of Titus Finch was estimated at £530 and that of Silas Montross at £571. . . .

Captain Sinclair did not conceal his displeasure at the wholesale destruction of private property, as on May 19 he wrote to the Secretary of the Navy:

They were two days on shore, succeeded in destroying several valuable mills, and some public property, with very little opposition; but I am sorry to learn that several private houses were also destroyed, which was so contrary to my wish, and to the idea I have of our true policy to those people, that I used every argument against it before his departure, and was under the impression that he accorded with me most fully. He has explained to me that he was urged to

> do so by people favorable to our cause, on that side, who pointed out those persons as old revolutionary Tories who had been very active, not only in oppressing our friends in Canada, but in aiding all in their powers the burning and plundering Buffalo. However much such characters may deserve our vengeance, I do not think it correct that our judgments should be past upon them from their being merely designated by a partisan officer or citizen who may, and no doubt are, in many instances, biast by individual motives. He (Campbell), however, will explain the whole affair to the Government, in the official report he makes. The impossibility of getting the militia to volunteer for the expedition without its being known to its fullest extent was no doubt the cause of the enemy being informed of the contemplated attack, and their having moved several thousand barrels of flour to the Niagara Frontier just before the arrival of our party.

Campbell's report has not been found, but in a letter in reply to an enquiry from General Riall whether the destruction of Dover had been authorized by the Government of the United States, he said: 'The whole business was planned by myself and executed on my own responsibility.'

His conduct was afterwards investigated by a court of enquiry, of which General Winfield Scott was president. The opinion rendered was that he was 'warranted in destroying the mills and distilleries under the laws and usages of war', and that the saw-mills and carding machine were necessarily involved from their proximity. But the court declared Colonel Campbell had erred in burning the dwelling houses and other buildings and that

> . . . he can derive no justification from the fact that the owners of these houses were actively opposed to the American interests in the present war, or from other facts that some of them were at the conflagration of Buffalo. In their partisan services it does not appear to the court that the inhabitants of Dover have done more than their proper allegiance required of them, and the destruction of Buffalo by a Lieut. General of the enemy's regular forces was emphatically the wrong of the British Government itself, rendered such by its subsequent adoption of the measure, and ought not to be ascribed to a few Canadians who were present at the time.

Campbell was mortally wounded at the battle of Chippawa, July 5, 1814, and nothing further was done to punish his offence. . . .

Immediately after the battle of Lundy's Lane the militia were permitted to return to their homes to assist in the harvest as a matter of vital importance, and small guards were posted for the protection of the grist-mills. Nothing seems to have occurred to excite further alarm until about the end of August. Writing from his camp before Fort Erie on September 5, Drummond reported a raid from Detroit upon Oxford, where a number of militia officers and other inhabitants were carried off as prisoners or paroled, and added:

> Several strangers have appeared lately in the neighbourhood of Dover. One armed, was fired at some nights since by a sentry. One Dickson and Simon Mabee, a fellow who made his escape from justice last year, entered the house of a person named John Muckle in Townsend and forcibly broke open a chest and robbed him of 200 dollars. Several persons are in pursuit of them, but hitherto without effect.

On September 5, the greater part of the settlement about Port Talbot was destroyed by another band of raiders who advanced eastward for fifteen miles along the Talbot road, plundering and maltreating the unfortunate inhabitants. Colonel Talbot, who was then at Charlotteville, despatched Captain John Bostwick with sixty men to check their further progress, but they quickly retreated to Delaware, stating their intention of returning when they received a reinforcement. . . .

About the middle of October, John Dixon again appeared in the county with a small band of refugees, and, besides committing other depredations, murdered Captain William Francis at his house in the township of Woodhouse in the most deliberate and cold-blooded manner. They then burnt the house with his body lying in it. Dixon was, however, mortally wounded in a skirmish with a guard of militia posted at the Sugar Loaf, a few days later, and died in Buffalo.

General Drummond had then been forced by bad weather and the weakness of his division to raise the siege of Fort Erie, and the army of the enemy, reinforced to eight thousand men, the largest body of troops yet put into the field, had advanced as far as the Chippawa River, behind which he awaited an attack. Their scouts had been seen near the Grand River, and information was received of an intended landing near the mouth of that river, or at Long Point, of a force intended to co-operate with another advancing from Detroit in an attack upon the supply depot at Burlington Heights. On October 25, orders were given to embody two-thirds of the Norfolk and Oxford militia and strengthen the guards posted at the mills, upon which the troops in the field were so largely dependent for their bread. A troop of the 19th Light Dragoons was stationed at Ancaster, and the Six Nation Indians and a part of the 5th Lincoln regiment were allowed to return to their homes as a measure of precaution, but the garrison at Burlington, which was very weak, was not increased.

In fact, a strong column directed against that post was already on the march from Detroit. It consisted of about eight hundred mounted riflemen under General McArthur. His movements were conducted with such secrecy that, on October 30, he arrived at Delaware without the least notice of his approach becoming known. Leaving his tired horses behind wherever they could be replaced by others taken from the inhabitants, his men pushed on with the utmost speed, sending on parties in advance to occupy the crossroads and prevent intelligence of their march from being forwarded. Recent rains had swollen all the streams and they were detained the greater part of two days in crossing the Thames. On the morning of November 4, two men from the Thames brought the news of McArthur's advance along the right bank of the river to Captain John Bostwick, commanding a detachment of the 1st Norfolk in the Township of Yarmouth. These men reported that 'the language in circulation with them at Moravians was that they were going to Burlington. But I cannot think', Bostwick added, 'their intentions are of that nature, but rather that they intend ravaging this district. They are composed almost entirely of Kentuckians and undisciplined.' He lost no time in sending on this information to Major Muir, who was stationed at William Culver's tavern in the township of Woodhouse. Muir received the message at one o'clock on the following morning, and sent it on to Lieut.-Colonel Parry at Burlington, by whom it was received twelve hours later. Being uncertain what direction the invaders would take, Muir ordered the Norfolk militia to assemble at Culver's in readiness to march. As the two regiments could not turn out more than three hundred men, he had small hopes of arresting the enemy's progress.

On the morning of November 4, McArthur's force rode into the little village of Oxford, and roughly ransacked the houses and barns in search of food and forage. Learning then that the Oxford militia had been ordered to assemble at Burford only a few miles distant, their commander announced that the property of any man who dared to send them any information would at once be destroyed. Undismayed by this threat, George Nichol, a farmer and Jacob Wood, a carpenter, stealthily left their homes at three o'clock next morning, and warned Lieut.-Colonel Bostwick at Burford three hours later of his danger. Their departure was made known to McArthur through the cowardice or malice of a neighbour, and their houses and buildings with all their contents were immediately burnt by his orders.

Colonel Bostwick retired from Burford to Malcolm's Mills on the road from Dover to Burlington, twelve miles from the crossing of the Grand River. During that day and the next he was joined by Lieut.-Colonel Ryerson and Major Salmon, with all the men of their respective regiments whom they had been able to collect, making a total force of four or five hundred, poorly armed and scantily supplied with ammunition. Muir went forward with fifty men to secure the ferry over the Grand River and assemble the Six Nations. He was soon joined by some of them, and by a troop of the 19th Light Dragoons from Ancaster. Parry at Burlington had not more than three hundred regulars, one-third of whom were invalids. As rumour had magnified the enemy's force to two thousand mounted men armed with rifles, tomahawks, and scalping knives, he believed his post was in serious danger and summoned the Indians and militia to its defence.

On the morning of November 5, McArthur advanced to Burford, which he found unoccupied, but instead of pursuing Bostwick he decided to move directly against Burlington. He reached the ferry before dark, but found the opposite bank occupied by an uncertain number of dragoons, militia, and Indians, prepared to dispute his passage. The river was high and rapid: Muir had destroyed the scow used for a ferry and there was no timber for making rafts at hand. Some desultory firing took place and McArthur encamped for the night. Before morning, he was informed that the U. S. army had begun to recross the Niagara, and determined to abandon his design of attacking Burlington. Leaving a hundred men behind to watch the river for a few hours, he rode off with the remainder to disperse the militia at Malcolm's Mills.

Bostwick had selected a good defensive position on high ground, overlooking a deep ravine. Its front was protected by an unfordable creek, crossed by a single narrow bridge. On the left was a large mill-pond. The road was obstructed by a barricade of logs. Possibly four hundred men were here assembled, but they were greatly dispirited by reports of the overwhelming numbers of the enemy.

When the head of McArthur's force came in sight, the planks of the bridge were removed and every preparation made to resist a frontal attack with a fair prospect of success. But McArthur was too shrewd to take any risks of failure. Leaving his battalion of Kentuckians to threaten this position in front and keep up a brisk fire across the creek, he dismounted the remainder of his men and led them on foot by a long circuit to a point below, where a dam of logs and driftwood afforded an easy passage. The whoops of his Indians disclosed this movement and enabled Bostwick to withdraw with small loss before it was too late. Sergeant Collins of the 41st Regiment, attached to the militia as an instructor, and Private Edwin Barton of the 1st Norfolk were killed, and privates Caleb Powell of the 1st Norfolk and Swaine Corliss were wounded. A few men were taken prisoners in the pursuit but most of them made their retreat so quickly that the affair was frequently referred to afterwards as 'the footrace'. However, McArthur's practice of paroling every male inhabitant who fell into his power along his line of march enabled him to state that he made prisoners during the day eight officers and one hundred and three other ranks. He admitted a loss of one man killed and six wounded. Malcolm's Mills were burned next day, as well as another mill two miles below, and the march was resumed towards Lake Erie. Every house along the road was searched for arms, and the men were forced to sign a parole under penalty of being carried off as prisoners if they refused. Sovereign's Mills were burnt in the afternoon and two others on the road to Dover about nightfall. McArthur encamped for the night at William Culver's tavern.

On the same day, Captain P. L. Chambers crossed the Grand River with the troop of the 19th Light Dragoons and a few militia and Indians. He followed the trail of the enemy cautiously next day to Malcolm's and thence to Sovereign's. Writing from the latter place on the morning of November 9, he said: 'The enemy have plundered the country in the most shameful manner, stole the horses, clothing, &c., and burned all the mills as far as this. Sergeant Collins of the 41st Regiment and Private Barton of the militia were killed and mutilated in the most horrible manner. Barton was actually butchered (no symptoms of having been shot) both scalped and cut shockingly.'

On the evening of the 9th, Colonel Talbot wrote from 'Bunnell's' that 'the enemy left Culver's yesterday morning about 9 o'clock and took the direction of Talbot Road, without completing the work of destruction; that is they have spared Tisdale's and Backhouse's mills through the entreaties of the American Marshal Long, who had remained at Long Point to deliver over the British prisoners. The enemy encamped last night at Browne's, ten miles from Culver's.'

On the 10th, Chambers, who had arrived at Long Point, reported that McArthur had retreated by Talbot's road 'with the greatest precipitancy', leaving a number of horses behind him.

> The avowed object of the enemy [he said] was to destroy all the mills in the country, (so as to prevent our advancing this winter to Amherstburg), which I happily defeated by the rapidity of my advance. I did not give them time to complete the work of destruction, three mills being left. Had we not arrived in time the whole of this valuable settlement must have fallen a prey to famine this winter. At present not a single barrel of flour is to be purchased in the district. The enemy have plundered the inhabitants most disgracefully and stole every horse they could find.

. . . The destruction of the mills was felt to be a matter of such importance that Drummond at once addressed a letter to Sir James Yeo, the naval commander on Lake Ontario, dated at Kingston on November 13, in which he said: 'Having just received an account of the destruction of all the resources (and the mills) of the country to the westward of the Grand River, from which we had calculated upon receiving the principal part of the supplies to support the regular troops and Indians during the approaching winter, it becomes absolutely necessary that the means of feeding them should be forwarding from hence before the close of navigation.'

. . . McArthur seems to have anticipated that the conduct of his troops would provoke censure, for he took care to state in his official letter, written immediately after his return to Detroit that 'of private property no more was destroyed than was absolutely necessary, for which regular payments or receipts were given,' but he added rather inconsistently, 'it is much to be regretted that there were some partial abuses produced by the unfortunate examples presented by the Indians, whose customs in war impel them to plunder after victory.'

. . . It will be seen from the preceding narrative that the militia of the county bore a creditable part in the defence of the province and that the losses of the inhabitants by invasion and their consequent privations were severe. Among the mill-owners, Nichol and probably some others were unable to obtain capital to rebuild, and the loss was permanent. The devastation of the settlement was not easily repaired for there were many abandoned farms for some time afterwards.

Tilly Buttrick,[5] a traveller from the U. S., who rode on horseback through the province from the Niagara River to Detroit in 1816, naïvely relates: 'I was most sensibly struck with the devastation which had been made by the late war, formerly in high cultivation, now laid waste; houses entirely evacuated and forsaken; provisions of all kinds very scarce; and, where once peace and plenty abounded, poverty and destruction now stalked over the land.'

FURTHER READING: W. C. H. Wood (ed.), *Selected British documents . . .* , volume 1, pages 406-7, 417-18; volume 3, part 1, pages 88-93, 106, 284-98; E. A. Cruikshank (ed.), *Documentary history . . .* , part VI, pages 181-6; part VII, pages 14-18; part VIII, pages 308-20; part IX, pages 206-10; R. C. Muir, *The early political and military history of Burford*, Part II (Quebec, 1913); E. A. Cruikshank, 'A sketch of the public life and services of Robert Nichol', *Ontario Historical Society*, volume 19 (1922), pages 6-81.

[5] [The reference is to *Voyages, Travels and Discoveries* by Tilly Buttrick, Jr. (Boston, 1831), page 53. The author had planned to travel from Niagara to Detroit in 1812 but was prevented by the war.]

Efforts to preserve authority within the beleaguered province necessitated control measures against American partisans. Though the authorities could not proceed against every instance of pro-American sympathies or every failure to co-operate with the war effort, they were prepared to visit the full rigours of the law on those adjudged guilty of treason. Yet even here the forms of civil authority were carefully observed. At Ancaster, nineteen persons were tried by justices of the Court of King's Bench under the statutes against treason and eight were afterwards executed. Judge Riddell's review of this unique trial will enable the reader to decide whether substantial justice was done, or whether the legal forms were prostituted for military ends – in short, whether the proceedings did or did not deserve the title of 'Bloody Assize'. . . . WILLIAM RENWICK RIDDELL *(1852-1945) was a justice of the Ontario Court of King's Bench and of the Ontario Supreme Court. Like his contemporary, Cruikshank, he was a life-long student of the history of Ontario and published scores of papers and articles on legal and historical subjects. This study is taken, with permission, from the 'Papers and Records' (volume 20, 1923) of the Ontario Historical Society.*

The Ancaster 'Bloody Assize' of 1814

BY WILLIAM RENWICK RIDDELL

The war of 1812-15 produced in the Province of Upper Canada many interesting results; one of the most interesting from a legal point of view was the session of the Court of Special Oyer and Terminer and Gaol Delivery holden at Ancaster in May and June, 1814, for the trial of certain inhabitants of the Province for the highest crime known to the law, High Treason.

We Canadians are rather given to vaunting the loyalty of our people; but it must be admitted that while the vast majority of Canadians in 1812, on the declaration of war and invasion of the Province, took their stand unflinchingly under the Old Flag, there were some in almost every section of the Province who were traitors – some openly joined the invading forces, some made their way across the lakes or boundary rivers to the United States.

It is not intended in this paper to discuss the question generally, but rather to deal with the prisoners who were called to stand at the Bar for trial at the Ancaster Special Court of Oyer and Terminer, sometimes in later days called the 'Bloody Assize'. . . .

[During November and December of 1813 the Norfolk militia conducted two successful operations against American raiders. One of these, already described on pages 231-2, was commanded by Lieutenant-Colonel Bostwick. The other, led by Lieutenant Henry Medcalf, surprised a group of marauders in a house near Chatham. Among the prisoners were fifteen residents of the province.]

All the prisoners who were inhabitants of Canada were sent down to York Gaol by Lieutenant Medcalf and Colonel Bostwick, his superior officer. Bostwick also sent down others charged with treason. Of course those from the United States were held as prisoners of war; they were not traitors. Some of these prisoners, on February 7, 1814, made a representation to the Governor that they had been taken by militia squads under command of Colonel Henry Bostwick about December 1, that they had been confined ever since, that they had families of small children in the County of Norfolk, and they asked for a trial if they were charged with crime, offering to furnish bail if the alleged offences were bailable.[1] The appeal was in vain.

The responsible law officers of the Crown at that time were John Beverley Robinson, Acting Attorney-General, and D'Arcy Boulton,[2] Solicitor-General: but Boulton was a prisoner in France, and the whole burden of the prosecution of the criminal law fell upon the shoulders of the young Attorney-General.

The representation of these prisoners was submitted to Robinson, then, be it remembered, not yet twenty-three years of age. Against one man[3] he had, indeed, no charge; but, thought that he was 'a person by no means proper to be set at large' – he was an alien taken under very suspicious circumstances and sent down in December 1813 by Colonel Bostwick with some others from the District of London under a military guard to Major Glegg at Burlington; and by Glegg sent to York, where he was committed to gaol under General Procter's orders. He was to be kept a prisoner of war. The rest were under charge of treason, a non-bailable offence, and would be tried at the proper time. The Court of King's Bench was busy in Term

[1] These were Joseph Fowler, Adam Chrystler, Griffis Collver, Isaac Pettit, William Carpenter, Dayton Lindsey, and Wadsworth Philips. We shall meet again Chrystler, Pettit, and Lindsey. William Carpenter was released in April, there being no evidence against him.

[2] D'Arcy Boulton, an Englishman, who had received a licence to practise under the Act of 1803, 43 Geo. III, c. 3, and had been called to the Bar, Easter Term of that year; he was appointed Solicitor General in 1805 on the death in the *Speedy* disaster of the first Solicitor General, Robert Isaac Dey Gray. On his way to England he was taken prisoner, 1810, by a French Privateer and taken as a prisoner to France, where he remained until the temporary peace of 1814.

[3] Wadsworth Philips.

and no other Court could, without a Commission, try Treason.[4] That Court might have a trial at Bar with all the Judges present on the Bench, but that practice had its disadvantages, and the usual course was to issue a Commission to certain persons, including a Judge or Judges of the King's Bench, authorizing those named in the Commission to try criminal cases. . . .

Robinson consulted the Judges and they agreed that, after the close of their Easter Term, they would take the cases whenever he was ready; and he quickened his movements, 'for I shall enjoy very little rest or comfort until these prosecutions are ended'; he sent a competent junior, a member of the Bar, to Niagara, to make all necessary research at that place. Then he made enquiry for a Court House, and at length 'the large house at Ancaster (the Union Hotel)' was secured. It was at the time in the possession of the military as a hospital, but the General agreed to give it up temporarily as a Court House. Provision was made for food, etc., for the jurymen, witnesses, etc.; that the military could see to from their adjoining posts on Burlington Heights; but Robinson had troubles which the military could not relieve him of. . . . 'You have no idea of the difficulty of carrying on a public prosecution here. At home everyone has his particular brand of duty assigned him, and he is able and willing to do it. Here every person stands in his place like a chessman waiting to be shoved. I have to look into every step of the proceedings in every department, for if anybody commits an error, the effect of it as regards the prosecution may be fatal.'[5]

. . . At first, it had been intended that only fifteen prisoners should be tried, but four more names were added to the list; jurors and witnesses were subpoenaed and everything made ready for May 23. In addition to those in custody it was intended that Indictments for Treason should be found against many others in order that they might be outlawed and their property forfeited to the Crown.[6]. . .

On May 23, the Court opened at Ancaster, the Commission was opened and read, and, as was the custom then and for some decades thereafter, the Court then adjourned. On the following days, Bills for High Treason were found in rapid succession against the nineteen accused persons in custody, and also against about fifty who had not been apprehended. A Copy of the

[4] Technically the General Quarter Sessions could try all felonies and misdemeanours, and during the times of the Tudor and Stewart Kings thousands were hanged by these Courts, but by the time Canada became British, the Quarter Sessions (in practice) sent all capital cases to the 'Assizes'.

[5] Robinson was often charged in times a little later with pressing the charges too strongly; that he was the mainspring of the prosecutions is beyond question, but there is no evidence that he acted more vindictively than was supposed at that time to be the duty of a Crown Counsel. His political enemies did not scruple to call this Assize the 'Bloody Assize' and to compare it, very unjustly, to the Bloody Assize of the infamous Jeffreys.

[6] [This was finally carried out on May 27, 1817.]

Indictment against him, with a list of the witnesses to be produced and of the jurors impanelled, was then delivered to each of the accused in custody, in the presence of two witnesses; and the Court adjourned until Monday, June 7. . . .

The Judges of the Court of King's Bench arranged to preside over the Court of Oyer and Terminer in rotation, and on Monday, June 7, Chief Justice Thomas Scott took his place on the Bench.

The first to be arraigned was Luther McNeal, whose trial occupied the whole Court day; he was acquitted, and the Court rose.

On Tuesday morning, the Bench was occupied by the Senior Puisne Justice, William Dummer Powell. Powell was of a different stamp from Scott. Scott was an amiable mediocrity without political ambition, and desirous only of being let alone; he imposed his personality on no one. Powell was of great learning, ambitious of power, and he dominated everyone he could, resenting the opposition of those who resisted. He was the real 'power behind the throne' at this time and at other periods of our history.

Jacob Overholtzer (or Overholser) was placed to the Bar, an elderly man, who had but a few years ago come from the United States. He had foolishly or heedlessly joined the enemy in arms, and could not possibly escape the verdict of Guilty.

Then Mr. Justice Campbell,[7] the Junior Puisne Justice, replaced Powell, and Robert Loundsberry was arraigned; he was acquitted, and the Court adjourned for that day. Campbell was not a strong judge; he seldom pressed for a conviction, but when a conviction had been secured he was generally ruthless and seldom recommended commutation.

Wednesday, June 9, the Chief Justice again presided. Aaron Stevens was called upon to plead: Stevens was a man of good reputation and standing in the community, and had actually been in the service of the Crown in the Indian Department. He confessed to acting as a spy for the enemy and was promptly convicted.

Then Mr. Justice Powell replaced the Chief Justice, and Garrett (or Garrat) Neill was arraigned. He also was a recent immigrant from the United States; he had made 'prisoners of the King's subjects in the London District to give them to the enemy' and he was found Guilty.

Thursday, June 10, brought Mr. Justice Campbell to the Bench, and John Johnston (or Johnson) to the prisoners' dock. He had been one of those in

[7] [William Campbell (1758-1834) served in the Royal Navy, settled in Nova Scotia, studied law and was attorney-general of Cape Breton from 1804 to 1807. In 1811 he was appointed a judge of the Court of King's Bench in Upper Canada and in 1825 chief justice and speaker of the legislative council. He was granted a knighthood on his retirement from the Bench in 1829.]

open and active rebellion in the London District, was one of Medcalf's prisoners, and could not escape conviction.

On the same day, before the Chief Justice, Samuel Hartwell and Stephen Hartwell were tried. They were young men lately from the United States who had on the outbreak of the war gone back to their native land, joined General Hull at Detroit, and were taken prisoner by Brock at that place; brought back to Canada, they were paroled by mistake. The overt acts in their case were attempts to take prisoner His Majesty's loyal subjects to deliver them over to the enemy. Guilty.

The next day, Friday, June 11, before Mr. Justice Powell came Dayton (or Daton) Lindsey (Lyndsay, Lindsay, Linsey). He was a ring-leader; he had openly joined the forces of the invader and had seduced others from their allegiance. He was convicted. Mr. Justice Powell finished out the day, and George Peacock, Jr., whose case was in almost every particular the same as Lindsey's, shared Lindsey's fate.

On Wednesday, June 15, Mr. Justice Campbell took his seat on the Bench, and Isaiah (Campbell calls him Jonah) Brink was set to the Bar. He had been in open rebellion, had joined the marauding party of the enemy, and had acted in a most atrocious way toward the loyal subjects. He was found guilty in a very short time. The same day Benjamin Simmons (or Simmonds) faced the Chief Justice and a jury. He had also been one of those who joined the enemy and helped to ravage their neighbours; he had been taken by Medcalf and had no chance of acquittal. Guilty.

The evening and the morning session exhausted that day; and Thursday, June 16, Mr. Justice Powell again presided. Robert Troup was tried; he seems to have been innocent, and, though some of his conduct had been suspicious if not equivocal, he was acquitted after a short trial.

In the afternoon, Campbell relieved Powell, and Adam Crysler (Chrystler) was brought before the Court. He was also one of Medcalf's prisoners; his conduct was even worse than that of his comrades and he was convicted.

Friday, June 17, Isaac Petit (Pettit) was placed in the dock before the Chief Justice. It was made to appear from the evidence that Petit had taken some part with the marauders, but he had refused to accompany them and had been branded as a coward; the case, however, was clear, and he was justly found guilty. The same day, Jesse Holly was tried before Mr. Justice Powell and acquitted. The Court sat on Saturday, June 18, when, before Mr. Justice Campbell, Cornelius Howey pleaded Guilty.

Monday, June 20, saw Mr. Justice Campbell again on the Bench; John Dunham was arraigned and the evidence proved him a ring-leader. Guilty. The following day, June 21, Noah Pyne Hopkins was proved before the Chief Justice and the jury, to have been the enemy's commissary and to have taken flour for their troops. He was found Guilty.

The list of prisoners was now exhausted; fourteen had been convicted on evidence, one had pleaded guilty, and four had been acquitted. For the unhappy fourteen, the law provided only one penalty; the hideous execution for High Treason had not been modified by legislation from the earliest times; that sentence was pronounced upon all on Tuesday, June 21. It then became the duty of the Sheriff to carry out the sentence on Thursday, unless the Judges should grant a respite.[8] The Judges had already met and had agreed that the sentences should be respited until July 20, to give all an equal opportunity of supplicating the Royal mercy, and that a report should be made to the President by the Chief Justice.

The report is extant; of those tried before the Chief Justice, the Hartwells, who had surrendered voluntarily for trial, were recommended to mercy; for the time being, none of those tried before Powell was so recommended, and, of those tried before Campbell, the Chief Justice says, 'Mr. Justice Campbell sees no circumstances of mitigation in the cases of those convicted before him unless the reluctance to continue with the party which Johnson appeared latterly to show, and the wish expressed of leaving them, and the confession and apparent penitence of Howey may be considered.' The Chief Justice, however, suggested that the opinion of the Executive Council should be taken.

The Attorney General, in his report, feared that Aaron Stevens, Dayton Lindsey, Benjamin Simmons, George Peacock, Jr., Adam Crysler, Isaiah Brink, and John Dunham must be executed. John Johnson, he thought an ignorant man who had been deluded by others and who had been humane to prisoners; the Hartwells, he said, were enemies and not British subjects. They had, on the outbreak of the war, gone to the United States, and had been taken prisoner by Brock at Detroit. They had been paroled by mistake, and the wise young Attorney General thought that though as residents of Upper Canada they were in law guilty of High Treason, it would be 'better not to strain the law to its utmost rigor'. Of the rest he would say nothing, but he suggested that the President should direct the Judges to order the immediate execution of one or two of the offenders, and that in any case no unconditional pardon should be granted.

Petitions had already begun to pour in. Jacob Overholzer was described as 'an unfortunate but honest old man' by many loyal inhabitants of the Township of Bertie as early as June 11. On June 20, many inhabitants of the District of Niagara pleaded for the Hartwells, who had been led to act as they did through ignorance and levity, and later on in July they were joined by many more. Poor Polly Hopkins, wife of Noah Payne Hopkins, on June

[8] At the Common Law the Sheriff was to execute the condemned within a convenient time, but in 1742, the statute 25 Geo. II, c. 37, directed that the Judge should direct execution the next day but one after the sentence.

29, pleaded her eleven years of marriage and her four children; and, July 8, a large number of the inhabitants of the Niagara District joined in her prayer; for John Johnson and Aaron Stevens, Samuel Hatt and Richard Beasley, J.P.s, and George Chisholm spoke. The Executive Council conferred with the Judges and the Attorney General, and, after anxious consideration and careful weighing of all the facts, it was determined that seven might be saved from death; these seven, the Hartwells, Cornelius Howey, Isaac Pettit, Jacob Overholzer, Garrett Neill, and John Johnson were respited till July 28, to enable proper enquiry to be made and proper terms fixed for commutation.[9] But Aaron Stevens, Dayton Lindsey, Noah Payne Hopkins, George Peacock, Jr., Isaiah Brink, Benjamin Simmons, Adam Crysler, and John Dunham must die the death of a traitor. The Chief Justice refused to advise whom to execute but he recommended that as the convicted men were all from the Niagara and London Districts, one at least from each District should be executed; at the same time he pointed out that the President had no power to pardon for Treason. The Executive Council asked the opinion of the Judges as to where the executions should take place. The Judges agreed that executions in the respective Districts where the overt acts had been committed would be of most salutary effect; but the majority were of opinion that this could not be legally ordered out of Niagara District in which the convictions were had except by bringing up the convictions into the Court of King's Bench, and that was an unusual proceeding, and should be avoided, if possible. They therefore advised that the Sheriff of the Niagara District should be directed to execute some on the boundary line between Niagara and London Districts, but that was not done; the unfortunate suffered the prescribed punishment,[10] July 20, 1814, at Burlington Heights,[11] and so ended the Ancaster 'Bloody Assize'.

What was to be done with the other seven? The Royal Instructions did

[9] Chief Justice Scott writes, York, July 14, 1814, complaining that the form of the reprieve is inaccurate; the sentence was to be 'hanged by the neck but not until his Death for he must be cut down alive and his Entrails taken out and burned before his Face, his Head then to be cut off and his Body divided into four Quarters and his Head and Quarters to be at the King's Disposal'.

[10] At that time the sentence for high treason was in the form presented for centuries by the Common Law:

(1) That you are to be drawn to the place of execution,
(2) Where you must be hanged by the neck, but not until you are dead, for you must be cut down alive
(3) And your bowels taken out
(4) And burned before your face (or your being still alive),
(5) Then your head must be severed from your body,
(6) Which must be divided into four parts, and
(7) Your head and quarters to be at the king's disposal.

Chief Justice Scott, in a letter to Drummond, July 14, 1814, says: 'In point of fact this not authorize the President oı any Governor to pardon for Treason, but gave 'power upon extraordinary occasions to grant Reprieves to the offenders, until and to the intent that our Royal pleasure may be known therein'. Accordingly, a reprieve was granted, and the matter submitted to the Home Government.[12]

The Gaol at York was crowded, and it was decided that these prisoners with others in like case offending should, pending removal to Quebec, be placed in the District Gaol at Kingston. And the seven were given by the Sheriff of the Home District at York, John Beikie,[13] to a Deputy Sheriff, to be delivered by him to the Sheriff of the Midland District at Kingston; with them went Calvin Wood, generally known as Dr. Wood, not quite in the same condition as themselves, but only committed on a charge of High Treason, making a cortège of eight prisoners under guard. They travelled by the Danforth Road, built by Asa Danforth fifteen years before from York to Kingston, and the melancholy cavalcade had got as far as Smith's Creek (now Port Hope) on the evening of July 31. Sergeant Montgomery and his small detachment of militia locked the door of the little hut in which the eight prisoners were confined about a quarter of an hour after midnight; but in the morning they found that four had escaped – Calvin Wood, who seems to have been an expert at breaking out of confinement, Cornelius Howey, the penitent, and the two Hartwells, U.S. citizens. Immediate pursuit was made, and all but Stephen Hartwell were speedily retaken. The seven remaining prisoners were safely delivered to the Sheriff at Kingston, and duly incarcerated in the Gaol there. The reward of $100 offered by Beikie was ineffective. Stephen Hartwell was never recaptured; he almost certainly was assisted to

sentence is never exactly executed; the executioner invariably taking care not to cut the body down until the criminal is dead, but the sentence of the law is always pronounced.'

[11] The *Quebec Gazette* of August 18, 1814, says that the execution took place at Burlington, *i.e.*, of course Burlington Heights, where the Hamilton Cemetery now stands.

[12] It may be worth while to quote the original despatch from Sir Gordon Drummond to Lord Bathurst. Writing from Kingston, U.C., July 10, 1814, he says: 'A band of Rebels in the District of London under a notorious partizan leader made incursions on unprotected parts of the country, a number of loyal inhabitants, Militia, volunteered, attacked and (January, 1814) took about 15 prisoners. To make an example of these miscreants and the like a Special Commission (of Oyer and Terminer) was issued for London, Niagara and Home Districts. The Court sat from May 23 to June 21, seventeen persons were tried out of seventy indictments for High Treason – fifteen were convicted and were to be executed, July 20. Mr. Robinson, Acting Attorney-General prosecuted and his conduct was highly meritorious and praiseworthy.' The Chief Justice and Acting Attorney-General advise, and Drummond agrees, that it is not necessary to execute all, and seven have been reprieved for His Majesty's pleasure as to their execution or perpetual banishment.

[13] [John Beikie (1767?-1839) was sheriff of the Home District 1810-15 and a member of the legislative assembly between 1813 and 1816. He became clerk of the executive council in succession to John Small. He was a captain in the 3rd York militia regiment.]

cross the lake by those secretly sympathizing with the enemy's cause, of whom there was, unfortunately, no lack in the Newcastle District.[14]

Communication with England was slow, and no instructions were to be expected until the arrival of the Spring Fleet at Quebec, as the war had put an end to the more speedy communication by post, *via* New York.

In the latter part of the winter there broke out in Kingston Gaol the dreaded Jail-fever which, under that name, or that of ship-fever, spotted-fever, etc., was the scourge of crowded gaols, ships, and other confined places. It was a virulent type of typhus fever, then and for long after believed to be 'generated out of filth and overcrowding, bad diet, and close, foul air'. . . .

Some of the unhappy prisoners were seized with the disease, and three died of it, Garret Neill, March 6, Jacob Overholzer, March 14, and Isaac Petit, March 16, 1815.[15] The other four received a pardon conditioned on their abandoning the Province and all other British possessions for life,[16] (which meant going to the United States). Their comrade, 'Dr.' Calvin Wood, did not wait for formal permission to take shelter across the international boundary. . . . He judged it wise not to wait for trial; and so, with two others, he made an escape from the Kingston Gaol, June 9, 1815; that was the third time he had escaped, and, as Sir Frederick Robinson,[17] the Administrator of the Government, complains, 'his being apprehended on the

[14] Robinson was very angry at the escape. He wrote to MacMahon, the Governor's Secretary, from Brockville, September 10, 1814, that the escape was due to the negligence of the Deputy Sheriff. 'It is punishable by a criminal prosecution for neglect and so frequent and inexcusable are his faults of this nature that I think the Sheriff of the Home District should be compelled to find a more efficient Deputy.' I cannot find the name of the Deputy Sheriff, and there is no record of any criminal prosecution or other proceedings against him.

[15] See the report of Charles Stuart, Sheriff of the Midland District, dated at Kingston, July 28, 1815. This report was sent to MacMahon. The overcrowding of Gaols at that time was notorious and probably unavoidable. In a Petition of the Justices of the Peace of the Eastern District at Cornwall, March 15, 1815, they say that in the Gaol at Cornwall there were confined three persons charged with murder, and seven charged with felony; that the Gaol had been and still was occupied as a barracks and that no part of the building was sufficient to hold prisoners in safety. They ask for a special Commission of Oyer and Terminer and General Gaol Delivery to deliver the Gaol.

[16] Banishment for crime came to an end in Canada in 1842 on the passing of the Statute 6 Vic., c. 5 (Can.), which, by sec. 4, enacted that instead of transportation or banishment there should be imprisonment in the provincial penitentiary or other prison.

[17] [Frederick Philipse Robinson (1763-1852) was an ensign in the Loyal Americans in 1778, became a captain in 1784 and a major in 1794. He served in the Revolutionary War, in the West Indies, and was a senior staff officer in the Spanish campaigns. In 1814 he returned to America with a brigade which he led at Plattsburg in September 1814. He later assumed command of the forces in Upper Canada and for a few months during 1815 he was administrator of the province. Afterwards he held appointments in the West Indies. He became a lieutenant-general in 1825 and a general in 1840. He was knighted in 1815.]

former occasions was not owing to any activity on the part of either the Gaoler or the Sheriff'. . . .[18]

After all the convicts had been disposed of, the next step was to proceed against those who had not been apprehended, but against whom indictments had been found for High Treason by the Grand Jury at Ancaster.

Robinson had gone to England to study for and be called to the Bar there, but D'Arcy Boulton returned from his prison in France, and became Attorney General on the last day of 1814. He did not delay, but he had the proper proclamations made under the Provincial Act of 1815; and, May 27, 1817, he had the satisfaction to have entered up judgments of outlawry against nearly thirty persons, amongst them the leader in treason, Abraham Markle; and many of these had lands which were forfeited to the Crown.

FURTHER READING: E. A. Cruikshank, 'John Beverley Robinson and the trials for treason in 1814', *Ontario Historical Society*, volume 25 (1929), pages 191-219; W. R. Riddell, 'An echo of the War of 1812', *Ontario Historical Society*, volume 23 (1926), pages 434-49.

[18] See Sir Frederick's letter to Col. Foster, the Military Secretary of the Governor-General, from Kingston, June 13, 1815. Can. Arch. Sundries, U.C., 1815. For the charges against the elusive 'Dr.' Wood, see Can. Arch. Sundries, U.C., 1813.

Like Norfolk, the provincial capital was open to invasion by troops convoyed across the lakes. Though it was of no great military importance, York was worth taking for reasons of morale, for the supplies and vessels that might be found there, and for the disruption its capture might cause to the British effort farther west. But control of Lake Ontario was essential, and only on two brief occasions did York fall to the enemy. This article examines the first occupation – the battle on April 27, 1813, the relations between the citizens and their conquerors, the official and unofficial treatment of private property, and the source and extent of looting and destruction during the six-day occupation. A seemingly trivial and in some ways farcical episode, the capture had a considerable effect upon the contest for Lake Erie. It also contributed to the growth of the Family Compact, and led to British reprisals against American centres. . . . CHARLES W. HUMPHRIES *is a member of the Department of History, Mount Allison University, Sackville, New Brunswick. His article appeared in volume 51 (spring 1959) of 'Ontario History' and is reprinted with his permission and with the permission of the Ontario Historical Society.*

The Capture of York

BY CHARLES W. HUMPHRIES

As afternoon yielded to dusk on April 26, 1813, two figures could be discerned tramping the two-mile stretch of road that ran from York to the fort. They were Quartermaster Finan, of the Royal Newfoundland Regiment, and his son, who had been in York for the day. A third person, Captain McNeale of the Grenadier Company of the 8th (King's) Regiment, hastened to catch up with them, and the trio continued toward the fort as the shadows lengthened. McNeale spoke of his plans for the next day and talked 'confidently of being in Fort George, the next town, on a certain day, as if no untoward circumstance could intervene'.

In town, the rector of York, the Reverend Dr. John Strachan, having earlier performed the pleasant ministerial chore of marrying a young couple, busied himself with the task of writing a letter to James Brown, a fellow clergyman. He complained that 'owing to the mismanagement of our little Navy we lost the command of the Lake last summer, and shall not regain it till we procure good officers from England, those we have do not belong to the Royal Navy and not having seen service are without experience'. He continued: '. . . this country cannot be defended, if we possess not the command of the Lakes. The weakness and imbecility of our Commander in Chief has produced all our defeats. We might have destroyed the enemies [sic] ships last winter but miserable forbearance and not vigour was at that time the order of the day. If this country fall Sir George Prevost and he only is to blame.'

In a bedroom of his large frame dwelling on the west side of Frederick Street, just south of King, Prideaux Selby, the Receiver General of Upper Canada, lay mortally ill. John Hunter, the messenger of the House of Assembly, was occupied with the job of stoking up the stove in the office of the Clerk of the Assembly. Before long, Hunter would be asleep in this office where he had spent every night during the winter months.

The normal routine of the little town was soon shattered by an alarming discovery. From the Scarborough bluffs, someone had sighted the American fleet to the east of York. By the time McNeale and his friends reached the fort, all was bustle and activity. The signal gun was fired to summon the militia to York and to battle. At his home in Markham Township, Matthias Saunders, sometime shipbuilder and owner, knew that something was amiss in York when he heard that gun booming out its alarm across the farms and fields. He quickly set out for the fort and his place as a private in John Willson's company of the First Regiment of York Militia. Behind him, Saunders left a wife and six children.

Ely Playter,[1] a lieutenant in the Third Regiment of York Militia, had just arrived home from the fort. He was soon summoned from his farm near the Don at the request of Major William Allan of the Third York Regiment, otherwise a leading merchant and postmaster of the capital. He hurried down to York to find both the troops and militia busy preparing – and sending out – guards and patrols. He set out to find Major Givins – the local official of the Indian Department – in order to obtain the assistance of the Indians in preparing the defences. Playter located him with Maj.-Gen. Sir Roger Hale Sheaffe, Brock's successor as commander of the forces in Upper Canada and as civil administrator at the Government House. Sheaffe, refusing to be overly alarmed by the appearance of the enemy, was confident that they would wait till sunrise before commencing any action. He told Playter to sleep at the Government House until morning, when there would be sufficient time to organize to resist the attack.

In the dark of that night, the pace of activity quickened in the little town. Donald McLean, the Clerk of the House of Assembly, made a hurried trip

[1] [Ely Playter (1775-after 1853) was a farmer on Yonge Street north of York. He became a captain in the Third York militia in 1816 and represented York and Simcoe in the legislative assembly from 1825 to 1828.]

to John McGill's home. He removed from there, in its owner's absence, the papers pertaining to the office which McGill held: Inspector General of Public Provincial Accounts.

At Sheaffe's behest Chief Justice Thomas Scott and Justice William Dummer Powell – like Selby and McGill members of the Executive Council – hastened to the house where Prideaux Selby lay in a state of insensibility. The public money, amounting to £3,109 .1 .8¾, which was at the Receiver General's, was uppermost in their minds. Determined that the Americans should have none of it, they counselled Mrs. Derenzy, Selby's daughter, to remove this sum to a safer place. Mrs. Derenzy agreed to this. However, before sending off an iron chest, containing the government funds, to a place of safe-keeping, Mrs. Derenzy removed a portion of it, supposedly six hundred dollars. This she put in a smaller iron container along with the public papers. The latter receptacle was then trundled off to Donald McLean's, since it was supposed that no one would suspect the Clerk of the Assembly of having much ready cash. The larger strong-box was secreted elsewhere.

William Warren Baldwin, York's practitioner in both law and medicine, fretted about what would happen to his valuables should the Americans land. His home at the corner of Frederick and Front Streets was next to the dockyards where a 30-gun ship was on the stocks; consequently his property was a likely mark for any pillager. Having hit upon a plan, he bundled up his silverware and someone's black silk gown and sent them out of town to a friend's barn. There, he was confident, they would be out of danger.

To the east of the town, at the head of the bay of York, were quartered Captain Eustace's company of the 8th (King's) Regiment and some of the York militia. They were left there to forestall any American attempt on that flank. The balance of Sheaffe's regulars, slightly over two hundred in number, were at the fort located on the triangular knoll which rose between Garrison Creek and the lakeshore; thus situated across from the western tip of the peninsula, it effectively commanded the entrance to the harbour. Yet, though its location may have been ideal, its defences were not. Despite Brock's complaint about the state of the post in 1811, only a stone magazine had been constructed in the interim, lack of supplies preventing further improvements. And the number of troops was never large; even the chance arrival of some of the 8th Regiment only increased the strength of the regulars at York to 300 men.

Uneasily the troubled town waited for the dawn. By four a.m. John Strachan was out of bed and, getting dressed, he was soon mounted up and almost eagerly looking for an excitement-filled day. In the grey light he could discern the ships of Commodore Isaac Chauncey's American fleet, some fourteen in number, lying close to the south shore of the peninsula in front of the town. The ship *Madison* of 28 guns, the brig *Oneida* of 18 guns, and twelve schooners, of from three to nine guns each, held about seventeen hundred soldiers in addition to an undetermined number of marines.

For the assault upon Fort York was a major American operation and was under the supreme command of Major-General Henry Dearborn. Some four thousand men had been assembled at Sackett's Harbour for an attack upon Kingston and York, the hope being that the capture of the two British naval bases on Lake Ontario would also allow Chauncey to win control of that vital body of water. The original plan had been to direct the attack against Kingston, but early in April Dearborn had become convinced that Prevost had reinforced the Kingston naval base with several thousand British regulars – a completely unfounded belief. Consequently he had decided to shift his attentions to York, a far less formidable enterprise but one that was not without its merits. If the vessel under construction in the dockyards could be destroyed and if the *Prince Regent*, the vessel of the Provincial Marine stationed at York, could be captured, the effect upon the British lake squadron would be most serious. In any event, since York was the capital of the upper province, some prestige at least was to be gained by its capture.

As the sun began to take a firm hold on the day, a fresh breeze sprang up from the east. The American ships weighed anchor and sailed for a position to the west of the fort. Shortly, they came to anchor off the point where old Fort Rouillé had once stood, a little more than a mile west of the fort.

Waiting on shore to see what the next enemy move would be, Sheaffe had another opportunity to assess his strength. He had a handful of regulars – two companies of the 8th (King's) Regiment, one of them under McNeale, about a full company of the Royal Newfoundland Regiment, a company of the Glengarry Light Infantry, a Bombardier and twelve Gunners of the Royal Artillery – the nearly three hundred militiamen, a few dockyard workers, and one hundred Indians under Major Givins. In all, he had no more than seven hundred soldiers at his disposal.

As eight o'clock approached, Sheaffe could see a considerable number of small boats gathering near the *Madison*. Taking his first concrete defensive step, he ordered the regular troops – except for Eustace's company, which was still to the east – into the ravine to the west of the fort. Major Givins and his Indians were sent into the woods west of Fort Rouillé, to oppose the enemy landing. The company of Glengarry Light Infantry was directed to support them. The lateness of this order considerably piqued Strachan and partially accounted for his feelings toward Sheaffe when this day was over. However, there was little else that Sheaffe could do but wait and allow the enemy the first move. The poverty of his force denied him any opportunity of placing it in some sort of lengthy line of defence. As a consequence, he had to let the Americans come to him. Strachan, who offered no alternative scheme, never forgave Sheaffe for his wait-and-see attitude.

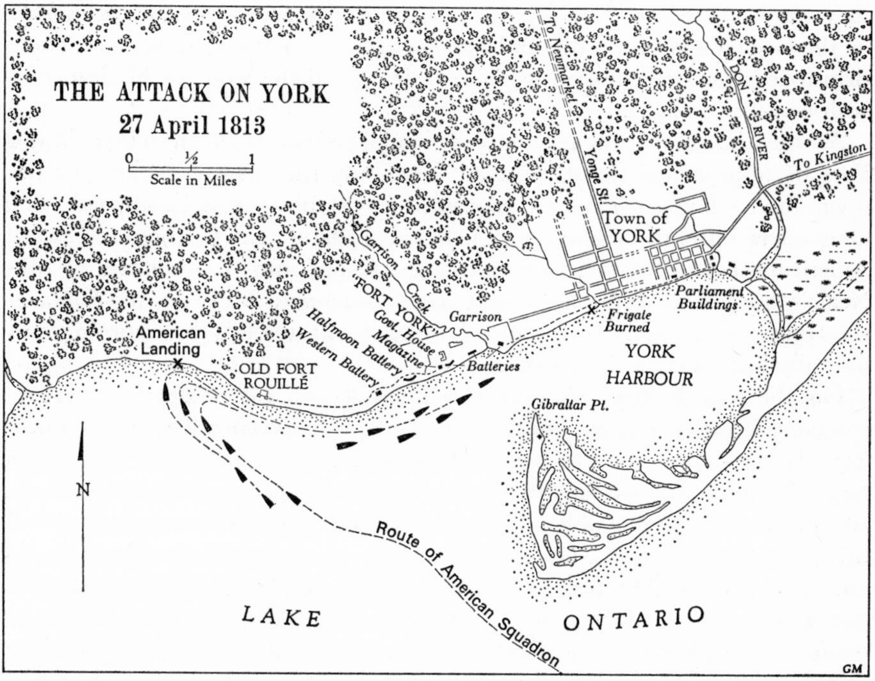

The militia failed to arrive on time in the ravine because of a general tardiness, probably the result of hesitancy about doing battle. This made it necessary for Sheaffe to send out the Grenadier Company of the 8th Regiment, under McNeale, and the Royal Newfoundland Regiment to aid Givins's group. Such an order saved the bulk of the 1st and 3rd York Regiments from encountering the enemy in any real engagement. Instead it was the Grenadier Company which found itself up against the landing Americans. As a result, the mettle of the militia never received a real test, and most of them were able to harvest the summer crops because they never fought the Americans that day.

The second company of the 8th, under Captain Eustace, with some of the militia, was ordered to come up to the assistance of the rest of the troops. Aeneas Shaw, Adjutant General of the Militia, led part of his force on to the Dundas Road, north of the woods, in order to protect the rear of the troops who were engaged. Shaw contributed to the success of the American landing by taking the Glengarry company with him on this project. Instead, the Glengarry Light Infantry should have been the first group to advance to the side of Givins and his Indians. This piece of bungling and the general slowness of the militia meant that when the Americans, taken off course by the east wind, landed above Fort Rouillé and nearly two miles west of the fort, they were opposed initially by the Indians alone, who were only supported by the Grenadiers of the 8th and the Royal Newfoundland Regiment. These British regulars, still unused to the terrain, found the woods a hindrance to both travel and battle.

As the American advance group, comprised of riflemen under Major Forsyth, approached the shore, there were only Indians present to open fire upon them. The enemy soon succeeded in establishing a beachhead. The Grenadiers hurriedly came up to help the Indians, but the now-reinforced Americans held their position and began to cut into the numbers of McNeale's company. McNeale himself fell, and Donald McLean, the Clerk of the House of Assembly, who had volunteered with the 8th that morning, was mortally wounded on the shore.

On the march, but still over two miles to the east, Captain Eustace's company heard the firing and increased its pace. Seven miles east of town, Ely Playter's group of 3rd York militiamen, vainly looking for Americans from that quarter, caught the sounds of the early firing and hastened back toward York on the double. Within half an hour, the American troops had driven back the Indians, Grenadiers, and Newfoundlanders, and had firmly established themselves, despite several rallies staged by the British under the personal direction of Sheaffe. By ten o'clock, over a thousand American soldiers were on shore and Brigadier-General Zebulon Pike, the noted explorer, assumed command. Fewer than two hundred British regulars had been on hand to oppose this landing.

Once the American troops were on shore, Commodore Chauncey ordered his ships to make sail into the bay, against a steady east wind. On shore, part of the battered 8th made its way to the fort for medical aid. Chauncey then commenced a fire both upon the western battery – about half-way between Fort Rouillé and Fort York – and the fort itself. To cope with the ever-increasing fire from the American vessels – which were now located nearly on a line between the point of the peninsula and Fort York – the British had only three twelve-pounders and two semi-obsolete eighteen-pounders.

What was left of the Grenadier company rallied around the western battery to meet the oncoming enemy. Disaster continued to stalk them: the battery's travelling magazine was accidentally ignited and, in the explosion which followed, about thirty-five men, principally Grenadiers, were killed and wounded. The battery platform was ripped apart by the force of the blast and one of the eighteen-pounders was overturned. Despite the ensuing confusion, the travelling magazine was replaced and sporadic firing was continued from this point. However, the western battery could no longer serve as a point of defence, and the loss of so many men made it highly doubtful that Sheaffe could withstand the Americans at any place.

The pounding by the American vessels, which went almost unanswered, was beginning to take its toll. Six American ships were now directly opposite the fort and pouring in a heavy bombardment. An attempt was made to rally the militia at the fort's guardhouse but the enemy fire became so heavy that this group was forced to hide under the cover of the fort's battery. The guns at Fort York were attempting to answer the American fire but their range was too short and the balls fell harmlessly into York Bay.

Many of the militia, on the scene for the first time, seemed finally ready for battle. An effort was made to form them up in the hollow next to the garrison. Some did organize, but they were more than discouraged in this work to find the tired and beaten British regulars passing by them on their way to town.

By this time, since he found his position untenable, Sheaffe had made his decision. He was scarcely able to reply to the ships' barrage and, although it had done little damage thus far, it would be foolish to suppose that it could remain ineffective much longer. He had seen one company of the 8th virtually wiped out and the heavy casualties of the other regular troops. A fight could be made at the fort, but the fire of the American vessels would probably weaken it first, and then the American troops would ultimately topple the fort by sheer weight of numbers if nothing else. What was to be gained by such a fight? Obviously nothing; York would be lost and, much more, further casualties would be sustained, and the military and civil leader of Upper Canada would probably become an American prisoner. A further stand by Sheaffe might have been quite heroic and in the finest tradition, but it would have been too costly and would have gained nothing. The die was cast for Sheaffe: he would retreat to Kingston and take with him those regulars still capable of performing the march.

Sheaffe refused to allow the advancing Americans to have anything that could be demolished. He gave the order to have the grand magazine blown up. Apparently this command was not general knowledge and, as this order was being executed, Ely Playter busied himself inside the fort, picking up his coat and advising the female cook to leave as the Americans were almost upon them. Matthias Saunders, also inside the post, struggled with a portable magazine that had served the twelve-pounder at which he had been stationed. He was eager to carry it off so that the Americans would have one less prize to claim. John Basil, the doorkeeper to the Legislative Council, was really too old for war, but he had gamely volunteered with the 3rd York that morning. His legs failed to keep him up with the rest of the retreating group and he lingered near the post.

Six hundred feet to the west of the fort, Pike led an eagerly advancing American force. The roar of the exploding magazine ripped the air apart, and then came the destruction. Stones filled the air; small ones bounced along the ground and large ones plummeted to earth and half buried themselves. Pike, struck [on the side and back] by one of the flying stones, fell mortally wounded. In the American 6th Regiment alone, thirteen were killed by the explosion and 104 wounded in varying degrees. As well, the 15th and 16th American Regiments suffered considerably. On the British side, Captain Loring, Sheaffe's aide-de-camp, had his horse killed underneath him. Saunders had his leg shattered by a large stone. Old Basil received wounds both in the head and knee. Joseph Shepard, a private in the 3rd York, dropped with a badly mangled left thigh and three broken ribs on his left side. It was now about twelve o'clock.

It has been stated that about one hundred regulars were killed or wounded by this explosion.[2] Obviously this is not an accurate accounting of the results of this blast, but some damage was done to the British side. It appears to have been the militia who suffered and were exposed to the greatest risk. It can thus be concluded that, although the regulars were ordered out of the area prior to the detonation, the militia were uninformed. Possibly Sheaffe underestimated the probable dimensions of the explosion when he gave his order. There seems to have been no thought, on Sheaffe's part, of crippling the enemy by this move, although he accidentally did so. Rather, the concern was to eliminate the possibility of valuable stores falling into their hands.

Following the explosion, the bulk of the American force came to an abrupt halt to take stock of the situation, but a few riflemen advanced to the fort and fired a few shots at the retreating regulars and militia. For many of the militia this was their first sight of the Americans and the only time that they were subjected to any sort of rifle fire. The disorganized British withdrew to the dockyards in town where, after further consultation between Sheaffe and his officers, the retreat to Kingston began. John Beikie, the sheriff of York, in writing of Sheaffe's departure, described the position of the residents and militia left behind when he noted that the regulars 'left us all standing in the street, like a parcel of sheep'.

With the regulars gone, the arranging of a surrender and terms of capitulation was left in the hands of the leading militia officers. Captain J. B. Robinson and Major William Allan set out for the American line with a flag of truce and returned to announce that they had been ordered by the Americans to come back in fifteen minutes. In the meantime, Ely Playter and his militia group, moving towards the town, encountered a regular officer who had turned back on Sheaffe's orders. This band went to the shipyard and fired the new vessel on the stocks and the marine stores. At two in the afternoon, the Union Jack was lowered at the fort and the Stars and Stripes replaced it.

Behind, Sheaffe left sixty-two regulars killed and seventy-six wounded. Forty-five of the killed and forty-nine of the wounded were in the 8th

[2] In his booklet, *The Yankees Capture York* (Detroit: Wayne University Press, 1955), Milo Quaife states on page 18 that forty British troops were killed.

Regiment. '. . . a few of the Indians (Missisagus & Chipeways [sic] were killed and wounded, among the latter were two Chiefs'. The record of the citizens of York is hardly impressive when placed next to that of the regulars. Ensign John Detlor of the 3rd York had his leg badly shattered and an amputation became necessary; he lost much blood both before and after the operation and died the day after the engagement. Private Daniel Murray, 3rd York, was killed during the battle. As has been noted, Matthias Saunders had his leg badly injured by the explosion of the grand magazine; an amputation followed, and he clung to life for close to a month before dying on May 25. Donald McLean, a volunteer, fell at the beach. John Basil never fully recovered from the concussion he received when the grand magazine exploded, and died during the summer.

Thus, five Upper Canadians died while fighting for Upper Canada, two of them as a result of the explosion of the grand magazine and not in actual combat. An equal number were wounded: William Jarvie, William Jarvis, Joseph Shepard, Patrick Hartney, and Andrew Borland. One of these had been injured when the grand magazine blew up. These figures dispel any visions of large losses by the militia, which, in this case, was defending its own land and town. Although there are no accurate figures for Indian losses during this contest, it is fairly safe to assume – on the basis of other battles where both Indians and militia participated – that the Indian casualties were probably just as severe as the Upper Canadian.

Now came the problem of working out a capitulation with the Americans. William Chewett,[3] a lieutenant-colonel of the 3rd York, and William Allan, a major in the same regiment, met with Col. Mitchell, of the 3rd Artillery of the U.S. Army, and Major King, of the 15th U.S. Infantry, in Mr. Crookshank's house on Front Street to detail the terms. J. B. Robinson was on hand to assist from a legal standpoint, and John Strachan hovered over the entire group like York's guardian angel. The American discovery that the ship on the stocks and the naval stores were on fire held up negotiations for a time. The United States officers looked upon this as a dishonest act, undertaken by the Canadians while the talks were in progress. However, since this order from Sheaffe had been executed by a group of the militia who had no knowledge of the capitulation talks, the Americans took no action. In any event, it seems likely that these stores had been fired before the discussion began. By four in the afternoon, the capitulation terms had been agreed upon, subject to ratification by Chauncey and Dearborn.

It was agreed that the regular and militia troops should surrender as

[3] [William Chewett (1753?-1849) came to Canada in 1771, became a government surveyor in Quebec, and was appointed deputy surveyor of Upper Canada in 1791. He held the position of deputy surveyor-general of the province from 1802 to 1832. After serving as a captain in the 1st Dundas and York regiments he became lieutenant-colonel of the 3rd York militia. He commanded at York at the time of the capitulation.]

prisoners of war and that the naval and military stores at York should be given up to the Americans. In return, the Americans guaranteed the safety of the private property of York citizens and the security of the civil papers of the province. In addition, any doctors attending the wounded regulars and militia would not be considered prisoners of war. While these talks were in progress, some of the militia who did not intend to be taken prisoners had time to stop at Jordan's Inn, on Front Street, for a quick drink before they travelled north to avoid capture and parole.

Upon completion of the terms of capitulation, Major Allan was made a prisoner of war. Because Allan had been under a flag of truce, Strachan was infuriated and, martyr-like, he accompanied Allan to the centre of town in the middle of an enemy column. There is little doubt that Strachan was glorying in this situation and his vocation meant that the Americans could do little with him. In town, the militia who were present were busy grounding their arms. Some were doing this quite willingly.

Isaac Wilson, writing home to his brother, described the scene in York: 'It struck my mind very forcibly the evening after the battle was over to see men who two hours before were doing their utmost to kill one another now convening together with the greatest familiarity. In the evening all seemed as settled and quiet in York as if nothing had happened.'

At dusk, the Americans left for the fort, except for Forsyth's rifle corps which stayed on as guards. Wilson noted: 'In the night they put a sentry over every store but they could not keep the inhabitants from it who made shameful work in some peoples houses.' As shall be seen, he was very much mistaken in what he said.

With the battle over, John Hunter returned to Donald McLean's office and 'found the enemy in possession of the House of Assembly whence they took . . . [Hunter's] chest, in which was the sum of one hundred and fifty dollars in army bills, and wearing apparel, books, and other small property. They likewise took a pair of blankets . . . the amount of which property, exclusive of the bills, was at a very moderate valuation twenty-nine dollars . . .'. Thus, before this eventful day was out, some Americans had found their way from the fort to the House of Assembly on Front Street. However, the bulk of the looting was done on the 28th and 29th of April.

On Wednesday, the 28th, John Strachan went forward to a full day of badgering and verbal sniping. He met Major King at Prideaux Selby's and immediately assailed him on the subject of Major Allan's capture and the matter of the non-ratification of the terms of capitulation by the American commanders, Chauncey and Dearborn.[4] At King's instigation the two men went to Fort York where the American officer in command, Colonel Pierce, was powerless to do anything about ratification. At the post, the captured

[4] Much of the preceding account has to be based on Strachan's letter.

militia were being kept in the blockhouse without food, and the wounded had had no attention. Pierce ordered food for the prisoners as the wrath of the rector increased.

Since the militia were still unparoled, Strachan demanded that he be taken on board the *Madison* to see Dearborn. However, Dearborn came ashore shortly, and Strachan, charging into the fray, met him and handed him the articles of capitulation for his signature. Strachan followed this with a demand for the parole of the militia and for permission to remove the wounded. Dearborn, his patience running short, told Strachan to leave him alone. The minister, never daunted, searched out Chauncey and told him in no uncertain terms that if the capitulation terms were not signed he would infer that it was a plot designed to give the riflemen time to loot, for the clause about respecting private property meant nothing while the articles remained unsigned. Strachan informed Chauncey that he would not permit this to happen, then, his dire threat uttered, he turned on his heel and stalked away from the American naval commander. It is difficult at this point to understand precisely who had won, and who had lost, in the battle of the previous day.

Word reached Dearborn of Strachan's statement to Chauncey, and to this Strachan attributed Dearborn's sudden appearance and the fact that he now signed the terms of capitulation in an amicable fashion. It is doubtful that Dearborn was actually giving in to Strachan. More likely, it was an act to be performed by Dearborn when it suited his purpose or he had the time. It was now possible to parole the officers and men in the blockhouse and it meant that the wounded could be removed from the fort and cared for.

This incident should not be brushed aside as merely an example of the Anglican minister's pomposity. It had deeper implications. Strachan had stood up to the Americans; he had been British. Here we have one source of his later, and greater, status. He had been present when the Americans had captured York and had not been cowed by the Yankee republicans. He had taken charge – or, at least, given the impression of doing this – when British authority had seemed to be disappearing with the retreating Sheaffe. After the war, he was to take charge in very real fashion in the form of the Family Compact. He had tasted power here, albeit the power of the vanquished, and he had liked it. Had he, in time of defeat, established himself for the next twenty-five years? Had he, by his actions, established some of those vague rules that governed entry into the Family Compact?

On Thursday, the 29th, the leading citizens of York had their memories jogged about the terms of capitulation by Major King. He reminded them that the articles necessitated the surrender of the public money in their possession and, if this was not done, the town would have to make up the difference. John Strachan, Chief Justice Scott, Dummer Powell, Major

Allan, and Duncan Cameron held a quick consultation and deemed it wise to hand over to the enemy the money which had been removed from Selby's home the night before the attack. The enemy was given £2,144.11.4 ($8,578) in army bills which was turned over to Captain Armstrong of the U.S. Infantry by the busy rector on behalf of Colonel Chewett and Major Allan.

Outside of this episode, Strachan, with W. W. Baldwin, spent the remainder of the day removing the sick and wounded from the fort to the hospital. North of town – near the Don River – as dusk was coming on, Ely Playter, who was determined not to be paroled, squatted in the woods near his farm and watched some American troops break down the door of his home and loot it.

Strachan wrote that on Friday 'the Govt. buildings [were] on fire, contrary to the articles of capitulation'. This notation leads into two major problems that were created by this period of occupation. Who burned the parliament buildings located on Front Street? Who did most of the looting which, by some accounts, was deemed to be extensive?

The burning of the parliament buildings is probably the more difficult question to answer. It is a fact that the American troops were in these buildings some time during their stay at York. It is also known that they took some loot from them, including that old conversation piece, a scalp. Except for the mention of the scalp, American accounts are vague on this subject or fail to note it. Later, Dearborn vigorously denied that he had ever given any order to fire these buildings.

Recently, Milo Quaife took a thorough look at this problem and, after a searching examination of documents and historical works, came to this conclusion:

> To sum up: . . . Save for the military works and the Parliament houses, no single building was destroyed in the town. No local contemporary charge was made that the Americans fired the Parliament houses, and such evidence as exists points strongly to the conclusion that the act was perpetrated by the Canadians themselves. Insofar as the destruction committed at Washington was based upon alleged prior American destruction at York, it was without justification. Finally, it is far from creditable to the American historical profession that for two generations its foremost spokesmen have been content to repeat, in more or less detail, the amazingly untrue statements of Henry Adams and John B. McMaster concerning the conduct of the American army at York, without troubling to examine for themselves the abundant and easily available contemporary evidence.

Despite his detailed work, Quaife is wrong.

Four local contemporary accounts *do* make the charge that the Americans burned the parliament buildings. The first of these is a letter from John Beikie, the sheriff of York, to his brother-in-law in Prescott. Beikie, who was in a position to know what really happened, made a very definite statement on this subject. What makes his statement important is that it was contained in a private letter which was not to be used for any polemic purpose. There would be no need to stretch the truth, whereas later declarations, used to arouse either controversy or patriotism, might be very suspect. Beikie wrote:

> They [the Americans] have burnt the Government House, two block houses, a barrack for soldiers, and other buildings. They have broken every door and window in the Council Office, which was Elmsby [Elmsley] House, and a schooner belonging to an inhabitant of York. They have carried off the 'Gloucester', which was undergoing repairs, and was to be converted into a transport, being too old for a ship-of-war. The new ship on the stocks we burnt ourselves, for otherwise, I dare say, they would have done it.

In his diary for April 30, Ely Playter wrote: 'The Town thronged with Yankies many busy getting off the publick [sic] stores the Council office with every Window Broke & pillaged of everything it contained the Government Building the Block House and the Building adjacent all burned to ashes . . .'. Playter's statement is almost identical to the first half of the quotation from Beikie's letter. By implication he is laying the damages done at the door of the Americans. Besides, if the Americans were burning government property and carrying off stores, why should not these buildings fall within their range of activities?

However, the case against the Americans does not end here. In two letters, appearing in successive issues [August 10 and 17, 1813] in the *Kingston Gazette*, there are further statements on this question. Both of these pieces of correspondence were written when the Americans showed alarm in June of 1813 over the proximity of the British fleet to Washington:

> We are not surprised at the 'anxiety, bustle and alarm', created by this approach to the Capital of the United States, when the barbarian conduct of the Americans is recollected in burning the Houses of Legislature, Courts, and Public Records, in their late occupation of York; and a private dwelling was sacrificed in the same manner, because it once had been a Government House [the writer is probably referring to Elmsley House].

> They [the Americans at York], it is true, entered into a formal stipulation not only that private property should be respected, but that papers belonging to the Civil Departments of the Government should not be removed or destroyed. Yet the first object they selected for depredation was the Printing Office. They broke and otherwise destroyed the Press; carried off or rendered useless the Types; and burned a large number of Copies of the Provincial Statutes that had been recently printed for general distribution. They then pillaged

> the Public Subscription Library kept at Elmsley House, carried away a great part of the Books, and did great injury to the house itself. And, to crown all, before they reembarked they set fire to the two houses erected for the accomodation of our Provincial Legislature and Courts of Justice, which . . . were neat and substantial buildings, and had been erected and fitted up at an expense of several thousand pounds. These with the Offices containing all the Journals, a large collection of Books and other appendages connected with such an establishment, were all consumed by the flames; and the bare walls alone remain, a monument of the Gothic ferocity and worse than Punic faith of our enemies.
>
> Of these exploits no notice has been taken in the States. They are not attended to in the dispatches of General Dearborn or Commodore Chauncey; though the latter, in order perhaps to vindicate what he is yet ashamed to avow, condescends to state in his dispatch that 'in the House of Assembly a Scalp had been found appended to the Mace', a most palpable falsehood, calculated for the prejudices of the most violent and ignorant only; and which it is impossible that he or any other man of common sense could believe.
>
> That they should have been silent on a subject so little to their honor is not surprising . . . .

Considering the reason for the writing of these two letters, it is interesting to note that, already, a reason for burning Washington had been created, although this did not occur until the following year.

The other charges against the American troops at York, except for the one pertaining to the burning of the parliament buildings, can be verified from a variety of accounts, including American ones, apart from these four. Why, then, should their statements about the parliament building be questioned? If it was common knowledge that the Americans were responsible for this act why would there be any need of propagating a commonly accepted fact? The people of York passed on little knowledge of the affair precisely because they knew all about it. Any argument that anyone, other than American soldiers, burned the parliament buildings is pure conjecture which cannot be substantiated by a solitary fact. What facts there are support the case against the Americans.

The question of looting is dealt with in a little-used group of volumes containing the War of 1812 claims for losses now in the Public Archives of Canada. Out of the total population of six hundred and twenty-five, twenty-two York residents deemed the damage sufficient to enter claims for their losses. As well, one person living beyond the town limits lost possessions to the pillagers. Judging from the character and size of some of the claims it would be safe to assume that everyone who suffered entered claims for losses. Of the twenty-three persons, thirteen had their homes or places of residence entered and looted; five had their stores robbed; two lost their carpenter's tools at the dockyards; two suffered livestock losses; and one had a schooner burned by the Americans. As has been noted, the Americans also destroyed the York printing press and looted the public library. Over twenty-two hundred claims, some of them inadmissible, were entered for losses during the entire war. Thus, just a shade over one per cent are for losses sustained when the Americans landed at York.

Who did this looting? Most of the claims are quite specific. Mary Marshall was the housekeeper at Elmsley House, the office of the Executive Council at the corner of King and Simcoe Streets, and was present when it was plundered by the Americans. They took £50 worth of silver articles as well as kitchen utensils, bedding, and wearing apparel belonging to her. In addition, the Americans also stole the baggage belonging to Sheaffe and Brock, and government stores kept there. Patrick Hartney, wounded in guiding the 8th Regiment to the attack, had his home looted by the Americans to the extent of £40. James Givins, who had departed from York with the retreating British, left behind a wife and seven children in their frame house at the head of what is today Givins Street. Their home was pillaged by the Americans. Some of these soldiers were stopped in the course of their looting by William Dummer Powell and Powell took Angelica Givins to Dearborn to ask for protection for herself, her family, and her property. Dearborn informed her that it was not in his power to protect her in her own house, and he recommended that she should take refuge with a citizen of York and not return home. Undeterred, Mrs. Givins went to Strachan's house for the man who had stood up to the American invaders but Strachan soon found out from Dearborn that it was beyond the general's power to guarantee protection to any persons connected with the Indians. The abandoned house was thoroughly plundered by the Americans.

John Small, clerk to the Executive Council, had his home entered and some silver items taken by the troops. John Dennison lost his Regimental sword, bedding, and family clothing to the Americans. Elizabeth Andrews and Jordan Post suffered minor losses at American hands. Grant Powell, who was an acting surgeon of the Marine Department and in the field with the forces at the time of the landing, had his home entered and plundered by the enemy. They took household furniture, bed and table linen, kitchen utensils, silverware, wearing apparel, books, and Powell's medical instruments; his total loss was £100. John Beikie, Powell's next-door neighbour on Front Street, saw the Americans take possession of the house on April 27th, and they retained possession of the house during their entire stay at York. After the enemy soldiers abandoned the House, Beikie rescued several articles from the hands of Canadian plunderers who were taking away what was left once the Yankees were gone.

William Shaw had his home looted of small items by the Americans. Ely Playter, who had just sent his family to Newmarket for safety, was preparing to remove his household valuables when the Americans approached the farm house. Forced to flee, he watched them pillage his home and take some army bills, his sword, a set of razors, a powder horn, a shot pouch, a box of jewellery, and some wearing apparel. Edward McMahon, secretary to Sheaffe, had his home plundered by the Americans to the sum of £70. Henry Brown, messenger to Sheaffe, lost £37 worth of personal and household items. John Hunter's loss has already been mentioned.

Among the store-owners, Quetton St. George and William Allan suffered the most severely. St. George lost £173.9 worth of goods, ranging from a 890-pound hogshead of sugar to one piece of Russian shirting and eight pounds of sewing silk. This was taken by the Americans on the 27th and 28th. The Americans looted Allan's storehouse on the 28th, while he was at the garrison busy taking care of the wounded soldiers and militia men. They took shot, soap, two barrels of Jamaica spirits, and other items. Near sundown, Allan saw them carting away several boxes from his storehouse to the place where they were collecting their plunder. He immediately went to one of the senior American officers and remonstrated about this looting which, he pointed out, was contrary to the terms of capitulation. The American replied that there was ammunition in his store which was always considered lawful booty, whether private property or not. This rule did not cover the rum and soap but, nevertheless, they too went missing.

Thomas Deary, another merchant, lost tobacco, hams, and liquor to the Americans. He entered his store while the soldiers were running amok and finally persuaded them to leave but, to his sorrow, they left the taps open on two casks of liquor, and the precious liquid served only to season the floor beneath. John S. Baldwin, who had yet to set up shop in York, had a hogshead of loaf sugar in St. George's store and this went with the Americans. The contents of Donald McArthur's store helped ease the parched throats of the U.S. troops when they lugged away from it a thirty-eight gallon barrel of whisky, along with some linen, soap, coffee, and chocolate.

Joseph Grenette's clothes and a complete set of carpenter's tools were taken from the York docks by the Americans before the eyes of a witness. Joshua Leach lost his set of tools at the same time, but the philanthropic Americans turned them over to another York inhabitant. Two farmers sustained losses: British Indians, hungry from the day's battle, killed seven cattle on one farm, and the Americans stole a horse from another.

Joseph Hendrick, proud owner of the schooner, the *Governor Hunter*, saw his possession go up in flames at the hands of the enemy. However, Dearborn eased his loss by leaving him £300 out of the public money which the Americans had acquired. This sum was delivered to him by the Chief Justice, Thomas Scott.

This, then, is the extent of the losses sustained by the York citizenry. Is there any pattern to it? In many of these cases, empty houses – apparently considered fair game by the looters – were entered and pillaged. The remainder of the sufferers, with the exception of the store-owners, were either connected with the government or lost personal items on government property. People like John Strachan, Alexander Wood, W. W. Baldwin, Elizabeth Russell, and Dummer Powell, who stayed with their homes, were not bothered. [Penelope Beikie] noted at that time: 'I kept my Castle, when all the rest fled; and it was well for us I did so, – our little property was saved by that means. Every house they found deserted was completely sacked. We have lost a few things, which were carried off before our faces; but as we expected to lose all, we think ourselves well off.'

With the exception of Grant Powell's house, there is no mention of Canadians participating in the looting of private homes, or, for that matter, government property. Why, then, does Quaife state: 'The article guaranteeing the sanctity of private property was violated to some extent by the Americans, and to a greater extent, probably, by criminal or disloyal Canadians.'? In doing this, he is merely reiterating an oft-repeated charge.

The answer to the question of why Canadians were suspected of looting seems to lie in finding out who ultimately obtained possession of some of these government stores and private property. A lead to providing a solution to this problem lies in the statements of two contemporary writers [Isaac Wilson and Penelope Beikie]:

> There was a large quantity of farming utensils which were sent by the Gov't which were sent for the use of settlers in this country. The authorities would not allow these to be given out except to favorites. The Americans distributed these generally to all settlers so their visit to York was very useful in this respect.

> I really attribute this visit to the vengeance of heaven on this place, for the quantities of stores, farming utensils, etc., sent from England . . . were allowed to remain in the King's stores, and nothing of them did they ever get. Now, our enemies have them, to do with them as they please.

These statements explain the necessity of Sheaffe's proclamation of June 4, 1813:

> Whereas it is made highly penal by various Statutes to retain possession of Public Stores and property of the Crown, by whatever means it may come into the hands of the possessor, unless through the channels pointed out by Law – And whereas it has been represented to me that large quantities of Public Stores, the property of the Crown, are actually in the hands of divers of his Majesty's Subjects not duly authorized to be possessed thereof – I have thought proper, by and with the advice of His Majesty's Executive Council, for the affairs of the Province, to issue my Proclamation, calling upon all persons so

possessed of Public Stores, the property of the Crown, forthwith to restore the same to the Sheriff of the District in which they may reside, or to some person appointed by me to receive and take charge of the same.

It is a fact that some Canadians did obtain a quantity of public stores from the Americans as gifts.[5] It would seem that the occupying army did what many such armies had done before, and have done since: they attempted to befriend or, perhaps, bribe the populace. Thus Canadians came into possession of goods, primarily government ones, that had been looted by the Americans. The settlers, some of them in difficult straits and some of them ex-Americans,[6] took what was given to them without asking any questions. In any age, how many people have done otherwise? The Americans looted York, not a motley crowd of pro-republican Canadians. The Canadians have to be characterized as the often willing recipients of stolen goods. Sheaffe's phrase – 'by whatever means it may come into the hands of the possessor, unless through the channels pointed out by Law' – substantiates this interpretation.

At the same time, this does not ignore the fact that there were some Canadians, predominantly ex-Americans with dubious loyalties, who, seeing a reward for their efforts, pointed out good places for plundering. Thus, Allan McLean was able to state: 'The Enemy were joined by a number of Vagabonds who gave them every information.' However, most of this group were prompted more by the thoughts of the booty to be given them, than by any dark designs in the direction of overthrowing the government.[7]

Undoubtedly, the activities of some Canadians led the magistrates of York to meet on April 30 and issue a proclamation designed to prevent anarchy. This document insisted that, despite the occupation, no change had taken place in the relation of the subject to the government and the law of Britain. It also pointed out that it was still high treason to aid the enemy in any way and that the powers of the magistrates continued to exist. As well, it noted that private property could not be subjected to looting.

There was good reason for this meeting because the criminal element of any society has a fine opportunity to run wild in the course of such a disruption as an enemy invasion. The laws of the country must be kept in force in order to prevent outbreaks of lawlessness. Also, the meeting was probably

[5] Public Archives of Canada, *Upper Canada Sundries, Traitors and Treason, War of 1812-14* (Record Group 5, Series A1), volume 16, containing materials relating to treason, verifies this fact in several of the depositions. As well, there are the Wilson and Beikie statements quoted above.

[6] Again, the depositions against supposedly treasonous individuals contained in this volume illustrate this point.

[7] Several of the documents in this volume illustrate that these people were more concerned about regaining the booty which the Americans had given them and which York officials had, in turn, taken from them, than they were interested in the cause of republicanism.

prompted by the fact that, already, public and private goods were sifting through into the hands of eagerly waiting Canadians. However, and this is important, anything that looks like treason was generally prompted by materialistic motives, not by any high flying ideals concerning republicanism.

On May 2, the Americans, having been held up by an adverse wind, were finally able to leave York. The stragglers were gathered together and taken out to the ships. The American venture had not been a complete success. The British ship they sought, the *Prince Regent*, had taken leave of York for Kingston on April 24. Large quantities of naval and military stores had not fallen into American hands because they had been previously fired by the British. The nearly finished ship on the stocks had been burned as well. The only British vessel which the Americans had taken was the *Duke of Gloucester* which was undergoing repairs, but Dearborn discarded the importance of this capture when he noted that there was 'no vessel fit for use'.

Sheaffe and his little band of regulars had escaped the United States forces. Although other British leaders criticized him either for leaving York or for not retreating to Fort George, the American strategists were annoyed that he had not been driven toward Newark. The American Secretary of War, John Armstrong, wrote: 'Taking then this fact for granted [the shortage of British regulars in Upper Canada], we cannot doubt but that in all cases in which a British commander is constrained to act defensively, his policy will be that adopted by Sheaffe – to prefer the preservation of his troops to that of his post, and thus carrying off the kernel leave us only the shell.'

The Secretary also stated that, if the Americans had landed between Fort York and the town, they would have driven Sheaffe to Fort George. He regretted that Sheaffe and his group had escaped to fight another day. Sheaffe's tactics displeased the British and Canadians, but they were equally unpalatable to the Americans. On the basis of whose displeasure should the success of the York venture be judged?

However, other consequences stemmed from the capture of York. Following his retreat from the capital of Upper Canada to Kingston, Sheaffe never again returned to York. Heavy criticism was directed against him for his course of action at the battle of April 27 and on June 19, 1813, he was succeeded as commander-in-chief and civil administrator of Upper Canada by Major-General Francis de Rottenburg. Baron de Rottenburg was a more forceful character than Sheaffe, but, until almost the end of his period of administration, things did not go too well for the British cause and the lack of supplies and men plagued him just as it had plagued Sheaffe. It was nearly the end of 1813, December 13, when he was replaced as commander and administrator by Lieutenant-General Sir Gordon Drummond, an able, dynamic individual, more in the tradition of Brock.

As a consequence of the battle of York, valuable naval supplies either had been burned by the British or carried off by the Americans. These stores had been intended both for shipbuilding purposes at York and for the British squadron on Lake Erie. When they were lost, Commander R. H. Barclay was seriously crippled before he even took charge of the little British fleet on Lake Erie; and the critical nature of these losses grew more and more evident as Barclay's position deteriorated during the summer months.

The capture of York and the looting that ensued must have left their imprint on the minds of the citizens of the little town. While the losses of individuals do not appear to have been large, they must have been unsettling to those who sustained them. And no doubt they long remembered the day the Americans took York.

In another way the occupation of York still was reverberating through the province as late as that fateful December in 1837, when two Scots, Strachan and Mackenzie, had their battle. The Family Compact was not created by the war, but the struggle, and notably the York occupation, gave tremendous prestige to the rector of York. At the time of the invasion, he had thought the right thoughts, had been desperately pro-British, had stood up to the conqueror. The capture of York was one of the first steps, and a big one, that took Strachan on his way to the top of the political ladder. Strachan, with Sheaffe gone, had the centre of the stage, and the view was much better than from the wings. He could see and be seen.

FURTHER READING: E. A. Cruikshank (ed.), *Documentary history . . .*, part III, pages 162-84 and 187-217, part IV, pages 3-4, part VI, pages 24-5; E. Firth (ed.), *The town of York*, 1793-1815 (Toronto, 1962); C. P. Stacey, *The battle of little York* (Toronto, 1963); M. Quaife, *The Yankees capture York* (Cass Lectures, Detroit, 1955).

PART THREE

Legacies of the War

Had the war continued into a fourth summer, the Americans would unquestionably have given a much better account of themselves, partly because of the steady improvement in military training and generalship, but principally because of a belated realization that their effort should be concentrated upon a single vital objective rather than being dissipated along four or more local fronts. The new strategy had its lessons for both sides. The Americans, after the war, built military roads to the Canadian border; the British replied by building fortifications and the Ottawa and Rideau canals. Fortunately, none of these were ever required to stand the test of war. The Rideau Canal found little use even as a transportation route. Instead, it has proved mainly a rustic memorial to the War of 1812 and a tourist attraction for American visitors. . . . This article is reprinted, with permission, from the 'American Historical Review', volume 46, (January 1941).

An American Plan for a Canadian Campaign

BY C. P. STACEY

The primary causes of the humiliating failure of the three American campaigns against Canada during the years 1812-14 were clear even to contemporaries. A few weeks after the return of peace, Sir James Yeo, who had commanded the British naval forces on the Great Lakes since 1813, summed the matter up in terms which, while unflattering to his late opponents, are nevertheless unexceptionable as a statement of the facts: 'The experience of two years' active service has served to convince me that tho' much has been done by the mutual exertions of *both Services*, we also owe as much if not more to the perverse stupidity of the Enemy; the Impolicy of their plans; the disunion of their Commanders, and, lastly, between *them* and their *Minister of War*.' Yeo considered the 'impolicy' of the Americans' strategy to have consisted mainly in their apparent failure to realize the paramount importance of the St. Lawrence communication and to strike a severing blow at this 'life-line', upon the integrity of which the defence of Canada west of Montreal entirely depended. From England came almost everything that made Canadian defence possible – the arms and munitions, the red-coated regiments, the fittings of the lake vessels, the seamen to man them; and from Montreal they passed to Upper Canada by the great river or by the primitive roads along its banks. There was no alternative means of communication, and the interruption of this line would necessarily cause the whole of Upper Canada west of the point of severance to fall into American hands.

Though one might expect these facts to be obvious to anyone after a glance at the map of North America, little appreciation of them is apparent in the American campaign plans of 1812-14. Far from concentrating every available man against the eastern section of the long Canadian line of communication, the American strategists frittered away their resources in ill-conceived enterprises in the west which, even if successful, could have had little positive result. At the end of the 1814 campaign, in consequence, the United States government was faced with the fact that in three seasons of offensive warfare it had failed to make any real impression upon British strength in Canada. In view of the nature of the demands which Britain had presented to the American negotiators at Ghent, the continuance of the war through 1815 seemed decidedly probable, and it remained to be seen whether in that event the American forces on the northern border would be employed to better purpose than in the preceding years.

As things turned out, of course, the arrival from Europe of the text of the treaty which had been signed on Christmas Eve of 1814 abruptly ended all warlike preparations and relegated strategical discussions to the realm of fantasy, and the value of the experience gleaned by American statesmen and soldiers from three years of trial and error was thus never demonstrated in practice. Nevertheless, it is possible to say with some conviction that before the good news from Ghent arrived the Administration had learned its lesson, for the confidential Letter Book of the Secretary of War contains evidence that in February 1815 a campaign plan was prepared at Washington which avoided the worst mistakes of earlier seasons and which, had it been adopted (and persevered in) in the beginning, might have altered the result very materially.

James Monroe had been in temporary charge of the War Department for a time in 1812-13 and had taken special interest in the plans for action against Canada. When the humiliation of the capture of Washington blew General Armstrong out of office, Monroe again became Acting Secretary of War, and he was appointed to full formal charge of the department, at his own earnest request, on September 26, 1814. . . .

While the new Secretary of War was evolving in his own mind the conception of a new and more effectual offensive campaign, one of the country's ablest and most aggressive soldiers, Jacob Brown, the only American major-general who had emerged from the Canadian operations with an enhanced reputation, was apparently similarly engaged. On December 19 he wrote a private letter to Monroe, asking permission to visit Washington in order to confer with him and with the President 'before the opening of the next

Campaign'. The Secretary warmly encouraged the idea, and Brown, after a leisurely journey from Sackett's Harbor, reached Washington on February 6. By that time, it appears, Monroe, lately returned to his duties after a severe illness, had already drafted the plan for the spring campaign, for on February 4 he had written to Governor Tompkins of New York describing the scheme and asking for 'not less than 20,000' militia to assist in executing it. When Brown left for the North on February 11 he presumably carried with him Monroe's letter laying down the general scheme of operations, which is published herewith. That the plan was Monroe's own is further indicated by comparison of this letter with his manuscript memorandum concerning the campaign plan of 1813, in which many of the same ideas appear – notably the two possible routes of invasion, the collection of supplies to be available on either or both, and the apparent hesitation between them.[1]

The superiority of the new scheme over those which had formed the bases of the actual operations of earlier years consisted primarily in the fashion in which it subordinated all other considerations to the need for a destructive concentration of force against the east end of the long British line of communications. There was to be no further waste of regular troops on operations on the Detroit or the Niagara; the forces there were evidently to consist almost exclusively of militia supplied by the neighboring states, and every possible regular was to be moved towards the St. Lawrence. Thus at long last the United States was adopting the strategic system which common sense should have dictated from the beginning.

The greatest weakness of Monroe's scheme is the hesitancy which it displays in deciding between the Sackett's Harbor and the Plattsburg lines of operation. The military history of the region, and especially, one would think, that of the year 1813, might have counselled the definite adoption of the latter. One's doubts are not lessened by Monroe's remark concerning the probability of there being 'important use for transportation on both routes'; this hint at another combined scheme of operations is not promising. Monroe seems to have been unwilling to abandon his ideas of 1813, and his perhaps too-simple faith in strategic expedients improvised at short notice and his apparently inadequate sense of the difficulty of concerting combined operations in a region of primitive communications seem to smack strongly of the amateur strategist. The further rather curious fact that none of his military letters or memoranda, at this time or earlier, appear to make specific mention of the function of the St. Lawrence as a British line of communication, makes one still more chary of rating Monroe's strategic acumen too high.

An additional feature of the plan, however, goes far to nullify these objec-

[1] This paper is undated, but the last sentence, apparently an addition, contains a clear reference to the military statute of January 29, 1813.

tions. It is pretty clear that General Brown was to be entrusted with its execution and that he was to have undisputed command of all operations against the St. Lawrence. On the day before Brown left Washington, Monroe wrote to General Macomb informing him that Brown's command would 'extend to the north, so as to include the state of Vermont, and all our troops on Lake Champlain'. It would seem probable that, within the rather broad limits laid down in Monroe's letter, Brown was to exercise complete authority and choose the actual line of operations. This impression may perhaps be strengthened by an observation in Monroe's memorandum of 1813: 'The plan of the campaign must be formed by the general who commands the expedition. He alone can best decide at what point to make attacks, and where to make feints, if any ought to be made.' Cynics, on the other hand, might recall that in 1813 Monroe himself aspired to the command of the northern army, and suggest that he might not have found it easy to refrain from interference. Had Brown actually been left a completely free hand, it cannot be doubted that his aggressive and determined spirit would have done everything possible to render the scheme successful. It may be added that we know that his experiences in the region in 1813-14 had left him with a lively sense of the inadequacy of the existing communications along the St. Lawrence eastward from Lake Ontario. This, combined with the pronounced views on the strategy of the Canadian border which he expressed in later years, suggests a strong probability that in 1815 a campaign under his direction would have taken the form of a concentrated attack by the line of Lake Champlain.

Of such an attack's chances of success, it is of course impossible to speak with certainty, but it seems likely that in 1815 the adoption by the United States of a sound strategic plan would have come too late. The national treasury was empty, the New England states were so disaffected as to be on the verge of secession; it was not certain that the 30,000 volunteers and militia from New York and Vermont, without which Monroe regarded the enterprise as hopeless, could be obtained. Finally, the great moment of opportunity had passed, for the threatened provinces were now swarming with veteran British troops. In the Canadas alone, there were available about 29,500 trained soldiers of all ranks.[2] It may be remarked, however, that had the war in America continued Britain would have been embarrassed by the renewal of hostilities in Europe after Napoleon's return from Elba, and the fashion in which the bulk of the forces in Canada were hastily withdrawn

[2] Return enclosed in Prevost to Bathurst, November 8, 1814. This total appears to include all permanently embodied units, imperial and local. The *Quebec Almanac*, 1815, lists thirty-six battalions of imperial and provincial regular infantry as stationed in the Canadas, and ten more, plus a detachment of another, in the Maritime Provinces, Maine, and Bermuda. In 1812 there had been seven battalions in Canada and five in the Maritimes.

to meet the emergency of the Hundred Days suggests how serious the embarrassment might have been.[3]

In the actual event, General Brown had scarcely left Washington to return to his command (a journey in the course of which he was to confer with the governors of Pennsylvania, New York, and Vermont) when the news of peace arrived. Brown's merits were recognized by his being retained in service as one of the two major-generals authorized by Congress (Jackson being the other), and he served the United States with distinction until his death, but he never took the field again.

The history of the campaign plan of 1815 does not, however, come wholly to an end with the conclusion of peace. The strategic conceptions which it embodied continued to dominate Brown's views and recur constantly in his letters as commander of the Northern Division (1815-21) and as commanding general of the Army (1821-8). A favorite project of his was the construction on the American bank of the St. Lawrence of a fortress which in the event of another war would facilitate the severance of the great British artery. This idea came close to realization in 1816 but was never actually carried out. It is interesting likewise to observe that in 1817 Monroe, who had now become President, himself made a tour of inspection of the northern frontier defences, of which one result was the commencement of two military roads to the St. Lawrence – one running west from Plattsburg, the other east from Sackett's Harbor.[4] This work was carried on by military labor for several seasons thereafter, and numerous references in the correspondence of Brown with Calhoun, who was Monroe's Secretary of War, leave no doubt that these roads were intended to enable American forces, in the event of further conflict, to undertake offensive operations on a plan similar to that which had been projected for 1815.[5]

While the Americans thus prepared for the next war, improving their natural facilities for a blow at British power in Canada, British soldiers there were not idle. In 1814-15 the military chiefs in the provinces had felt great anxiety for the St. Lawrence communication, not merely on account of the danger of its interruption by American action but also because of its natural inadequacy for its function – a circumstance then emphasized by the diffi-

[3] No less than twenty-one battalions were ordered back from Canada in March 1815.

[4] The President's original plan was for a complete road connection between Plattsburg and Sackett's, but Brown recommended instead one road from Plattsburg to French Mills (Fort Covington, New York), as an avenue for offensive operations against the St. Lawrence line, and a second from Sackett's to the vicinity of Morristown, as a means of maintaining communication with his proposed fortress on the river.

[5] It is interesting to note that in 1840 a group of American officers, in a comprehensive report on the country's military problems, noted that Lake Champlain was 'undoubtedly the avenue by which the British possessions may be most effectually assailed', and also revived Brown's scheme of a fort on the St. Lawrence.

culty of obtaining the labor necessary for moving up the rapids the increasing mass of supplies required by the ever-growing military and naval forces in Upper Canada. In the course of the last winter of the war exploratory surveys were undertaken to determine the possibility of developing an alternative inland route between Montreal and Kingston (the naval station at the foot of Lake Ontario) by the Rideau Lakes and the Ottawa River.[6] The most definite lesson which British soldiers derived from the war was the imperative need for opening this route.

Before 1815 was out they had at their command a particularly telling argument. In the last weeks of hostilities Sir George Prevost had apparently suspected an American design against the St. Lawrence line. Now information came to hand that left no doubt that such a scheme had been in contemplation. On July 29 Major-General Sir Frederick Robinson, the general officer commanding in Upper Canada, wrote to Lord Bathurst as follows:

> Had the War continued it was the intention of the American Government to have interrupted our Transport Communication by the St. Lawrence to the Lower Province in the event of which an attempt at inland conveyance must have been made, or we must have endeavoured to dislodge the Enemy from the South Shore of the River by transferring the seat of War thither. The American General Brown, thinking secrecy no longer necessary, explained to me all that had been in contemplation for the ensuing Campaign, which in my opinion would have answered their expectations.

Bathurst was decidedly impressed. Informing the lieutenant governor of Upper Canada early in 1816 that 'His Majesty's Government are most desirous that preparatory measures should be taken for the performance of this important Work', he applauded the steps already taken for settling 'industrious and useful families' in the Rideau region and ordered the local government to advertise for the construction of the canal by contract. This was done, but without producing any tangible result.

In 1819 the Duke of Wellington turned his attention to Canadian defence and in a forceful memorandum addressed to Bathurst urged the importance of the Ottawa-Rideau project; and in the same year work actually began, when the governor in chief (the Duke of Richmond) authorized the Royal Staff Corps to break ground at Grenville on the Ottawa.[7] The most important and costly leg of the project – that between the Ottawa and Lake Ontario – was postponed until after the report of the board of officers sent out at Wellington's instance, in 1825, to consider the defences of British North

[6] It appears that the investigation was undertaken at the orders of Sir Gordon Drummond, in command in Upper Canada.

[7] Wellington's memorandum grew out of recommendations by Richmond.

America generally.[8] It was begun in 1826 and completed in 1832. The whole great scheme cost vastly more than had been anticipated in the beginning. In 1819 a sanguine officer had estimated the cost of improving the Ottawa at £16,740; the commissioners of 1825 hoped that the Rideau link could be built for £169,000; but the total expenditure notified to parliament in 1835, when the accounts for both enterprises were closed, was no less than £1,069,026.[9] The Ottawa-Rideau canals thus constitute by far the most costly and important military work ever undertaken by the British government in North America. This expenditure lavished upon the business of providing a substitute for the communication by the St. Lawrence is the best evidence of the soundness of the general strategic conception underlying Monroe's campaign plan of 1815.

The document below is transcribed from pages 53 to 58 of volume 309 of the series of Secretary of War's Letter Books formerly in the Old Records Division of the Adjutant General's Office in the War Department at Washington but now in the National Archives. This volume, formerly labeled 'Confidential, War Office' and now entitled 'Confidential Letters', was used for preserving copies of secret letters written by successive secretaries on a wide variety of subjects from 1814 to 1835. In addition to the letter presented herewith, it contains on the same topic the letters of Monroe to Tompkins and Macomb, referred to above, and also letters written by him to the governors of Pennsylvania and Vermont, introducing General Brown and requesting their assistance in collecting forces for the projected campaign.

MONROE'S LETTER

Department of War, February
10th 1815.

Major Genl,
Brown. *Sir*,

Having had much personal communication with you, relative to the operations of the next campaign, there remains little to be said in this letter, more than to give a general outline of the preparatory measures which it is necessary to adopt, to give effect to the plan which it is intended to pursue.

The great object to be attained, is to carry the war into Canada, and to

[8] *Copy of a Report to His Grace the Duke of Wellington . . . relative to his Majesty's North American Provinces by a Commission of which M. General Sir James Carmichael Smyth was President* (lithographed copy in Toronto Reference Library, dated September 9, 1825). On this report see James J. Talman (ed.), 'A Secret Military Document, 1825', *American Historical Review*, volume 38, pages 295-300.

[9] The total may include the comparatively small contributions made by the imperial government to the cost of the Lachine and Welland canals. In saying that 'little or nothing' had been done as a result of the 1825 project, Lord Stanley in 1844 was not perhaps strictly accurate; but the inflated cost of the Rideau scheme made the government unwilling to proceed with the rest of the commission's recommendations.

break the British power there, to the utmost practicable extent. After making due allowance for the number of British forces, for the difficulties attending the passage of the St. Lawrence, and the immature state of our preparations, I think that we may enter Canada, and gain a decided superiority this next campaign. To what extent it may be carried, is uncertain, as it will depend on many circumstances, of which we can form no estimate at this time. It seems probable, however, that if we secure the landing of a great force, and beat them completely in the field at any point between Kingston and Montreal, or wherever we may select, we shall be able to drive them into Quebec.

The formation and collection of this force, is the first thing to be attended to, on our part. On that, our success must altogether depend. If we fail to raise a force which will put the result beyond hazard, so far as certainty is attainable, we ought not to make the attempt, but rest satisfied with making a defensive, inglorious war for the nation, however honorable it may be for the gallant officers who conduct and may be employed in it.

It is believed, that the British commander cannot bring into the field, between the points above mentioned, an army of more than 20,000 regular troops, and 10,000 militia; and that to do this, he must weaken his posts above and below those points. I am satisfied, that this is an high estimate of the British force now there. If we can form an army of 40,000 men, to bear on that district of country, of which 15,000 are regular troops, and the residue volunteers organized as regular troops, and militia, we must beat their main army.

At every other point above Kingston, our superiority may be whatever we choose to make it; and altho' it will [not] consist principally, or in any considerable force of regular troops, it will be of a character to press the enemy, interrupt his supplies, fight and demolish him.

There are two routes by which we may enter Canada, one by passing the St. Lawrence at some point between Kingston and Montreal, the other by lake Champlain. The force relied on, in aid of the regular troops, must be raised principally in the states of New-York and Vermont. Other aid may be drawn to a certain extent, from Pennsylvania, Ohio, and the western parts of Virginia, if necessary, and perhaps from some of the more eastern states; but our chief dependence will be, on New-York and Vermont.

It is proposed to raise in these two states for this service, 30,000 men, 20,000 of which, in New-York, and 10,000 in Vermont. The state of New-York has already passed an act for raising 12,000 state troops: of these, if raised, a considerable part may be applied to this service. The rest must be collected, if possible, under a late act of Congress, authorizing the President to accept the service of volunteer corps. As many volunteers must also be raised in Vermont, as possible. The deficiency, if any, in both states, must be supplied from the militia. . . .

After placing as many troops as may be proper on lake Champlain, and near Sackett's harbour, the two routes leading to Canada, it will be proper to establish a camp at some place in the rear of the mountains which separate those routes, either at Greenbush,[10] Johnston,[11] or some other point. At this latter station, the troops, now to be formed, may be collected with advantage, in many respects. They will be supplied with provisions there with great facility. While there, the enemy will be held in suspense as to the route they mean to take, and finally, they may be moved by surprize, on either route, as may be most advisable.[12]

If we succeed in the invasion of Canada, we take the war from our seaboard at once. It is only by making a defensive war there, that we enable the enemy to detach troops here. I shall not, however, dwell on the subject, in this view.

Your attention will necessarily be drawn to the provision which ought to be made of ordnance, arms, and munitions of war, of every kind, and likewise, to the means of transportation on whatever route our troops may be led. Preparations for the latter purpose, often serve to amuse the enemy, and mask from him the true object. It is, however, probable, that we may have important use for transportation on both routes.

In promoting the organization of the volunteer corps in Vermont, to raise the force contemplated, which ought not to be less than 10,000, this species of force ought to be preferred. Too much care cannot be taken in the selection of the field officers or of the company officers of each corps. It may be useful for you to fix on some highly meritorious character in that state, and recommend [him] to the President for the rank of a brigadier general. From him much aid may be derived in the organization of these corps, and officering of them. With him you may correspond in your absence. Other generals, in case the whole force be raised, will be necessary. You will enquire into the pretensions of different characters there, and communicate them to this department, without compromitting yourself to the parties. I communicate to you in particular confidence, a copy of a letter to general Dearborn, on a similar subject, in relation to the eastern states, the instructions, in which, so far as they are applicable, you will observe. You will see, that it is desired not to be governed in these appointments by party considerations; but to confide in, and associate in command, with those who have supported the government, any meritorious, honorable men, who, jealous of the rights and honor of their country, are willing to vindicate them in the present controversy. To the governor of Vermont, you will shew great respect, and consult with him on all subjects which you may find conducive to the public interest.

I will forward to you by an early opportunity, a law prohibiting under new and severe penalties all commerce and intercourse with the enemy,[13] to which you will pay particular attention. You will not, however, delay the

[10] On the east bank of the Hudson, opposite Albany.

[11] Johnstown, in the Mohawk valley (Fulton County, New York).

[12] At this point the letter, as first copied into the letter book, ended, but the signature is erased and the text continues.

[13] Presumably the statute approved on February 4, 1815, six days earlier than the date of this letter.

suppression of this practice for the receipt of the law: the existence of war authorises us to do it. The supplies which the enemy have received from us, have given them great aid in the prosecution of the war. It is important to the public interest, as well as to our national character, that it be completely suppressed.

I am, &c.
Jas Monroe.

FURTHER READING: G. S. Graham, 'Views of General Murray on the defence of Upper Canada, 1815', *Canadian Historical Review*, volume 34 (1953), pages 158-65; C. P. Stacey, 'The myth of the unguarded frontier, 1815-71', *American Historical Review*, volume 56 (1950), pages 1-18; E. Green, 'War-clouds over the Short Hills', *Welland County Historical Society*, volume 5 (1938), pages 153-62; R. Leggett, *Rideau Waterway* (Toronto, 1955).

Among the monuments of the War of 1812 were the sizeable war fleets built and based at Kingston and Sackets Harbor. The Rush-Bagot agreement gave them a continuing potential value while reducing the likelihood of their actual return to service. The vessels, built in haste during the heat of the conflict, were gradually consigned to oblivion as their value diminished to the vanishing-point. The naval establishment devoted to their upkeep gave Kingston a continuity as a naval and military centre, spanning the sixty years between the Treaty of Ghent and the beginnnings of the Royal Military College. The study is of further interest as revealing the uses of paintings, charts, and physical remains in reconstructing the historic past. . . . RICHARD PRESTON *has published widely, particularly in the histories of Canada and the United States before 1812. He has been a member of the departments of history at the University of Toronto and Cardiff University College, and at the Royal Military College of Canada. This study is taken, with permission, from 'Ontario History', volume 44 (summer 1952).*

The Fate of Kingston's Warships

BY R. A. PRESTON

The fact that old wooden warships dating from the War of 1812 now lie beneath the waters of Lake Ontario in the vicinity of Kingston is well known locally. They are believed by many people to have been sunk as the result of the Rush-Bagot Agreement of 1817 which prohibited the keeping of large naval forces on the Great Lakes. Sometimes it is added that the ships were sunk in such fashion that they could, if need be, be raised again for use against an American attack.[1]

At various times investigations have been made into the state of the sunken fleet; but no complete survey has ever been made and no full account of their disposal by sinking has ever been pieced together from what documentary

[1] Other explanations of the sinking have been forthcoming: (a) that after the Rush-Bagot Agreement was signed the ships were sold to junk dealers, stripped of their copper and other valuable metals, set on fire, and sunk; (b) that the ships were dismantled in accordance with the agreement, laid up in port until they began to rot, and then sunk to preserve their timbers from further decay; (c) that 'the ships that were afloat also rotted in Navy Bay and were sold under hammer when they were condemned'.

evidence remains. The most persistent observer has been Mr. C. H. J. Snider of the Toronto *Telegram* who has kept watch over the remains of the largest of the wrecks from 1909 to 1950. . . . In 1937 and 1938, when Fort Henry was being restored, Mr. Ronald L. Way, the director, used a diver to examine the *St. Lawrence* and wreckage in Navy Bay and Deadman Bay on either side of Point Henry. Two large vessels and one small one were located in Deadman Bay in such a state of preservation that the diver was able to enter beneath the lower deck of the largest of them. In Navy Bay, where Royal Military College cadets in the past had been busy with underwater demolition charges, piles of debris in several places showed where old hulks had been fast in the mud. From measurements made by the diver it was clear that the two vessels in Deadman Bay were among the largest after the *St. Lawrence,* but no closer identification could be made with any certainty.

In 1951 a third investigation into the state of the sunken fleet was undertaken. It was at first hoped that by the use of 'frogman' diving apparatus in place of the more conventional type a more thorough survey could be made of Navy Bay and Deadman Bay. . . . Lt.-Commander W. H. Willson, R.C.N., . . . made about twelve dives, mainly to the two larger hulks in Deadman Bay which had been reported by Mr. Way's diver in 1938. The position of these was not at first known accurately; but the vessels were located by information from cottagers on the neighbouring shores, by the use of a newspaper photograph of the operations in 1938, by the use of a specially made 'viewer' (a tube with a glass bottom), and by dragging an anchor. The only things recovered during the diving operations in 1951 were some small timbers, a section of a beam about 24 inches by 18 inches thick, and a large number of hand-wrought spikes. The wood was examined by the Forest Products Laboratory of the Department of Mines and Resources and shown to be local white oak which, when water-logged, sinks straight to the bottom. This partly accounts for the sinking of the 1812 fleet. By chance, a section of timber examined in the laboratory showed interesting evidence of the haste with which the ships were built in the pressure of war. There was a streak of decay running through the beam which the scientists declared to have been already in the growing tree before it was shaped for use in ships. There was no evidence of the effect of fire on the timbers retrieved.

The two wrecks examined in 1951 were accurately located by use of a sextant and were marked on a chart. One lies towards the head of Deadman Bay in about 13 feet of water. This vessel, which was called for convenience 'Wreck Able', measures about 93 feet in length and 34 feet in beam. Its transverse frames, 18 inches square, stand about eight feet from the silt in some parts of the vessel. The highest frames are about five feet below the high-water level of the summer of 1951.

The second hulk, 'Wreck Baker', lies about a hundred yards from the shore of Point Henry, opposite to Cartwright Point, in about 20 to 30 feet of water. It measures some 134 feet long and is also over 30 feet in beam. Both wrecks stand out of silt accumulated along their sides and are filled with piles of debris. In some parts of the vessel, piles of stones seemed to lend support to the theory that the ships were sunk deliberately; but of course the stones may only be the normal ballast of the vessels. All the decks have collapsed into the interior and it seems clear that there has been considerable deterioration since 1938. For instance, it does not now seem possible to get below the lower deck in Wreck Baker as Mr. Way's diver did.

Commander Willson also made brief examination of some of the wreckage in Navy Bay and of structures which appear to be on the site of the slips from which the ships were launched, but no complete examination of this wreckage has yet been made.

Parallel with the practical task of examining the wrecks by diving, research into the later history of the fleet was undertaken by more normal techniques. The purpose of the research was to ascertain which vessels were likely to have been disposed of by sinking in Deadman Bay, to find out why they were sunk, and to attempt an identification by co-ordinating the information obtained by diving and by research. This paper gives the results of that research. It does not give a complete answer to these problems. Because of the state of the records it may never be possible to be certain of the fate of particular ships. However, rough identification on the basis of probability can be attempted. . . .

The British Provincial Marine, an inland naval service operated by the army, began the war with a small three-masted sloop-of-war, the *Royal George* (22 guns), and several brigs and schooners. Some of the latter were converted into brigs when war broke out because square sails were more suitable for armed vessels. The Royal Navy took over both construction and operation of the fleet at Kingston in 1813. At the end of the war the British had one first-rate three-decker bigger than Nelson's *Victory* in the water, two on the stocks, and a number of frigates and brigs, as well as schooners, gunboats, and row-boats which could carry a single gun.

In passing, some tribute should be made to the enormous effort undertaken in the remote interior of a continent still in the pioneer stages of its development by the men who built there a battle-fleet worthy of the seven seas. Lieutenant Francis Hall, in his *Travels in Canada, 1816-17*, comments on the magnitude of the resources called into action. The *St. Lawrence* alone was said to have cost £300,000. Another vessel, the *Psyche*, a frigate and the third largest of the vessels launched by the British, was built in England of 'fir', and was transported in 'frames', i.e., without her planking, to Quebec from whence she was carried by water and land to Kingston to be completed. The *Psyche*'s transportation from Quebec to Kingston cost £12,000.[2] After the war ended, the dockyard at Kingston was said to be costing £25,000 per annum and employing 1,200 labourers. Many of the carpenters and sailors who came to Kingston to build and operate the ships stayed on to become pioneer settlers in Upper Canada; and the ship-building activity begun for war became an important part of the peace-time economy of Kingston and district in the nineteenth century.[3]

It must be fully realized that while ships which existed at the beginning of the war could be described as 'small and poor of their class',[4] those built during the war were comparable in construction and size with the ships built for ocean warfare. Their construction plans, which are extant, show that, in the main, the builders followed conventional models. They had a tendency to have a greater 'deadrise' than ocean vessels, to make them faster and weatherly; and the construction plan of one of the bigger vessels, the *Princess Charlotte*, which was begun by the Provincial Marine as a brig but completed as a frigate by the Royal Navy, show that she had a bottom that was much less flat than most naval vessels. This is the only major variation from normal ship-designs.[5] The lake vessels probably carried a greater armament than vessels of similar size on the ocean because they did not have to carry such large quantities of water, rations, and beer and could carry guns instead. The American ships, built at Sackett's Harbour by the great shipwright Eckford, were finished with 'no other polish than what is given them by the axe and the adze' and were rushed into the water in about a month from the time the trees were standing in the forest. The British vessels, almost all built on Point Frederick at Kingston where the master-builder was John Dennis, were finished up to the standards of ocean vessels. But like the American fleet, the British ships were also built with green timber; and it was fully realized at the time by men who knew the vessels that 'ships built on this lake will not last more than five or at most six years of actual service'. Furthermore, in fresh water the ships were believed to suffer more from 'worm' than in the salt oceans. The condition of the timber of which the

[2] A popular story says that the Admiralty sent *Psyche* to the lakes complete with an apparatus for distilling sea-water. Travellers nearer the time said that she carried casks for fresh-water when all that was necessary was to throw a pail over the side.

[3] As late as 1875-6 the skill of the naval dockyard men was being exploited in the district. In that year Henry Roney, who had been formerly employed in the dockyard on Point Frederick, was in charge of building the first salt-water vessel to be built on Garden Island.

[4] E. E. Vidal's water-colour of Kingston dockyard, 1815, now in the Royal Military College, includes this comment.

[5] Photostat copies of the construction plans of most of the vessels are to be found in the Public Archives of Canada.

ships were built is, of course, an important consideration in any investigation into the disposal of the vessels after the war.

The vessels in existence in the Kingston fleet at the end of the war can be ascertained from several sources. A water-colour of the fleet by Emerich Essex Vidal, the naval purser, shows the fleet lying in Navy Bay in July 1815. The artist shows the two uncompleted three-deckers (*Wolfe* and *Canada*) on the stocks. The great, first-rate *St. Lawrence*, and the frigates *Prince Regent*, *Psyche*, and *Princess Charlotte* are shown in Navy Bay and are also identified by name. *Psyche*, which had probably never sailed, was housed-over for protection. Vidal commented: 'Besides these ships we have two corvettes (one condemned and one a transport) and two brigs. These four vessels are small and poor of their class.'[6] In contemporary usage, a 'corvette' was a small ship-rigged sloop-of-war or small frigate. Vidal was referring to the *Royal George* and the *Wolfe* which had been built by the Provincial Marine and of which he, as a Royal Navy man, thought very little. The schooners and gun-boats were not mentioned.

Vidal's picture confirms the report made by the British commissioners who negotiated the Rush-Bagot Agreement. They told the Americans that Britain had on Lake Ontario the *St. Lawrence*, *Psyche*, and *Princess Charlotte* which were 'laid up in ordinary', i.e., in reserve, and the *Prince Regent*, which was 'in commission but unequipped'. They gave more information about the 'corvettes' mentioned by Vidal. *Montreal* (formerly the *Wolfe*) was in commission as a transport but carrying only six of her twenty-odd guns. *Niagara* (formerly the *Royal George*) was 'condemned as unfit for service'. Of the two brigs, the *Netley* (built at York in 1812 as the schooner *Prince Regent* and operated during the war as the brig *General Beresford*) was now 'attached for the most part to the surveyors' and unarmed, and the *Star* (formerly the *Lord Melville*) now carried only four of her fourteen guns and was declared by the commissioners to be 'unfit for actual service'. In addition to these vessels mentioned by Vidal, the commissioners told the Americans that Britain had also the *Charwell* (formerly the *Earl of Moira*) which was 'hauled up in the mud, condemned', some row-boats capable of carrying long-guns, and one transport of 400 tons.

Although many of the ships were in bad condition, it is clear that, up to the time of the Rush-Bagot Agreement, the British were planning to preserve the fleet. A new transport, the *Beckwith*, was launched in July 1816 on Point Frederick, and a schooner, the *Brock*, in April 1817. Furthermore, a naval commander, Sir Robert Hall, appointed to take over the command of the Ontario fleet in 1816, was understood to have been ordered to preserve a 'respectable naval force' on the lakes with the *Star*, *Netley*, *Montreal*, and *Kingston* in commission on Lake Ontario. In 1817 it was reported that 'the

[6] Vidal's picture of Point Frederick is in the Royal Military College, Kingston.

British gun-boats on the lakes are to be reinforced and their crews increased' and the following ships were to be commissioned: *Kingston* (a new name for the frigate *Prince Regent*), *Burlington* (formerly the *Princess Charlotte*) and *Charwell.* The latter, being a hulk, was possibly a powder-ship.

The Rush-Bagot Agreement signed in April 1817 and proclaimed by President Monroe on April 28, 1818, brought inevitable changes in British policy. The pertinent section referring to Lake Ontario reads as follows:

> The naval force to be maintained up the American lakes by His Majesty and the Government of the United States shall henceforth be confined to the following vessels on each side, that is: On Lake Ontario to one vessel, not exceeding 100 tons burden, and armed with one 18 lb cannon . . . All other armed vessels on these lakes shall forthwith be dismantled, and no other vessels of war shall be there built or armed.

To carry out the agreement the big ships did not have to be sunk or demolished. They were laid up in reserve, or 'in ordinary', as the contemporary phrase described it. To emphasize the fact that he now commanded a shore station, the naval commander on the lakes became the 'Acting Commissioner of His Majesty's Navy on the Great Lakes'; and for the next ten years Britain did not even commission the single gun-boat allowed her by the treaty. A traveller in 1818 described the scene on Point Frederick in these words: 'These huge and ghastly skeletons, these gloomy hulks in Kingston Dockyard.'

In reality, the picture was not one of complete neglect and decay. A new Commissioner, Commodore Robert Barrie, was appointed to the Kingston post in July 1818. Barrie had a brilliant operational record during the Napoleonic Wars and his letter-books testify to his vigour in his new post. For several years he spent £10,000 a year in the dockyard. From 1823 to 1830 he spent £6,000.

His first major task was the building of a huge stone warehouse to store the gear from the fleet. This was the building now known as the 'Stone Frigate', a dormitory of the Royal Military College. It was built between 1819 and 1820. John Howison, of the East India Company, visited the storehouse soon after it was built and was impressed by the systematic arrangement of the material kept there. He said that the fleet could be equipped in a few hours. Another visitor, in 1826, similarly impressed by the ship-shape order of the store, was a little more realistic. He said that the fleet could be put to sea in a month. A third visitor, in 1828, the Duke of Saxe-Weimar, gave a full description of the storehouse and said that it was intended to fireproof the floors by covering them with iron.

Meanwhile, the ships had been housed-in and lay in Navy Bay near to the 'stone store'. John Creighton, a mayor of Kingston, remembered seeing them there when he came to Kingston in 1823 as a boy of six. A water-colour painted about 1817 by Lieutenant William Bayfield shows the bay as it must have appeared during much of this time. The housed-in ships were tied up a little to the north of the pier now known as St. Lawrence Pier and quite close to the stone store which held their rigging.[7] A chart made by Lieutenant A. T. E. Vidal, a brother of the artist-purser, and by Lieutenant Bayfield, shows the exact location of all the vessels much as they appear in Bayfield's picture. . . .

In 1827 Barrie had commissioned a small 70-ton gunboat, the *Cockburn*, obviously that allowed by the agreement with the United States, and this act seems to mark a new stage in British naval policy on the lakes. The struggle to keep the big ships in repair had come to be seen as a losing battle. There were ten or eleven other gun-boats on the stocks and for some years Barrie's men worked to keep them in repair. It seems as if the new policy was to keep one gun-boat in commission but to back that boat by a fleet of small vessels held in reserve.

The victory of the Whigs in England in 1830 on a programme of reform and retrenchment confirmed a change in policy. Economy was the watchword. The grant for the dockyard was cut to £3,000 in 1830 and the money for repairing the big ships was discontinued the following year. In 1831 rumours circulated in Kingston that the dockyard was to be closed down.[8] Barrie was ordered to break up the four largest vessels in the water, namely *St. Lawrence*, the frigates *Kingston* (*Prince Regent*), *Burlington* (*Princess Charlotte*), the corvette *Montreal* (*Wolfe*), and also the two great ships on the stocks, namely *Wolfe* and *Canada*. A few weeks later his orders were changed. He was to sell them by auction. When the advertisement appeared in Canadian papers, the Kingston *Chronicle* commented sadly: 'However useless and unnecessary they have latterly been, we cannot avoid expressing our regret that one of the great bulwarks of our Province, and which formed an object of curiousity to travellers, should be removed.'

The standing and running rigging of the four vessels brought £1,400 and was declared to be in excellent condition, fit to make the best oakum ever imported into the province. But the ships themselves attracted only one bid. Mr. Robert Drummond bid £25.00 for the *St. Lawrence*, which the *Chronicle* declared had cost 'upwards of a million' to build. The great vessel was

[7] Water-colour of Navy Bay by Lieutenant William Bayfield, later Admiral Bayfield. Admiral Bayfield was the famous sailor who surveyed the waters of the Great Lakes system from the head of the lakes to Newfoundland. The picture is now in the Royal Military College, Kingston.

[8] The appointment of a new Master to Kingston in October was hailed as a sign that the dockyard was not to be closed down altogether.

knocked down to him for that paltry sum. The other hulks, and the frames of the *Canada* and *Wolfe*, could not be sold at all.

Robert Drummond was a prominent Kingston contractor and merchant who had just completed the Kingston Mills locks of the new Rideau Canal. He owned a ship-building yard in Kingston opposite the foot of Gore Street. Before his death from cholera in 1834 he had sold that yard and had begun to open a new one at Portsmouth.[9] He bought the *St. Lawrence* at the beginning of the freeze-up and she was still in Navy Bay in late May or early June of 1832 when an army surgeon, posted to Kingston, reported his arrival by river as follows: 'But we are now in sight of Fort Henry – presto – we are abreast of it. Anon the three-deckers on the stocks and the miserable remains of the *St. Lawrence* of 104 guns, make their appearance.' In August, however, she was gone. A British subaltern on holiday in Kingston wrote in his journal in that month that she had been sold a few months previously.[10] Presumably Mr. Drummond had her towed away.

No contemporary report of the removal of the great hulk has been found and we have to rely on hearsay. One old man in 1909 is reported to have said that he remembered seeing her towed away by a paddle-steamer. A grand-daughter of Mr. Drummond, who is still alive, says that her mother used to tell of seeing the ship anchored one fine summer evening off their house, St. Helens, and that during the night a great storm cast her on shore. It is certain that for many years afterwards she lay close to St. Helens and was used as the end of a pier attached to 'Morton's Distillery'. The cordwood burned by the steamers which had driven the great sailing vessels from the lakes was stored in her hull.

Many old Kingstonians remember diving to her for souvenirs and as late as 1938 Mr. Way's diver recovered from her vicinity an eight-foot anchor of the type used at the beginning of the nineteenth century. Although too small to be one of the warship's great anchors, this might have been a secondary anchor or have belonged to one of her cutters. It may even have been the anchor by which she was held when the storm rose and drove her to her last resting place.

The other first-rates, *Wolfe* and *Canada*, did not long survive the *St. Lawrence*. In May of 1832, just before they had been seen by the army surgeon who had reported their presence along with the *St. Lawrence*, Barrie

[9] Robert Drummond was a Director of the Commercial Bank of the Midland District. Among his many enterprises he operated a distillery. He built and owned steam-boats which operated on the Rideau Canal. When he died the *British Whig* was edged in black as a sign of respect.

[10] Lt. E. T. Coke in *A Subaltern's Furlough* (London, 1833), page 320, said that a 'seventy-four' had been sold. This was a phrase commonly used for a first-rate ship-of-war. He also said that the *St. Lawrence* had split down the middle when he meant the *Wolfe*. Travellers frequently confused one ship with another.

had arranged for their standing rigging, which had never been installed, to be sent back to England. On July 31, 1832, between five p.m. and six p.m., there came a terrific storm. The props which supported the sides of the *Wolfe* gave way, either as a result of the wind or because the ship was struck by lightning. *Wolfe* split right down the middle and collapsed into a heap of matchwood. A few days later an observer recorded that the timbers of four or five other ship-frames on the stocks were also 'in a very advanced state of decay, partly owing to the want of proper care, and being run up hurriedly and of unseasoned timber'. Barrie's efforts to keep the fleet in condition for launching had failed. An Admiralty record shows that the *Wolfe* was listed to be 'sold or broken up' between November 1832 and January 1833. At the same time the *Canada* was listed as 'broken up'. It seems that all the great British three-deckers passed from the scene about the same time. The American first-rate *New Orleans,* which had been enclosed by a great shed on 'Shiphouse point' at Sackett's Harbour, long outlived them. It was sold on the stocks in 1883, having remained on the Navy List all that time.

When the first-rates were sold or broken up, some of the frigates and brigs lay in the water of Navy Bay and the remainder had been pulled up on to the stocks and stripped of their planking. The fate of individual vessels is not easy to determine but the general policy and programme is clear. During 1832 Barrie worked on the task of cutting down the naval establishment at Point Frederick. His men were 'embarking the stores ordered to England' but, at the same time, to preserve the naval strength on the lakes which he himself believed was essential to Canadian security, he also had them 'repairing the gun-boats'. He worked in vain. In December 1833 the decision to down the naval dockyard completely had been taken and rumours of this soon reached Canada. On March 11, 1834, the Kingston *British Whig* commented on a report 'that we fear has some foundation for its truth', that the Naval Establishment at Point Frederick was to be closed down on August 1. The *Whig* wrote: 'The town of Kingston will lose a warm friend and kind patron in the passing of Commodore Barrie.' Two days later, the Kingston *Spectator* reported that the dockyard would be closed during 1835.

Actually Barrie had already received instructions to sell off all the naval stores left in his charge. A reserve price of one-quarter of their value was to be set on them and, if that price was not received, some were to be sent to Montreal and the remainder left in the dockyard. One suit of *Psyche*'s sails (which had never been used) were not to be offered for sale but sent at once to Montreal. The sale took place in May 1834; but it does not appear that the ships were put up to auction at the same time. Barrie left for England soon afterwards, and the dockyard, ships, and stores passed into the charge of Mr. John B. Marks, the naval clerk at Kingston. Towards the end of the year the Admiralty and the Colonial Office came to a general agreement covering all the stores in the dockyards which the navy was relinquishing. Material and dockyards were to pass into the care of the Ordnance, subject to the proviso that they should not be disposed of without the sanction of the Secretary of State. There was no specific mention of the ships.

It seems, however, that both ships and stores at Kingston were included. On June 27, 1836, Marks put everything left in the dockyard at Kingston up for sale. Along with the store he advertised 'all the . . . ships and vessels, sloops, schooners, gun-boats, and boats remaining at the station, viz., one frigate in frames, 56 guns, one ship in frames, 22 guns, one brig in frames, 14 guns, and one schooner in frames, 4 guns'. We can identify these vessels. An Admiralty list of 1837 tells that the *Psyche*, *Niagara*, and *Netley* were 'in frame on slip' in that year.[11] Marks also offered for sale in 1836 the new schooner *Cockburn*, ten unfinished gun-boats 'in good condition', an old schooner lying at the Wharf, and 'four old ships of war lying aground in the harbour'.

The four vessels on the stocks were those which had been seen in 1832 by the army subaltern who reported the collapse of the *Wolfe*. At that time they were already in a decayed condition. Nevertheless, an English newspaper report suggested that the British Admiralty still regarded them as having operational value. The Portsmouth *Herald*, discussing the closing-down of the Great Lakes Naval Establishment, said that there were 'no ships afloat on those lakes but there are three in a state for launching on the stocks, viz., the *Psyche*, 50 guns, *Star* 14, and an 18-gun sloop'. The Montreal *Gazette* carried the Portsmouth *Herald*'s report and commented: 'the Admiralty certainly know little of the state of those vessels'; and the Kingston *Chronicle* in its turn carried both report and comment on February 12, 1832, without, from its closer knowledge, denying the insinuation that the ships were unfit for service. It is not known whether the vessels were sold at the auction in 1836; but an Admiralty list of 1837 shows *Niagara* 'in frame on slip. Sold for £7.10.0'; and *Netley* 'in frame on slip. Sold for £11.0.0'. Furthermore, all the ships at Kingston were listed as 'Establishment broken up in July 1834 and the ships left in charge of a Warrant Officer'. An Admiralty Order July 14, 1838, stated that they were 'to be left off the Navy List, it appearing that they have been either broken up or sold'. Presumably *Star* and *Psyche* were similarly disposed of at this time. At any rate, no further record of them has been found.

One of these vessels had more service life left. In the spring of 1838, as a result of the rebellion of the previous year, Commodore William Sandom, R.N., with a party of several officers and enough men to man a frigate, were sent to Kingston. They found no vessel afloat, and, although the dockyard

[11] The fourth was *Star*, which had been reported on the stocks in 1832. *Niagara* had been listed as ordered to be broken up in 1817. If this order was carried out then the vessel on the stocks in 1837 must have been a new vessel which had replaced the old *Royal George* (*Niagara*).

had recently been declared unhealthy, took up their quarters in the old stone warehouse. Sandom's letters were written from 'H.M.S. Niagara' and this has sometimes led to the assumption that the Stone Frigate was commissioned as the *Niagara*. John Creighton, in a letter to which reference has already been made, said the building was named 'Her Majesty's Ship Niagara'. Another Kingstonian recalled that when Sandom came to Kingston there was still a *Niagara*, a hulk from the War of 1812, in the harbour, and he said that the sailors, while living in the warehouse, were technically assumed to belong to the hulk. When Sandom acquired steam-vessels and gun-boats the men were posted to them and they became the *Niagara*'s tenders. What actually happened can be seen from Admiralty records. Sandom rebought the *Netley* (the former schooner *Prince Regent* and brig *General Beresford*) which had been used by the surveyors before being pulled out of the water. He paid £33 for her and two gun-boats as they lay on the stocks, not having been removed by their purchaser in 1837. He commissioned her as the *Niagara*, a fifth-rater, and she stayed on the navy list until 1843 when she was 'put out of commission on the arrival of crew in England'. It is not known whether Sandom put her into the water. His men, living in the Stone Frigate, were on the books of old *Niagara*.

While it may be possible that the *Netley*-cum-*Niagara* went back into the water, it seems very unlikely that the other old ships on the stocks, *Psyche*, *Niagara*, and *Star* were planked simply to float them around to Deadman Bay and resink them. It seems most likely, then, that none of these three vessels are among those found in Deadman Bay, and it is also unlikely that the unplanked frames would have been pushed off the stocks to sink in the mouth of Navy Bay. The identity of the vessels now under the water must therefore be sought elsewhere among the hulks which were in the mud in Navy Bay at the time of the sale in 1832. These include the frigates *Kingston* (*Prince Regent*) and *Burlington* (*Princess Charlotte*), the corvette *Montreal* (*Wolfe*), the brig *Charwell* and the old snow *Duke of Kent*. An Admiralty record states that the *Kingston*, *Montreal*, and *Star* (which was on the stocks) were 'to be broken up or sold, 1832'. *Burlington* was listed as 'supposed taken to pieces, January 1833'. From the advertisement of the sale in 1836 it is clear that some of these hulks actually remained in Navy Bay after the time when they were written off by the Admiralty. However, from the difference in the description of their fate, it may be assumed that it was less likely that the *Burlington* survived than the remainder. She was 'supposed taken to pieces', which is a little more definite than the record of the fate of the others. The *Charwell*, described as 'hauled aground rotten to the water edge', was sold for £21 in 1837, and the *Magnet*, a sloop of which no other post-war record remains, was also struck off the Navy List at this time; but the manner of her disposal is not recorded.

In August 1838 a British artist, W. H. Bartlett, visited Kingston and made a sketch of Navy Bay. This picture, one of the 'Bartlett prints', shows two peculiar structures in the water which resemble short wooden sheds. It was Bartlett's custom to make rough sketches on the spot and to paint the picture when he returned to England. What obviously happened was that when he got back to England he had forgotten the precise nature of the structures in Navy Bay (which were actually housed-in hulks), and he made them too short in the finished picture so that they no longer looked like ships at all. Probably what Bartlett saw were some of the hulks which Sandom found in Navy Bay. They may even be the two vessels which later found their way round to Deadman Bay.

We can only guess what happened to the hulks in the following years. No doubt the wrecks cluttering up Navy Bay were a menace to navigation, if only to the races in which Sandom's men delighted. Some of the vessels were therefore pulled out of the mud and abandoned in Deadman Bay, which was not used by ships. The period of Sandom's tenure of the Kingston post is the time when it is most likely that this occurred, when there were plenty of men to do the job and when there was little useful work for them to do. . . .

The two big ships in Deadman Bay measure roughly 134 feet (Wreck Baker) and 93 feet (Wreck Able), respectively. The hulks that were in the water and which therefore may have been moved round to Deadman Bay measured as follows, in descending order of length.

Kingston (or *Prince Regent*) 155 feet deck, 131 feet keel.
Burlington (or *Princess Charlotte*) 121 feet deck, 100 feet keel.
Montreal (or *Wolfe*) 101 feet 9 inches deck, 86 feet 1 inch keel.

Of these, as shown above, it is more probable that the *Burlington* was demolished in Navy Bay between 1832 and 1833. Therefore it seems likely that the two big vessels in Deadman Bay can be identified in this way. Wreck Able, at the head of the bay, is the *Montreal* (formerly Yeo's flagship *Wolfe*), and Wreck Baker is the *Kingston* (formerly Yeo's flagship *Prince Regent*). The third small vessel in Deadman Bay cannot be identified. The remainder of the fleet, or at any rate of those vessels not broken up on land, now lies under the water in Navy Bay.

On June 21, 1852, under the heading 'End of a gallant chapter', the *British Whig* reported that the steamship *Mohawk* had been paid off and that her officers and men were to be sent back to England immediately. The report concluded dramatically: 'Thus ends the naval establishment on the Great American Lakes.' A picture dating from this same year shows traces of what may be the wreckage of some of the ships in the bay.[12] The dockyard was actually still occupied by military and naval authorities in 1855 when the editor of the *Whig* commented that he could not walk freely on Point Frederick or speak freely of what went on there. Kingston was again used as a

[12] Lithographed engraving by Aug. Kollner, 'Kingston at King's River' (*sic*) published 1851.

naval base at the time of the Fenian raids in the sixties; and naval stores were kept in the Stone Frigate until 1870 when they were cleared out as part of the process of withdrawal of the Imperial forces from Canada. The land on Point Frederick was transferred to the Dominion of Canada in that year on the condition that it should be put to no other than 'naval purposes' and for the naval defence of Canada. Apparently this restriction was interpreted loosely. A picture dated 1871 shows the militia encamped on Point Frederick.[13] This picture again shows traces of wreckage in Navy Bay. A photograph taken in 1873 is clearer. Close to the present Royal Military College boathouse, where the debris of two small vessels were located by Mr. Way's diver in 1938, hulks can be seen sticking out of the water.[14] The Stone Frigate, near by, became the dormitory of the first class of cadets who came to the Royal Military College in September, 1876.

The history of the dockyard and of the fleet after the War of 1812 has thus been followed from the close of the War of 1812 to the opening of the Royal Military College in 1876. . . . The legend that the ships of 1812 were sunk as a result of the Rush-Bagot Agreement in such fashion that they could be raised again is definitely not true. The old fleet was kept in existence by the Kingston Dockyard until it deteriorated to a point where it was no longer serviceable. The *St. Lawrence* was sold and put to menial use off St. Helens where her remains now lie. The rest of the fleet was abandoned, part of it in Navy Bay and the remainder round Point Henry in Deadman Bay, where their timbers lie as a reminder of the magnitude of the effort made by Britain to defend the integrity of Canada in the War of 1812.

FURTHER READING: R. A. Preston, 'Broad pennants on Point Frederick', *Ontario History*, volume 50 (1958), pages 81-90; C. P. Stacey, 'The myth of the unguarded frontier', *American Historical Review*, volume 56 (1950), pages 1-18; C. H. J. Snider, 'Recovery of H.M.S. "Tecumseth" of the Upper Canada naval department . . .', *Ontario History*, volume 46 (1954), pages 97-105; G. F. G. Stanley, 'Historic Kingston and its defenders', *Ontario History*, volume 46 (1954), pages 21-35.

[13] Engraving of Point Frederick, dated 1871, now at Fort Henry, Kingston.

[14] Photograph in Royal Military College Library.

The war actually stimulated the economy of Upper Canada by increasing the local demand for and the prices of goods, and by providing payment in the form of heavy British military expenditures. The colony was helped over a difficult period of reduced foreign investment and reliance upon distant export markets, and was enabled to proceed to a higher and more prosperous stage of economic development. This pioneer study was written more than half a century ago, but much still remains to be done on economic aspects of the War of 1812. . . . ADAM SHORTT *(1859-1931) was a professor of philosophy and political science at Queen's University and for many years a distinguished federal civil servant. Termed 'the founder of the study of economic history in Canada', he published many works in this field and also collaborated with Dr. A. G. Doughty to edit the monumental 23-volume 'Canada and Its Provinces' (1914). This article has been taken with the Ontario Historical Society's permission from volume 10 (1913) of its 'Papers and Records'.*

The Economic Effect of the War of 1812 on Upper Canada

BY ADAM SHORTT

In considering the economic conditions of any country, and especially of a new country, many considerations have to be taken into account besides a mere survey of prices, rates of profit, or volume of trade. Only when we know the social and economic atmosphere of the various districts, the conditions of transportation, labour local production, etc., can we come to any rational conclusions. Thus, in dealing with the economic condition of Upper Canada before, during, and after the War of 1812, we require to know not only the isolated facts as to prices and values, but the general setting of the country, geographical, social, and commercial.

In its early days there were two or three important general conditions which vitally affected the economic development of the Province of Upper Canada. In the first place, the frontier settlements of Ontario were planted much earlier than the corresponding regions of the adjoining states to the south of the lakes. The first settlers, being for the most part United Empire

Loyalists, enjoyed the benefit of having been especially outfitted by the British government and partially supported at its expense for several years. For various reasons, partly accidental and partly of an international nature, the government established strong garrisons along the Canadian frontier, contributed largely to the support of the civil government, and undertook certain public works. The requirements of these establishments created very profitable local markets for the limited produce of the early settlers, much of which could not support the expense of shipment from the country. They furnished also a strong market for labour, so that, during the first ten years of Upper Canada's existence as a separate province, the economic condition of the country was on the whole very satisfactory, especially along the frontier settlements, where the people had access to both local and central markets. The most important trade of the province in both exports and imports was conducted for a considerable time by Messrs. Cartwright and Hamilton, who were originally partners and always close business associates. In various capacities, the Honourable Richard Cartwright[1] was associated with practically all the business of Upper Canada. These varied interests are fully represented in his commercial and general letter-books, which constitute the most extensive and accurate sources of information as to the more important affairs of Upper Canada, between the first settlement of the province in 1785 and the close of the War of 1812. This information is supplemented and confirmed by many special papers in the Canadian Archives, and by more fragmentary letters and records drawn from various private sources.

From these various sources we find that the early settlers of Upper Canada were by no means dependent upon their own resources for the establishment and development of the province. In other words, they were not compelled to pay for what they imported by furnishing exports to be disposed of in distant markets. Otherwise, their struggle for existence would have been much harder than it was, for few of them had much capital and not many of them had much experience in making their way in the wilderness. The most successful element from the point of view of individual resources, with a knowledge of agricultural conditions in a new country, were the subsequent American immigrants, such as the Quakers and others, who settled in Prince Edward County, and in other districts along the Bay of Quinte, the Niagara region, and at various points along the north shores of Lakes Ontario and Erie.

[1] [Richard Cartwright (1759-1815) came to Quebec during the American Revolution and settled at Niagara, moving soon afterwards to Carleton Island and then to Kingston where he became a leading merchant, shipbuilder, and contractor. He was appointed a justice of the Court of Common Pleas in 1788 and a member of the legislative council of Upper Canada in 1792. During the war he commanded the militia of the Midland District and was colonel of the Frontenac militia.]

When the American settlers began to develop along the south shore of the lakes, they naturally depended upon the Canadians for the larger part of their food supplies, as well as for much of their imported European goods. These settlements proved to be very valuable and high-priced markets for Canadian produce. Thus it was, that, except for an odd year now and again, the greater part of the Upper Canadian agricultural produce found local markets. In such cases the price of agricultural produce in western Canada, instead of being determined by the price in Britain less the cost of transportation, insurance, commission and duty, expressed a local demand only, the limit of which was the price in Britain plus these items; because in those days, and occasionally in the future, Canada found it necessary to import food supplies from Europe.

It is a common mistake to suppose that, since the forests have been largely cleared from the basin of the Great Lakes, the rainfall has been lessened and drouth is more common. The fact is that drouth was at least as common and the rise and fall of the lakes was as much commented upon over a hundred years ago as today. The period from 1794 to 1797 was an exceptionally dry one, and the people, with little past experience, were alarmed at the prospect of the permanent lowering of the Great Lakes. Crops suffered severely from drouth, as also from the ravages of the Hessian fly. In consequence, the harvests were light and prices high. At this time flour sold in Upper Canada at $4.00 to $4.50 per cwt., and on the American side of the lakes at even higher prices. Peas brought $1.00 per bushel, and very inferior grades of salt pork cost $26.00 per barrel. At the same time, the government was importing food supplies from Europe to feed the troops in Lower Canada. When it is remembered that the cost of transporting a barrel of flour from Upper Canada to Montreal, up to 1802, had not been reduced below 80 cents, even when taken on rafts and scows, one can understand what difference it would make when the cost of transport was deducted from the price of provisions in Upper Canada. Cartwright summed up the situation very well when he said, 'As long as the British Government shall think proper to hire people to come over to eat our flour we shall go on very well, and continue to make a figure, but when once we come to export our produce, the disadvantages of our remote inland situation will operate in their full force, and the very large portion of the price of our produce that must be absorbed by the expense of transporting it to the place of export, and the enhanced value which the same cost must add to every article of European manufacture, will give an effective check to the improvement of the country beyond a certain extent.'

A few good harvests in the early part of the nineteenth century, and the rapidity with which the Americans brought their side of the lakes under cultivation, greatly changed the situation in Upper Canada. The price of wheat fell in the Upper Province because it had now to bear the cost of transportation to the Lower Province, and sometimes to England. It was estimated that between 1800 and 1810 the normal difference in the price of a barrel of flour as between Kingston and Montreal, including commission and freight, would range from $1.00 to $1.50. When, therefore, the price of grain fell, the people of Upper Canada turned their attention to the lumber and timber trade, and to the production of staves and potash. The timber, in particular, could be cheaply transported down the St. Lawrence.

The era of the Orders in Council, after 1808, and the increasing trouble with the United States before the outbreak of the war, coupled with returning short harvests, led to a revival of prices, between 1808 and 1811. Having regard to the price of wheat alone, one would infer that the province must have been increasingly prosperous during this period, but such was not the case. Prices, it is true, in Upper Canada were practically the same as in Lower Canada, because there was little to export, the wheat crop having been particularly poor during 1810. Moreover, as indicated, agriculture had suffered considerably for the past few years on account of the settlers going in for lumber and staves, but now there was a severe fall in the prices of these articles, as also of potash. The high price of staves during the years 1808 and 1809 had induced many settlers to go into that line very extensively, but in 1810 prices fell from forty to sixty per cent.

Owing to the slowness and uncertainty of transport, and the closing of the Canadian ports in winter, merchants required to order their supplies of goods considerably in advance. The result was that in 1810 the merchants found themselves overstocked with European goods, which the public were unable to purchase, or for which the merchants could not secure returns. The commercial distress first manifested itself at Montreal, but spread more or less rapidly to the outlying districts dependent upon it, and especially to Upper Canada. As Cartwright put it, 'The large returns heretofore made in lumber have occasioned an immense quantity of goods to be brought into this country, and sudden depression in the price of that article would occasion great deficiency in remittances.' The reaction caused even the price of food to drop. Flour, which had been $11.00 and $12.00 per barrel in April, fell to $8.40 in Montreal and $7.50 in the Kingston district. As a natural consequence of the depression, specie became very scarce, while merchant bills were a drug on the market. For lack of a better medium of exchange, notes of hand were in circulation in local centres. Towards the latter part of 1811 things were looking very blue indeed in all parts of Canada. Montreal merchants could not collect their debts from their western correspondents, because they in turn could not collect from their debtors. Bills of exchange, accepted by the merchants, were not met when due, and the cost of protesting them was heavy. Early in 1812 Cartwright was offered pork at $18.00

per barrel and flour at $9.00. In June it could be had at $8.00 delivered in Montreal. Early in July, however, it was learned that war had been declared and prices immediately took an upward turn. As the summer advanced, supplies of every description rapidly rose in price. In September flour had risen to $12.00 per barrel and in November to $13.00. In the spring of 1813 shipments of provisions down the St. Lawrence had quite ceased, everything available being in demand for the supply of the troops and others in the service of the government. When the army bills went into circulation in August 1812, they furnished an easy and safe means of meeting the immediate obligations of the British government without the danger of shipping specie to Canada, while their being convertible into bills of exchange enabled the merchants to meet their obligations in Britain without expense. Towards the close of 1812, we find Cartwright beginning to receive quite a stream of payments from all parts of the province in commissariat bills and army bills, which he, in turn, was sending down to Montreal to pay off his indebtedness there.

From the beginning of 1813 to the close of the war, there was little or nothing going down the river beyond furs from the west and an ever-increasing stream of bills of exchange and army bills. The whole movement of commerce was up the river, and the rates of freight were correspondingly high. In 1814 freight from Montreal to Kingston amounted to $12.50 per barrel of miscellaneous goods. The conditions referred to by Cartwright in the early nineties were reproduced in an exaggerated form. The British government had sent large contingents of troops and marines to Canada, including Upper Canada. It was also employing men and horses wherever available from Cornwall to Detroit. It paid famine prices for all kinds of produce and hired men to consume it in the province. Owing to the great volume of exchanges drawn against Britain, the very unusual experience was realized, from the beginning of 1814, of government exchange on Britain being at a discount. Thus we find Cartwright, in July 1814, buying a bill of exchange on England for £61 2s. 2d. sterling for which he paid only £55 currency, a pound currency being rated at $4.00. Real estate and other property in the frontier towns had gone up enormously in value.

As supplies on the Canadian side began to grow scarce during the last two years of the war, those who had to furnish provisions for the troops, particularly in the lines of flour and meat, found it necessary to devise means of obtaining supplies from the adjoining districts of the United States. This was accomplished, as a rule, by the connivance of people of influence, military and other, on both sides of the line. This trade, once established, continued very briskly for nearly a couple of years after the war; the Province of Upper Canada in particular having been practically stripped of everything saleable in the food line.

During the war, certain permanent changes were made in the methods of conducting business. Money being very plentiful in all parts of the province, trade brisk, and the returns rapid, the old system of long credits, extending to at least a year and over, were gradually abolished, and at the close of the war the business of the province was pretty well established on a cash basis. On this basis the purely commercial business of the country remained, though in some of the newer sections and in minor retail trade longer and more irregular credits once more prevailed. Again, in consequence of the universal employment of the army bills and the facilities which they afforded for effective exchange, the people had grown accustomed to the use of an efficient and reliable paper currency. Hence, when the war terminated and the army bills were withdrawn, the people were in a proper frame of mind for the establishment of banks. Thus, the Bank of Montreal appeared in 1817, and in the following year the Quebec Bank, the Bank of Canada at Montreal, and the Bank of Upper Canada at Kingston.

On the other hand, there were certain unfortunate consequences which, if they did not originate from the exceptional prosperity of the war period, were at least greatly fostered by it. Merchants, wholesale and retail, transporters, labourers, and farmers had all alike grown accustomed to obtaining large profits, good wages, and high prices, and all without any special enterprise, foresight, or industry on their part. When the fertilizing stream of British expenditure, all of it extracted from the pockets of the British taxpayer, had ceased to flow, the people could not believe that the prosperity which they had enjoyed must cease, and that they must henceforth largely depend upon their own exertions and enterprise for such wealth as they might acquire. Many people who had cultivated expensive tastes and who found it difficult to severely prune their expenditure, fell into financial difficulties and were ultimately ruined. Much wealth was, of course, left in the country when the war ceased, and so long as it lasted prices declined but slowly. Upper Canadian markets were therefore especially attractive to enterprising American producers. For fully three years the upper province imported quite abnormal amounts of American goods. Lastly, the war had not improved the social condition of the people. The lack of means to gratify their tastes accounted for the relative sobriety of a considerable element in the population during the early years of provincial history. Many of these persons, however, were quite unable to stand prosperity; hence drunkenness and other forms of vice flourished throughout the province in proportion to the diffusion of British wealth. Naturally, the later state of these people was much worse than the first, and the existence of a regular pauperized class dates from the close of the war.

It is difficult to determine whether Canada was, on the whole, benefited or the reverse by the exceptional period of prosperity which the war had brought to her doors. It may be said, however, that the more thrifty elements of the population, and those who had not lost their heads through sudden wealth, utilized their savings for the establishment of permanent enterprises, while for the more unbalanced and incapable the war period had proved their undoing. A great change, therefore, was observable in the personnel of the leaders in economic and social life after the war, as compared with the period before it. On one point, however, there is no doubt whatever, namely, that the War of 1812, instead of being the occasion of loss and suffering to Upper Canada as a whole, was the occasion of the greatest era of prosperity which it had heretofore enjoyed, or which it was yet to experience before the Crimean War and the American Civil War again occasioned quite abnormal demands for its produce at exceptionally high prices.

FURTHER READING: J. Stevenson, 'The War of 1812 in connection with the Army Bill act', *Literary and Historical Society of Quebec*, 1892-1900, pages 1-79.

As with every war, there were ballads to commemorate the events of 1812-14 though no extensive repertoire seems to have been inspired by the Upper Canadian phase. This ballad survives in at least one other version, attributed to a Private Flumerfelt of the York Volunteers, which is also printed in the 'Papers and Records' of the Ontario Historical Society, volume 23. A brief explanatory note by Dr. R. I. Warner (1848-1924) on the background of the version printed below is included.

The Bold Canadian

A BALLAD OF THE WAR OF 1812

On July 17th, 1924, [James H. Coyne] received from the late Rev. Dr. Robert Ironsides Warner a type-written copy of the ballad which is reproduced in this paper, together with his own explanatory note. Accompanying it was a brief statement in these words: 'I learned this when a boy, by hearing my grandfather, Captain John Lampman, sing it. He was in the Detroit Expedition. – R. I. Warner.'

Come all ye bold Canadians,
  I'd have you lend an ear
Unto a short ditty
  Which will your spirits cheer,
Concerning an engagement
  We had at Detroit town,
The pride of those Yankee boys
  So bravely we took down.

Those Yankees did invade us,
  To kill and to destroy,
And to distress our country,
  Our peace for to annoy.
Our countrymen were filled
  With sorrow, grief and woe,
To think that they should fall
  By such an unnatural foe.

At length our brave commander,
  Sir Isaac Brock by name,
Took shipping at Niagara,
  And unto York he came.
Says he, ye valiant heroes,
  Will ye go along with me
To fight those proud Yankees
  In the west of Canada?

And thus we replied,
  We'll go along with you,
Our knapsacks upon our backs,
  Without further adieu.
Our firelocks we did shoulder
  And straight did march away
With firm and loyal purpose
  To show them British play.

At Sandwich we arrived,
  Each man with his supply,
With a determination
  To conquer or to die.
Our General sent a flag to them
  And thus to them did say:
'Surrender up your garrison,
  'Or I'll fire on you this day.'

They refused to surrender,
  But chose to stand their ground:
We opened on them our great guns,
  And gave them fire all round.
Our troops, they crossed over,
  Our artillery we did land,
And marched up toward their town
  Like an undaunted band.

Those Yankee hearts began to ache,
  Their blood it did run cold
To see us marching forward
  So courageous and so bold.
Their general sent a flag to us,
  For quarter he did call,
Saying, 'Stay your hand, brave British boys,
  'I fear you'll slay us all.'

'Our town, it is at your command,
'Our garrison likewise.'
They brought their arms and grounded them
Right down before our eyes.
Now prisoners we made them,
On board a ship they went,
And from the town of Sandwich
Unto Quebec were sent.

We guarded them from Sandwich
Safe down unto Fort George,
Thence unto the town of York
All safely we did lodge.
Now we've arrived at home once more,
Each man is safe and sound.
May the news of this great conquest
Go all the province round.

Come all ye bold Canadians,
Enlisted in the cause,
To defend your country,
And to maintain your laws;
Being all united,
This is the song we'll sing:
Success unto Great Britain,
And God save the King.

[Dr. R. I. Warner writes:] This was, I believe, a popular barracks and camp-fire song during the War of 1812-1815. My grandfather [Captain John Lampman] told me that he never saw it in print or writing, but had picked it up by hearing the men sing it. He would usually sing it when he drew his pension, and on the great battle dates of the war, including Waterloo. Captain John Lampman was attached to Brock's Detroit expedition, in connection with a convoy overland of cattle and army supplies. The impression I retain is, that the convoy heard of the capture of Detroit, while following the River Thames near Chatham. At least part of the convoy was turned back at news of the victory.

FURTHER READING: J. Bennett, 'Perry's victory on Lake Erie', *Inland Seas*, volume 2 (1946), pages 155-8; E. Fowke and A. Mills, *Canada's story in song* (Toronto, 1960).

Laura Secord's story is known to every Canadian schoolchild – how a courageous woman risked her life to carry the news that saved Upper Canada in the gloomy days of June 1813. From an undoubted foundation in fact, Laura Secord's exploit was enlarged upon and dramatized, and a campaign was launched to erect a monument to her memory. Since then scholars have sought to rediscover the truth lying behind the latter-day accretions. . . . The first excerpt, a traditional account, is by MRS. SARAH ANNE CURZON *(1833-1898), a leading literary figure of the 1880s and 1890s who has been credited with kindling Canadian interest in the War of 1812 by her writings; as a leading champion of women's rights, she may be assumed to have found this a particularly congenial subject. It comes from a pamphlet, 'The story of Laura Secord, 1813', published in 1891 under the auspices of the Lundy's Lane Historical Society. The remaining extracts, by* JOHN S. MOIR, *Professor of History at Carleton University, indicate the sort of historical detective work required to locate the most relevant documents and interpret their meaning and significance. They appeared in 'Ontario History', volume 51 (spring 1959) and volume 54 (September 1962) and are presented by permission of Dr. Moir and of the Society.*

Laura Secord

THE STORY OF LAURA SECORD, 1813

BY S. A. CURZON

. . . The first year of the war was past, and the invaders had gained nothing. Irritated by the want of success of their arms, the American people, always excepting the saving few, rated the Government, and the Government replied by throwing into the field all the money and forces it could raise. By land and water the struggle was continued, and during the first portion of the campaign of 1813 the Americans scored several important successes. In June they held Fort George, and it had become the headquarters of their general, who, irritated at finding he had picked up a shell with nothing in it, inflicted on the inhabitants within his limits, which covered Queenston and reached on towards Burlington, many unnecessary restrictions. Every male from the age of the boy to that of the octogenarian was put on parole, and forbidden to leave his immediate home on any pretence whatever.

General Vincent had retreated before the invading force to Burlington

Heights, and the situation looked very unpromising, mainly owing to the absence of necessary reinforcements, when a brave man, Col. Harvey, turned the scale of events in some measure by a successful night sortie upon the enemy, on the 6th of June, at Stoney Creek. Seeing that the Loyalists, though cast down, were by no means destroyed, Dearborn thought to crush them in another quarter, and in some measure retrieve the *prestige* lost at Stoney Creek, and it seemed a very easy thing to do. At the cross-roads at Beaver Dams, by which only could Vincent receive supplies or reinforcements, was posted, in Decau's (or DeCew's) stone house, Lieutenant FitzGibbon with a picked company of thirty men, volunteers from the 49th, Brock's old regiment – in charge of certain stores. To take this post was to open up the whole peninsula, and for this errand Col. Boerstler, a gallant officer who had already distinguished himself, was ordered to prepare himself. He was in command of the 14th United States Infantry, one twelve and one six-pounder field gun, with ammunition, wagons, etc., a few cavalry, and volunteers; in all, six hundred and seventy-three men – a mountain to crush a mouse! But so confident were the Americans of their ultimate success in annexing Canada, 'the people' indeed regarding it for some time as a mere walk-over, that they were heedless of certain precautions in an enemy's country, *and talked* – among themselves to be sure, but the old proverb that says 'stone walls have ears' was exemplified on this occasion; for hints of the intended night surprise fell from the lips of certain of the American soldiers in the house of James Secord, where by the right of might the invaders were wont to make themselves free of such comforts as it afforded.

James Secord had been desperately wounded at the Battle of Queenston Heights, and was at home under parole. But Lieutenant FitzGibbon must be warned; his chance against the force that was to surprise him was *nil*. Moreover, the country must be saved. And who could do it? The dilemma was soon settled; the loyal heart of the devoted wife was touched to the core at the peril of the time, and Laura Secord,[1] rising to the occasion, essayed a task from which strong men might justly shrink.

Whoever now should travel from Queenston to Beaver Dams would find a fine stone road to traverse all the way. Skirting the lovely and fertile vale of St. David's, he would be filled with admiration, not more of the natural scenery than of the fine agricultural district dotted with substantial homes that would greet his eye on every hand. On the north-west, as he advanced, another fertile valley of great extent would come into view. At three points within the valley the spires and tall chimneys of manufacturing villages

[1] [Laura Ingersoll Secord (1775-1868) came to Upper Canada with her father, a land speculator, in 1793. Soon afterwards she married James Secord, a United Empire Loyalist, who was wounded at Queenston Heights while serving as a sergeant in the First Lincoln militia regiment. After the war he was appointed to the Customs service, and he died in 1841.]

would meet his vision, while on the shores of the blue waters of Lake Ontario, stretching away in the distance, two considerable port towns would be distinguishable. At the back of the valley the traveller's eye would rest upon high bluffs, richly wooded, curving south-westerly and losing themselves in the high plateau on which he was advancing. He would also observe with much admiration the stupendous piece of engineering that crosses the valley from the high land at his feet to the lake shore, the locks of the Welland Canal; and, travelling a little further, until the canal itself crosses his path, he would be stopped by a magnificent cantilever bridge. Turning to the left of the bridge, about fifty yards from the river-bank, he would see a fine memorial stone to the memory of the killed at Beaver Dams.

Not such was the valley nor such the road in 1812, when Laura Secord essayed her journey of patriotism and mercy. The whole of the valley was a black swamp traversed by innumerable creeks, full of wild creatures, and across which no path led. The road was a quagmire, and, moreover, was not open to peaceful travel. To have pursued a direct route to FitzGibbon at DeCew's would have been a trying and toilsome journey indeed, but the delicate woman, the mother of four little children, was forbidden even that. The enemy's pickets were out on all the roads; she would have to travel through the swamp, climb the heights at Twelve-Mile Creek, push her way through the beech woods, and reach DeCew's from the back. The distance involved was the smallest item of the terrible journey. The thickets of the swamp, with its dense underbrush, the lurking-places of the wolf, the wildcat, the bear, and the rattlesnake; the pathless wilderness with its oozy bottom, its solitude, its terror – these were the real hardships. Even the mountain, its steep sides, its brawling stream, its dark mantle of virgin forest, was not so terrible, for once upon it she might meet a British picket; she did not count on Indians, a sufficient terror in themselves if come upon unawares.

But duty had to be done, and Laura Secord did it. Leaving her home, her sick husband and young children – not without many a scalding tear, we may be sure, though all signs of agitation had to be concealed – the brave woman set forward on her journey, all unprepared for it indeed, for she did not dare alter her usual morning attire by one iota, and had to circumvent three American sentries before she reached St. David's – one at her own gate, where the pretence of a strayed cow sufficed, the others by the true story of a sick brother at St. David's.

At St. David's she entered the swamp, through which she guided herself by the signs of the points of the compass known to most settlers in those times. But she lost herself more than once, and the moon was rising as she reached the further end. All that long, hot summer's day, from daybreak to moonlight, on the 23rd of June, she had traversed the haunted depths of an impenetrable swamp, alone, hungry, faint, and, for the most part of the way, ragged and shoeless. Even today we can judge how long it would take to destroy every article of attire in a thicket full of thorns and burrs, of branches and fallen trees, of water and bog. Wild creatures alarmed her, for the rattlesnake often strikes as he springs his alarum, and the wild-cat drops from the high branch without warning, or pursues his prey perseveringly until he is sure of his aim. Once only she faltered, and it was at the dread cry of wolves; but they passed her by, and she went on, trusting more than ever to the Hand that guides the world.

Crossing by means of a fallen tree the Twelve-Mile Creek, then a swollen and considerable stream, for rains had been heavy for days previous, the heroine climbed slowly and painfully the steep sides of 'the mountain', and on the ridge encountered a British sentry. O, joyful sight! A friend once more! By him she is directed to FitzGibbon, still, however, some miles distant. Her heart is lighter, for she is within British lines. But oh, how heavy are her feet! She enters at length upon a little clearing, the trees having been felled, and their twigs and branches strew the ground: they crackle beneath her tread. Suddenly she is surrounded by ambushed Indians, and the chief throws up his tomahawk to strike, regarding the intruder as a spy. Only by her courage in springing to his arm is the woman saved, and an opportunity snatched to assure him of her loyalty. Moved by pity and admiration, the chief gives her a guide, and at length she reaches FitzGibbon, delivers and verifies her message, *and faints.*

It is a wonderful story. Today, when we are lost in admiration of the pluck of a Stanley, a Jephson, and a Stairs, with their bands of men diving into the heart of Africa, we may reasonably ask ourselves which was the greater – theirs or Laura Secord's. The distinction is only a difference of climatic conditions; the end was the same, the unity and glory of the British Empire, and the heroism is surely equal.

FitzGibbon's prompt action, his success, and his promotion for it, are matters of history. To Mrs. Secord he was ever grateful, and never failed to show it on occasion. Promotions came to him, but there was no reward for Laura Secord, whose self-denying devotion to her king and country led to it. Nor did she look for reward, save that achieved by the success of her errand. But today, when we are gradually awakening to a better appreciation of the heroes who gave us, by preserving to us, our liberties, we know that Laura Secord ought to find a place among them. We have been less susceptible to greatness than the ancients, in whose Pantheon the deities were not all gods. Nevertheless, we have not been wholly unmindful; we have contemplated doing the memory of Laura Secord some honor; we have approached our Provincial Legislature for a grant to be expended on marking her last resting-place, in Drummondville Cemetery, with a memorial stone somewhat worthy of her and of us. We are ready to open a subscription list on the part of the men and women of Ontario, if it should be desirable to supplement such grant as we may obtain, in order to carry out to the full our sense of the heroine's deserts.

Within the last decade a great awakening of interest in the details of our history has been remarked in our literature, and it is not to be wondered at that the romantic story of Laura Secord's heroism has touched the imagination of our poets. Mair, Machar, Jakeway, and others have sung of her in harmonious strains, while many a green leaf has been laid on her lonely tomb.

AN EARLY RECORD OF LAURA SECORD'S WALK

By John S. Moir

Over a quarter of a century has passed since the appearance of Dr. W. S. Wallace's small pamphlet, *The story of Laura Secord: a study in historical evidence* (Toronto, Macmillan, 1932). If Dr. Wallace did not entirely 'debunk' the Secord 'myth', he at least threw grave doubts on the credibility of many of the details, and on the true importance of the episode for Canadian history in general and for national secular hagiography in particular. Dr. Wallace found the *fons et origo* of the Secord story of the prelude to the Battle of Beaver Dam in the financial objects of Mrs. Secord's two memorials to the government – that of 1839 which prayed for a lease of a ferry at Queenston on preferred terms, and the second of 1841 for a pension on account of the services of herself and of her lately deceased husband. Dr. Wallace is justifiably skeptical of the accumulated stories of Mrs. Secord's exploit, particularly as his earliest documentary evidence – Colonel FitzGibbon's testimony on behalf of Mrs. Secord in support of her petition of 1837 – was written almost twenty-four years after the event, and, as FitzGibbon confesses, 'in a Moment of much hurry and from Memory'. Dr. Wallace's primary evidence consists of FitzGibbon's certificate of 1837, of the two petitions of 1837 and 1841, and of Mrs. Secord's personal account, as first published in the *Anglo-American Magazine* in 1853.[2]

The points with which Dr. Wallace takes issue are three in number. First, there is the question of time, the exact date of Mrs. Secord's perambulation being nowhere specified. Secondly, there is the question of attendant circumstances – her passing through the American picket lines, and the later gloss about her cow and milk pail (now indispensable parts of Canadian folk lore and apparently considered essential parts of her disguise). Finally, as to results, the question is, simply, did the warning which Mrs. Secord brought to

[2] This document is reprinted in E. Cruikshank's *Documentary History of the Campaign upon the Niagara Frontier in 1813* (Welland, n.d.), part II, pages 127-8, along with the official reports on the engagement.

FitzGibbon really enable him to save Canada for the Crown, as our heroine so modestly suggests in her narrative of 1853?

Dr. Wallace points to the very confused chronology of Mrs. Secord's trip which might suggest that she did not reach FitzGibbon until after the battle. Further, according to the above documents, FitzGibbon took no defensive measures on the basis of Mrs. Secord's warning, supposing that she did in fact reach him before the battle. Therefore Dr. Wallace feels that 'Mrs. Secord's claim that she enabled FitzGibbon to "save the country" is too absurd for further discussion'. He is convinced that Mrs. Secord's narrative 'fails therefore by all the tests we have applied to it'. But he does not reject the story as a fabrication:

> FitzGibbon's certificate would seem to establish beyond reasonable doubt that Mrs. Secord did 'in the month of June, 1813' make an attempt to convey some information to the British troops at Beaver Dam; and it must be confessed that her picture of her encounter with the Indians has about it a strong air of verisimilitude. Of her courage and patriotism there is no question. But truth compels one to say that the story she told from memory in later years (and no doubt sincerely believed) was seriously at variance with the facts, and that she played no part in determining the issue of the battle at the Beaver Dam.[3]

The document appended hereto compels us, however, to reassess both the story of Laura Secord and Dr. Wallace's interpretation of the previously known documents. This earlier certificate, written in FitzGibbon's own hand, is to be found in volume 84 of the Upper Canada Sundries in the Public Archives of Canada. It does not answer all the questions raised by Dr. Wallace – in fact it raises at least one new issue – but it does settle the problem of the date of Mrs. Secord's walk, of the success of her mission, and perhaps throws a more charitable light on the motives of the Secords in their recurrent pleas to the government for pecuniary relief. FitzGibbon does not mention the American pickets, or the hallowed cow and pail, nor Mrs. Secord's meeting with the loyal Indians, and these may be dismissed as accretions of later vintage. Further, FitzGibbon does not place the same explicit importance on the results of her action. But he does acknowledge his personal indebtedness, which may conceivably be interpreted as implicit recognition that she had some claim to share in the fame which he had acquired as a result of the victory at Beaver Dam. The most significant fact about this document is that it predates any of the hitherto known evidence by a decade, and so considerably narrows the time-lag between the event and the record.

Two interesting points do arise from this statement by FitzGibbon. Although, as Dr. Wallace shows, the American operation orders were not issued

[3] Wallace, W. S., *The story of Laura Secord: a study in historical evidence* (Toronto, 1932), pages 25-6.

at Fort George until the morning, or more probably the afternoon, of June 23, it is quite conceivable that the American plan for a surprise attack was common knowledge to the officers at Fort George. The fact that despite the precautions of secrecy the plan became known to the British is perhaps a mute commentary on the democratic spirit of the American militia who made up such a large part of Boerstler's force. Further, the encounter between the American force and the Indian scouts early on the 24th gave warning of the Americans' approach, and this new document suggests that the encounter resulted from FitzGibbon's defensive steps taken *after* the receipt of Mrs. Secord's warning. The belated arrival of FitzGibbon and his detachment of the 49th on the scene of battle suggests either that the trial of arms had commenced earlier and at a more distant point than FitzGibbon had anticipated, or that the delay of one day by the Americans in putting their plan into operation had led him to doubt the veracity of Mrs. Secord's information.

The second point is that Mrs. Secord's 'circuitous route' is given here as twelve miles – elsewhere in the primary material the distance is given as 19 or 20 miles. If Mrs. Secord did, as she says, leave her home 'early in the morning' and reach FitzGibbon by moonlight, some explanation for her slow progress is required. The discrepancy in the distance may be explained by a confusion arising over Mrs. Secord's point of departure. If she left from St. David's a 'circuitous route' of twelve miles is reasonable, if from Queenston the trip would be more than sixteen miles. A niece of Mrs. Secord asserts that her aunt left Queenston before sunrise, stopped at the home of her mother-in-law in St. David's, and then proceeded via St. Catharines to FitzGibbon's camp.[4] This would account for a walk of approximately 20 miles following the then-existing roads and paths as shown on the contemporary map reprinted by Wallace. FitzGibbon apparently assumes that Mrs. Secord had commenced her walk at St. David's. Assuming that these two versions are compatible, not only the discrepancy in distance is explained but also the temporal length of the journey, for Mrs. Secord would obviously stop with her relatives at St. David's to refresh herself.

We still face the contradiction of FitzGibbon's statements about the time that the warning was delivered. In his official report he says he was warned about 7 a.m. on the 24th. In the following document he states that Mrs. Secord reached him on the 22nd. FitzGibbon was by nature ambitious, and he may have felt no obligation to share the honours of victory when he sat down to pen his official report. It is regrettable that the flower of Canadian womanhood and patroness of the national confectionery industry cannot be

[4] Emma A. Currie, in *The story of Laura Secord and Canadian reminiscences* (St. Catharines, 1913).

completely vindicated, but in fact this new document seems to confound rather than clarify confusion.

PAC, U.C. Sundries, v. 84, (R.G. 5, A 1)

York 11th May 1827

I do hereby Certify that on the 22d. day of June 1813, Mrs. Secord, Wife of James Secord, Esqr. then of St. David's, came to me at the Beaver Dam after Sun Set, having come from her House at St. David's by a circuitous route a distance of twelve miles, and informed me that her Husband had learnt from an American officer the preceding night that a Detachment from the American Army then in Fort George would be sent out on the following morning (the 23rd.) for the purpose of Surprising and capturing a Detachment of the 49th Regt. then at the Beaver Dam under my command. In Consequence of this information I placed the Indians under Norton together with my own Detachment in a Situation to intercept the American Detachment, and we occupied it during the night of the 22d. – but the Enemy did not come until the morning of the 24th when his Detachment was captured.

Colonel Boerstler, their commander, in a conversation with me confirmed fully the information communicated to me by Mrs. Secord, and accounted for the attempt not having been made on the 23rd. as at first intended.

The weather on the 22d. was very hot, and Mrs. Secord whose person was slight and delicate appeared to have been and no doubt was very much exhausted by the exertion She made in coming to me, and I have ever since held myself personally indebted to her for her conduct upon that occasion, and I consider it an imperative duty on my part humbly and earnestly to recommend her to the favourable consideration of His Majesty's Provincial Government.

I beg leave to add that Mrs. Secord and her Family were entire Strangers to me before the 22d. of June 1813, her exertions therefore could have been made from public motives only.

[signed] James FitzGibbon

LAURA SECORD AGAIN!

By John S. Moir

Mr. Robert Gordon of the Manuscript Division, Public Archives of Canada, has drawn my attention to a document concerning Laura Secord's famous walk which antedates by seven years the account printed in my note 'An Early Record of Laura Secord's Walk' (*Ontario History*, volume 51, spring 1959, pages 105-8). This latest discovery is another attestation by James FitzGibbon, made at 'York, 26th February, 1820', and contained in the Upper Canada Sundries, v. 46 (R.G.5, A 1). Although this earlier statement is much briefer than the one given in 1827, and adds no new information to our meagre stock of factual evidence, it does corroborate his later statement on two points. In this document of 1820 FitzGibbon says categorically that Mrs. Secord came to him two days before the engagement with Boerstler, (although the date is not fixed), that she arrived at his headquarters 'about sunset of an excessively warm day, after having walked twelve miles. . .'.

The contents of this document certainly add further support to the tradition that Mrs. Secord's warning facilitated FitzGibbon's victory, and casts further doubt on the veracity of FitzGibbon's official report. The reference to a walk of twelve miles seems to imply, as did the 1827 document, that Laura Secord's immediate point of departure was St. David's rather than Queenston.

FURTHER READING: E. A. Cruikshank (ed.), *Documentary History . . .*, part IV, pages 110-37, 140-4, 150-4; E. A. Cruikshank, 'The fight in the Beechwoods, a study in Canadian history', *Lundy's Lane Historical Society*, volume 1, part VI, 1895; J. H. Ingersoll, 'The ancestry of Laura Ingersoll Secord', *Ontario Historical Society*, volume 23 (1926), pages 360-4.

Ernest Cruikshank followed his military career by becoming in 1919 the first chairman of the Historic Sites and Monuments Board of Canada. In this capacity he unveiled a tablet to the memory of the last wartime administrator of Upper Canada at which he gave the following review of Drummond's military career. There have been countless anniversary celebrations in which praise passes far beyond the bounds of accuracy and balanced judgment. This article has a tendency to lean in this direction, but with some justification, for Drummond's great services have seldom received their proper due. It may be read as one of the better examples of the oratory inspired by the commemoration of people and events of the War of 1812. It was published in 1933 by the Ontario Historical Society ('Papers and Records' volume 29) and appears here by permission of Mrs. Cruikshank and of the Society.

Sir Gordon Drummond, K.C.B.

BY ERNEST A. CRUIKSHANK

AN ADDRESS AT THE CEREMONY OF UNVEILING
A TABLET IN THE PARLIAMENT BUILDINGS, TORONTO
OCTOBER 27, 1932

This tablet[1] commemorates the public services, civil and military, in Canada, of the first native Canadian to attain high rank in the British army and to fill the highest civil offices, first as President of the Executive Council and administrator of the government of this province, and afterwards as acting governor-general of the British provinces in North America.

[1] This tablet . . . bears the following inscription:

SIR GORDON DRUMMOND

Commemorating the eminent public services of General Sir Gordon Drummond, who was born in Quebec in 1771, and administered the Government of this Province 1813-1815. His daring and skilful winter campaign in December, 1813, resulting in the Recovery of the Niagara Peninsula, the Capture of Fort Niagara, Lewiston, Schlosser, Black Rock, and Buffalo, and Destruction of Part of the Hostile Fleet on Lake Erie transformed Public Feeling from deep depression into well grounded confidence.

He commanded in person at the capture of Oswego, the victory of Lundy's Lane, and the siege of Fort Erie.

Erected 1932.

The tablet was unveiled by Mrs. Geo. S. Henry, the wife of the Premier, and the Hon. Mr. Henry, himself, accepted it on behalf of the Province.

After distinguished service in Holland, Egypt, and Minorca, as well as some uneventful years in Lower Canada, he returned to his native country, with the rank of lieutenant-general, at the age of forty-two, to act as second in command to the governor-general. The Commander-in-Chief, announcing his appointment, stated that 'effectual aid' was expected from his 'zeal, intelligence, and local knowledge'.

He was at once directed to take command of the troops in Upper Canada, and assume the civil government of the province. On arriving at Kingston on the 5th December, 1813, he found that the situation was decidedly gloomy. The three western districts, extending from the Niagara to the Detroit river, had been abandoned to the enemy, whose foraging parties were roaming about and pillaging the inhabitants. The 'Right Division' of the army, which had defended its western frontier so long and well, had been almost annihilated, all the regular troops who had been employed in the defence of the Niagara peninsula had retired to Burlington Heights and most of them had been sent to Kingston or were on the march in that direction. The enemy had obtained undisputed possession of Lake Erie and the temporary command of Lake Ontario. Their most formidable army had gone into winter quarters near the St. Lawrence, nearly midway between Ogdensburg and Montreal, in a position menacing his line of communications with his base of supplies. The loyalists in the province were dispirited and the disloyal were triumphant and aggressive. The farmers east of Kingston were discontented and resentful about the tactless enforcement of martial law for the impressment of provisions and forage.

His first act was to countermand the orders for retiring and direct that the scattered detachments should be assembled at Burlington for a vigorous offensive. Three days later he resumed his tiring journey westward. Arriving at this place on December 12, he was at once sworn as president of the Council. Within forty-eight hours he learned that the rapid advance of less than four hundred men in sleighs from Burlington had so alarmed the enemy that they had abandoned the entire peninsula, burning the town of Niagara before retreating. These events were announced in an inspiriting general order and he decided to follow up this advantage by an immediate invasion of the enemy's territory, where they seemed to think themselves secure from any attack. In another forty-eight hours he had established his headquarters in the secluded village of St. David's, where preparations for that movement could be made with little risk of discovery. Boats were brought forward by water from Burlington to the mouth of the Four Mile Creek and then secretly conveyed overland in sleighs to a ravine on the river, where its passage was to be attempted and there concealed. Rough weather caused a day's delay, but on the morning of December 19, before daylight, he wrote a letter from Fort Niagara, announcing the capture of that fortress by assault with its whole garrison and munitions valued at a million dollars, and stating that he would at once accompany another body of troops to attack the fortifications on Lewiston Heights. This operation was equally successful and the pursuit was continued for fifteen miles, in severe wintry weather, until halted by the destruction of a bridge over Tonawanda Creek, which interposed an unfordable obstacle.

Before resuming his offensive it became necessary to convey his boats around the Falls to the upper river to effect its passage once more. Extremely cold weather and the want of warm clothing for his soldiers, none of whom had fur caps and some were without overcoats, caused a delay of ten days, but on the morning of December 30, Black Rock and Buffalo were taken, a more numerous opposing force was completely dispersed, with the loss of all its artillery, and four ships of the hostile squadron on Lake Erie were destroyed. In retaliation for the destruction of Niagara, the whole of the opposite frontier was laid waste. Thus in less than three weeks the complexion of affairs had been totally changed and leisure obtained for attention to his most important civil duties.

As president of the Council he was obliged to combine the duties of a prime minister with those of a lieutenant-governor. On December 28, he published a proclamation convoking a meeting of parliament on February 12, but on January 6 this was amended by changing the date to February 15. On January 11, he prohibited the exportation and distillation of grain as a measure of necessity. He then returned to Kingston, where fifteen hundred shipwrights were employed in the navy yard, to confer with Sir James Yeo on the best means of regaining the mastery of the lakes, which he considered a matter of supreme importance. On January 25 he rescinded the proclamations declaring martial law in force in the Midland, Johnstown, and Eastern districts, for procuring provisions and forage, thereby allaying great discontent. An expedition for the destruction of the remaining ships of the enemy's squadron on Lake Erie at Put-in Bay and Erie, where they were ice-bound, was carefully planned to be carried out by the swift and secret movement of eighteen hundred soldiers and seamen in sleighs from near Niagara to Amherstburg and then across the lake on the ice. Preparations were made and both commanders intended to accompany this force but the enterprise was frustrated by the unusual mildness of the month of January, which prevented ice from forming of sufficient thickness to admit of a passage upon it. This project was in consequence reluctantly abandoned.

The little garrison at Mackinac was reported to be menaced with starvation and would probably be attacked by a strong force as soon as navigation from Detroit became possible. The safety of the very valuable fur-trade in the North West depended upon the retention of this post. Reinforcements and supplies must be sent across Lake Huron in boats for that purpose before the other route became practicable. A road was opened from Lake Simcoe to Nottawasaga river, where boats were built and supplies collected. An expedition was fitted out there, which, after battling with fields of floating ice for nineteen days, reached Mackinac and enabled the commandant to equip a second expedition, which captured the fort at Prairie du Chien and gained control of the upper course of the Mississippi. The subsequent attack on Mackinac itself was successfully repelled.

Returning to the seat of government for the opening of the session of parliament, it became Drummond's duty to frame the outline of a programme of legislation. The successful defence of the province was necessarily the most important subject. He recommended the immediate organization of incorporated battalions of militia for twelve months' service, the repair of one great road through the province to facilitate the transport of military stores, and an increase of contributions levied upon conscientious objectors excused from military service. He remarked upon the desertion to the enemy of two members of the Legislative Assembly and urged parliament to strengthen the power of the executive government. He advised the passage of a bill of attainder for the punishment of such traitors by the forfeiture of their estates for the relief of sufferers by the war. He considered it would be indispensably necessary to prolong the act prohibiting the exportation and distillation of grain.

Four members of the assembly were prisoners in the hands of the enemy and another was absent through sickness, but those present responded cordially by the passage of the measures proposed in an acceptable form and in the enactment of an emergency law authorizing the summary arrest and detention of persons suspected of treason, misprision of treason, and treasonable practices, which Drummond felt warranted in interpreting as a virtual suspension of the Habeas Corpus Act.

As soon as parliament was prorogued on March 14, Drummond again transferred his headquarters to Kingston to keep in close touch with Yeo and make all practicable arrangements for the rapid movement of troops and supplies to the Niagara frontier, where he thought another invasion would be made, and possibly for an attack on the enemy's naval base at Sackett's Harbour. But the most reliable intelligence described that place as being strongly fortified and well garrisoned. It was decided that an attempt upon it, to succeed, would require a stronger force than could be prudently assembled. But it seemed that the capture of their secondary depot at Oswego would have the effect of delaying the equipment of their fleet on Lake Ontario. This was accomplished by a combined naval and military attack on May 6, and, as forecast, proved a factor in preventing the co-operation of that fleet with their invading army at Niagara when most needed during the first three weeks of July, and permitted the undisturbed employment of four of the smaller British ships in the conveyance of troops and supplies so efficiently as to decide the result of the campaign.

The governor-general refused to credit Drummond's warning that another invasion of the Niagara peninsula was imminent and declined to reinforce him adequately until too late. When it actually began, Drummond was still at Kingston and too deeply involved in the transaction of civil business to proceed at once to the seat of operations, although the initial success of the invaders seemed very alarming. On arriving here he learned that they were preparing to besiege the forts at Niagara, and at once framed detailed instructions for an immediate offensive, of which he intended to assume the personal direction.

With this object he sent all the troops available, about 400 of the 89th Regiment, and the new battalion of Incorporated Militia, across the lake to Fort Niagara and followed them on the evening of the next day. Arriving there at daybreak, on July 25, he was informed that the invaders had retired hastily beyond the Chippawa, with the apparent intention of retreating still further. General Riall had sent a strong advanced body in the night to observe their movements and occupy the high ground and important road junction at Lundy's Lane, which he intended to reinforce with the remainder of his division that day. Drummond at once resolved to expel the enemy from Lewiston, where they had established a supply depot, and then join Riall for the pursuit of the retreating force. Lewiston was occupied without difficulty, a part of his troops was sent back to the forts, and after resting the others at Queenston, he began his march forward on the river road late in the afternoon. On the way he received a message from General Riall that a strong force was advancing against him from Chippawa. Riding quickly forward he learned that Riall had ordered a retreat by the St. Catharines road, on which the main body of his division had advanced some miles, and the heights had already been abandoned. These orders were immediately countermanded, and the position was reoccupied barely in time to place the guns on the hill in a situation to command the road to Chippawa. His own column was brought forward as quickly as it could be moved and formed on the left of Riall's, making a total of about fifteen hundred of all ranks and arms. Still, as the road was narrow and the men were tired by a long march on a hot day, this took much time, and was not done without some disorder.

The battle opened badly. When the battalion of Incorporated Militia, which was in rear of the column advancing from Queenston, and formed nearly half of it, was deploying into line on the extreme left, it was suddenly and unexpectedly attacked in flank from the woods, and broken up with heavy loss. Its commander was disabled and more than a hundred men were killed, wounded, or taken, with several officers. About the same time General

Riall was badly wounded and, in riding to the rear, he was made a prisoner with his staff officer. The artillery, however, succeeded in repelling the main attack and holding it at bay for almost three hours, until darkness had fully set in. This enabled a fresh body of assailants to approach nearly unseen, when sustained musketry, followed by a determined and well-led charge, forced Drummond's much-tried centre from its position and drove it down the slope into the fields below. Some of the gunners of the small party of Royal Artillery were bayoneted where they stood and it was nearly annihilated. All the guns were taken and the commanding heights and road junction were occupied by the enemy in very superior numbers. They had been steadily reinforced until their entire army was brought into action.

At nine o'clock the battle seemed to be lost. Drummond had lost a third of his fifteen hundred men and the weary remnant had been forced down into the low ground, from which the ascent was much more difficult than from the opposite side. His second in command was missing and several of his most experienced officers had been disabled. The situation appeared almost hopeless, but his courage never wavered. The main body of Riall's division was then coming up, but very tired and angered by their march, countermarch, and final advance which brought them to the field of battle. As they appeared they were flung into action, yet two or three resolute assaults failed to recover the lost position, from which their own guns, as well as those of the enemy, were firing upon them. Drummond, himself, was severely wounded in the neck, but he still remained undaunted in his determination to continue the struggle, which lasted, with brief intermissions, until nearly midnight, when the hill, with all the lost artillery, except a single gun, and two of those brought up by the enemy, was retaken by a final desperate charge. Their infantry was then in full retreat, having received orders to retire.

Drummond's name is naturally associated with this hard-fought and dearly-won battle, the crisis of the campaign, which was certainly gained by his invincible will to conquer. Brock has been called the saviour of Upper Canada and his fame is known to all who have the least acquaintance with our military history. But Drummond equally deserves that title. He had a much more formidable enemy to contend with both in numbers and in military value. He proved himself a resourceful and indomitable leader of men, noble minded and stout hearted.

As a recent American writer, General Lewis Babcock, justly remarks: 'He inspired his command with his own contempt for danger and his own confidence in the final result. His name should be held in grateful remembrance by the people of Canada.'

FURTHER READING: E. A. Cruikshank, 'Drummond's winter campaign, 1813', *Lundy's Lane Historical Society*, volume I, part III, n.d.

The centennial celebrations of the War of 1812 occurred during a period of intense national pride, when Canadians felt a strong desire to see Canada achieve a full, independent, national life and win recognition from the world at large as a national entity. These addresses reflect the contemporary currents, coloured by the personalities of the orators. The soldier saw the war as demonstrating the need for continuing close association with Britain and for military preparedness; the Member of Parliament found Brock a worthy national hero and an inspiration to future generations; and the educator felt that study of the war could be used to mould character and inculcate a patriotic spirit. . . . The speeches are taken from the commemorative volume, 'Brock Centenary, 1812-1912: account of the celebration of Queenston Heights, Ontario, on the 12th October, 1912', edited by Alexander Fraser and published in Toronto in 1913.

A Century Later – Canadian Memories of the War

Addresses at the Brock Centenary, 1912

BY COLONEL G. STERLING RYERSON

This meeting today is held to commemorate the death of a brave and wise man who died in the defence of his country. It is not a paean of victory we sing but a requiem. We are not here to glorify war; nor is our object to exult over our brave but defeated adversary. Rather is it an occasion when Canadians should pause and look back over the past and give praise to God that in the days of stress and storm He raised up great, good, and brave men who were willing and able to fight for their king and country in order that they might enjoy civil and religious liberty under the British flag, and that they might hand down to their posterity a fair and goodly heritage which they had won from the primeval forests by their labour and sacrifices. The United Empire Loyalists came to this country not as those who desired to better their condition in life, nor were they possessed by land hunger, nor by ideas of political and social aggrandisement. They came solely because of their devotion to the British Crown and Constitution, and because they preferred to live in peace and poverty under a monarchical government rather than in wealth and discord under republican institutions. It was to these men that Brock appealed, nor did he appeal in vain when war was declared. It was on July 27th, 1812, that in reply to an address from the Assembly of Upper Canada he said:

> Gentlemen: When invaded by an enemy whose avowed object is the entire conquest of the Province, the voice of loyalty as well as of interest calls aloud to every person in the sphere in which he is placed, to defend his country. Our militia have heard the voice and have obeyed it. They have evinced by the promptitude and loyalty of their conduct that they are worthy of the king whom they serve, and of the constitution which they enjoy; and it affords me particular satisfaction, that while I address you as legislators, I speak to men who, in the day of danger, will be ready to assist not only with their counsel, but with arms.

He concluded as follows:

> We are engaged in an awful and eventful contest. By unanimity and despatch in our councils, and by vigour in our operations, we may teach the enemy this lesson, that a country defended by free men, enthusiastically devoted to the cause of their king and constitution, can never be conquered.

We know the response, and others who will follow me will speak of it in greater detail. With the Canadian poet we can say and sing:

We boast not of the victory,
But render homage, deep and just,
To his and their immortal dust,
Who proved so worthy of their trust –
No lofty pile nor sculptured bust
Can herald their degree.

No tongue need blazon forth their fame –
The cheers that stir the sacred hill
Are but the promptings of the will
That conquered then, that conquers still;
And generations yet shall thrill
At Brock's remembered name.

Nor must it be supposed that the United Empire Loyalists and their children were the only men who responded to Brock's call to arms. Our gallant French-Canadian compatriots were not a whit behind in their hearty response. Coming from a brave and adventurous race, they performed deeds of valour and endurance equal to the best in the defence of our country. The hardy Highlanders of Glengarry, too, were rallied to the flag by the Macdonells. Not the least active among these Scottish Roman Catholic Loyalists was the Rev. Alexander Macdonell, a priest who afterwards became the

'Good Bishop', a brave and loyal man whose country's welfare was ever near to his heart. Another Macdonell, George, was second in command of the Glengarry Regiment, and still another, Colonel John Macdonell, was aide-de-camp to Brock in addition to being Attorney-General of the Province. He, alas, lost his life in his gallant efforts to second his chief at this battle which we commemorate today. Scotsmen are ever brave and loyal, and we have in the Scottish population of the country an element on whom we can rely in time of danger.

Let us not forget that we owe not a little to our Indian allies in the War of 1812. Tecumseh and Brant played great parts. Nor was Brock niggardly in his praise. After the fall of Detroit he says in his despatch to the Governor-General:

> The conduct of the Indians, under Colonel Elliot, Captain McKee and other officers of the department, joined to that of the gallant and brave of their respective tribes, has since the commencement of the war been marked with acts of true heroism, and in nothing can they testify more strongly their love for their King, their great Father, than in following the dictates of honour and humanity by which they have hitherto been actuated.

Why do we single out Brock as a hero among so many who have rendered good service to the country? I think that it is because he was a man of loyalty, vigour, energy and administrative ability; because he was the embodiment of the patriotism and loyalty of the people; because he had within him the power to inspire others with the spirit of patriotism and self-sacrifice; and above and beyond all, it is due to his efforts, and to the spirit of resistance and Imperialism to which he gave form and substance, that Canada today is an integral part of the British Empire, and a daughter nation within that great galaxy of the nations known as the British Empire.

What does it mean to be a British citizen? What benefits accrue to us by having this status? Are not the paths of the sea open to us and to our commerce by the grace of the British navy? Can we not go to all parts of the world as individuals, knowing that the Union Jack protects us? Is it a small privilege to share in the brave deeds of the British army? Are we not proud of our common literature, and are not Shakespeare and Milton and Tennyson our very own? Not borrowed plumes we are wearing, but our own. And are not the benefits of British civil, religious and political liberty ours also? Is not British justice and administration of the law something to be proud of and to be thankful for? What should we do to maintain our status as a partner, a full partner, in the Imperial concern? Is it not our bounden duty to contribute directly to the support of the British navy? Are we to lag behind the other self-governing nations of the Empire in this essential duty? A thousand times No! A government which will subscribe twenty-five millions of dollars for this purpose, and at once, can go to the polls in perfect confidence when their time comes to ask the people for their verdict.

Some good people seem to think that the time of universal peace is at hand. One has only to look at the state of affairs in Europe on this very day, to perceive how far we are removed from the millennium. In time of peace we must prepare for war; preparation for war is the best insurance policy against it. We wish to live at peace with all nations, but at all costs and at all hazards we must defend our shores. Universal military service is the duty of the Canadian people in the near future. The people will be better for it morally and physically. It will surely come, for the policy of the future is the maintenance of the integrity of the British Empire. We love our country, we believe it has a great future; we must make it secure. What says a sweet singer of Canada:

> O strong hearts guarding the birthright of our glory,
> Worth your best blood this heritage ye guard:
> Those mighty streams resplendent with story,
> These iron coasts by rage of seas unjarred –
> What fields of peace these bulwarks well secure:
> What vales of plenty these calm floods supply:
> Shall not our love this rough, sweet land make sure,
> Her bounds preserve inviolate, though we die:
> O strong hearts of the North
> Let flame your loyalty forth,
> And put the craven and the base to open shame
> Till earth shall know the Child of Nations by her Name.

BY ANGUS CLAUDE MACDONELL, M.P.

We have gathered here today as Canadians to commemorate an event which will be ever dear to us and our posterity. One hundred years ago Sir Isaac Brock, the hero of Upper Canada, died in battle upon this field in defence of his country and the flag. In the past we have learned and heard altogether too little of this truly great man, and of what he accomplished; it is not too much to say that he preserved Canada to the Empire and at the same time created a national sentiment in Canada which has ever grown and expanded to the present day. The national importance of the battle of Queenston Heights, following the capitulation of Detroit, cannot be over-estimated; national sentiment or a feeling of nationhood was even then manifesting itself in this young colony. The peoples who had settled in Canada sprang from races which had always stood out strongly for national identity – the English glory in their historic past; the Scottish race, to which my forefathers belonged and which to some extent I represent, on this occasion, are noted for their love of country; and so with the other races which made up the United Empire Loyalist settlers of Upper Canada at the time of the War of 1812-14. Our national heart was created and stirred in this century-old war, and the heartbeats have ever become stronger down to this day, and we now look back through the mists of one hundred years to Sir Isaac Brock as the first true source of national sentiment which fertilized our country, and stamped it as British and Canadian forever.

Our object in coming here today, after we have enjoyed one hundred years of blessed peace with our neighbours to the south, is not to perpetuate national hostility, or even to cherish a mere military spirit; we hope and pray and fully believe that this peace will ever exist between us and our American brothers. Our object in coming here today is to honour the name and memory of one who was chiefly instrumental in bringing about that blessed peace, and in preserving our country to enjoy it; and in the name of peace we say that the ground upon which we stand today is consecrated and distinguished by the valour of our soldier hero, who gave up his life on this spot in the first great battle of the War of 1812 to purchase that peace which a grateful country has ever since enjoyed.

This monument under which we stand is a fit emblem of everlasting peace and at the same time it fittingly commemorates the glorious death of the man in memory of whom it was raised. We Canadians should ever be grateful to Divine Providence for having favoured us with such an able civil and military chief, because Brock was both the chief executive in our civil affairs and Commander-in-Chief of the forces. As Administrator of the Province of Upper Canada he was able and prudent; as Commander-in-Chief he was experienced and fearless. It remained, however, for the great chief Tecumseh to read the true character of the man as man. When they first met, Tecumseh turned to his fellow chiefs and allies, and, pointing to Brock, who stood by him, said, 'This is a man!' The correctness of this opinion was borne out in both the life and death of Brock.

Our hero was ever dutiful. He always performed his duty and saw that others did likewise. The performance of duty was ever uppermost in his mind, and his ideals were always high, his aspirations noble. Permit me to quote here one of his first General Orders issued to the troops immediately upon his taking the field on the 4th of July, 1812:

> The Major-General calls the serious attention of every militiaman to the efforts made by the enemy to destroy and lay waste this flourishing country; they must be sensible of the great stake they have to contend for and will, by their conduct, convince the enemy that they are not desirous of bowing their necks to a foreign yoke. The Major-General is determined to devote his best energies to the defence of the country, and has no doubt that, supported by the zeal, activity and determination of the loyal inhabitants of this Province, he

> will successfully repel every hostile attack, and preserve to them inviolate all that they hold dear.

The result of the war proves how well Brock himself lived up to these sentiments.

Let us always remember that the War of 1812 was not of our making. On the 18th of June, 1812, President Madison declared war against Great Britain, with Canada as the point of attack. The 'Right of Search', the power to search for contraband or for deserters on board of American ships, was claimed by Britain, but was resisted by the United States. Strange to say, this claim was abandoned by Great Britain the very day [sic] before war was declared by President Madison, yet the war was declared and went on. It will be readily seen that Canada had absolutely nothing to do with this war or its alleged cause, the 'Right of Search'; and yet, in making this war on Canada, the United States placed itself on record as approving a forcible invasion of a neighbouring peaceful country and of involving it in all the horrors of war. At that time the United States had eight million people, Upper Canada had barely eighty thousand. At the very outset the Americans placed upon a war footing one hundred and seventy-five thousand men, whereas there were less than ten thousand men of all kinds capable of bearing arms in Upper Canada. These figures give us an idea of the very great disparity both in numbers and fighting strength between the two peoples so far as we in Upper Canada were concerned. During the two and a half years of the war there were no less than twelve separate and distinct invasions of Canada, and fifty-six military and naval engagements, the great majority of which were won by our forces. While Brock lived, his genius and spirit guided and inspired the defence of the country, and after his death his noble example and the preparations he had made for war during his life encouraged and enabled the people to repel the invader.

Under the guise of strict discipline and the grim visage of a soldier and fighting man, Isaac Brock possessed a warm human heart; he was ever solicitous for the comfort and well-being of his people and especially of his militia soldiers, and on every occasion consistent with the safety of the Province he relaxed the rigours of war and would permit the militia to return to their homes and farms. This is evidenced by many of his Militia General Orders. An extract from Militia General Orders of 26th of August, 1812, immediately after the capture of Detroit, reads as follows:

> Major-General Brock has ever felt anxious to study the comforts and conveniences of the militia, but the conduct of the detachments which lately accompanied him to Detroit has if possible increased his anxiety on this subject. The present cessation of hostilities enables him to dispense with the services of a large proportion of them for a short period.

We very naturally ask ourselves who these troops were for whose welfare General Brock was always so solicitous. There were of course some British regular troops in Canada, noticeably the Forty-ninth, Brock's own regiment, but during the earlier stages of the war, and while Brock lived, the men of the province, militia and yeomanry, had to be relied upon mainly; these chiefly were the men of the York, Glengarry, Norfolk and other militia regiments; every loyal man capable of bearing arms in the province turned out to fight, or to help those who fought. The York and Glengarry militia served with great distinction, and I may perhaps be permitted to refer to the fact that forty-three gentlemen of my own name and family connection held commissions in the various regiments in that war. In connection with this I might further mention a somewhat curious incident. My own grandfather, Colonel Alexander Macdonell, was taken prisoner by the Americans at the Battle of Niagara, and was confined as a prisoner at Lancaster, Pennsylvania, in the very same prison in which his own father, Captain Allan Macdonell, had been confined by the Revolutionary States as a prisoner of war during the Revolutionary War, 1776-83.

Now, happily, all is peace; we have enjoyed one hundred years of peace and we thank Divine Providence for it. We have had preserved to us by Brock and those who fought and fell with him a rich kingdom; we possess it in peace and happiness and great prosperity. This is an age of peace, and in this age and generation it is fit that we should advance all the works and arts of peace; a very great trust in this respect has been handed down to us and confided to our safe-keeping. In these days of our prosperity we must protect and defend and develop this great country, this rich heritage which the heroism of our forefathers has preserved to us. We must not only conserve it, but we must better it and develop it, and make useful to man all these possessions which have been given us. Our ideals and ambitions must always be high, and if we find ourselves faltering let us look upon this splendid monument and think of the hero in honour of whom it was raised; and let us at all times remember that now as in 1812 in unity we possess our strength; we must become one people if we are to be a great people, with one great common country. We have many provinces but only one Canada.

It has been well said by one of Brock's biographers that 'it remains for the youth of Canada to profoundly cherish the memory of Isaac Brock and to never lose an opportunity to follow the example set for them by his splendid deeds.' It has also been truly said that 'he fell ere he saw the star of his country rise', and, although the sky over this battlefield upon which his eyes closed forever one hundred years ago was cloudy and overcast, yet because he lived and died those who came after him enjoy the cloudless sunshine of peace and happiness.

Brock's family motto was, 'He who guards never sleeps.' We know how faithfully he guarded and safeguarded his country in life, and let us pray that in death under this monument he sleeps well.

BY DR. JAMES L. HUGHES

I had the honour of requesting the Hon. Dr. Pyne, Minister of Education, to call the attention of the School Boards of Ontario to the importance of celebrating the hundredth anniversary of the victory so gallantly won on these heights, and of paying due tribute to the brave men and women who so nobly and heroically struggled to preserve for us the blessings of British liberty, and of unity with our motherland. To these men and women of firm faith and strong heart we give gratitude and reverence today, and especially to the statesman and hero who at the foot of these heights died a hundred years ago while leading Canadian volunteers to drive back invaders who without just cause had dared to come to Canada with the avowed purpose of forcibly taking possession of our country.

In the judgment of the committee that arranged for the celebration of the glorious deeds of our early history, it is most important that Canadian children should be trained to revere the memories of the great and true men and women of one hundred years ago, and to rejoice because of the victories won by them for freedom and for imperial unity.

There are men who have written to the newspapers objecting to the course we adopted. They seem to think it improper to let our children know that our country was ever in danger, and that it was saved by the unselfish devotion and the brave deeds of our ancestors. However, in spite of their protests, based on weak and unpatriotic sentiment, we intend to teach young Canadians to remember the patriotism and valour of the founders and defenders of Canada, and to train them to become worthy successors to the men and women who made such sacrifices for them.

We have no wish to fill the hearts of the pupils in our schools with animosity towards the great nation whose fertile fields and happy homes we see beyond the great river that separates it from our own fair land. We wish to develop in our children a spirit that will lead them to say to the people across our borderland not, 'Hands off Canada', but, 'Hands together to achieve for God and for humanity the highest and broadest and truest ideals that have been revealed to the Anglo-Saxon race.'

We do not wish to make our children quarrelsome or offensive, but we do wish them to be patriotic Canadians, full of loyalty to their flag, their Empire, and their King. We wish them to understand what their predecessors did in order that they may have faith in themselves and in their country; and we intend that they shall learn the achievements of the past in order that they may have a true basis for their own manhood and womanhood.

True reverence for courage and self-sacrifice, fidelity to principle, and devotion to home and country in time of need, is a fundamental element of strong, true character. The facts of history may have little influence in developing character, but the noble deeds of our ancestors performed for high purposes are the surest sources for the development of the strong and true emotions that make human character vital instead of inert. Emotions form the battery power of character, and among the emotions that give strength and virility and beauty to character, reverence for the dead who wisely struggled and nobly achieved is surely one of the most productive of dignified and transforming character.

The history of the past is valuable chiefly for the opportunities it gives to be stirred to deep, true enthusiasm for heroism, for honour, for patriotism, for love of freedom, for devotion to duty, and for sublime self-sacrifice for high ideals. Whatever else we may neglect in the training of the young, I trust we shall never fail to fill their hearts with profound reverence for the men and women of the past to whom they owe so much.

We should teach other lessons from the War of 1812. We should fill each child's life with a splendid courage that can never be dismayed, by telling how a few determined settlers scattered widely over a new country successfully repelled invading armies coming from a country with a population twentyfold larger. We should teach reverence not only for manhood but for womanhood by recounting the terrible hardships endured willingly by Canadian women generally, as well as by proudly relating the noble work done by individual women, of whom Laura Secord was so conspicuous an example.

A certain class of thoughtless people call us 'flag-wavers' if we strive to give our young people a true conception of the value of national life, and of their duty to have a true love for their country and for their Empire. If a flag-waver means one who is proud of a noble ancestry, and determined to prove worthy of the race from which he sprung; one who knows that his forefathers gave a wider meaning to freedom, and who intends to perpetuate liberty and aid in giving it a still broader and higher value; one who is grateful because his Empire represents the grandest revelation of unity yet made known to humanity and who accepts this revelation as a sacred trust – then I am a flag-waver, and I shall make every boy and girl whom I can ever influence a flag-waver who loves his flag and waves it because it represents freedom, and honour, and justice, and truth, and unity, and a glorious history, the most triumphantly progressive that has been achieved by any nation in the development of the world.

We do well to celebrate the great deeds of the men and women of a hundred years ago, and teach our children to give them reverence, but it is far more important for us to consider what the people a hundred years hence will think of us than to glorify the triumphs of a hundred years ago. The work of the world is not done. Evolution to higher ideals goes ever on. Each succeeding generation has greater responsibilities and higher duties than the one that preceded it. The greatest lesson we can learn from the past is that we should prove true to the opportunities of our time; that we should with unselfish motive and undaunted hearts accept the responsibilities that come to us as partners in our magnificent Empire, and share in the achievement of greater triumphs for freedom and justice than have ever been recorded in the past.

Inspired by the records of such men as Brock, at the foot of whose monument we stand today and look with reminiscent glance over the marvellous progress of a hundred glorious years, let us determine that we shall do our part to make the coming century more fruitful than the past.

FURTHER READING: *The centenary celebration of the Battle of Lundy's Lane* (Lundy's Lane Historical Society, Niagara Falls, Ontario, 1919); J. M. Harper, *In commemoration of 'The Century of Peace': the annals of the war, illustrated by a selection of historical ballads* (London and New York, 1913); George D. Emerson (ed.), *The Perry's victory centenary* (Perry's Victory Centennial Commission, Albany, New York, 1916).

The following paper was read at a session of the annual meeting of the Ontario Historical Society, held in Midland, Ontario, in June 1958, and was afterwards published in 'Ontario History', volume 50 (1958). It appears here by permission of the Society and of the author.

The War of 1812 in Canadian History

BY C. P. STACEY

The War of 1812 is one of those episodes in history that make everybody happy, because everybody interprets it in his own way.

The Americans think of it as primarily a naval war in which the pride of the Mistress of the Seas was humbled by what an imprudent Englishman had called 'a few fir-built frigates, manned by a handful of bastards and outlaws'. Canadians think of it equally pridefully as a war of defence in which their brave fathers, side by side, turned back the massed might of the United States and saved the country from conquest. And the English are the happiest of all, because they don't even know it happened.

This evening I should like to look at that war as an episode in Canadian history and try to discover what its real significance for our country was. It's a suitable subject to discuss in this society, because so far as Canada was concerned it was largely Ontario's war. Quebec was constantly threatened but never really seriously invaded. The Maritime Provinces were protected by British sea-power, and the war gave them a not unwelcome opportunity of showing their patriotism by relieving their New England neighbours of some of their property. The seafarers of Nova Scotia and New Brunswick went out privateering, and what with that and other things the war years were prosperous ones down east; the Maritimes could probably have managed to put up with it if the war had lasted five years longer.

But here in Upper Canada the war was serious business. The province was a battlefield; large parts of it were devastated by invading armies; its people were kept in fear for three years; its capital was twice occupied by the enemy. It was inevitable that the whole incident should leave a deep impression on Ontario's history, and the nature of that impression is my subject tonight.

A few years ago, when staying at the Royal Empire Society in London,

I found in its library a Canadian book I had never seen before. It was *The Report of the Loyal and Patriotic Society of Upper Canada*, printed at Montreal in 1817. It's a volume of something like 400 pages, and it tells you quite a bit about what this war was like to the people who went through it. The Loyal and Patriotic Society was formed at York late in 1812. Its first task was to provide winter clothing for the militia then defending the frontier; it went on to the job of helping the families of serving militiamen, and later it provided relief for people who had suffered by what it called the 'predatory incursions of the enemy'. It got a lot of help in its good work from benefactors in other colonies and, still more, in England. Indeed, in the end it had several thousand pounds left over, and this money, donated by patriotic Englishmen to help the much-tried citizens of a distant province that had paid a heavy price for its loyalty to the Crown, was used to found a Provincial Hospital at York. That was the beginning of the Toronto General Hospital.

Every country has its historical legends, and Canada is no exception. One of the most durable of our legends is what I may call the Militia Legend of 1812. By that I mean the idea that during that war the country was defended by 'the Militia' with only a little help from regular troops. I think this idea is still pretty widespread, and I suspect you can still find it in some school textbooks; but it isn't in accordance with the facts. It's perfectly true that the militia played an essential part in the defence of Canada, but it was still a secondary part. The country was not saved in 1812 merely by youngsters fresh from the tail of the plough. It was scientifically defended by men trained for the job. The battles on the border, particularly in the early days, were essentially a contest between ill-organized numbers on the American side and professional skill on ours. You won't find this in the schoolbooks: but Upper Canada was saved in the campaign of 1812 because the province was actually better prepared for war than the United States. It was better prepared because the British taxpayer had provided in Canada the essentials for successful defence. These were a naval force on the Lakes; an efficient body of regular troops, small, it is true, but equal to the job; and trained officers who could provide skilful and energetic professional leadership.

The regulars did more than supply the leadership. They usually did the lion's share of the actual fighting. Take a look at the casualty lists for the fiercest battle of the war, Lundy's Lane. The unit that lost most men there was the 89th Foot, a British regular regiment which is now the Royal Irish Fusiliers (Princess Victoria's). It had no less than 254 casualties, including 29 killed. Upper Canada's single battalion of Incorporated Militia, a long-service unit enlisted on a basis similar to regular troops, had 142 casualties, including seven killed. But the local units of the so-called Sedentary Militia, who had about 500 men present at the battle, had only 22 casualties and had exactly one man killed. These were the actual lads from the plough tail; and that pretty well tells the story.

Please note one thing. I am not suggesting that Canadians did not play an important part in the defence of Canada. I am merely saying that the trained soldier was the key figure in the whole affair, and that the amateur soldier was much less important than he has been made out to be. The fact is that a good many of the trained regular soldiers were Canadians. There were five regiments of 'Fencibles', regulars raised in British North America. One of them was the Glengarry Light Infantry Fencibles, which everyone has heard of. They were not part of the Canadian Militia, but a regular unit of the British Army, raised here in Canada for the defence of Canada. And some of the individual Canadians who most distinguished themselves in this war were regular soldiers too. One of them was the famous Colonel Charles de Salaberry, the hero of Châteauguay. He was a Canadian, right enough, born at Beauport just outside Quebec City; but he was also a professional soldier, who had entered the British Army as a youngster and learned his trade in long years of hard service in the 60th Rifles.

All the same, let's give credit where it's due. And the chief credit for the saving of Canada in 1812 is due to British soldiers. No one can read the documents that tell the story of the events in Upper Canada in the summer of 1812 without realizing that this is so. It is at least possible that this province would be part of the United States today had it not been for the presence here in that year of one single battalion of British regular infantry – the 41st Foot, now The Welch Regiment – and an able and energetic British major-general, Isaac Brock. Every Ontario schoolboy, I hope, still knows the name of General Brock; but how many of them have heard of the Welch Regiment?

The point I am trying to make is one that is important not merely historically but from the point of view of national defence. It is simply that a Canadian does not become a good soldier merely by putting on a uniform and simply because he is a Canadian. He has to learn the business like other people. The reputation won by our Army in the two world wars was not won by untrained troops. By the time the army of 1939-45 got into action, it was actually better trained than any peace-time regulars have ever been.

I have sometimes wondered, if these things are true, just when and how the story got going that this country was saved in 1812 by 'the Militia' single-handed. I found part of the answer, at least, in that book I spoke of, the *Report of the Loyal and Patriotic Society.* For in an appendix to it there is a document headed 'York, 22d November, 1812. An Exhortation pronounced after the Sermon, or rather in continuation of it, to induce the Inhabitants to contribute to the comfort of the Militia fighting upon the Lines. . . .' The speaker's name is not given, but he can only have been the Rector of York, the Reverend John Strachan. He said:

> It will be told by the future Historian, that the Province of Upper Canada, without the assistance of men or arms, except a handful of regular troops, repelled its invaders, slew or took them all prisoners, and captured from its enemies the greater part of the arms by which it was defended. . . . And never, surely, was greater activity shewn in any country, than our militia have exhibited, never greater valour, cooler resolution, and more approved conduct; they have emulated the choicest veterans, and they have twice saved the country.

Thus Dr. Strachan in November 1812. I cannot help comparing this statement with one written by General Brock only four months before, just after the outbreak of war:

> My situation is most critical, not from any thing the enemy can do, but from the disposition of the people – The population, believe me is essentially bad – A full belief possesses them all that this Province must inevitably succumb. This prepossession is fatal to every exertion – Legislators, Magistrates, Militia Officers, all, have imbibed the idea, and are so sluggish and indifferent in their respective offices that the artful and active scoundrel is allowed to parade the Country without interruption, and commit all imaginable mischief. . . .
>
> What a change an additional regiment would make in this part of the Province!! Most of the people have lost all confidence. I however speak loud and look big. . . .

What a change actually did take place in four months! What happened to transform the discouraged and hopeless community of July into the bouncing, optimistic, almost self-complacent province of November? What had happened, of course, was that General Brock, defying discouragements that would have hamstrung a lesser man, had taken the offensive. He had moved west with his tiny central reserve, and with a force composed partly of regulars, partly of militia and partly of Indians, but whose most formidable component was the 41st Regiment, he captured Detroit and with it an American army. This extraordinary and quite unexpected victory changed the whole aspect of affairs in Upper Canada. Brock himself wrote soon afterwards, 'The militia have been inspired, by the recent success, with confidence – the disaffected are silenced.' The province's spirits were further raised by the triumph at Queenston Heights in October, even though this cost Brock's life; and Canadians surveying the remarkable change that had taken place in their fortunes, seem to have had comparatively little trouble in convincing themselves that their militia had done it all. I suspect that if Brock had lived to hear that 'Exhortation' delivered by John Strachan, it would have given him a lot of quiet amusement. He might have been even more surprised by the description of himself which I found last week in a new American history textbook: 'the brilliant Canadian General Isaac Brock'.

So much for that national legend. Another thing struck me still more forcibly as I read this yellow old volume published over 140 years ago. It presents a striking picture of a devastated province. Page after page of the appendices are lists of houses burned, property destroyed and people plundered, on the Niagara frontier, at Long Point, in the Talbot Settlement and elsewhere. We count up the 80 houses burned in the town of Niagara, the 14 houses burned in the village of St. Davids. (These two communities were victims of what were perhaps the most genuine 'atrocities' committed by the Americans in Upper Canada. They were exceptional, for the war in general was conducted in a fairly gentlemanly way. But let's face it: no war is very gentlemanly. Warfare is an essentially ungentlemanly activity.)

We read only too clearly, between the lines of the accounts of the society's gifts to the sufferers, the bitterness and anger of Upper Canadians against the invader who had brought these distresses upon them. We catch a suggestion or two of their delight in the 'retributive justice' visited by General Drummond upon the equally unfortunate inhabitants of the American shore of the Niagara. We realize suddenly what a miserable experience this war was for many of the people of this province. It was a far worse experience than anything England had in the Napoleonic Wars; for England was never invaded. It was an ordeal calculated to leave an enduring mark on the minds of the generation of Upper Canadians who had lived through the struggle.

I turn again to the *Report of the Loyal and Patriotic Society of Upper Canada*, to the lists of directors who attended the society's meetings; and I suddenly realize that what I am reading sounds like a roll-call of the Family Compact. The lists are full of the names of men who were members of the Legislative Council, or the Executive Council, or both, in the Compact's heyday. William Campbell, John Strachan, John Beverley Robinson, Peter Robinson, William Allan, Duncan Cameron, Thomas Ridout – one could go on much longer. These, and men like them, were the local leaders of Upper Canada during the war; and later they were the leaders of the Compact.

This was probably not accidental. It is quite likely that these men, who had helped to save Upper Canada, in the field and at the council table, in the greatest crisis in her history, felt themselves entitled to some gratitude and some privilege. But I think it likely that thev also felt that they knew more than other people about the facts of life in North America. The people who had lived through the invasions had no inclination to take any chances on the British connection, and it is not surprising that they made the maintenance of the connection the central feature of their political creed. The prospect of any violent breach with Britain was abhorrent to them, largely I suspect because they considered it would be tantamount to annexation to the United States.

It is interesting, too, to note that not all the names of the directors of the society are those of members of the Compact. We find among them also that of 'Doctor Baldwin'. William Warren Baldwin, we all know, was no Tory; neither was his son Robert. Both were reformers, but they were constitutional ones. The day was to come when a great Governor-General was to say of Robert Baldwin, 'I consider him of more importance to the [British] connexion than three regiments.' Is it mere fancy to suggest that the Baldwins' moderation owed something to a provincial political atmosphere strongly influenced by the war?

One name, of course, is missing from the roll. It could not possibly have been there, for William Lyon Mackenzie came to Canada only in 1820. He was brought up in the United Kingdom in a political atmosphere very different from that in which Robert Baldwin was nurtured, and one in which of course Canadian experience had no part: the atmosphere of radical reaction against Tory repression in the days before and after Waterloo. Mackenzie being the emotional character he was, it is at least possible that if he had shared the experiences of the people who were living in Upper Canada in 1812-15, his political career might have taken a quite different turn. I am almost tempted to suggest that he might have become a pillar of the Family Compact!

The American invasions of Canada in 1812-15 did much, I am sure, to prevent the ultimate annexation of the country to the United States. The Americans, if annexation can really be said to have been their policy, played their cards extraordinarily badly. Before 1812, Upper Canada was getting more American every year as settlers from the States poured across the border. If the United States had only held its hand and refrained from violence, it would have had an excellent chance of absorbing the country peacefully at an early date. But the unsuccessful and destructive invasions of 1812-14 reversed the whole trend. A deep prejudice against the United States was created, or perhaps it would be truer to say, was revived and intensified. All the forces in Canada making for the maintenance of the British connection were immeasurably strengthened. The events of the war years made the permanent survival of British North America much more probable.

Turning to domestic matters, I feel certain that the memory of the War of 1812 was enormously important in the political life of Upper Canada in the next generation. It loaded the dice against Upper Canadian political radicalism and in favour of conservatism. It did a very great deal to strengthen the Loyalist tradition. It provided the stuff of a nascent Canadian nationalism – and I do not doubt that the militia legend of which I spoke, however shaky its foundation in fact, itself made a very considerable contribution to national feeling.

After all, it was the sober truth that the colony had been successfully defended against heavy odds. Upper Canada had come through a fiery trial. Great deeds had been done, and good blood spilled, upon its soil; and future generations of Upper Canadians would look back to the years 1812-14 as a heroic age, whose symbol was the tall shaft they erected on the battlefield of Queenston Heights. It is experiences and memories like these that make nations.

FURTHER READING: H. Craig, 'The Loyal and Patriotic Society of Upper Canada and its still-born child – the "Upper Canada Preserved" medal', *Ontario History*, volume 52 (1960), pages 31-52; E. A. Cruikshank, 'Post-war discontent at Niagara in 1818', *Ontario Historical Society*, volume 29 (1933), pages 14-46; A. Dunham, *Political unrest in Upper Canada, 1815-36* (London, 1927); R. E. Saunders, 'What was the Family Compact?' *Ontario History*, volume 49 (1957), pages 165-78; G. F. G. Stanley, 'The contribution of the Canadian militia during the war', *After Tippecanoe* (P. P. Mason, ed.), pages 28-48.

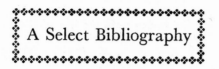

A Select Bibliography

Nearly every printed work in the field of American or Canadian history during the early nineteenth century touches in some fashion upon the War of 1812. The following list omits purely derivative or survey works as well as writings concerned with the fighting in the southern United States, Lower Canada, and the oceans, or the causes and consequences of the war for Anglo-American relations. Apart from a number of basic reference works this bibliography is restricted to those articles and books that deal with the impact of the war upon the region surrounding the Great Lakes, and Upper Canada in particular.

To avoid undue repetition items are listed only once even though their content might warrant their being included under several of the ten general categories. This should be kept in mind when seeking out references for a particular subject or aspect of the War of 1812 and Upper Canada.

A. GENERAL ACCOUNTS

ADAMS, HENRY. *The War of 1812.* Edited by H. A. De Weerd. Washington: The Infantry Journal, 1944.

An impartial and correct history of the war between the United States of America and Great Britain . . . carefully compiled from official documents. New York: John Low, 1816.

AUCHINLECK, GILBERT. *A history of the war between Great Britain and the United States, during the years 1812, 1813, and 1814.* Toronto: Maclear, 1855.

BEIRNE, FRANCIS F. *The War of 1812.* New York: E. P. Dutton, 1949.

BRACKENRIDGE, HENRY M. *History of the late war between the United States and Great Britain: containing a minute account of the various military and naval operations.* Baltimore: Cushing, 1817.

BROWN, SAMUEL R. *An authentic history of the second war for independence . . . .* 2 vols. Auburn, N.Y.: J. G. Hathway, 1815.

CHRISTIE, ROBERT. *A history of the late province of Lower Canada . . . .* 3 vols. Quebec: T. Cary, 1848. Vol. II.

———. *The military and naval operations in the Canadas, during the late war with the United States . . . .* Quebec: publisher not identified, 1818.

COFFIN, WILLIAM F. *1812; the war, and its moral: a Canadian chronicle.* Montreal: J. Lovell, 1864.

CRAIG, GERALD M. *Upper Canada; the formative years, 1784-1841*. ('The Canadian Centenary Series'.) Toronto: McClelland and Stewart, 1963.

CULLUM, GEORGE W. *Campaigns of the war of 1812-15, against Great Britain, sketched and criticised; with brief biographies of the American Engineers*. New York: James Miller, 1879.

DAVIS, PARIS M. *An authentic history of the late war between the United States and Great Britain* . . . . New York: E. F. Baker, 1836.

DAWSON, HENRY B. *Battles of the United States by sea and land: embracing those of the Revolutionary and Indian wars, the War of 1812, and the Mexican War*. 2 vols. New York: Johnson Fry, 1858. Vol. II.

FORTESCUE, SIR JOHN W. *A history of the British army*. 13 vols. London: Macmillan, 1910-35. Vols. VIII, IX and X.

GILLELAND, J. C. *History of the late war between the United States and Great Britain* . . . . Baltimore: Schaeffer and Maund, 1817.

HANNAY, JAMES. *History of the War of 1812, between Great Britain and the United States of America*. Saint John, N.B.: John A. Bowes, 1901.

HEADLEY, JOEL T. *The second war with England*. 2 vols. New York: C. Scribner, 1853.

INGERSOLL, CHARLES JARED. *Historical sketch of the second war between the United States of America and Great Britain* . . . . 2 vols. Philadelphia: Lea and Blanchard, 1845-9.

JOHNSON, ROSSITER. *A history of the war of 1812-15 between the United States and Great Britain*. New York: Dodd, Mead, 1882.

KINGSFORD, WILLIAM. *The history of Canada*. 10 vols. Toronto: Rowsell and Hutchison; and London: Trübner, 1887-98. Vol. VIII.

LOSSING, BENSON J. *The pictorial field-book of the War of 1812* . . . . New York: Harper and Brothers, 1869.

LUCAS, SIR CHARLES P. *The Canadian War of 1812*. Oxford: Clarendon, 1906.

MCAFEE, ROBERT. *History of the late war in the western country* . . . . Lexington, Ky.: Worsley and Smith, 1816.

MASON, PHILIP P. (ed.). *After Tippecanoe: some aspects of the War of 1812*. East Lansing: Michigan State University; and Toronto: Ryerson, 1963.

PAINE, RALPH D. *The fight for a free sea; a chronicle of the War of 1812*. ('The Chronicles of America'.) New Haven: Yale University, 1920.

PERKINS, SAMUEL. *A history of the political and military events of the late war between the United States and Great Britain*. New Haven: S. Converse, 1825.

RADDALL, THOMAS H. *The path of destiny: Canada from the British conquest to home rule, 1763-1850*. ('Canada History Series'.) Toronto: Doubleday, Canada, 1957.

RYERSON, ADOLPHUS EGERTON. *The loyalists of America and their times, from 1620 to 1816*. 2 vols. Toronto: W. Briggs, 1880.

SHORTT, ADAM, AND DOUGHTY, ARTHUR G. (eds.). *Canada and its provinces, a history of the Canadian people and their institutions* . . . . 23 vols. Edinburgh: printed for the Publishers' Association of Canada, 1914-17. Vol. III, etc.

STANLEY, GEORGE F. G. *Canada's soldiers, 1604-1954: the military history of an unmilitary people*. Revised edition. Toronto: Macmillan, 1960.

THOMPSON, DAVID. *History of the late war between Great Britain and the United States of America* . . . . Niagara, U. C.: T. Sewell, 1832.

THOMSON, JOHN LEWIS. *Historical sketches of the late war between the United States and Great Britain* . . . . Philadelphia: Desilver, 1818.

TUCKER, GLENN. *Poltroons and patriots; a popular account of the War of 1812.* 2 vols. Indianapolis: Bobbs-Merrill, [1954].

WOOD, WILLIAM C. H. *The war with the United States; a chronicle of 1812.* ('The Chronicles of Canada'.) Toronto: Glasgow, Brook, 1915.

B. PUBLISHED DOCUMENTARY COLLECTIONS.

(BOYD, JOHN PARKER). *Documents and facts relative to military events, during the late war.* Publisher not identified, [1816].

BRANNAN, JOHN (comp.). *Official letters of the military and naval officers of the United States, during the war with Great Britain in the years 1812, 13, 14, & 15.* Washington: Way and Gideon, 1823.

(BROCK, SIR ISAAC). 'District General Orders of Maj-Gen. Sir Isaac Brock from June 27th, 1812 - Oct. 16th, 1812', *Women's Canadian Historical Society of Toronto Transactions*, no. 19 (1920), 5-48.

Buffalo Historical Society. 'Papers relating to the burning of Buffalo, and to the Niagara frontier prior to and during the War of 1812', *Buffalo Historical Society Publications*, vol. 9 (1906), 309-406.

BULGER, ALFRED E. (ed.). 'The Bulger Papers', *State Historical Society of Wisconsin Collections*, vol. 13 (1895), 1-162.

CANADA. PUBLIC ARCHIVES. 'Anticipation of the War of 1812', *Public Archives of Canada Report for 1896* (1897), B, 24-75.

CRUIKSHANK, ERNEST A. (ed.). *Documents relating to the invasion of Canada and the surrender of Detroit.* ('Publications of the Canadian Archives', no. 7.) Ottawa: Government Printing Bureau, 1912.

———. (ed.). 'Documents relating to the invasion of the Niagara Peninsula by the United States army, commanded by General Jacob Brown, in July and August, 1814', *Niagara Historical Society Publications*, no. 33 (1920).

———. (ed.). 'Records of Niagara – a collection of contemporary letters and documents, 1812; and January to July 1813', *Niagara Historical Society Publications*, no. 43 (1934); and no. 44 (1939).

———. (ed.). *The documentary history of the campaign on the Niagara frontier . . . 1812 [-1814].* 9 vols. Welland: Lundy's Lane Historical Society, 1902-8.

'Dickson and Grignon papers, 1812-1815', *State Historical Society of Wisconsin Collections*, vol. 11 (1888), 270-315.

DOBBINS, WILLIAM W. (ed.). 'The Dobbins papers', *Buffalo Historical Society Publications*, vol. 8 (1905), 255-379.

FAY, HEMAN A. (comp.). *Collection of the official accounts in detail, of all the battles fought by sea and land between the navy and army of the United States and the navy and army of Great Britain during the years 1812, 13, 14 & 15.* New York: E. Conrad, 1817.

(HULL, WILLIAM.) *Report of the trial of Brig-General William Hull . . . by a court martial held at Albany on Monday, 3d January, 1814 and succeeding days, taken by Lieut.-Col. Forbes.* New York: Eastburn, Kirk, 1814.

(IZARD, GEORGE.) *Official correspondence with the Department of War, relative to the military operations of the American army under the command of Major-General Izard, on the northern frontier of the United States in the years 1814 and 1815.* Philadelphia: Thomas Dobson, 1816.

LONDON GAZETTE. *Bulletins of the campaign 1812*, etc. Westminster: R. G. Clarke, annual.

MICHIGAN PIONEER AND HISTORICAL SOCIETY. 'Copies of papers on file in the

Dominion archives at Ottawa, Canada, pertaining to Michigan, as found in the Colonial Office Records, Indian Affairs, and other official papers', *Michigan Pioneer and Historical Society Historical Collections*, vol. 23 (1893) and vol. 25 (1894).

———. 'Copies of papers on file in the Dominion archives at Ottawa, Canada, pertaining to the relations of the British government and the United States during the period of the War of 1812', *Michigan Pioneer and Historical Society Historical Collections*, vol. 15 (1890) and vol. 16 (1892).

MILLS, GEORGE H. (comp.). 'Documents relating to the battle of Stoney Creek', *Wentworth Historical Society Papers and Records*, vol. 2 (1899), 94-102.

MURRAY, JOHN M. (ed.). 'A recovered letter: W. W. Baldwin to C. B. Wyatt, 6th April, 1813', *Ontario Historical Society Papers and Records*, vol. 35 (1943), 49-55.

NILES' WEEKLY REGISTER. 30 vols. Baltimore, 1811-28. Volumes II-IX.

PALMER, T. H. (ed.). *The historical register of the United States.* 4 vols. Philadelphia: G. Palmer, 1814-16. Vols. I and II – From the declaration of war in 1812 to January 1, 1814; Vols. III and IV – For 1814.

PAULLIN, CHARLES O. (ed.). *The battle of Lake Erie, a collection of documents, chiefly by Commodore Perry . . . .* Cleveland: Rowfant Club, 1918.

QUAIFE, MILO M. (ed.). *The John Askin papers.* 2 vols. Detroit: Detroit Library Commission, 1928, 1931. Vol. II.

SEVERANCE, FRANK H. (ed.). 'Papers relating to the War of 1812 on the Niagara frontier', *Buffalo Historical Society Publications*, vol. 5 (1902), 21-109.

(SHEAFFE, ROGER HALE.) 'Documents relating to the War of 1812; the letter-book of Gen. Sir Roger Hale Sheaffe', *Buffalo Historical Society Publications*, vol. 17 (1913), 271-381.

SNIDER, CHARLES H. J. (ed.). *Leaves from the war log of the 'Nancy', eighteen hundred and thirteen.* Toronto: Rous and Mann, 1936.

SPRAGGE, GEORGE W. (ed.). *The John Strachan letter-book*, 1812-1834. Toronto: Ontario Historical Society, 1946.

STACEY, CHARLES P. (ed.). 'Upper Canada at war, 1814: Captain Armstrong reports', *Ontario History*, vol. 48 (1956), 37-42.

(TOMPKINS, DANIEL D.) *Public Papers of Daniel D. Tompkins, governor of New York 1807-1817, Military – Volumes I-III. With an introduction by Hugh Hastings, state historian.* New York, Albany: Wynkoop, Hallenbeck, Crawford, 1898-1902.

The War. Being a faithful record of the transactions of the war between the United States of America . . . and the United Kingdom . . . . Declared on the eighteenth day of June 1812. 3 vols. New York: published as a weekly by S. Woodworth.

UNITED STATES. *American State Papers, Volume 16. Class V: Military Affairs, Vol. I.* Washington: Gales and Seaton, 1832.

———. *American State Papers, Volume 23. Class VI: Naval Affairs.* Washington: Gales and Seaton, 1834.

———. Congress. House of Representatives. Committee appointed to enquire into the spirit and manner in which the war has been waged by the enemy. *Barbarities of the enemy exposed in a report . . . and the documents accompanying said report.* Worcester, Mass.: R. Dunnell, 1814.

———. President (James Madison). *Message from the President of the United States . . . in obedience to a resolution of the 31st of December last, requesting such information as may tend to explain the causes of the failure of the arms of the United States, on the northern frontier*. Albany: Websters and Skinners, and H. J. Southwick, 1814.

UPPER CANADA. Commissioners appointed to investigate the claims of certain inhabitants of this province for losses sustained by them during the late war with the United States of America, and for other purposes therein mentioned. *Report*. York, U. C.: J. Carey, [1825].

———. Legislative Assembly. 'Journals of Upper Canada: Legislative Assembly, 1812, 1814', *Ontario Bureau of Archives Report*, no. 9 (1912), 1-164.

———. Legislative Council. 'Journals of Upper Canada: Legislative Council, 1812, 1814', *Ontario Bureau of Archives Report*, no. 7 (1910), 399-457.

WESTERN RESERVE AND NORTHERN OHIO HISTORICAL SOCIETY. 'Papers relating to the War of 1812', *The Society Tracts,* nos. 1, 3, 7, 12, 15, 17, 18, 19, and 28 (1870-5).

WOOD, WILLIAM C. H. (ed.). *Select British documents of the Canadian War of 1812*. 3 vols. in 4. Toronto: Champlain Society, 1920-8.

C. ACCOUNTS BY PARTICIPANTS

(AN OHIO VOLUNTEER [JAMES FOSTER?]). 'The capitulation, or, A history of the expedition conducted by William Hull, Brigadier-General of the North-Western Army', in Milo M. Quaife (ed.), *War on the Detroit*. Chicago: Lakeside, 1940, 179-320.

ANDERSON, THOMAS G. 'Personal narrative of Capt. Thomas G. Anderson: early experiences in the north-west fur trade – British capture of Prairie du Chien, 1814', *State Historical Society of Wisconsin Collections*, vol. 9 (1880-2), 136-261.

ARMSTRONG, JOHN. *Notices of the War of 1812*. 2 vols. New York: G. Dearborn, 1836; and Wiley and Putnam, 1840.

ATHERTON, WILLIAM. *Narrative of the suffering & defeat of the north-western army under General Winchester* . . . . Frankfort, Ky.: A. G. Hodges, 1842.

BOURNE, COL. ALEXANDER. 'The siege of Fort Meigs, year 1813: An eye-witness account by Colonel Alexander Bourne', *Northwest Ohio Quarterly*, vol. 17 (1945), 139-54, and vol. 18 (1946), 39-48.

BROWN, SAMUEL R. *Views of the campaigns of the north-western army*. . . . Philadelphia: William G. Murphey, 1815.

BULGER, ANDREW H. *An autobiographical sketch of the services of the late Captain Andrew Bulger of the Royal Newfoundland fencible regiment*. Bangalore, India: Regimental Press, 1865.

BURGES, TRISTAM. *Battle of Lake Erie, with notices of Commodore Elliot's conduct in that engagement*. Philadelphia: W. Marshall, 1839.

(BYFIELD, SHADRACK.) *A narrative of a light company soldier's service in the 41st regiment of foot during the late American war, together with some adventures amongst the Indian tribes, from 1812 to 1814*. Bradford, Wilts.: John Bubb, 1840.

CROOKS, JAMES. 'Recollections of War of 1812', *Niagara Historical Society Publications*, no. 28 (n.d.), 28-41.

CRUIKSHANK, ERNEST A. (ed.). 'Campaigns of 1812-14; contemporary narratives by Captain W. H. Merritt, Colonel William Claus, Lieut.-Colonel Matthew Elliott and Captain John Norton', *Niagara Historical Society Publications*, no. 9 (1902).

Darnell, Elias. *A journal containing an accurate and interesting account of the hardships, sufferings, battles, defeat and captivity of those heroic Kentucky volunteers and regulars, commanded by General Winchester, in the years 1812-13* . . . . Philadelphia: Lippincott, Grambo, 1854.

Douglass, David B. 'Reminiscences of the campaign of 1814, on the Niagara frontier', *Historical Magazine*, Series Three, vol. 2 (1873), 1-12, 65-76, 127-42, 216-24.

Dunlop, Dr. William. *Recollections of the American war, 1812-14.* Toronto: Historical Publishing, 1905.

Finan, Patrick. *Journal of a voyage to Quebec in the year 1825, with Recollections of Canada during the late American war, in the years, 1812-13.* Newry, Ireland: Alexander Peacock, 1828.

Grignon, Augustin. 'Seventy-two years' recollections of Wisconsin', *State Historical Society of Wisconsin Collections*, vol. 3 (1856), 197-295.

(Hamilton, Robert). 'The expeditions of Major-General Samuel Hopkins up the Wabash, 1812: the letters of Captain Robert Hamilton', *Indiana Magazine of History*, vol. 43 (1947), 393-402.

Hatch, William S. *A chapter in the history of the War of 1812 in the Northwest . . . with a description and biographical sketch of the celebrated Indian chief Tecumseh.* Cincinnati: Miami Printing and Publishing, 1872.

Hull, William. *Defence of Brigadier-General W. Hull. Delivered before the general court martial . . . at Albany, March, 1814* . . . . Boston: Wells and Lilly, 1814.

———. *Memoirs of the campaign of the north western army of the United States, A.D. 1812* . . . . Boston: True and Greene, 1824.

Lethbridge, Robert. 'Despatch from Colonel Lethbridge to Major-General Brock, by Lieut.-Colonel Cole', *Ontario Historical Society Papers and Records*, vol. 10 (1913), 57-9.

Lord, Norman C. (ed.). 'The war on the Canadian frontier, 1812-14; letters written by Sergt. James Commins, 8th Foot', *Journal of the Society for Army Historical Research*, vol. 18 (1939), 199-211.

Lucas, Robert. *The Robert Lucas journal of the War of 1812 during the campaign under General William Hull.* Edited by John C. Parish. Iowa City: State Historical Society, 1906.

Merritt, William Hamilton. *Journal of events principally on the Detroit and Niagara frontiers, during the War of 1812.* St. Catharines: Historical Society, 1863.

Parsons, Usher. *Battle of Lake Erie; a discourse delivered before the Rhode-Island Historical Society, on the evening of Monday, February 16, 1852.* Providence: Benjamin S. Albro, 1854.

Procter, Henry A. *Defence of Major-General Proctor, tried at Montreal by a general court martial upon charges affecting his character as a soldier* . . . . Montreal: John Lovell, 1842.

Richardson, John. *The War of 1812*, with notes and a life of the author by A. C. Casselman. Toronto: Historical Publishing, 1902.

Ritchie, M. K. and C. 'A Laker's Log', *American Neptune*, vol. 17 (1957), 203-11.

Scott, Winfield. *Memoirs of Lieut.-General Scott, written by himself.* 2 vols. New York: Sheldon, 1864.

Severance, Frank H. 'The case of Brig.-Gen. Alexander Smyth, as shown by his own writings . . .', *Buffalo Historical Society Publications*, vol. 18 (1914), 213-55.

SHAW, JOHN. 'Personal narrative of Col. John Shaw, of Marquette County, Wisconsin', *State Historical Society of Wisconsin Collections*, vol. 2 (1855), app. 7, 197-232.

VAN RENSSELAER, SOLOMON. *A narrative of the affair of Queenston in the War of 1812* . . . . New York: Leavitt, Lord, 1836.

VERCHÈRES DE BOUCHERVILLE, THOMAS. 'The journal of Thomas Verchères de Boucherville', in Milo M. Quaife (ed.), *War on the Detroit.* Chicago: Lakeside, 1940, 3-178.

(VIGER, JACQUES.) *Reminiscences of the war of 1812-14, being portions of the diary of a captain of the 'Voltigeurs canadiens' while in garrison at Kingston, etc.* Translated from the French by J. L. Herbert Neilson. Kingston, Ont.: News Printing, 1895.

WALKER, ADAM. *A journal of two campaigns of the Fourth regiment of U.S. infantry, in the Michigan and Indiana territories, under the command of Col. John P. Boyd, and Lt. Col. James Miller during the years 1811, & 12.* Keene, N.H.: the author, 1816.

WHITE, SAMUEL. *History of the American troops during the late war, under the command of Cols. Fenton and Campbell* . . . . Baltimore: the author, 1829.

WHITTLESEY, CHARLES. 'Gen. Wadsworth's division, War of 1812', *Western Reserve and Northern Ohio Historical Society*, Tract no. 51 (1879), 115-23.

WILKINSON, JAMES. *Memoirs of my own times.* 3 vols. Philadelphia: Abraham Small, 1816.

WILLIAMS, MENTOR L. 'John Kinzie's narrative of the Fort Dearborn massacre', *Journal of the Illinois State Historical Society*, vol. 46 (1953), 343-62.

(WINCHESTER, JAMES.) *Historical details, having relation to the campaign of the north-western army, under Generals Harrison and Winchester, during the winter of 1812-13* . . . . Lexington, Ky.: Worsley and Smith, 1818.

WITHERELL, B. F. H. 'Reminiscences of the north-west', *State Historical Society of Wisconsin Collections*, vol. 3 (1856), 299-336.

WOOD, ELEAZER D. 'Journal of the Northwestern campaign of 1812-13 under Major-General William H. Harrison', in George W. Cullum, *Campaigns of the war of 1812-15* . . . . New York: James Miller, 1879, 362-412.

D. BIOGRAPHIES

BETHUNE, ALEXANDER N. *Memoir of the Right Reverend John Strachan, D.D., LL.D., first bishop of Toronto.* Toronto: Rowsell, 1870.

BOND, BEVERLEY W. 'William Henry Harrison in the War of 1812', *Mississippi Valley Historical Review*, vol. 13 (1926-7), 499-516.

(BRENTON, E. B.?). *Some account of the public life of the late Lieutenant-General Sir George Prevost, bart., particularly of his services in the Canadas* . . . . London: Cadell, 1823.

BURT, A. BLANCHE. 'Sketch of Captain Robert Heriott Barclay, R. N.', *Ontario Historical Society Papers and Records*, vol. 14 (1916), 169-78.

CAMPBELL, MARIA. *Revolutionary services and civil life of General William Hull* . . . . New York: D. Appleton, 1848.

COLQUHOUN, A. H. U. 'The career of Joseph Willcocks', *Canadian Historical Review*, vol. 7 (1926), 287-93.

CRAMER, C. H. 'Duncan McArthur: the military phase', *Ohio State Archaeological and Historical Quarterly*, vol. 46 (1937), 128-47.

CRUIKSHANK, ERNEST A. 'A sketch of the public life and services of Robert Nichol . . .', *Ontario Historical Society Papers and Records*, vol. 19 (1922), 6-81.

———. 'Additional correspondence of Robert Nichol', *Ontario Historical Society Papers and Records*, vol. 26 (1930), 37-96.

———. 'Robert Dickson, the Indian trader', *State Historical Society of Wisconsin Collections*, vol. 12 (1892), 133-53.

———. 'Sir Gordon Drummond, K.C.B.', *Ontario Historical Society Papers and Records*, vol. 29 (1933), 8-13.

———. 'The military career and character of Major-General Sir Isaac Brock', *New York State Historical Association Proceedings*, Albany, vol. 7 (1909), 67-90.

CURRIE, EMMA A. *The story of Laura Secord and Canadian reminiscences*. St. Catharines: publisher not identified, 1913.

CURZON, SARAH ANNE. 'The story of Laura Secord, 1813', *Lundy's Lane Historical Society Publications*, vol. 1, part 9 (1891).

DRAKE, BENJAMIN. *Life of Tecumseh, and of his brother the prophet . . . .* Cincinnati: E. Morgan, 1841.

DUTTON, CHARLES J. *Oliver Hazard Perry*. New York and Toronto: Longmans, Green, 1935.

EAYRS, HUGH S. *Sir Isaac Brock*. ('Canadian Men of Action'.) Toronto: Macmillan, 1924.

EDGAR, MATILDA RIDOUT. *General Brock*. ('The Makers of Canada'.) Toronto: Morang, 1904.

ELLIOTT, CHARLES W. *Winfield Scott, the soldier and the man*. New York: Macmillan, 1937.

FITZGIBBON, MARY AGNES. *A veteran of 1812; the life of James FitzGibbon*. Toronto: W. Briggs, 1894.

GOEBEL, DOROTHY B. 'William Henry Harrison, a political biography', *Indiana Historical Collections*, vol. 14 (1926).

GURD, NORMAN S. *The story of Tecumseh*. ('Canadian Heroes Series'.) Toronto: W. Briggs, 1912.

HITSMAN, J. MACKAY. 'Sir George Prevost's conduct of the Canadian War of 1812', *Canadian Historical Association Report*, 1962, 34-43.

INGERSOLL, JAMES H. 'The ancestry of Laura Ingersoll Secord', *Ontario Historical Society Papers and Records*, vol. 23 (1926), 360-64.

JACOBS, JAMES R. *Tarnished warrior; Major-General James Wilkinson*. New York: Macmillan, 1938.

JENKINS, JOHN S. *The generals of the last war with Great Britain*. (Biographies of Jacob Brown, E. P. Gaines, W. H. Harrison, Andrew Jackson, Alexander Macomb, Z. M. Pike, and Winfield Scott.) Auburn, N.Y.: Derby, Miller, 1849.

JONES, F. L. 'A subaltern of 1812', FitzGibbon, *Canadian Army Journal*, vol. 9, no. 3 (July 1955), 59-68.

JOSEPHY, ALVIN R., JR. *The patriot chiefs; a chronicle of American Indian leadership*. ('Tecumseh, the greatest Indian', 129-74.) New York: Viking, 1961.

KLINCK, CARL F. (ed.). *Tecumseh: fact and fiction in early records*. Englewood Cliffs, N.J.: Prentice-Hall, 1961.

LAMB, W. KAYE. 'Sir Isaac Brock: the hero of Queenston Heights', in Philip P.

Mason (ed.), *After Tippecanoe*. East Lansing: Michigan State University; and Toronto: Ryerson, 1963, 17-27.

———. *The hero of Upper Canada*. Toronto: Rous and Mann, 1962.

LYMAN, OLIN L. *Commodore Oliver Hazard Perry and the war on the lakes*. New York: New Amsterdam Book, 1905.

MACDONELL, J. A. 'Major-General Sir Isaac Brock, K.B.', *Ontario Historical Society Papers and Records*, vol. 10 (1913), 5-32.

MACKENZIE, ALEX S. *Commodore Perry . . . his life and achievements*. (Written in 1840.) Akron: J. K. Richardson and sons, 1910.

METCALF, CLARENCE S. 'Daniel Dobbins, Sailing Master, U.S.N., Commodore Perry's right-hand man', *Inland Seas*, vol. 14 (1958), 88-96, 181-91.

MEYER, LELAND W. *The life and times of Colonel Richard M. Johnson of Kentucky*. New York: Columbia University, 1932.

MILLS, JAMES C. *Oliver Hazard Perry and the battle of Lake Erie*. Detroit: John Philps, 1913.

MUIR, ROBERT C. 'Burford's first settler, politician and military man – Benajah Mallory', *Ontario Historical Society Papers and Records*, vol. 26 (1930), 492-7.

MURRAY, JOHN M. 'John Norton', *Ontario Historical Society Papers and Records*, vol. 37 (1945), 7-16.

NILES, JOHN M. *The life of Oliver Hazard Perry, with an appendix, comprising biographical sketches of the late General Pike and Captain Lawrence, etc. . . .* Hartford: William S. Marsh, 1820.

NURSEY, W. R. *The story of Isaac Brock, hero, defender and saviour of Upper Canada, 1812*. ('Canadian Heroes Series'.) Toronto: W. Briggs, 1908.

OSKISON, JOHN M. *Tecumseh and his times: the story of a great Indian*. New York: G. P. Putnam's Sons, 1938.

PARSONS, USHER. 'Brief sketches of the officers who were in the battle of Lake Erie', *Inland Seas*, vol. 19 (1963), 172-89.

PRATT, FLETCHER. 'Sword of the border', (General Jacob Brown). *Infantry Journal*, vol. 44 (1937), 387-93.

QUAIFE, MILO M. 'An artilleryman of old Fort Mackinac', (James Keating). *Burton Historical Collection Leaflets*, vol. 6, no. 3 (1928), 33-48.

READ, DAVID B. *Life and times of Major-General Sir Isaac Brock, K.B.* Toronto: W. Briggs, 1894.

REDWAY, JACQUES W. 'General Van Rensselaer and the Niagara frontier', *New York State Historical Association Proceedings*, vol. 8 (1909), 14-22.

RICHARDS, GEORGE H. *Memoir of Alexander Macomb, the major-general commanding the army of the United States*. New York: McElrath, Bangs, 1833.

RIDDELL, WILLIAM RENWICK. 'Benajah Mallory, traitor', *Ontario Historical Society Papers and Records*, vol. 26 (1930), 573-8.

———. 'Joseph Willcocks, sheriff, member of parliament and traitor', *Ontario Historical Society Papers and Records*, vol. 24 (1927), 475-99.

ROBINSON, SIR CHARLES W. *Life of Sir John Beverley Robinson, bart., C.B., D.C.L. . . .* Toronto: Morang, 1904.

SMITH, ARTHUR D. H. *Old fuss and feathers: the life and exploits of Lt.-General Winfield Scott . . . .* New York: Greystone, 1937.

THOMPSON, MABEL W. 'Billy Green, the scout', *Ontario History*, vol. 44 (1952), 173-82.

TUCKER, GLENN. *Tecumseh, vision of glory*. Indianapolis: Bobbs-Merrill, 1956.

TUPPER, FREDERICK BROCK. *The life and correspondence of Major-General Sir*

Isaac Brock, K.B. . . . Second edition. London: Simpkin, Marshall, 1847.

WALLACE, W. STEWART. *The story of Laura Secord; a study in historical evidence.* Toronto: Macmillan, 1932.

WILLIAMS, CHARLES R. 'George Croghan', *Ohio Archaeological and Historical Society Publications,* vol. 12 (1903), 375-409.

E. THE ORIGINS OF THE WAR (as pertaining to Upper Canada)

BURT, ALFRED LEROY. *The United States, Great Britain, and British North America from the revolution to the establishment of peace after the War of 1812.* ('The Relations of Canada and the United States'.) New Haven: Yale University, 1940.

CREIGHTON, DONALD GRANT. *The commercial empire of the St. Lawrence, 1760-1850.* Toronto: Ryerson, 1937. Republished as 'The empire of the St. Lawrence'. Macmillan, 1956.

CRUIKSHANK, ERNEST A. 'The "Chesapeake" crisis as it affected Upper Canada', *Ontario Historical Society Papers and Records,* vol. 24 (1927), 281-322.

GOODMAN, WARREN H. 'The origins of the War of 1812: a survey of changing interpretations', *Mississippi Valley Historical Review,* vol. 28 (1941-2), 171-86.

HACKER, LOUIS M. 'Western land hunger and the War of 1812: a conjecture', *Mississippi Valley Historical Review,* vol. 10 (1923-4), 365-95.

HORSMAN, REGINALD. 'British Indian policy in the Northwest, 1807-1812', *Mississippi Valley Historical Review,* vol. 45 (1958-9), 51-66.

———. *The causes of the War of 1812.* Philadelphia: University of Pennsylvania, 1962.

———. 'Western war aims, 1811-12', *Indiana Magazine of History,* vol. 53 (1957), 1-18.

KELLOGG, LOUISE P. *The British régime in Wisconsin and the Northwest.* Madison: State Historical Society of Wisconsin, 1925.

PERKINS, BRADFORD. *Prologue to war; England and the United States, 1805-12.* Berkeley and Los Angeles: University of California, 1961.

———. (ed.). *The causes of the War of 1812: national honor or national interest?* ('American Problem Studies'.) New York: Holt, Rinehart and Winston, 1962.

PRATT, JULIUS WILLIAM. *Expansionists of 1812.* New York: Macmillan, 1925.

———. 'Western aims in the War of 1812', *Mississippi Valley Historical Review,* vol. 12 (1925-6), 36-50.

UTTER, WILLIAM T. 'The coming of the war', in Philip P. Mason (ed.), *After Tippecanoe.* East Lansing: Michigan State University; and Toronto: Ryerson, 1963, 9-16.

F. ACCOUNTS OF THE MILITARY CAMPAIGNS

BABCOCK, LOUIS L. 'The siege of Fort Erie', *New York State Historical Association Proceedings,* vol. 8 (1909), 38-59.

———. *The War of 1812 on the Niagara frontier.* Buffalo: Buffalo Historical Society, 1927.

BAYLISS, JOSEPH AND ESTELLE. *Historic St. Joseph Island.* Cedar Rapids, Iowa: Torch, 1938.

BUELL, WILLIAM S. 'Military movements in eastern Ontario during the War of 1812', *Ontario Historical Society Papers and Records,* vol. 10 (1913), 60-71.

CLARK, THOMAS D. 'Kentucky in the Northwest campaign', in Philip P. Mason (ed.), *After Tippecanoe*. East Lansing: Michigan State University; and Toronto: Ryerson, 1963, 78-98.

CLARKE, JAMES FREEMAN. 'History of the campaign of 1812, and surrender of the post of Detroit', in Maria Campbell, *Revolutionary services and civil life of General William Hull*. New York: D. Appleton, 1848, 295-482.

CLEARY, FRANCIS. 'Defence of Essex during the War of 1812', *Ontario Historical Society Papers and Records*, vol. 10 (1913), 72-8.

COUTTS, KATHERINE B. 'Thamesville and the battle of the Thames, October 5, 1813', *Ontario Historical Society Papers and Records*, vol. 9 (1910), 20-5.

CRUIKSHANK, ERNEST A. 'Battle of Fort George, 27th May, 1813', *Niagara Historical Society Publications*, no. 1 (1896).

———. 'The battle of Lundy's Lane, 25th July, 1814', *Lundy's Lane Historical Society Publications*, vol. 1, part 7 (1893).

———. 'The battle of Queenston Heights', *Lundy's Lane Historical Society Publications*, vol. 1, part 4 (1891).

———. 'The battle of Stoney Creek and the blockade of Fort George, 1813', *Niagara Historical Society Publications*, no. 3 (1898).

———. 'Battle-fields of the Niagara peninsula during the war 1812-15', *Canadian Military Institute, Welland, Selected Papers*, no. 2 (1890-1), 25-48.

———. 'Drummond's winter campaign, 1813', *Lundy's Lane Historical Society Publications*, vol. 1, part 3 (n.d.).

———. 'The fight in the beechwoods, a study in Canadian history', *Lundy's Lane Historical Society Publications*, vol. 1, part 6 (1895).

———. 'General Hull's invasion of Canada in 1812', *Royal Society of Canada Transactions*, series 3, vol. 1 (1907), section 2, 211-90.

———. 'Harrison and Procter; the River Raisin', *Royal Society of Canada Transactions*, series 3, vol. 4 (1910), section 2, 119-67.

———. 'The siege of Fort Erie, August 1 - September 23, 1814', *Lundy's Lane Historical Society Publications*, vol. 1, part 14 (1905).

———. (ed.). 'Laura Secord's walk to warn FitzGibbon', *Niagara Historical Society Publications*, no. 36 (1924), 64-74.

CUMBERLAND, FREDERIC B. *The battle of York; an account of the eight hours' battle from the Humber Bay to the old fort in the defence of York on 27th April, 1813*. Toronto: W. Briggs, 1913.

CURRY, FREDERICK C. 'Little Gibraltar', *Ontario Historical Society Papers and Records*, vol. 33 (1939), 39-44.

ERMATINGER, CHARLES O. Z. 'The retreat of Proctor and Tecumseh', *Ontario Historical Society Papers and Records*, vol. 17 (1919), 11-21.

GILPIN, ALEC RICHARD. *The War of 1812 in the old Northwest*. Toronto: Ryerson, 1958.

HAMIL, FRED COYNE. 'Michigan in the War of 1812', *Michigan History*, vol. 44 (1960), 257-91.

HEFLINGER, W. M. 'The War of 1812 in northwestern Ohio: the year of disaster', *Northwest Ohio Quarterly*, vol. 22 (1950), 158-72.

———. 'The War of 1812 in northwestern Ohio: the year of victory', *Northwest Ohio Quarterly*, vol. 23 (1951), 195-210.

HORSMAN, REGINALD. 'Wisconsin and the War of 1812', *Wisconsin Magazine of History*, vol. 46 (1962), 3-15.

HOUGH, FRANKLIN B. *A history of St. Lawrence and Franklin counties, New York, from the earliest period to the present time*. Albany: Little, 1853.

James, William. *A full and correct account of the military occurrences of the late war between Great Britain and the United States of America.* 2 vols. London: Black, 1818.

Johnston, Charles M. *A battle for the Heartland: Stoney Creek, 6 June 1813.* Stoney Creek: Pennell Printing, 1963.

———. *The head of the lake; a history of Wentworth County.* Hamilton, Ont.: Wentworth County Council, 1958.

Jones, F. L. 'The Long Woods', *Canadian Army Journal*, vol. 12, no. 2 (April 1958), 64-76.

Kellogg, Louise P. 'The capture of Mackinac in 1812', *State Historical Society of Wisconsin Proceedings*, 1912 (1913), 124-45.

Ketchum, Mrs. J. 'The battle of Lundy's Lane', *Women's Canadian Historical Society of Ottawa Transactions*, vol. 1 (1901), 168-72.

Kirby, William. *Annals of Niagara.* Welland, Ont.: Lundy's Lane Historical Society, 1896.

Land, J. H. 'The battle of Stoney Creek', *Wentworth Historical Society*, vol. 1 (1892), 21-7.

Landon, Harry F. *Bugles on the border.* Watertown, N.Y.: Watertown Daily Times, 1954.

Lauriston, Victor. 'The case for General Procter', *Kent Historical Society Papers and Addresses*, vol. 7 (1951), 7-17.

Lindley, H. (ed.). 'Captain Cushing in the War of 1812', *Ohio Historical Collections*, vol. 11 (1944).

Mather, J. D. 'The capture of Fort Niagara, 19 December 1813', *Canadian Defence Quarterly*, vol. 3 (1925-6), 271-5.

Near, I. W. 'The causes and results of the failure of the American campaigns on the Niagara frontier in the second war with England', *New York State Historical Association Proceedings*, vol. 8 (1909), 91-102.

Oman, Sir Charles. *Studies in the Napoleonic Wars.* London: Methuen, 1929.

Pearkes, George R. 'Detroit and Miami', *Canadian Defence Quarterly*, vol. 11 (1933-4), 456-66.

Pratt, Julius William. 'Fur trade strategy and the American left flank in the War of 1812', *American Historical Review*, vol. 40 (1934-5), 246-73.

Quaife, Milo M. *Chicago and the old Northwest, 1673-1835.* Chicago: University of Chicago, 1913.

———. 'The story of Brownstown', *Burton Historical Collection Leaflets*, vol. 4, no. 5 (1926), 65-80.

Rheaume, Mme. 'Battle of Chrysler's Farm', *Women's Canadian Historical Society of Ottawa Transactions*, vol. 1 (1906), 173-6.

Sellar, Robert. *The U.S. campaign of 1813 to capture Montreal: Crysler, the decisive battle of the War of 1812.* Huntingdon, Que.: Gleaner, 1913.

Stacey, Charles P. *The battle of Little York.* Toronto: Toronto Historical Board, 1963.

Stanley, George F. G. 'British operations in the American north-west 1812-1815', *Journal of the Society for Army Historical Research*, vol. 22, no. 87 (1943), 91-106.

Wilner, Merton M. *Niagara frontier: a narrative and documentary history.* 4 vols. Chicago: S. J. Clarke, 1931. Vols. I and II.

Young, Bennett H. 'The battle of the Thames, in which Kentuckians defeated the British, French, and Indians . . .', *Filson Club Publications*, no. 18 (1903).

G. THE WAR ON THE LAKES

BREITHAUPT, WILLIAM H. 'Some facts about the schooner "Nancy" in the War of 1812', *Ontario Historical Society Papers and Records*, vol. 23 (1926), 5-7.

CHAPELLE, HOWARD I. *The history of the American sailing navy*. New York: Norton, 1949.

CRUIKSHANK, ERNEST A. 'An episode of the War of 1812, the story of the schooner "Nancy" ', *Ontario Historical Society Papers and Records*, vol. 9 (1910), 75-126.

———. 'The contest for the command of Lake Erie in 1812-1813', *(Royal) Canadian Institute Transactions*, vol. 6 (1899), 359-86.

———. 'The contest for the command of Lake Ontario in 1812 and 1813', *Royal Society of Canada Transactions*, series 3, vol. 10 (1916), section 2, 161-223.

———. 'The contest for the command of Lake Ontario in 1814', *Ontario Historical Society Papers and Records*, vol. 21 (1924), 99-159.

CUMBERLAND, FREDERIC. 'The navies on Lake Ontario in the War of 1812 . . .', *Ontario Historical Society Papers and Records*, vol. 8 (1907), 124-42.

CURRY, FREDERICK C. 'Six little schooners', *Inland Seas*, vol. 2 (1946), 185-90.

CUTHBERTSON, GEORGE A. *Freshwater, a history and a narrative of the Great Lakes*. Toronto: Macmillan, 1931.

DOBBINS, WILLIAM W. *History of the battle of Lake Erie (September 10, 1813), and reminiscences of the flagships 'Lawrence' and 'Niagara'*. Erie, Penna.: Ashby Printing, 1913.

FORESTER, C. S. *The age of fighting sail: the story of the naval War of 1812*. Garden City, N.Y.: Doubleday, 1956.

HANFORD, FRANKLIN. *Notes on the visits of American and British naval vessels to the Genesee River, 1809-1814*. Rochester, N.Y.: Genesee, 1911.

HATCHER, HARLAN. *Lake Erie*. ('The American Lakes Series'.) Indianapolis: Bobbs-Merrill, 1945.

HITSMAN, J. MACKAY. 'Alarum on Lake Ontario, winter 1812-1813', *Military Affairs*, vol. 23 (1959), 129-38.

———. 'Spying at Sackets Harbor, 1813', *Inland Seas*, vol. 15 (1959), 120-2.

JAMES, WILLIAM. *A full and correct account of the chief naval occurrences of the late war between Great Britain and the United States of America* . . . . London: Egerton, 1817.

LANDON, FRED. *Lake Huron*. ('The American Lakes Series'.) Indianapolis: Bobbs-Merrill, 1944.

MACLAY, EDGAR S. *A history of the United States Navy from 1775 to 1901*. 3 vols. New York: D. Appleton, 1907-10. Vol. I.

MACPHERSON, R. R. 'List of vessels employed on British naval service on the Great Lakes, 1755-1875', *Ontario History*, vol. 55 (1963), 173-9.

MAHAN, ALFRED THAYER. *Sea power in its relations to the War of 1812*. 2 vols. Boston: Little, Brown; and London: Sampson Low, Marston, 1905.

'PERRY'S VICTORY CENTENNIAL NUMBER', *Journal of American History*, vol. 8, no. 1 (1914).

POUND, ARTHUR. *Lake Ontario*. ('The American Lakes Series'.) Indianapolis: Bobbs-Merrill, 1945.

PRESTON, RICHARD A. 'The first battle of Sackets Harbor', *Historic Kingston*, no. 11 (1963), 3-7.

ROOSEVELT, THEODORE. *The naval war of 1812* . . . . New York: G. P. Putnam's Sons, 1883.

SNIDER, CHARLES H. J. *In the wake of the eighteen-twelvers* . . . . London: John Lane, 1913.

———. *The story of the 'Nancy', and other eighteen-twelvers.* Toronto: McClelland and Stewart, [1926].

STACEY, CHARLES P. 'Commodore Chauncey's attack on Kingston Harbour, November 10, 1812', *Canadian Historical Review*, vol. 32 (1951), 126-38.

———. 'Naval power on the Lakes', in Philip P. Mason (ed.), *After Tippecanoe.* East Lansing: Michigan State University; and Toronto: Ryerson, 1963, 49-59.

———. 'The ships of the British squadron on Lake Ontario, 1812-14', *Canadian Historical Review*, vol. 34 (1953), 311-23.

'WINTON-CLARE, C.' (Dr. R. C. Anderson). 'A shipbuilder's war', *Mariner's Mirror*, vol. 29 (1943), 139-48.

H. THE MEN UNDER ARMS

BEAL, VERNON L. 'John McDonnell and the ransoming of American captives after the River Raisin massacre', *Michigan History*, vol. 35 (1951), 331-51.

BRADY, WILLIAM Y. 'The 22nd Regiment in the War of 1812', *Western Pennsylvania Historical Magazine*, vol. 32 (1949), 56-60.

CALLAHAN, EDWARD W. *List of officers of the navy of the United States and of the Marine corps from 1775 to 1900 . . . compiled from the official records of the Navy Department.* New York: L. R. Hamersly, 1901.

CANADA. DEPARTMENT OF MILITIA AND DEFENCE. *Statement showing the name, age, and residence of militiamen of 1812-15 who have applied to participate in the gratuity voted by Parliament in 1875, with the name of the corps or division and rank in which they served.* Ottawa: Maclean, Roger, 1876.

CHAMBERS, ERNEST J. *The Canadian militia, a history of the origin and development of the force.* Montreal: L. M. Fresco, 1907.

CRUIKSHANK, ERNEST A. 'Record of the services of Canadian regiments in the War of 1812 – I, The Royal Newfoundland Regiment; II, The Glengarry Light Infantry; III, The 104th Regiment; IV, The Provincial Cavalry; V, The Incorporated Militia; VI, The Canadian Voltigeurs; VII, The Canadian Fencibles; VIII, The Frontier Light Infantry; IX, The Lincoln Militia; X, The Militia of Essex and Kent; XI, The Militia of Norfolk, Oxford, and Middlesex; XII, The York Militia (12 parts)', *Canadian Military Institute, Welland, Selected Papers*, nos. 5 to 16 (1893-4 to 1908): 5-15 (1893-4); 9-23 (1894-5); 9-20 (1895-6); 9-26 (1896-7); 70-80 (1897-9); 9-21 (1899-1900); 9-22 (1901); 9-19 (1902); 9-41 (1904); 43-60 (1906); 47-71 (1907); 31-54 (1908).

———. 'The employment of Indians in the War of 1812', *American Historical Association Annual Report*, 1895, 319-35.

———. 'The garrisons of Toronto and York, 1750-1815', *Canadian Military Institute, Toronto, Selected Papers*, no. 31 (1934-5), 17-65.

CUMMINS, J. F. 'Notes on the military history of Toronto', *Canadian Defence Quarterly*, vol. 5 (1927-8), 478-85.

DOUGLAS, JOHN. *Medical topography of Upper Canada.* London: Burgess and Hill, 1819.

GREAT BRITAIN. ADMIRALTY. *The navy list.* London: John Murray, etc., annual.

———. WAR OFFICE. *List of the officers of the army and royal marines on full and half pay* (title varies). London: various publishers, annual.

GREEN, ERNEST. 'Upper Canada's black defenders', *Ontario Historical Society Papers and Records*, vol. 27 (1931), 365-91.

HAMILTON, C. F. 'The Canadian militia: universal service', *Canadian Defence Quarterly*, vol. 5 (1927-8), 288-300.

HORSMAN, REGINALD. 'The role of the Indian in the war', in Philip P. Mason (ed.), *After Tippecanoe*. East Lansing: Michigan State University, and Toronto: Ryerson, 1963, 60-77.

HUNTER, A. T. 'How Upper Canada was saved in the War of 1812', *Canadian Defence Quarterly*, vol. 8 (1930-1), 400-4.

IRVING, L. HOMFRAY. *Officers of the British forces in Canada during the war of 1812-15*. Welland, Ont.: Tribune Print, 1908.

KOKE, RICHARD J. 'The Britons who fought on the Canadian frontier: uniforms of the War of 1812', *New York Historical Society Quarterly*, vol. 45 (1961), 141-94.

KYTE, E. C. 'Fort Niagara in the War of 1812: side-lights from an unpublished order-book', *Canadian Historical Review*, vol. 17 (1936), 373-84.

LOMAX, D. A. N. *A history of the services of the 41st (the Welch) Regiment . . . from its formation, in 1719 to 1895*. Devonport, England: Hiorns and Miller, 1899.

MANN, JAMES. *Medical sketches of the campaign of 1812, 13, 14 . . . .* Dedham, Mass.: H. Mann, 1816.

MARTIN, JOHN D. P. 'The Regiment de Watteville: its settlement and service in Upper Canada', *Ontario History*, vol. 52 (1960), 17-30.

PETRE, F. LORRAINE. *The Royal Berkshire Regiment (Princess Charlotte of Wales') 49th/66th Foot*. 2 vols. Reading, England: the regiment, 1925.

POWELL, WILLIAM H. *List of officers of the army of the United States from 1779-1900 . . . compiled from the official records*. New York: Hamersly, 1900.

ROBINSON, RALPH. 'Retaliation for the treatment of prisoners in the War of 1812', *American Historical Review*, vol. 49 (1943-4), 65-70.

SHERK, A. B. 'Early militia matters in Upper Canada 1808-1842', *Ontario Historical Society Papers and Records*, vol. 13 (1915), 67-73.

SQUIRES, WILLIAM AUSTIN. *The 104th Regiment of Foot (the New Brunswick regiment) 1803-1817*. Fredericton, N.B.: Brunswick, 1962.

STANLEY, GEORGE F. G. 'The contribution of the Canadian militia during the war', in Philip P. Mason (ed.), *After Tippecanoe*. East Lansing: Michigan State University; and Toronto: Ryerson, 1963, 28-48.

———. 'The Indians in the War of 1812', *Canadian Historical Review*, vol. 31 (1950), 145-65.

———. 'The New Brunswick Fencibles', *Canadian Defence Quarterly*, vol. 16 (1938-9), 39-53.

———. 'The significance of the Six Nations participation in the War of 1812', *Ontario History*, vol. 55 (1963), 215-31.

STEWART, CHARLES H. (comp.). *The service of British regiments in Canada and North America; a resumé . . . .* ('DND Library Publication no. 1'.) Ottawa: Department of National Defence, 1962.

WHITEHORNE, A. C. *The history of the Welch Regiment*. Cardiff, Wales: Western Mail and Echo, 1932.

WHITTON, FREDERICK E. *The history of the Prince of Wales's Leinster Regiment (Royal Canadians)*. 2 vols. Aldershot: Gale and Polden, 1924. Vol. I.

I. THE PEOPLE IN THE WAR

CRUIKSHANK, ERNEST A. 'A study of disaffection in Upper Canada in 1812-15',

Royal Society of Canada Transactions, series 3, vol. 6 (1912), section 2, 11-65.
———. 'John Beverley Robinson and the trials for treason in 1814', *Ontario Historical Society Papers and Records*, vol. 25 (1929), 191-219.
———. 'The county of Norfolk in the War of 1812', *Ontario Historical Society Papers and Records*, vol. 20 (1923), 9-40.
EDGAR, MATILDA RIDOUT. *Ten years of Upper Canada in peace and war, 1805-1815; being the Ridout letters with annotations* . . . . Toronto: W. Briggs, 1890.
ERMATINGER, CHARLES O. Z. *The Talbot regime; or, The first half century of the Talbot settlement.* St. Thomas, Ont.: Municipal World, 1904.
FIRTH, EDITH G. (ed.). *The town of York, 1793-1815.* Toronto: Champlain Society for the Government of Ontario, 1962.
GREEN, ERNEST. *Lincoln at bay; a sketch of 1814.* Welland, Ont.: Tribune-Telegraph, 1923.
HAMIL, FRED COYNE. *The valley of the lower Thames, 1640 to 1850.* Toronto: University of Toronto, 1951.
HUMPHRIES, CHARLES W. 'The capture of York', *Ontario History*, vol. 51 (1959), 1-21.
KERR, WILLIAM B. 'The occupation of York (Toronto), 1813', *Canadian Historical Review*, vol. 5 (1924), 9-21.
LANDON, FRED. *Western Ontario and the American frontier.* ('The Relations of Canada and the United States'.) Toronto: Ryerson, 1941.
LAURISTON, VICTOR. *Romantic Kent* . . . . Chatham, Ont.: City of Chatham, 1952.
LOYAL AND PATRIOTIC SOCIETY OF UPPER CANADA. *The report of the Loyal and Patriotic Society of Upper Canada, with an appendix, and a list of subscribers and benefactors.* Montreal: William Gray, 1817.
MARTELL, J. S. 'Nova Scotia's contribution to the Canadian Relief Fund in the War of 1812', *Canadian Historical Review*, vol. 23 (1942), 297-302.
MUIR, ROBERT C. *The early political and military history of Burford: Part II: The first one hundred years of Burford's military history, 1798-1898.* Québec: Imprimerie commerciale, 1913.
QUAIFE, MILO M. *The Yankees capture York.* ('The Cass Lectures'.) Detroit: Wayne University, 1955.
RIDDELL, WILLIAM RENWICK. 'An echo of the War of 1812', *Ontario Historical Society Papers and Records*, vol. 23 (1926), 434-49.
———. 'The Ancaster "Bloody assize" of 1814', *Ontario Historical Society Papers and Records*, vol. 20 (1923), 107-25.
———. 'The first Canadian war-time prohibition measure', *Canadian Historical Review*, vol. 1 (1920), 187-90.
SMITH, MICHAEL. *A geographical view of the British possessions in North America . . . with an appendix containing a concise history of the war in Canada* . . . . Baltimore: P. Mauro, 1814.
———. *A geographical view of the province of Upper Canada and promiscuous remarks on the government* . . . . Boston: Hale and Hosmer, 1813.
STEVENSON, JAMES. *The War of 1812 in connection with the Army bill act.* Montreal: Foster, Brown, 1892.
WEEKES, WILLIAM M. 'The War of 1812: civil authority and martial law in Upper Canada', *Ontario History*, vol. 48 (1956), 147-61.

J. THE AFTERMATH OF THE WAR

An account of the organization & proceedings of the Battle of Lake Erie Monument

Association, and celebration of the 45th anniversary of the battle of Lake Erie, at Put-in-bay Island, on September tenth, 1858. Sandusky, Ohio: Henry D. Cooke, 1858.

AHEARN, M. H. 'Battlegrounds of the Niagara peninsula', *Women's Canadian Historical Society of Ottawa Transactions*, vol. 5 (1912), 19-36.

BOTSFORD, DAVID P. 'Old Fort Malden and the modern museum', *Western Ontario Historical Notes*, vol. 10 (1952), 76-82.

CRAIG, HAMILTON. 'The Loyal and Patriotic Society of Upper Canada and its stillborn child – the "Upper Canada Preserved" medal', *Ontario History*, vol. 52 (1960), 31-52.

CRUIKSHANK, ERNEST A. 'The negotiation of the agreement for disarmament on the lakes', *Royal Society of Canada Transactions*, series 3, vol. 30 (1936), section 2, 151-84.

———. 'Post-war discontent at Niagara in 1818', *Ontario Historical Society Papers and Records*, vol. 29 (1933), 14-46.

CURZON, SARAH ANNE. *Canada in memoriam, 1812-14; her duty in the erection of monuments in memory of her distinguished sons and daughters.* Welland, Ont.: Telegraph Steam Printing, 1891.

DUNHAM, AILEEN. *Political unrest in Upper Canada, 1815-1836.* ('Imperial Studies, no. 1'.) London: Longmans, Green, 1927.

EAMES, F. 'Gananoque block house, 1813-1859', *Ontario Historical Society Papers and Records*, vol. 32 (1937), 85-91.

FOWKE, EDITH, AND ALAN MILLS. *Canada's story in song.* Toronto: W. J. Gage, 1960.

FRASER, ALEXANDER (ed.). *Brock Centenary, 1812-1912; account of the celebration at Queenston Heights, Ontario, on the 12th October, 1912.* Toronto: Briggs, 1913.

GATES, M. 'The west in American diplomacy, 1812-15', *Mississippi Valley Historical Review*, vol. 26 (1939-40), 499-510.

GOURLAY, ROBERT. *Statistical account of Upper Canada, compiled with a view to a general system of emigration.* 2 vols. London: Simpkin and Marshall, 1822. Vol. I.

GRAHAM, GERALD S. 'Views of General Murray on the defence of Upper Canada, 1815', *Canadian Historical Review*, vol. 34 (1953), 158-65.

GREEN, ERNEST. 'War-clouds over the Short Hills', *Welland County Historical Society Papers and Records*, vol. 5 (1938), 153-62.

HARPER, JOHN M. *In commemoration of 'The Century of Peace', the annals of the war, illustrated by a selection of historical ballads.* ('Studies in Verse and Prose'.) London, New York: Musson Book, [1913].

KLINCK, CARL F. 'Some anonymous literature of the War of 1812', *Ontario History*, vol. 49 (1957), 49-62.

LEGGETT, ROBERT F. *Rideau Waterway.* Toronto: University of Toronto, 1955.

LUNDY'S LANE HISTORICAL SOCIETY. *The centenary celebration of the battle of Lundy's Lane, July twenty-fifth, nineteen hundred and fourteen; compiled by a committee of the Lundy's Lane Historical Society.* Niagara Falls, Ont.: the society, 1919.

MCCALL, CLAYTON W. 'A British medal of Michigan interest', *Michigan History*, vol. 29 (1945), 51-8.

NEW YORK STATE. PERRY'S VICTORY CENTENNIAL COMMISSION. *The Perry's victory centenary. Report of the Perry's victory centennial commission, state of New*

York. Comp. by George D. Emerson, secretary. Albany: J. B. Lyon, 1916.

PRESTON, RICHARD A. 'Broad pennants on Point Frederick', *Ontario History*, vol. 50 (1958), 81-90.

———. 'The fate of Kingston's warships', *Ontario Historical Society Papers and Records*, vol. 44 (1952), 85-100.

ROBINSON, SIR CHARLES W. *Canada and Canadian defence; the defensive policy of the Dominion in relation to the character of her frontier, the events of the war of 1812-14, and her position to-day.* Toronto: Musson [1910].

SAUNDERS, ROBERT E. 'What was the Family Compact?', *Ontario History*, vol. 49 (1957), 165-78.

SEVERANCE, FRANK H. 'Collections of historical material relating to the War of 1812', *Ontario Historical Society Papers and Records*, vol. 10 (1913), 43-56.

SHORTT, ADAM. 'The economic effect of the War of 1812 on Upper Canada', *Ontario Historical Society Papers and Records*, vol. 10 (1913), 79-85.

SNIDER, CHARLES H. J. 'Recovery of H.M.S. Tecumseth of the Upper Canada naval department, succeeding His Majesty's provincial marine . . . ' , *Ontario History*, vol. 46 (1954), 97-105.

STACEY, CHARLES P. 'An American plan for a Canadian campaign; Secretary James Monroe to Major General Jacob Brown, February, 1815', *American Historical Review*, vol. 46 (1940-1), 348-58.

———. 'Myth of the unguarded frontier, 1815-71', *American Historical Review*, vol. 56 (1950-1), 1-18.

———. 'The War of 1812 in Canadian history', *Ontario History*, vol. 50 (1958), 153-9.

STANLEY, GEORGE F. G. 'Historic Kingston and its defences', *Ontario History*, vol. 46 (1954), 21-35.

SYMONS, JOHN (ed.). *The battle of Queenston Heights . . . with notices of the life of Major-General Sir Isaac Brock, K.B., and description of the monument erected to his memory.* Toronto: Thompson, 1859.

WARNER, MABEL V. 'Memorials at Lundy's Lane', *Ontario History*, vol. 51 (1959), 43-8.

WAY, RONALD L. 'Old Fort Henry, the citadel of Upper Canada', *Canadian Geographical Journal*, vol. 40 (1950), 148-69.

———. *Ontario's Niagara parks, a history.* Fort Erie: Niagara Parks Commission, 1960.

Index